Contents

Fixers

Fixers

AGENCY, TRANSLATION, AND
THE EARLY GLOBAL HISTORY
OF LITERATURE

Zrinka Stahuljak

The University of Chicago Press CHICAGO AND LONDON

The University of Chicago Press, Chicago 60637
The University of Chicago Press, Ltd., London
© 2024 by The University of Chicago
Published 2024
Printed in the United States of America

33 32 31 30 29 28 27 26 25 24   1 2 3 4 5

ISBN-13: 978-0-226-83039-1 (cloth)
ISBN-13: 978-0-226-83040-7 (paper)
ISBN-13: 978-0-226-83041-4 (e-book)
DOI: https://doi.org/10.7208/chicago/9780226830414.001.0001

The University of Chicago Press gratefully acknowledges the generous
support of the University of California, Los Angeles, toward the publication
of this book.

Library of Congress Cataloging-in-Publication Data

Names: Stahuljak, Zrinka, author.
Title: Fixers : agency, translation, and the early global history
of literature / Zrinka Stahuljak.
Description: Chicago : The University of Chicago Press, 2024. |
Includes bibliographical references and index.
Identifiers: LCCN 2023028623 | ISBN 9780226830391 (cloth) |
ISBN 9780226830407 (paperback) | ISBN 9780226830414 (ebook)
Subjects: LCSH: Translating and interpreting—Social aspects. |
Translating and interpreting—History—To 1500. | Translators—
History—To 1500. | Mediators (Persons)—History—To 1500. |
Intercultural communication—History—To 1500. |
Literature, Medieval—History and criticism.
Classification: LCC P306.97.S63 S73 2024 | DDC 418/.02—dc23/
eng/20230721
LC record available at https://lccn.loc.gov/2023028623

For Andreja, Janja, Višnja,
and for my mother, Ivanka, because
motherhood may be a fixer's biggest job

Figures

On Translations and Terminology

For translations, "fixer" is the term I commonly use instead of "interpreter" to denote linguistic agents. In translation of primary sources, especially when citing published translations, I retain "dragoman" and "interpreter" for "drogman" (and its western European variants) and "interpres."

The term "Holy Land" is used when quoting or referring directly to the primary source, and to denote the Christian conception and geographic delineation of the Near East. Otherwise, whenever possible, the preferred term is "medieval Syria" or "the Near East" and, when designating the continent, "Asia Minor."

Medieval names "Moor/s" and "Saracen/s" are retained when they appear in the primary source. "Moors" usually refers to Andalusi Muslims; "Saracens" is a term for Arab Muslims; both indicate Muslim faith.

The term "Tartar" is retained when quoting from primary sources or referring directly to the medieval usage. Otherwise, I refer to the people and the institutions as "Mongol." The exception is made in reference to the language, as "Tartar" usually designates a Turkic language (like Uighur), whereas Mongolian does not belong to the same language group.

"Orient" is retained from the primary sources.

Translation into English from published translations is provided for all the primary sources, when available. A double-notation system is adopted throughout, referring to the published English translation, then to the published original text. For all original texts with a single reference to the published edition, the translations from Latin, from Middle and modern French, and from medieval and modern Italian are mine. For bilingual editions, a single reference includes both the original and a translation, and this is noted at first mention of each such item, to distinguish references to these sources from references to original texts without a published translation. Any errors in transcription or translation are my sole responsibility.

In the introduction, I use the term "premodern" to denote two European periodizations, medieval and early modern; Europeanists commonly separate the periods, but I consider them continuous for the purposes of this book. "Medieval" refers generally to the European Middle Ages throughout the book. In the conclusion, "precolonial" refers to medieval European writing prior to European colonization of the late fifteenth and early sixteenth centuries but also aims at other non-Western cultural production (oral, written, artistic) before European colonization. "Early" is the term suited to describing premodern and precolonial writing.

✳ INTRODUCTION ✳

Fixers

TOWARD AN ALTERNATIVE HISTORY OF TRANSLATION AND LITERATURE

Why Fixers?

This book exists for two reasons. On the one hand, most scholars of translation do not read work by medievalists, which results in the separation of the history of translation from translation studies. On the other hand, most medievalists interested in translation take the formalism and precepts of translation studies as a given, despite the foreclosure of this discipline to the social history of translation and to the history of translation more generally, which often results in translation studies being an uncomfortable fit to the European medieval setting. This book therefore proposes a paradigmatic shift for medieval literary history and for the history of translation that counters the accepted standard grounding of European medieval studies and translation and interpreting studies (T&IS) in the modern notions of authorship as origin, and translators and interpreters as a neutral conduit. This paradigm shift is operated through the figure and concept of "the fixer."

"Fixer" is a journalistic term that became commonplace during the twenty-first-century wars in Afghanistan and Iraq (2001–21) and has gained an ever wider acceptance since the start of the war in Ukraine (February 24, 2022).[1] Among journalists, fixers are known as the unsung heroes of foreign reporting. They are agents who perform a range of tasks, acting as interpreters, local informants, guides, brokers, personal assistants, and more. I think of them as multifunctional intermediaries with multiple linguistic, social, cultural, and topographical skills and knowledge. They are enablers, facilitators, and mediators—linguistic, logistic, cultural, religious, military, commercial—who negotiate and work through spaces of unintelligibility and, as a consequence, enable various networks of exchange: informational, commercial, artistic, and so on.

Using this contemporary journalistic and, for the general public, mostly unfamiliar term, I follow neither the disciplinary dogma of translation studies to talk about "translation" (which privileges language instead of persons) nor the historical terminology true to the medieval and early modern periods (e.g., the well-attested "dragoman"). The prism of the fixer allows me to reread, first, historical communication and cultural encounter in the medieval period as a form of commensuration and intermediation (rather than translation). Consequently, this historically grounded reading enables me to propose an alternative history of literature, manuscript illumination, and translation, from the perspective of the fixer (rather than author). There is heuristic value in the "fixer" as a historical figure, but there is also cross-disciplinary and revisionary value of this term for different disciplines; thus, in this book, medieval studies and translation studies not only are connected in a transdisciplinary fashion but are used to confront and interrogate each other in their core disciplinary assumptions. The high stakes of the book are thus also its risks: challenging the traditional assumptions and disciplinary pillars of European medieval studies and translation studies will inevitably create discomfort, perhaps even rejection, among readers and specialists. But this discomfort can hardly be greater than what I believe early, that is premodern, studies face every day in their struggle to contribute to contemporary studies.

Often the biggest hurdle medievalists encounter is precisely how to negotiate the underlying tension in the scholarship, between the on-the-ground, empirical, and granular evidence of the premodern periods and the paradigms that remain silently beholden to modern and contemporary translation studies. The first and foremost among them are the term and the paradigm of "interpreter." The difference between contemporary and early accounts of interpreting, and the conceptual differences that the two mobilize, quickly and often become a stumbling stone because we are dealing with two different configurations that are designated by the same term, "interpreter," but that do not share the same semantic field of "interpreting."

Contemporary translation and interpreting (T&I) has operated in a singularly ahistorical, asocial, apolitical, and acultural discourse because it identifies translational activity as extrasituational, that is, it does not account for situational specificity. Simultaneous and consecutive translation activity most commonly occurs at international congresses and meetings, at bilateral or multilateral diplomatic meetings or summits, in international organizations (e.g., the UN), and within supranational state forms (e.g., the European Union). There, interpreting is guided by strict protocols of deontology, which require adherence to the content and form of the translated discourse, without possibility of intervention related to the situation. Deontology is a set of objective rules and responsibilities that guide the linguistic behavior of interpreters with disregard for the material, psychological, or other circumstances. It stipulates noninterventionism, impartiality, and neutrality, what, in short, Lawrence Venuti had called the "translator's invisibility" (Venuti 1995; see also Delsaux 2019). The interpreter is to be a mere conduit, neutral, guided by this objective, extrasituational professional code; he or she is never a third party to a dialogue. Focus on meaning given in language (rather than in an utterance), on linguistic work alone (rather than on multifunctionality in a context), and translator neutrality (rather than agency) are encoded in the deontology of the profession.

By contrast, early accounts offer many pieces of evidence of the interpretative function that is inscribed in the vagaries of its situation, that is nonprofessional, and that depends on improvisation, informality, and accommodation to particular settings. It quickly becomes clear that interpreting has never been extrasituational and decontextual in the past. The complexity of medieval interpreting comes to full light in an overview of the terminology used in pilgrimage and missionary accounts, which demonstrates that medieval "interpreters" performed multiple functions beyond a purely linguistic service. In 1384, the Florentine pilgrim Giorgio Gucci speaks of "our dragoman who guided us" (nostro turcimanno che ci guidava; Gucci 1948, 121 / Gucci 1862, 348). In 1420 an anonymous Frenchman mentions "dragomans to guide the pilgrims" (trussemans pour les [pellerins] conduire); and in 1485, burgomaster Georges Lengherand speaks of "those who have already contracted dragomans to take them to the monastery of Saint Catherine" (desja avoyent fait marchié aux truchemans pour les y mener [à Sainte-Catherine]; "Un pèlerinage en Terre Sainte" 1905, 82; Lengherand 1861, 142). In 1483, the Dominican Felix Fabri provides the most elaborate definition:

> dragomans—that is to say, protectors, conductors, or guardians of the Christian pilgrims. Indeed, in every city there are some men to whom the Sultan grants the privilege of guiding Christians through the land and defending them from wrong, which men are officers of the Government, and are called dragomans. In like manner, also, the Jews have their own dragomans or Calini. (Fabri 1896, 9:105)

> (dicuntur Trutschelmanni, i.e. defensores et ductores, sive provisores Christianorum peregrinorum. Sunt enim in qualibet civitate aliqui, quibus Soldanus concedit, ut Christianos per terram ducant et eos

protegant, et sunt magistri officiales de curia domini Soldani et dicuntur Trutschelmanni. Sic etiam Judaei habent suos Trutschelmannos sive Calinos.) (Fabri 1843–49, 2:108)

These functions of protection and defense are also attested in a slightly earlier account by Anselm Adorno (1470): "First and above all, one must acquire a loyal and wise dragoman, that is interpreter, who will accompany them, attend to each of their affairs faithfully, defend them and guide them as a good pastor his sheep" (Primum atque summum est de fideli ac prudente trucemanno, sive interprete, providere que nobiscum eat ac fideliter singula negocia peregrinorum faciat ac eos defendat et regat velut pastor bonus oves suas; Adorno 1978, 210). Many other sources attest to the fact that dragomans perform multiple functions beyond a linguistic— interpreting—service. A German knight, Arnold von Harff, for instance, traveled in the Near East and Egypt between 1496 and 1499 and hired his dragoman in Venice:

Item, they [the German merchants] helped me to find a dragoman, that is a guide knowing many languages. He was called Master Vyncent, a Spaniard; he was a renegade Christian. . . . He knew many languages such as Latin, Lombard, Spanish, Wendish, Greek, Turkish and excellent Arabic. . . . He was to take me from Venice to Cairo, further to St. Catherine's and through all the heathen lands to Jerusalem. Item, as soon as I had made my contract with him, he went to buy everything which would be necessary for us in the ship.

(Item van stunt an hulffen sij mir an eynen trutzselman, dat is eyn geleytzman kunnende vil spraichen, her hiesch myschier Vyncent eyn hyspaneoler, he was eyn verlueckener kryst. . . . Hee kunt gar vyllerleye spraiche, as latijn lumbartz hyspanioils wyndichs greex turcks ind guet arabs . . . des suyldt he mich voerent van Venedich bys zo Alkayr, voert zo sijnt Katrijnen ind durch alle heydensche landen bys zo Jherusalem. Item doe ich dit verdynckenysse mit ime gemaich hatte gynck hee ind kuefft mir alles wes wir noitturfftich in dem schyff waeren.)[2]

Not only does "my dragoman," as von Harff calls him throughout, purchase all the provisions, but he passes off the knight as a merchant in Cairo and as a Muslim on several occasions, allowing him access to sights otherwise forbidden to Christians.

"Dragoman," derived from the Hebrew *targum*, via Arabic *tarjumān* or *turjumān*, is just one of a number of different vernacular terms used in different regions in the premodern period to designate a fixer: alongside the many variants of the Latin *dragomannus* (in Romance languages, Persian, and Turkish), we can find, by way of example, Old High German *tolmetsche* (Venetian It. *tolomaci*; see chapter 2); Proto-Slavic *tъlmačъ* (and its variants in Hungarian, Russian, Polish, Croatian) and Turkic *tilmäč, kelemürči* and *kälämäči* (Mongol, medieval It. calamanci); along with *lengua* (Spanish), *tangomão* (West African Creole), and *túlkur* (Old Norse and its variants in Dutch, Middle High German, and Baltic languages).[3] They, like the Old and Middle French "latinier," convey the complex interaction of translation and interpreting that exceeds the linguistic skills and outlines the role of the premodern linguistic agent.[4] In the mid-fourteenth century *The Book of John Mandeville* (*Le livres des merveilles du monde*), whose first part is based on the lived experience of a pilgrim's physical travel that includes the distances from one holy site to the next, the dependence of pilgrims on the "latiniers" is foregrounded: "And whoever wants to go through this country or another over there always takes *latiniers* until he knows the language. It is necessary to have carried through this desert all the essentials of life" (Et toutdis amene homme des lathomers [latiniers] qe voet aler par ceo païs ou par autre de la jusques a tant qe homme sache la langage. Y covient faire porter par cest desert les necessaires pur vivers).[5] "Latiniers" are as essential as provisions and the only means to go from one place to another. Crucially, they are only a temporary fix for the traveler, so to speak, as they serve him only until he learns the language himself. In his *Chronicles*, written in the last third of the fourteenth century, Jean Froissart likewise shows that "latiniers" are mobile figures who create intelligibility in their movement. At Nicopolis, the defeated Burgundian and French nobles "were examined by the *latiniers* of the king [Sultan Bajazet]" (furent bien examinés des lattiniers du roy). There is palpable materiality in what Froissart says: "The emir [Sultan Bajazet] spoke to the Count of Nevers, that is by the mouth of a *latinier* who carried over the speech" (Le dit Amourath parla au conte de Nevers, voire par la bouche d'un latinier qui transportoit la parole).[6] The mouths of "latiniers" carry words: languages are brought from one to the other by the actions of "latiniers and dragomans who carry over the languages from one to the other" (les latiniers et trucemans qui portent les langaiges de l'un à l'autre; Froissart 1867–77, 16:67). We are faced with the materiality of translation: premodern linguistic agents, whom I call fixers, are bodies that transport languages, mouths that carry words; these bodies have agency in space and time, and they gain in intelligibility only within a context.

Even when nonprofessional premodern interpreting begins to be institutionalized, for example, in the Ottoman Office of the Dragoman or in the

Office of General Interpreter in Spanish America, one finds that these "interpreters" carry out more than one function. Despite attempts to qualify and theorize in their full complexity what is "alongside and beyond the linguistic function," scholarship on these premodern linguistic agents either reverts to reconciling them to the function of "interpreter," by explaining away their multifunctionality, or subsumes them under other recognizable functions such as secretary, ambassador (or diplomat), or, more paradigmatically, trickster or cultural broker, while it deals uncomfortably with their "mixed loyalties."[7] Their multifunctional positionality compromises any notion of neutrality or fidelity, especially as these linguistic intermediaries are often social agents who act as subjects, advancing their own ends, thereby creating and occupying a third space. Crucially, then, these rich premodern descriptions clash with our perception of what translation is: interpreters today are viewed in relation only to the linguistic service they provide; they are linguistic instruments. Language use—a tool or skill—is dissociated from its context or action, that is from history, agency, and culture. It is this dissociation—the extrasituationality of languages—that provides the grounds for the regulation of present-day interpreting with professional and deontological rules of source-to-target—neutral and faithful—interpreting. Calling such premodern figures "interpreters" does not correspond to their premodern situations and multifunctional agency, because they do much more than interpretation between languages.

For scholars of the premodern, a continued acceptance of modern terms and paradigms requires a constant description of these figures in the negative mode: they were not neutral, not professional, not faithful; they were "informal interpreters," and so on (Nesvig 2012). We spend time justifying the existence of the "more-than-linguistic" as if it were a problem, without ever resolving the problem of how to talk about the more-than-just-the-linguistic as a situated phenomenon of the premodern. More problematically, defining the premodern in relation to the norms of the modern does not allow us to see these intermediary figures in a situated social history of premodernity. In fact, when "lengua," "dragoman," and "túlkur" are translated with "interpreter," the situated history of premodernity is not given its due but continues to labor within categories of modern, European translation. These "interpreter-like" figures are neither neutral nor instrumentalized but are agents and subjects who insert themselves in the translational process and create a third space. Instead of being seen as "in-between," the third space that fixers create should be acknowledged in its own right.[8]

Fixing Translation (1): Decolonizing Middle Ages and Translation Studies

A new history of translation that is social and decolonial, and that this book advances, must therefore begin with the acknowledgment that there is hardly any equivalence between the past and present term "interpreter." The contemporary "interpreter" may be a cognate of the Latin "interpres," or a Latinate translation of the Arabic "turjumān" (*dragomannus, turchu-manni*), but in reality "interpres" and "interpreter" are "false friends." In writing this book, I have moreover reached an even more radical con-clusion: a decolonized history of translation requires abandoning both the modern terminology of "interpreter" and the historical terminology used in premodern sources, because, although terminology we find in our sources is situated and rich, it has been systematically translated and equated with the modern term "interpreter." It has thus become too re-ductive in modern scholarship and is ultimately forcing us into partially tautological readings: *túlkur* or *drogman* means "interpreter"—one who performs a linguistic service—which requires a justification of their multifunctionality, nonprofessionalism, and nonneutrality in relation to modern norms of interpreting, which further disables us from analyzing them on their own terms within the fabric of the social phenomenon that these linguistic intermediaries or agents not only are an element of but are coconstitutive of. That is, the focus on intermediary figures that we would no longer call interpreters, and that I call fixers, could free us to see what premodern translation was made of and how it generated the fabric of a society and created a world.

On the one hand, fixers are intermediaries who always do linguistic work, something that is not a constant for a more generic "intermediary." On the other hand, fixers are never just interpreters—a function that they are often erroneously reduced to—since their work encompasses the work of intermediation broadly conceived, as described above. Intermediation can in fact be defined as creating intelligibility. In the activities they ex-ercise, the linguistic skill is the medium but not the end in itself. Fixers' multifunctionality is the response to the multifaceted nature of situations of unintelligibility, whereby unintelligibility exceeds linguistic nonunder-standing. Recent scholarship in history and anthropology has used "in-termediary," "go-between," or "broker," terms often also used interchange-ably. Unlike "fixer," these terms do not easily denote or incorporate the linguistic element; moreover, "fixer" is more exact than "interpreter" (or "secretary" or "emissary") given the scope of fixers' activities. Fixer is also an existing term, neither overly familiar nor overused (and thus over-determined, as is "interpreter"), that describes exactly what these histori-cal persons did and the third space their activity created for them. Because of the relative unfamiliarity of the term, but also because of its limited journalistic use designating multifunctional linguistic agents, "fixer" is thus a potentially fresh paradigmatic term.

I deploy this term with the aim of providing a more inclusive ap-proach to translation studies whereby the history of oral, interpersonal translation—interpreting—is not only a legitimate object of study but an indispensable lens. The book takes a comprehensive look at transla-tion that includes communication and interpreting, and all their atten-dant features (intelligibility, commensurability, agency, ethics). This ap-proach questions the legacy of the philosophy of translation, of textual approaches to literature and biographical approaches to history, and is an attempt to adapt the concepts of contemporary T&IS to the lived ex-perience of medieval actors and agents. Showing the Middle Ages as a dynamic field of experience, the book moves the conversations that often characterize medieval studies from the textual and intertextual to the oral and interpersonal; from requirements of accuracy and fidelity (likeness) to parameters of intelligibility, commensurability, and loyalty in transla-tion; from the sole focus in translation studies on interpreters to fixers; from fixers as persons (and biographies) to fixers as apparatus (*dispositif*). It aims to provide a grid for reading, a protocol—the apparatus of the fixer—that can be applied to a number of contexts and periods, although I focus on two.

On the one hand, for medieval studies, I show how fixer as apparatus can be used in the historical study of communication and contact in the Middle Ages and how this historical apparatus changes the method and content with which we have been reading medieval European writings of all genres. The premise is that our scholarship on translation and com-munication in the medieval period has been contaminated by modern frameworks of translation: original, accuracy, method, author, (aesthetic) genres, textuality, rather than commensurability, relationality (ethics), col-laboration, translators, orality, situational clusters. Looking through the prism of fixers works toward emancipating the study of the European Mid-dle Ages from modern, national categories of analysis, which are also co-lonial by virtue of the European colonization that imposed them as silent norm across the globe and time periods. Ultimately, this book proposes a new literary history from within this new paradigm of a fixer, implicitly breaking down the imbrication of the author name with the history of the nation-state. Rather than as the slow emergence of the author, the literature and society of northwestern medieval Europe are viewed as the long death of the fixer. The fixer paradigm can thus denationalize and de-canonize the Middle Ages. Since our current categories of analysis silently partake in the national and colonial norms, the book also contributes to the reflection on the early global literatures and cultures.

On the other hand, the historical dimension of this book intervenes in contemporary T&IS and literary criticism to undo the entanglement of the nation-state and translation that have led to an impasse between Western (and Anglophone-dominated) market structures and theories of world literature. The book also provides both a parallel example and an analysis that respond to the contemporary calls in favor of a more formal and recognized interpreter agency in communicative contexts that are ethically challenging, based on a set of carefully defined ethical impera-tives. For literary criticism, the book reveals ways in which translation (to the exclusion of interpreting and translators) is complicit in the ongoing national and colonial relationship of domination of Western epistemic and aesthetic modes, while the fixer paradigm has the potential to enrich our understanding of the early global period—going beyond the Global Middle Ages—with simultaneous lateral and vertical thinking, providing ways to interface what otherwise frequently remains juxtaposed, not con-nected, or contiguous.

The remainder of this introduction is dedicated to substantiating the above claims and concludes with the presentation of the book's structure.

Fixer, an Apparatus: Translating Unintelligibility

For me, a fixer is a body, and not a biography. It designates an apparatus, *dispositif* in the Foucauldian sense. He or she is a site of multiple discourses and techniques, of biology (life, death, survival), communication (to give or restore meaning vs. to do or to act), economy (market, gift, indebted-ness), ethics (fidelity, loyalty, professional codes, deontology, experience), politics (state and individual, means and ends), and aesthetics (the beauti-ful and the true). The apparatus of the fixer organizes different discourses and techniques. Such a history of intermediation corresponds more to a history of networks and processes than to a connected history of persons; in the European Middle Ages, the human is a vehicle, before he or she is a biography or an institution. Thus a book on fixers is neither a genealogy of a profession or trade (from nonprofessional to diplomat, to interpreter, etc.), nor a biography of a person or of a social life of a (translated) object. Instead it is a book that identifies situations in which people occupy po-sitions, in which they are functions and, often improvised, interfaces or nodes of exchange; once identified, the networks these nodes command can be analyzed. Language is seen as an agentive object that is used by men as much as it acts on men. Fixers have agency; they are not tools, simply charged with transmitting content from source to target language, and they are not invisible. The fixer apparatus sees translation as not just a linguistic, but a total social phenomenon in order to understand how a culture thinks the activity of translating, of transmitting; how it relates to and sees the world through translation; and how translation organizes the world. Importantly, understanding fixers as an apparatus makes them into an interface, rather than into a new center.

The fixer apparatus is constituted between language use and situational inscription.[9] It is built on three principles. Unlike intermediaries, go-betweens, or brokers, as the disciplines of anthropology and history have understood such figures, fixers always operate between at least two languages, and more precisely, between people speaking two mutually unintelligible languages.[10] Linguistic difference—bilingualism and multilingualism—is an essential context for the fixers' intermediation. The linguistic skill is the medium but not the end in itself; it is just one of the functions performed. The second principle is that fixers operate in what I call conflict zones. Conflict zones are contact zones, because war is neither continuous in activity nor with an impermeable frontline. A good example of permeability and frequency of contact in medieval conflicts comes from *Apollonius of Tyre*, a hagiographic romance and one of the most widespread medieval narratives, rewritten across the Mediterranean from the eleventh well into the fifteenth century: in the middle of a siege, a merchant caravan passes through it and occasions a rich scene of communication despite, or perhaps because of, conflict. Zones of contact are zones of conflict because they are by definition hostile. They are hostile not because there is an active armed confrontation, but because one is unfamiliar with the language, customs, and codes, all factors of unintelligibility. Language, indeed, is only one element of unintelligibility. In other words, zones of contact are hostile because of various, often simultaneous, forms of nonintelligibility. I thus use "conflict" to indicate situations that evolve in a state of tension and hostility, in high-risk areas, with the potential for misunderstanding, escalation, and outright armed confrontation. A third principle is that being a fixer is not a profession; rather, it is a job that requires multiple skills for which there is no received training and which, in order to create intelligibility, needs a lot of improvisation in a situation of contingency. To be a fixer is more akin to holding a position more than to pursuing a career or a trade; this is certainly the case with contemporary fixers. It is a multifunctional positionality with agency. The premodern is thus a natural mold for the concept of fixers; as is the case for diplomacy, interpreting is not yet a distinct profession in medieval Europe and will not be for quite some time (perhaps not even until the nineteenth century). Language difference, conflict, and multifunctional positionality (with agency) are thus the three principles that determine the apparatus of "fixer."

In conflict, as a rule, fixers' work is about survival and life-and-death situations; the contact zone is a conflict zone. To acknowledge the materiality of these situations, and the fixers' work that makes them intelligible, is to see that interlingual communication does not happen because one wants it (because one would be eager for some cross-cultural "discovery" and "exchange"), but because one needs to obtain something through interpersonal communication; missionary and pilgrim accounts and crusade treatises show that this "something" can be as essential as water or shelter. In conflict zones, the material approach reveals that communication is first a question of survival, before it is a question of exchange and transmission. In other words, cultural contact and exchange (of objects and ideas) hinge on material conditions; they are an effect and not the cause. But if cultural translation and, subsequently, cultural production are an effect of material conditions and fixers' work in them, then several correctives are necessary. First, when it comes to medieval cultural translation, interlingual, interpersonal communication must be treated on par with textual translation. Second, the material approach of "conflict zone" reveals that translation was first thought of as a relational system that depended on human agency. Third, this relational system implied a different notion of fidelity, one based on loyalty, rather than on equivalence, likeness, or accuracy.

Unintelligibility makes visible the ways in which our relationship to the world is made. The situations in which fixers intervene are (almost without exception) extreme and limit cases—survival is in question—but these are not exceptional situations, nor are fixers, in that sense, exceptional. What these situations of unintelligibility make visible is what is always in play in our relationship to the world, that is, how the intermediary intervenes in and organizes our relationship to the world, how communication is the basis of relationality. While one may think of conflict zones as extreme situations of life and death, the focus on forms of unintelligibility and commensurability shows that there is a form of banality, or a form of universality; the apparatus of fixers makes visible what is relevant to most, if not all, human interactions.[11]

Communication and Commensuration (Nicole Oresme)

The focus on fixers—bodies not texts—brings to the fore the premise of modern Western translation: rejection of translation as communication and insistence on fidelity in translation. Since Saint Jerome, the faithful transfer from one language to another has been the dominant concept in the West. Usually understood as a faithful transfer of meaning, rather than word-for-word translation, Saint Jerome's definition, we must remember, was double, both free translation and word-for-word translation. Namely, he translated the Scripture word for word because its sense is hidden: "in my translations of Greeks, I try to render well sense with sense, rather than word for word, *except* in the translation of the Holy Scripture, where even in the order of words there is mystery" (con me in interpretatione Graecorum, *absque* Scripturis sanctis, ubi et verborum ordo mysterium est, non verbum e verbo, sed sensum exprimere de sensu; my emphasis; Jerome, n.d.). What if we were to understand Saint Jerome's method as a form of loyalty, rather than look for confirmation of the translator's fidelity either to sense or to literal meaning?[12] To that end, we can think of translation not as fidelity and equivalence, but as a form of commensuration of unintelligibility acted via the *third term of intermediary*. In other words, rather than focusing on the meaning (sense), we can privilege the intelligible as the outcome of commensuration.

Nicole Oresme, who coined the word "communicacion" in the fourteenth century, sheds light on the idea of translation as commensuration and communication. Oresme was an accomplished linguist and translator for Charles V of France. In his translations of Aristotle's *Nichomachean Ethics* (*Éthique à Nicomaque*, 1370–73), *Politics* (*Politique*, 1374), *Economics* (*Économique*, misattributed to Aristotle, 1374), and *On the Heavens and the World* (*Du ciel et du monde*, 1377), all from Latin (rather than from Aristotle's Greek), he created an impressive number of neologisms in French (and, by extension, in English), for example: abstraction, function, identity, object, relation, subject (*Ethics*); action, dialogue, hierarchy, impossibility, presidency, technique (*Politics*); complication, indifference, observation, transformation (*On the Heavens*).[13]

Oresme coins "communicacion" in his translation of *Nichomachean Ethics*. "Communicacion" replaces the Latin "societas," "respublica," "amicitia," "urbanitas," "communitas," all terms that we use to refer to communities or political organizations.[14] That is to say that Oresme chooses "communicacion" instead of "communité," a term he uses only to describe a polity, "cité ou communité." Before the invention of "communicacion," in French there existed only the term "communion" (Balibar 1998, 23–27;

Berman 2012, 29, 54). "Communion" signaled that via the language of the church (Latin), the faithful integrated the body of Christ; there was an inherence of knowledge to the universality of Latin and a relationality— via communion—among the same. In contrast, "communicacion" posits something else: relationality because of difference.

Here is how Oresme translates Aristotle: "And if there were no com-mutation, there would be no communication. And there would be no commutation without equality, and no equality without measure" (Et se il n'estoit nulle commutacion, il ne seroit nulle communicacion. Et nulle commutacion ne seroit qui ne feroit equalité, et nulle equalité ne seroit se elle n'estoit faite par mesure; Oresme 1940, 5.9:297). Communication is born out of human need for things; need can be satisfied by communicat-ing. But in order to communicate, one has to commute, that is convert. Conversion and hence communication are made possible by a measure of equality between things that are different, a third term that will at once make it possible for a carpenter to be compensated by a cobbler, and for a farmer to obtain wine from a vintner regardless of when his wheat har-vest is finished. The measure of equality resolves the problem of barter (how many shoes for a house?), and the problem of time (buying wine as needed, asynchronously from the harvest): "One should measure such things by some other thing, whatever it may be" (Donques convient il teles choses mesurer par une autre chose quelle que elle soit; Oresme 1940, 5.9:295). In other words, if there is to be a conversion, different things have to enter into a relationship by a measure of comparison. This artificial measure (mesure artificiel; Oresme 1940, 5.9:295) is money: "It is neces-sary that all the things that are being commuted somehow be compared and evaluated one with the other. Money was first invented for this reason and comes from this [need]" (Convient il que toutes choses de quoy l'en fait commutacion soient comparees aucunement et avaluees l'une a l'autre. Et pour ce fu premierement trouvee monnoie et de ce vint elle; Oresme 1940, 5.9:294).[15]

Money is the third term that makes commutation and, consequently, communication possible: "if there were no commutation, there would be no communication" (se il n'estoit nulle commutacion, il ne seroit nulle communicacion; Oresme 1940, 5.9:297).[16] In Oresme's translation, com-munication and commutation are cosubstantive: "les communications ou commutacions" (Oresme 1940, 5.9:295); one is at once the condition and the effect of the other. Need creates both communication (relation among people) and conversion (relation among things).

Thus communication is the outcome of a commutation that is a com-mensuration; communication is a commensuration, a relationality of difference. What is "comeasured" are two things on the scale of difference, from comparable (similar, lowest degree of difference) to incomparable (dissimilar, largest degree of difference). Communication emerges between two points of difference that require commensuration and transit via a common third term, *measure*. In other words, we are not dealing with direct equivalence and identity (communication is not a communion), nor are we dealing with binaries; commensuration produces "equality," not fidelity (likeness). Communication is therefore not a direct relation of equivalence, but a ternary relation of commensuration, of loyal production of equality in the relationship of difference. The ternary translational structure also means that commensuration permits a comparison of incomparables. As a form of conversion, long before identity and fidelity, translation was a commensuration of discourses, and the need for communication its first condition. It was ternary, relational, loyally commensurating the incomparables (or the untranslatables).

In his gloss on Aristotle, Oresme connects money to social and political organization: "It becomes clear that the custom of money is as if necessary to civic communication" (il appert que usage de monnoie est aussi comme neccessaire en communicacion civile; Oresme 1940, 5.9:297n15). Relating two things via a third term—that is, communication or conversion—is the condition of possibility of civil society. In other words, community comes after communication; if community is political, communication is what makes the political become. If, as we observed, Oresme prefers "communicacion" to "communité," it is because communication—commensuration—is a form of relationality by which there is "commonness," a "with-ness."[17] Communication is the first condition even before identity—one does not communicate an identity, but one does form an identity in communicating. Medieval communication, in Oresme's understanding, is about community, not messaging and meaning, formed in the constant effort of commensuration via a third term: an intermediary. The fixer is the third term, which cannot be elided or silenced because she or he is the common measure.

The Legacy of the Nation-State: Walter Benjamin, Marco Polo, and Christopher Columbus

Yet, commensuration—a ternary process—is not the way we see translation, since for the moderns, translation is binary, nor do we take communication to be the goal of translation. Both these views are a legacy of modernity's relationship to translation and interpreting that began in the Age of Romanticism, the time of nation-states. In the opening lines of his 1923 canonical essay "The Task of the Translator," Walter Benjamin posits what will influence and shape translation studies, literary studies, Continental philosophy, comparative and postcolonial literatures: the superiority of literary translation to all other forms of translation. At the same time, he excludes communication—that is translation or interpreting for the sake of communication—from the realm of sanctioned and legitimate linguistic study: "For what does a literary work 'say'? What does it communicate? It 'tells' very little to those who understand it. Its essential quality is not statement or the imparting of information. Yet any translation which intends to perform a transmitting function cannot transmit anything but information—hence, something inessential" (Benjamin 1969, 69–70). These were two significant moves: in his search for "pure" language via translation, Benjamin opposed translation to communication. He characterized communication as nothing more than an inessential function of transmitting meaning and information. Tangentially, he erased the person of the translator, who appears only in the title to his essay, in favor of (agentless) translation attaining "pure" language. In the European-influenced philosophy of translation, and much of twentieth-century European critical theory, Benjamin's essay was taken to confirm the prestige of literary translation and to downgrade communication to messaging (technical or social communication) and public relations spin (Berman 1984, 12). In this way, Benjamin's essay cemented the notion of elitism of literary translation that went back to Friedrich Schleiermacher's 1813 distinction between art and scholarship (literary translation) and commerce (interpreting and technical translation). Interpreting was devalorized as "a merely mechanical task that can be performed by anyone with a modest proficiency in both languages" (Schleiermacher in Inghilleri 2012, 125). This created a long-standing twentieth-century hierarchy between translation studies and interpreting studies, in favor of translation and to the point of exclusion of interpreting from translation studies. The narrow, elitist, and highbrow identity of translation as literary, not as commensuration, is a recent, modern, national development, the exclusionary politics of interpreting from translation studies its heritage.

This legacy explains perhaps much of why so few historical studies of premodern intermediaries center on languages of communication: for much of modernity, communication has been a discredited linguistic function, and interiorized as unworthy of the status of translation. In short, historical studies often focus on brokers and intermediaries (although they do not always foreground their analysis in language difference), and literary studies define language difference mainly through an agentless translation and transmission of texts; historians study intermediaries, while literary historians study translations. A good number of premodern historical studies of the Mediterranean have investigated circulation and exchange through interpersonal contact of brokers and go-betweens—soldiers and spies; pirates and corsairs; merchants and emissaries; captives and slaves; missionaries, pilgrims, and converts—who were instrumental in facilitating the commercial, political, and cultural traffic across wide swaths of land and sea.[18] But only some scholars have positioned language(s) of communication as central to their studies, and especially for the early modern period.[19] In parallel, in literary history the attention to textuality and literary (textual, manuscript) traditions prevails, since interpreting does not accede to the status of literature and literary translation. Medievalists have especially remained confined to the text, exploring translation as a form of written exchange and interaction but without much attention to oral, interpersonal contact and communication. Worldwide, beyond Anglophone medieval studies, scholarship of medieval European literature has been characterized by a classical philological approach to manuscript traditions, that is, cataloging the transmission of texts into different languages and cultures and a comparative study of literary genres. It suffices to mention the oft-quoted transfer of the ancient Greek medical and philosophical corpus into Latin via Arabic and Hebrew. Instead of the connectivity to the world, literary studies have too often presented a connectivity of texts in isolation from the world.[20] Textuality, tradition, fidelity between the original and its translation, and authorship have been the predominant lens of medieval literary studies. This almost exclusive emphasis on manuscript traditions and textual translations has tended to neglect communication, the oral dimension of contact between persons, making the study of orality a particularly thorny problem for European medieval textuality.

The fixer apparatus allows a different approach to the sources. Consider the example of Marco Polo in his *Description of the World* (*Le Devisement du monde*), dictated in 1298. There is not a single instance of interpreting in it, although translation makes possible Polo's travels and their narrative. The mention of language difference is reduced to Polo's formulaic assessment of peoples who "have their own language" (ont langajes por elz; Polo 2016, 172 / Polo 1982, 579). The only other indication of language difference occurs early in the narrative: "Now it so happened that Marco, Messer Niccolò's son, learned the Tartars' customs, languages, and writing so well that it was a marvel; for I tell you in all truth that not long after coming to the great lord's court, he learned to read and write [four] languages" (Or avint que Marc, le filz messer Nicolao, enprant si bien le costume de Tartars et lor langajes et lor leteres [que c'estoit mervoille]; car je voç di tout voiremant que, avant grament de tens puis qu'il vint en la cort dou grant segnor, il soit de [quatre] langaies et de quatre letres et scriture; Polo 2016, 10 / Polo 1982, 317–18). Although to this day scholars are unsure what the four "Tartar" languages are—three of the four are thought to be Mongolian, Uighur, and Persian[21]—Marco Polo uses his linguistic and cultural knowledge to place himself at the center of the narrative: at the Great Khan Qubilai's court he translates stories about the West, and, later, in Genoa he translates for his European audience stories about Asia. In both courts, Polo is the fixer who speaks directly into a translated language, whether Tartar or Franco-Italian. This resembles the account of the mission to the Mongols by John of Plano Carpini, dictated in October 1247 by Brother Benedict the Pole (Benedictus Polonus), Carpini's "companion in our tribulations and interpreter" (nostre tribulationis socius et interpres).[22] Benedict, who was Carpini's official interpreter for German and Slavic languages, makes not a single mention of translation in his account. Since a fixer does not need an interpreter because he himself is one, we are led astray if we look for evidence of interpreters, rather than of fixers.[23] The case of being one's own fixer is "invisible" through the lens of interpreting defined in contemporary terms. These two examples are central to the way in which we have been (mis)reading translation in the medieval period, focusing on the presence of interpreters while leaving out entire networks of interlinguistic exchange and social organization. While it is easy to spot language difference when narratives highlight the role of interpreters, there are many more occasions—unmarked—where communication through translation occurs without the narrative ever drawing our attention to it. Fixers are not just hired interpreters but organize a whole network of relations and actions.

In adopting a new paradigm, we can cast a wide net wherever we encounter unintelligibility and conflict across a variety of sources, whether fictional or factual. I therefore do not maintain as strict a separation between sources as would history and literature respectively. Fixers recalibrate the modern categories that separate imagination from history, literature from document. Christopher Columbus is my most eloquent example: he traveled with a copy of Marco Polo's Description of the World when he sought the western route to the Great Khan and, beyond, to Jerusalem, since access was cut off by the Ottoman advances in the Mediterranean. Alongside Marco Polo, Columbus read the crusade treatises and John Mandeville, author of a largely imaginative narrative of the "Far East." These readings of Columbus—a description of the world, crusade treatises, and a (fictional) travelogue—are quintessential "fixer literature"— literature of the fixers by the fixers for the fixers—that gave Columbus direction and motive for travel. Columbus made no distinction between what we call documents and fictions.[24] If equality is the goal of commensuration, we have to reevaluate medieval writing of all genres and forms whose value modernity has based in notions of fidelity between text and event and between an original and "its" translation. In fact, these writings were called in the twelfth century "letreure," a reference to the written, textual production, and to knowledge production through books. In this book, I therefore treat all writing, "letreure," as an archive of fixers. Imagined fixers, of whom we have a record, were no less important, as we shall see, than "real" fixers of whom we have no record. In this commensuration of fiction and fact, documented historical fixers provide the necessary point of comparison and measure (for modern audiences).

Translatio(n) in the Middle Ages: Teleology of Europe's Rise or Precarity of Human Knowledge?

Throughout its recent history, translation has also been analyzed as a specifically European model of transmission. This model incorporates *translatio*, a central medieval political and cultural notion and theory. The medieval Latin term *translatio* stands for transfers of power (*translatio imperii*), knowledge (*translatio studii*), physical objects or materials (such as relics in *translatio reliquiarum*), and linguistic translation. A canonical twelfth-century description of *translatio* shows it as an inexorable movement of knowledge and power through space and time in different material forms, from the East to the West. We find this movement in the frequently cited example taken from the twelfth-century verse romance *Cligés* (ca. 1176), a Byzantine-Arthurian chivalric adventure by the author known as Chrétien de Troyes: "Our books have taught us that chivalry and learning first flourished in Greece; then to Rome came chivalry and the sum of knowledge, which now has come to France. May God grant that they be maintained here and may he be pleased enough with this land that the glory now in France may never leave" (Ce nos ont nostre livre apris / Que Grece ot de chevalerie / Le premier los et de clergie: / Puis vint chevalerie a Rome / Et de la clergie la some, / Qui or est an France venue. / Dex doint qu'ele i soit retenue / Tant que li leux li embelisse / Si que ja mais de France n'isse / L'ennors qui s'i est arestee).[25] *Translatio* presented this way—the move from east to west, from Greece to Rome to France or to French-speaking England—is the ideology of legitimation that educated medieval people wanted to believe (Jongkees 1967). What is more, this articulation gave this transmission a sense of inevitability and predestination, since the linearity of *translatio* reads as a hereditary genealogy of sorts. Such a narrow idea of what medieval *translatio* was—a linear, as if genealogical, transmission from east to west—hews closely to the narrowness of the modern understanding of translation as linguistic, from source to target; as if, indeed, the West always had been the final destination for power and knowledge. It also corresponds to the idea that translation of knowledge, or *translatio studii*—in written or book form—is preeminent. Finally, it introduces the idea that translation is a tool of conquest and colonization. This articulation of *translatio* thus lends itself easily to a teleology of the rise and eventual expansion of Europe, the ideological claim that the West was always destined to concentrate the knowledge and the power of the world.

Such a configuration has made it difficult to recognize that on a European continuum, translation was first about transmission, understood in much broader terms of "transfer" than our modern translation. *Translatio* as an ideology of European ascent to domination is, in fact, a retrospective interpretation privileged in modern scholarship of the European Middle Ages, best exemplified in the classical work of Ernst Robert Curtius.[26] To grasp an expansive—and different—notion of translation in the Middle Ages, we have to consider how a culture *thinks* the activity of translating and of transmitting.

Translation in the Middle Ages was a crossroads of multilingual and multicultural contacts and encounters.[27] *Translatio* describes a range of transfers across time, space, and matter that exceed by far the linguistic translation of texts. A teleological reading of *translatio*, often privileged in literary studies, neglects the fact that these transmissions occurred alongside and thanks to changes in language: linguistic translation was both a cultural and a material translation. Medieval translation was a nexus of a will to knowledge (*studium*) and technologies of power (*imperium*), while registering a historical version of their origin (in the East) and the effect of their transmission (in the West); the effect of transmission was neither determinism nor election. Wace's *Romance of Brutus* (*Roman de Brut*; 1155), itself a translation of Geoffrey of Monmouth's Latin work *History of the Kings of Britain* (*Historia regum Britanniae*; ca. 1135), portrays translation as a process of change of dominions. The changes in rule coincide with the changes in names: "Through many great acts of destruction that foreigners committed, who often held, conquered, and lost the land, the names of cities and regions are completely different from the names given to them by the ancestors who first founded them" (Par plusurs granz destruiemenz / Que unt fait alienes genz / Ki la terre unt sovent eüe, / Sovent prise, sovent perdue, / Sunt les viles, sunt les contrees / Tutes or altrement nomees / Que li anceisor nes nomerent / Ki premierement les fonderent; Wace 1999, lines 1239–46). In his later *Romance of Rollo* (*Roman de Rou*; 1160–74), Wace makes clear that name changes are caused by language changes, as each conqueror imposes their language: "By the length of time and their antiquity, and by the changes of languages, towns, cities, and regions have lost their first names" (Par lunc tens et par lungs aages / e par muement de langages / vnt perdu lur premerains nuns / viles, citez e regiuns).[28] In the 1380s and 1390s, Jean Froissart chronicled politics and conflicts of fourteenth-century Europe and the Mediterranean. He framed his *Chronicles* with the *translatio* of prowess, that is of chivalry (*imperium*), which had begun in Chaldea and Judea, then came to Persia and Greece, and, in his time, France and England. Froissart pointed to the vagaries of power shifts and indeterminacy of *translatio:* "I do not know if it wants to advance [westward] or return [eastward]" (Or ne sçai pas se elle voelt encores aler plus avant ou retourner).[29] There is nothing that guarantees that the migration of chivalry (*imperium*) will continue beyond the European West or even return eastward.

Contrary to a teleological reading, this mutation—and migration—has little to do with hereditary succession but is rather a way of tracing successions that result from a shifting power differential: it is a transmission, but it is not a genealogy.[30] It is a succession but not historical determinism. Moreover, migration and mutation are not governed by fidelity to an original. The materiality, and the precarity, of *translatio*—that power migrates and mutates with language change—means that translation is not faithful to an "original," but that we call "translation" that which precedes and mutates. This translation now surpasses—by supersession—what is only a precedent (but not an "original"). Finally, preservation of knowledge and memory from death and destruction happen only thanks to human agency: "Of the transformations of the names and the deeds of which we speak, we would have little or nothing to say, if man did not have them be recorded" (Des tresturnees de ces nuns, / e des gestes dunt nus parluns, / poi u nïent seüssum dire, / si l'um nes eüst feit escrire; Wace 1877, vol. 2, part 3, lines 81–84). Although not a creator in the sense of an "original" work, the human translator is key to the process of preservation.

A teleological reading of *translatio* has also neglected that knowledge was a means to power for all the rulers who encouraged and supported translation movements. In the Middle Ages, knowledge was seen as the foundation of all power; in the West, its language had been Latin. Translation into a vernacular meant transfer of power (empire) away from Latin (the church). Regardless of the language of transfer, sponsorship of a translation movement and using it to fashion oneself as a great ruler were a shared impulse across cultures. Caliph al-Mansur (r. 754–75) and the

FIGURE I.1: Giovanni of Monte Cassino, *Sultan of Tunis Sending al-Razi's Book in Arabic; Charles of Anjou Receiving the Book from Messengers; Charles of Anjou Commanding a Translation from Faraj ben Salim and Faraj ben Salim Translating.* From Faraj ben Salim, *Liber Elhavy* or *Continens Rhazis* (books 1–25), translation of the Persian physician al-Razi's *Comprehensive Book on Medicine (Kitāb al-hāwī),* Naples, 1279–82. Paris, BnF, Latin 6912, vol. 1, fol. 1v. Photograph: Bibliothèque nationale de France.

translation movement in Baghdad during the Abbasid caliphate (eighth to thirteenth centuries), King Roger II in Norman Sicily (r. 1130–54), Alfonso X the Wise, king of Castile and Leon (r. 1252–84), Charles V of France (r. 1364–80), and Philip III of Burgundy (r. 1419–67) are just some of the rulers who wielded effectively the power of translation. Empire (*imperium*) could be within reach of the one who invested in translation (Kinoshita 2008b). Moreover, translation was a dynamic process, in which a book was a relational and a transitional object. A frontispiece miniature in a 1279 Latin translation of *Liber Elhavy* or *Continens Rhazis* (books 1–25), by Faraj ben Salim, of the Persian physician al-Razi's *Comprehensive Book on Medicine* (the *Hawi, Kitāb al-hāwī*), made for Charles d'Anjou of Sicily, is a case in point (fig. I.1). The miniature is composed of three frames, moving from right to left: the upper right-hand frame pictures the sultan of Tunis giving al-Razi's book in Arabic to three emissaries of Charles I; the upper left-hand frame then shows the three emissaries presenting the manuscript to the king; the single bottom frame, split in two, shows Charles commissioning a translation from Faraj, and Faraj translating alone at his desk. The pivot on which this image stands is the translator and the open book; this frame serves as the initial E, the opening of the prologue and of the translation. The translator obeys a princely order, at origin of his translation is a prince, but the translator and the book are pivotal; they are the base, the pivot of the initial. Translation is secondary only to the patron's command, by order of succession, but it is not derivative of an "original." As pivot and first letter (initial E) of the text, the bottom frame of the miniature highlights translation as primary; it is the origin from which flows the text. By virtue of migrations and mutations, it is not proprietary. Most of all, translation depends on interpersonal communication, as each frame of the image shows.

Translation, Coloniality, and Untranslatability

Throughout the Middle Ages, it was translation, and not authorship, that served as the primary model of cultural and knowledge production, based on a radically divergent notion of equivalence and fidelity defined by the preservation of content and its migration. Overall, medieval translation (especially, scientific translation)[31] was accurate, but its "infidelity," according to modern standards, stems from the fact that either not everything or too much was translated—one proceeded by adaptation, appropriation, abbreviation, and amplification. Much of medieval (theological and philosophical) translation was interlinear, via commentary and gloss. This process of accretion was in essence a collective and collaborative text,

creative but not original. Conversely, the notion of an original did not pre-
vail. Instead of originality, the merit of a precedent to be translated came
from past authority. What mattered were preservation and access (of and
to authority), not accuracy. Accuracy was based in relation to authority:
that which was worth preserving in translation was truthful, "accurate."
This primacy and prestige of translation were such that they led to the
vogue of pseudotranslation, whereby authors pretended to be translators
instead of original creators. Miguel de Cervantes's *Don Quixote* (1605–15)
is a late, and perhaps the most famous, albeit far from the sole or last,
example of writers seeking prestige in the guise of translators rather than
in their own right, as authors.

It is usually said that on the cusp between the late Middle Ages and the
Renaissance (fourteenth to sixteenth centuries), the hierarchy between
the translation and an "original" changed; the emergence of the author
is customarily credited with this reversal. There is another way of looking at this, seeing the author emerge from the translational impetus to
vernacularization, the secularization of power through vernacularization,
and the simple linguistic fact that anything becomes translatable (not only
the church authorities). Authors evolved from fixers, and authorship from
translation (see chapter 5).

Philological humanism introduced new attitudes to translation, embodied in Leonardo Bruni's treatise *De interpretatione recta* (*On the Right
Way to Translate*, 1420): "I say that the full power of a translation resides
in the fact that what is written in one language should be rightly [or cor-
rectly] translated into another" (Dico igitur omnem interpretationis vim
in eo consistere, ut, quod in altera lingua scriptum sit, id in alteram recte
traducatur).[32] According to Bruni, linguistic competence must complement a competence in style and form that can be acquired only through
the mastery of the letters, the requirement for translator's competence and
expertise in source and target languages: "the translator transforms himself into the original author with all his mind, will, and soul, and he also
ponders the problem of how to transform the shape, the stance, the gait,
the style, and all the other features, and how to express them" (interpres
quidem optimus sese in primum scribendi auctorem tota mente et animo
et voluntate convertet et quodammodo transformabit eiusque orationis
figuram, statum, ingressum coloremque et liniamenta cuncta exprimere
meditabitur; Bruni 1992, 84 / Bruni 2008, 44–46). A new method, "optima
interpretandi ratio" (the highest rule of translation), recommends instead
"that the shape of the original text should be kept as closely as possible,
so that understanding does not lose the words any more than the words
themselves lose brilliance and craftsmanship" (si figura prime orationis

quam optime conservetur, ut neque sensibus verba neque verbis ipsis nitor ornatusque deficiat; Bruni 1992, 85 / Bruni 2008, 48). In other words, philological humanism in its return to the "original" language—the one in which a text was first written—imposes a new concept of translation as linguistic equivalence, a single (not multiple) translator activity, and opposes accuracy in translation to the previous relative autonomy of the text and translator(s). The translational worth of a text was no longer established by authority and access, but by method of linguistic and historical accuracy; thus method created the original and the original displaced authority as the source.

Method also made room for claims of authorship. The two-hundred-year difference between Nicole Oresme, clergyman and translator of Aristotle for Charles V of France (1370–77), and poet and emissary Joachim du Bellay, in 1549, is one between a translator and an imitator (author). Oresme tells the readers that "then it was so that Greek was to the Latin of Rome as Latin is now to our French" (Or est il ainsy que, le temps de lors, grec estoit en regard de latin quant aux Rommains si comme est maintenant latin en regard de françois quant a nous). Translation into French is "for the public good" (pour le bien commun) and therefore "to be praised" (est à recommander; Oresme 2013). It is also the first step in the transformation of the French vernacular into a learned language of Latin's stature. But by the time of du Bellay, the motivation is no longer to make Aristotle speak French to permit access to content, but to cannibalize and become a French Horace and Petrarch: "If the Romans . . . did not devote themselves to this labour of translation, by which means then were they able to enrich their language even to make it almost equal to Greek?" (Si les Romains . . . n'ont vaqué à ce labeur de traduction, par quels moyens donc ont-ils pu ainsi enrichir leur langue, voire jusques à l'égaler quasi à la grecque?) Instead of translating, the Romans imitated "the best Greek authors, transforming themselves into them, devouring them; and, after having well digested them, converting them into blood and nourishment . . . and these like shoots, as I have already said, they grafted and applied to their own tongue" (imitant les meilleurs auteurs grecs, se transformant en eux, les dévorant, et après les avoir bien digérés, les convertissant en sang et nourriture . . . et icelles comme greffes, ainsi que j'ai dit devant, entaient et appliquaient à leur langage).[33] We go from Oresme's indifference to language—Oresme translated from Latin and not from Aristotle's Greek—and nonproprietary translation devoted to the common good to du Bellay's language as the tool of domination and marker of origin (property and identity) and, ultimately, to linguistic nationalism.

Du Bellay signals what will be a long process of changing attitudes to translation and language in a process of retraction from global relationality (*translatio*, or migration and mutation of content irrespective of language, accuracy, origin, and ownership). It will culminate in modern European nation-state prominence (translation as method; language as property and instrument of domination; author as origin). Concomitantly, a move toward fidelity (likeness) and accuracy in translation can be understood as property demarcation, the colonial mode. Henceforth, translation could play only the supporting role to the property of the original and the name of the author; where translation had been content, authorship was first imitation of forms and ultimately development of style autochthonous to a vernacular language and rise of the modern aesthetic value judgment.

Faithful translation—the basis for our modern method of translation—and the institution of the original, the resulting claims to authorship, and colonization go hand in hand. This can be easily observed in the curious, and little remarked on, change of attitudes toward language acquisition and translation right around the time when notions of original, author, and linguistic property begin to emerge. In the late medieval period under study here, from the mid-thirteenth to end of fifteenth century, *translatio* was a free-form translation (less about inaccuracy of translation than about at-will abbreviation or amplification) and often a collective enterprise, a workshop. At the same time, foreign language acquisition was the desirable norm. It was felt that those who wanted to engage with the other should learn their language; interpreters were not enough for proselytism or conquest, and occupiers and preachers needed to learn the language of the conquered or of those targeted for conversion if they were to succeed in their missions (see chapters 1 and 2). When translation attitudes shift to historical and linguistic fidelity, translation engages in the colonial mode, because it not only sets the right of ownership in the target language, but moreover it sets the norm, the standard, whereby the dominant judge the dominated. Acquisition of the foreign language loses its appeal for colonizers, who impose massively their language on the conquered natives, often through missionaries; colonizers are no longer displaced into a foreign language but domesticate the colonized into their own. Even though this change was gradual and slower than we usually think, nevertheless, by the nineteenth century translation became synonymous with the assumption and appropriation into the language of the (European) colonizer.

Concordant with the idea of European colonial expansion, Pascale Casanova showed that du Bellay's rejection of translation as a creative process was also the beginning of the constitution of an autonomous—transnational—literary space, regulated by an inherent, though invisible,

European and national aesthetic value system, the norm for world literature, which has led to the late twentieth- and twenty-first-century world
literature in translation. Other, non-European or lesser European (Europe's minor languages), often heterogenous, forms of literature can be
candidates for translation into dominant languages (of western Europe)
only if they correspond to those norms, seen as universal values of literature. Specifically, Anglophone capitalist markets, the most dominant, set
and drive almost exclusively the publication into English of translatable—
palatable—works from other cultures. It has led to the very problem, seemingly unsolvable, of world literature today that is English-dominated and
evaluated by the norms of Anglophone academic and book markets. The
problem of world literature is not just that it is culturally Eurocentric, but
that it is Eurocentric by virtue of the economic (capitalist, that is, European) system. In the twenty-first century globalized, transnational world,
capitalist book and translation markets erase the heterogeneity of world
forms of knowledge and knowledge systems by conditioning the regimes
of writing (themes, styles, genres) and their translation (into English), a
colonial nature of European expansion and domination that continues to
impose the silent (European) national model as universal. Literature, of
course, is not merely a market phenomenon, although its norms of universality are uncontestably linked to colonialism and capitalism. In other
words, this kind of literary history and translation, where literature and its
forms are defined by equivalence, aesthetics, authorship, and debasement
of translation, is and remains wedded to colonial expansion and domination of European nation-states.

In recent years, scholars have responded to this problem of world literature regulated on the single—Eurocentric—translational mode with the
concept of untranslatability. Deployed at first in the context of philosophy
of translation and translation of philosophy, "the idea was to replace ontological nationalism with an approach that emphasized the shapes of language assuming a national silhouette or personality."[34] How do languages
express and differ concepts in their untranslatable particularity without
owning them, since each language has its own form to translate the untranslatable concept? The impact and value of untranslatability has been
immense in the move to revalorize philosophizing in non-European languages. But what about non-European philosophies; what about radically
different systems of thought built around notions such as character (in
African languages: Akan, Ewe, Igbo, Yoruba, Shona, South Soto) and that
diverge from a European philosophy that places morals and morality, not
character, at its core?[35] And what about thought systems where comparison
is in the service of translation (rather than the Western reverse view) and

translation occurs as "transversal communication between perspectives in which the position of the human is in constant dispute"? (Viveiros de Castro 2014, 87, 151). Is untranslatability the last line of (ethical and practical) defense in the name of Indigenous and heterogenous discourses?

Thinking untranslatability, even when one is open to other philosophies and translations, posits translation of texts as the norm, whose very source is in Bruni's (and Petrarch's) notions of historical and linguistic propriety and later, in the nineteenth century, in property. Untranslatability also grounds us in Eurocentric literary and philosophical translation, because literature and philosophy that are being translated are inherently European, not Indigenous. Untranslatability does not include, or come close to resolving, what happens to cultures of orality and our inability to commensurate oral culture, theory, and history with western European writing and truth regimes. What happens when we question writing and literary translation as the norm? In this light, the concept of untranslatability appears as too narrow a question and too thin of a line of defense of heterogeneity of cultural forms and modes of inquiry. Untranslatability needs to be unmoored from its premises of translation as equivalence, by which it also maintains essentialist and incommensurable positions of postcolonial asymmetries. It also needs to unyoke from the philosophy of translation where the norm is still the written word. Neither the Republic of Letters defined by the expansion of Europe and its rise to global domination (Casanova) nor untranslatability (Cassin; Apter) is adequate to the circulation of multiple discursive forms in the present-day context of minority challenges to classical Western imperialism and its forms of cultural hierarchy. But most importantly, they reflect the communicative situations neither of the premodern—precolonial—nor of the contemporary—decolonial—situations that turn on collective, ephemeral, migrant, digital "authorship"[36] and that let speak the Indigenous voices. If we are to have world literature, then oral literatures and cultures, songs, sounds, relational acts, ephemeral literary forms, rituals, emergent literatures, and other media literatures must all be included but not according to the norms of the written word. That is, untranslatability needs to relinquish the hallowed notion of "original," in order to open up to non-European systems of knowledge and thought.

Fixing Translation (2): Decolonizing the Middle Ages and Translation Studies

The fixer lens provides a more inclusive approach to translation studies whereby the history of oral, interpersonal translation—interpreting—is not only a legitimate object of study but an indispensable lens. Fixers disrupt the notion of translation as literary—the basic, silent, principle of elite European culture—and expand it to all translational forms, oral and written, literary and nonliterary, Indigenous and heterogenous forms of thought and knowledge. Moreover, fixers reveal the inadequacy of the basic premise of translation as binary, occurring between source and target and premised on the notion of equivalence and fidelity, and they dispel the notion of translation being in the service of an "original."

New forms of interpreting recognize that interpreters take an active social-linguistic role in the interpreting process and that their intervention is often culturally and ethically necessary. Globalization, beyond mere internationalization and multilateralism, has produced situations that have multiplied exponentially in recent decades because of increased humanitarian work, migration, asylum proceedings, and international armed interventions across the globe. There now exists legal, healthcare, military, news, and community interpreting, often performed by civilian, nonprofessional, or not professionally trained interpreters (Baker and Saldanha 2020). Meaning is not central to these activities: "'meaning' of an utterance is not given in language via some form of direct correspondence, but is an outcome of the relationship between utterances in specific contexts where 'language' is but one of many tools used by participants to communicate" (Inghilleri 2012, 8). Extreme conditions (working on the front line, in the hospital, in a courtroom, all situations that may determine life and death) differ from the conference context where interpreters are protected by professional norms and union contracts, inside soundproof cabins. Nonconference contexts often require interventions that contradict the traditionally defined deontology and "fidelity" of the translated discourse. A case of one fixer on the ground, Janis Shanwari, is a case in point.[37] He worked for eight years as interpreter for the US military. Four years into his service, his unit was ambushed by the Taliban; he joined the firefight and saved lives of American soldiers. The interpreter's actions were an ethical choice that exceeded by far the conditions posed by the deontology of interpreting.

The work described in these situations is the work of fixers; their agency exceeds the sole linguistic function attributed to interpreters by the deontology of interpreting. Instead of communicating meaning, they collaborate over meaning: "in communicative contexts where mutual recognition and understanding are at stake, there is no place for positions of impartiality or incommensurability; inter-subjective verifiability is possible only through the ethnographic encounter itself" (Inghilleri 2012, 45). To collaborate is to make commensurable, in other words, intelligible. This is the foundation of an ethical translation that is not based in property and possession. Commensuration is the core of a translation between minority-majority discourses, between the Indigenous and underrepresented and the elite, between the heterogenous and the translatable, between the East and the West, between the present and the past.

Fixers do the work of commensuration in the real world. As analytical lens, they also enable an alternative account of translation and the Middle Ages, one that has repercussions for modern and contemporary translation and disciplinarity. An alternative history of translation as commensuration reckons with the narrow and elitist definition of translation studies (that excludes history of translation; commensuration; orality), and its continued participation in the dominant, capitalist academic and literary market discourses. It lends its support to the current efforts by scholars to bring an ethical activist methodology to T&IS via interpreting.[38] While translation studies took on the ethical role in the critique of postcolonial and transnational asymmetries in translation, the predominantly linguistic definition of interpreting relegated interpreting studies to technique and deontology. And yet, new situations of interpreting give interpreters agency and power, while they also pulverize notions of extrasituational deontology and require an ethical thinking of commensuration. These scholars of interpreting have thus called for the visibility and agency of interpreters to be more explicitly based on ethical considerations in meaning negotiation in political and social communicative contexts, in which interpreters are the sole points of access to all sides of the conflict (understood broadly along the spectrum from disagreement to armed conflict). This book contributes to the efforts to decolonize classical notions of translation by including interpreting in the history of translation.

At the same time, an alternative history of interpersonal communication and fixers as a principal lens to view the medieval world aims to decolonize the Middle Ages from the stranglehold of modernity and its teleology, and from modern translation—fidelity, ownership—as the European colonial mode. As we saw, *translatio* was a major political theory and a main mode of knowledge transmission and production before translation became a European colonial mode of appropriation and ownership. To decolonize the Middle Ages is to decolonize translation from fidelity and equivalence, and the attendant notions of origin, authorship, genre, ownership, linguistic nationalism, and the original, to take our disciplines down from the mounting on which they stand. This also hopefully breaks through the disciplinary presentism that turns on itself: untranslatability does not undo the stranglehold of European norms because it still stands on the premise of Renaissance and Romantic notions of translation as literary and philosophical, and as subservient to an original. Two of the most important critical works of world literature, Pascale Casanova's *La République mondiale des lettres* (1999) and David Damrosch's *What Is World Literature?* (2003), begin with du Bellay and Goethe respectively.

To make the premodern relevant, it does not suffice to reestablish a different genealogy or a literary history that would not start at the Renaissance but begin in the Middle Ages. To make the medieval modern, it has not been enough to show that modernity has its origins in the medieval— with concepts such as author, genre, nation, or race.[39] "Seeing modernities in premodernity" (Heng 2015, 363) across the globe is a call to raising the modernity's awareness of its own lack of exceptionalism—it is a necessary effort. But to change the heuristic value of the premodern, perhaps we must break with the modern, rather than continue inventing the Middle Ages from within the contemporary, modern, and nationally and colonially produced categories. The fixer paradigm is one way of going about it because it forces us to break with the familiar (familial and teleological) modern categories of analysis. In turn, this gives us a standing from which to see the modern with unfamiliarity, rather than seeing it from the teleology of the familial. Hence the double project of decolonizing translation and the Middle Ages is a double commensuration.

Fixers, an Alternative History: Sources and Structure

Undoing these modern norms that keep a stranglehold over medieval studies and T&IS with the fixer apparatus is the goal of the introduction and the conclusion. These sections of the book operate between the medieval and the contemporary, with a simultaneous consideration and cross-pollination of medieval and twenty-first-century fixers, medieval communication and contemporary interpreting, medieval and world literature, to move toward an alternative early global history of literature and translation. The book is then divided into two parts. While the first part presents the historical figure of the fixer and culminates in the articulation of the fixer apparatus, the second part mobilizes the conceptual force of the fixer paradigm. The two parts thus move from a historical to a conceptual analysis, in order to propose a paradigm shift and put the paradigm to work.

The core of the book focuses on medieval texts and experiences, circa 1250–1500. Geographically, the book has the Mediterranean Sea at the center, from the European Northwest across the Mediterranean and the Adriatic Seas to the Near East and North Africa. Alongside crusade treatises and travel reports of missionaries, pilgrims, and spies, I rely on histories, chronicles, and romances, written in prose and in verse, in Latin and Middle French, as well as on sources in Italian, Spanish, and German. Manuscript illumination is another rich archive that I use. Although my sources were written in European languages, fixers in these textual and visual sources are the interface between European and non-European linguistic worlds. In this role, they show the ways in which permeability and porousness between opposing cultures, religions, or languages operate; they reveal how unintelligibility can imply a dynamism of communication, and how cross-linguistic issues in exchange are formulated, analyzed, and resolved. As an interface between different worlds, the fixer brings out themes in common, shared concerns, regardless of the language in which they were recorded and written or, perhaps more accurately, because of linguistic difference.

Part 1, "Historical Realities: Strategy, Loyalty, and Gift," serves principally as a study of fixers' historical presence in primary sources that begin in 1245, the first year of Christian missionary travel to the Mongols, continuing with crusade treatises written after the fall of Acre in 1291, the last Western Christian foothold in Asia Minor. Numerous pilgrim accounts from the fourteenth and fifteenth centuries—with the last travelogue under consideration from a pilgrimage completed in 1499, just before a more widespread and systematic printing of travel reports from the recently discovered parts of the globe—complement the corpus. The propositions of politics and economy are organized around corresponding analytical concepts of strategy (language acquisition), loyalty, and gift.

I define the historical figure of fixers in chapter 1, "The Politics of Translation: Foreign Language Acquisition, Conversion, and Colonization (Thirteenth- and Fourteenth-Century Crusade Treatises)." Religious and political treatises on the reconquest of the Holy Land, written between 1291, the year of the loss of Acre, the last Christian outpost in the Near East, and 1453, the year of the loss of Constantinople to the Ottomans, theorize the centrality of language acquisition and interpreting to medieval legal theory, governmental policy, and military strategy, in relations with Eastern Christians and Muslims, in contradistinction to colonial translation and imposition of language in the Americas. Main sources include the writings of Humbert of Romans, Riccoldo of Monte Croce, Roger Bacon, Fidentius of Padua, William of Adam, Pseudo-Brocardus, Pierre Dubois, and Ramon Llull.

As we have seen in this introduction, linguistic interpreting was only one of the services that fixers rendered to their clients. Fixers were multifunctional, and interpreting was not yet a profession regulated by a set of extrasituational rules. Crusade treatises and missionary travel reports were thus not concerned with describing the method for training the people that we could call "interpreters" and who would be faithful practitioners of their profession, bound by their professional, occupational ethics—a deontology. Instead, they focused on the creation of multifunctional linguistic agents who were loyal and obedient, but who had agency and were therefore autonomous, able to react in unscripted situations. The aim of the early indoctrination of fixers born and trained on the Christian European mainland, to be shipped out, as it were, for service in overseas lands, was to obtain, on the one hand, an autonomous, agentive translation of the faith that would lead to the conversion of the colonized and, on the other, a total obedience on the part of the fixers that would prevent their acculturation and assimilation into the ways of the colonies.

While "The Politics of Translation" shows the centrality of the fixer to European medieval political thought and the building of new overseas state forms, chapter 2, "The Economy of Translation: Missionaries to the Mongol Empire, Pilgrims to the Holy Land, and the Gift of Languages (Thirteenth to Fifteenth Centuries)," complements these geopolitical theories with the lived experience told in missionary accounts of travel to the thirteenth-century Mongol Empire and in accounts of pilgrimages to the Holy Land written between 1330 and 1500. The main sources are the missionary accounts of John of Plano Carpini and William of Rubruck, and pilgrim accounts of Niccolò da Poggibonsi, Lionardo Frescobaldi, Giorgio Gucci, Georges Lengherand, Anselm Adorno, Felix Fabri, Bernhard von Breydenbach, and Arnold von Harff. In this chapter, I trace forms of relationality, from affiliative networks of affinity for missionaries to the "purchasing" power of gifts and a contractual translation market for pilgrims to the Holy Land. In doing so, I focus on communication and demonstrate that translation is a ternary process and a commensuration. A relation of "gift giving" between all the parties—missionaries and their hosts, and pilgrims, fixers, and Arab officials—emerges as the sole condition of possibility for communication. I propose furthermore an intervention in the anthropology of gift exchange that posits that the giver indebts the receiver of the gift. The situations described by missionaries and pilgrims offer an inverse reading: the giver is indebted when his life is saved by the receiver. Fixers hold the lives of gift givers in their hands, putting them in a position that nevertheless does not give them absolute power over life and death, because they themselves are in a circulation of gifts.

Part 2, "Disciplinary Realities: Authorship, Genre, and Literary History," is concerned with larger disciplinary and methodological questions of European medieval studies that emerge from the historical analyses in part 1. The book shifts from the historical, descriptive analysis of the fixer as a figure and an apparatus to a conceptual and paradigmatic use of the fixer to shed light on social, cultural, and artistic phenomena of the medieval, precolonial period and our scholarly narratives and disciplinary assumptions about them. Here, fixers provide a vantage point for the writing of a new literary history of the European Middle Ages, and a rethinking of literary history in its relation to art history (medieval manuscripts). Chapters 3–5 are intended to be read together as a unit. Chapter 3 discusses the relationship of event and writing through multiple levels of intermediation and commensuration: from fixers to writers to literary forms (verse, prose, allegory), as they appear in fourteenth-century writings of Guillaume de Machaut, Philip of Mézières, and Jean Froissart. Chapters 4 and 5 then follow the implications of seeing the relationship between event and text through the lens of fixers, first as they are translated in the literature of (pseudo)translation, in manuscript illumination, and as state building in the Burgundian Netherlands of the fifteenth century (chapter 4). Then, by bringing back the writers discussed in chapter 3, Machaut, Froissart, and Mézières, and understanding their place in the inventory of the library of the Valois Burgundian dukes, I draw the implications of the fixer paradigm toward a revision of modern categories of author and genre (chapter 5).

Chapter 3, "The Ethics of Translation: Loyalty, Commensuration, and Literary Forms in the Fourteenth Century (Machaut, Froissart, Mézières)," picks up the discussion of commensuration from the introduction to understand the articulations of loyalty in the European Middle Ages. Loyalty, and not likeness (fidelity), was the primary interest of medieval "employers." The chapter is structured around two key events, the brief Western capture of the Egyptian city of Alexandria (1365) and the Christian defeat of the Franco-Burgundian and Hungarian armies by the Ottomans at Nicopolis (1396), two events that strongly marked the late fourteenth-century European consciousness. These events, and the role that different multilingual fixers had in their preparation and aftermath, were described by three near contemporaries, Guillaume de Machaut in a verse history, Jean Froissart in a prose chronicle, and Philip of Mézières in a number of allegorical works and one biography. Other writers, like Roger de Stanegrave, also used allegory to write their crusade manuals and to describe the role of fixers.

Loyalty is the basis of ethics in the medieval period, and it is on this concept that truth regimes are erected: the actors in the events no less than historians of these events ground their claims to truthfulness in loyalty. If personal loyalty organized much of European medieval ethos and sociality, we have to reevaluate medieval writing of all genres and forms whose value is based in notions of fidelity between event and text, event and its translation. That is, if writers and their audiences were not preoccupied with fidelity of translation, but their own truthfulness and allegiance to chivalry and Christianity, if the loyalty of fixers is the parameter of truth regimes, then how does this affect our modern reading of medieval historical writing, the poetic forms that it takes, and our modern writing of literary history? The figure of the fixer provides us with a different perspective on medieval history writing, where verse form and historical narrative are not opposed but inform each other. The modern understanding of fidelity of translation implies a difference in form (verse vs. prose) or in genre (history vs. allegory) that shifts the premodern evaluation of "fidelity" between text and event, where the loyalty of fixers and whether their translation is faithful, is under scrutiny. This allows us to commensurate prose, verse, and allegory and better understand the equal use of these forms to record and translate contemporary events.

Chapter 4, "Fixer Literature: (Pseudo)Translation and Manuscript Illumination (the Fifteenth-Century Court of Burgundy)," offers one possible definition of the fixer: an interpreter in the world, a fixer who is in full possession of agency precisely because he or she is in the world. This applied to the Duchy of Burgundy too: as power brokers dealing in many languages, the Dukes of Burgundy officiated as a small fixer state between the East and the West. At that time, the second half of the fifteenth century, the Burgundian Low Countries, or the Burgundian Netherlands, were the hub of luxury manuscript illumination and production in Europe. Fifteenth-century illuminations in Netherlandish manuscripts owned by the Burgundian dukes and its entourage depict translation as a process, show fixers in the world, and affirm translation as primary. By positing translation as originary and a process, they also made translation into an agent of the new world order, one that the Valois Dukes of Burgundy will accomplish in Duke Philip the Fair's ascension to the Spanish throne and culminating in the coronation of his son, the Habsburg Charles V, first as king of Spain (1516) and then as Holy Roman emperor (1519). Rather than an incomplete Kingdom of Burgundy that never became, translation brought about the Valois-Habsburg Empire. The Middle Ages did not wane in Burgundy, but Burgundy transformed itself, in the process of translation, into a flourishing Spanish Empire, the largest of its time. Using the fixer paradigm, this chapter proposes a wholesale reinterpretation of political, social, and cultural (artistic and literary) phenomena in fifteenth-century Valois Burgundy.

Chapter 5, "The Hermeneutics of Translation: Authorship and Genre (the Fifteenth-Century Court of Burgundy)," returns to writers first discussed in chapter 3. Machaut, Froissart, and Mézières wrote under the influence of their individual positions as fixers in the court and government: before there were authors, there were fixers. This is indeed how Burgundian readers saw them in their book collections, which privileged a "fixer literature": literature of the fixers, by the fixers, for the fixers. And before there were genres of romance, epic, and chronicle, there were situational, provisional genres that can be analyzed through the inventories of book collections. The situational clusters of the library of the Dukes of Burgundy give an alternative reading of medieval writing before modern aesthetics—a new literary history. Categories of the inventory of the ducal library free us from reading medieval literature through the literary categories of national and colonial provenance. The library inventory thus enables us to see translations and literature not only as a historical record of a culture and its practices, a representation, but as agentive in such categories as "books of deeds"; beyond representation and in the proper sense of "cultural production," translations "produce" events, generate actions into happening, and reactualize the past as a future. How can the medieval be read as modernity's future anterior, instead of as precursor or origin, its "premodern?" (Agamben 2009c; Stahuljak 2020a). Modernity would then be the speculative future of the medieval instead of the medieval being modernity's past.

The conclusion, "Fixers: Early World Literature in the Age of the Global," picks up the challenge of formulating a world literature of the early world. It first shows that translation is deeply incompatible with nation. I reread the role of two translators and book agents, David Aubert and Colard Mansion, who orchestrated manuscript production in fifteenth-century Burgundian Netherlandish workshops, and at the role of William Caxton, who was at once a translator, a printer, and a merchant, whose first printing shop was in Flanders (present-day Belgium), and who later had a shop in Westminster (England). In modern literary history, Caxton is portrayed as an author; Aubert and Mansion are not. The crucial difference between those who ascend to authorship and those who remain translators lies in the writing of national literary histories: literary history of present-day Belgium is not that of England. That is, medieval translation is uncomfortably "translated" into literary histories of emerging national literatures.

The apparatus of fixer opens onto a series of questions on the relationship of literature and history, textuality and orality, empire, periodization, and world literature. Reading medieval literature through the lens of the fixers, placing translation as commensuration at the center, allows us to unyoke, first, from linear forms of literary history and, second, from national and colonial notions of the disciplinarity of European medieval studies, defined by aesthetics, authorship, and the debasement of translation. Through "fixer literature," early literature reverses the teleology of national literary histories; rather than serving as the (genealogical) origin to national literatures, it can be read as world making; early literature not only would represent and describe the world, but would have imagined and shaped it. It is an early world literature.

In the final instance, the fixer apparatus allows a paradigmatic shift not just of disciplines but of the methodology of the Global Middle Ages. If a claim to early world literature is made, then it behooves us to find other ways of writing new world literary histories in the age of the global, ways that emancipate from national and colonial categories of thinking. Fixers ask us to confront the definition of "the global" that is premised on connectivity (likeness) and contiguity (proximity) and invite us to rethink histories of translation and histories of literature with the notion of commensuration:[40] instead of global, commensurate. That is the ultimate objective of this book.

PART I

Historical Realities: Strategy, Loyalty, and Gift

The Politics of Translation

FOREIGN LANGUAGE ACQUISITION, CONVERSION,
AND COLONIZATION (THIRTEENTH- AND
FOURTEENTH-CENTURY CRUSADE TREATISES)

The thirteenth century was the century of foreign language acquisition in western Europe. A long record of language study going back to at least the Carolingian times preceded this development, when ancient Gothic was studied by scholars, as were Greek, Arabic, and Hebrew, for matters of theology, philosophy, and science. Likewise, practical, non-erudite language study for survival and self-preservation was also first recorded in the ninth century. Elementary dictionaries and phrase books became part of travel guides (sg. *itinerarium*), later also supplemented with maps.[1] But in the early thirteenth century, two new mendicant orders emerge: in 1209 the Franciscans, the Friars Minor; and in 1216 the Dominicans, the Friar Preachers. The Dominicans were active in evangelization and also focused on reunification with the Greek and other Eastern Christians; but preaching (and living) the Gospel in their efforts to incite Latin Christians to repentance and Muslims to conversion was the main ministry of the Franciscans.[2] They established the province of the Holy Land in 1217; the Dominicans did so in 1228 (Jackson 2009, 1). In 1342, the Franciscans became the official custodians of the holy places in the name of the Catholic Church.

The nature of their missions and the locations of their work required the learning of foreign languages, heavily advocated by the Dominicans. The Dominican order was founded by a Castilian Catholic priest, Domingo de Guzmán, in Albigensian southern France. In other words, the Dominican order was formed during the anti-Cathar crusade in the Occitan-language area at a time when Dominic's native Iberia was still a borderland fought over by Christians and Muslims; one was easily attuned to language difference in Occitania and in Castile.[3] The first Dominican circular on language learning dates to 1236. Jourdain of Saxony, master general of the order, recommended: "We exhort that in every province and convent brothers learn the languages of those to whom they are close" (Monemus

quod in omnibus Provinciis et conventibus Fratres linguas addiscant illorum, quibus sunt propinqui; qtd. in Cortabarría-Beitia 1970, 196, 215).
The Dominican Humbert of Romans, master general of the Order of the
Preachers (1254–63), in his *De vita regulari* encouraged his brothers "in the
learning of Arabic, Hebrew, Greek, and pagan languages" (ad linguam arabicam, hebraicam, graecam, et barbaras addiscendas).[4] For about seventy
years, Dominican schools existed in Tunis, Murcia, Barcelona, Valencia,
and Jativa, while those in the east, in Pera and Caffa, continued into the
fifteenth century (Cortabarría 1970). Arabic, Hebrew, Greek, Tartar, and
Armenian were the Dominicans' main languages of study. The Franciscans did not follow suit at first. In a famous case, the Dominican Thomas
Aquinas fought with Franciscans in Paris over the teaching of Greek (and
Aristotle). Nevertheless, by the latter part of the thirteenth century, the
Franciscans accepted the need for language study. Around 1270, the Franciscan Roger Bacon advocated the study of the most common languages
for diplomacy, trade, and conversion of non-Christian peoples (Lusignan
1987, 62–77).

Linguistic acquisition by friars was accompanied by broader training,
especially on differences in doctrine, but also on practical communicative
issues (Cortabarría-Beitia 1970, 218). In fact, the practical needs of communication quickly exceeded the missionary framework. From the fourteenth century onward, travel accounts and reports increasingly resembled
manuals and guides to future travelers, be they pilgrims, missionaries, or
would-be crusaders. The loss of Acre in May 1291, the main port through
which the Latin trade and pilgrims transited after the definitive loss of
Jerusalem in 1244, made visits to pilgrimage sites and communication a
complex endeavor (see chapter 2). Although Christians had had regular
interactions with Muslims ever since the First Crusade and the foundation
of the Latin Crusader kingdoms, it is striking that a greater awareness of
linguistic, cultural, and religious differences, and the necessary apparatus
to overcome them, whether by learning the foreign languages or by hiring
fixers, came into focus at the moment when Christians became wholly
dependent on Muslims for access to the Holy Land, after Acre, in the fourteenth century. For infrequent visitors, such as pilgrims, the best choice
was hiring a fixer: "My advice is to pay whatever price to retain a good
and loyal [fixer] wherever you encounter him, for he will spare you many
dangerous situations" (Nullo igitur precio, bono ac fideli aliquo quovis in
loco invento, quo plura evadatis pericula, dimitti consulo; Adorno 1978,
210). At the very end of the fifteenth century, a German knight, Arnold
von Harff, found a fixer who spoke German and "many languages such as
Latin, Lombard, Spanish, Wendish, Greek, Turkish and excellent Arabic"

(vyllerleye spraiche, as latijn lumbartz hyspanioils wyndichs greex turcks ind guet arabs); moreover, his pilgrimage account included alphabets and nine dictionaries.[5]

By the time of the fifteenth century, new linguistic and logistical realities that the manuals and guides convey likewise placed these enablers, the fixers, at the core of medieval "fiction." Burgundian romances of the second half of the fifteenth century often read like travel itineraries. This is especially true of two types of narratives, both new Burgundian productions and prosifications of earlier verse romances written between 1450 and 1470. They are inventoried in the category "Livres de gestes" (Books of deeds) in the 1467–69 inventory of the Dukes of Burgundy (see chapter 4; Falmagne and van den Abeele 2016). For instance, the *History of the Lords of Gavre* (*Histoire des seigneurs de Gavre*; 1456) displays a great precision for northern Italian, Adriatic, and Greek geography and ethnicity (Stuip 1993). It was mapped closely on the Venetian interests in northern Italy, from Istria, down the Adriatic Sea to the Aegean, while it provided an extraordinary road map to the Duchy of Athens, in reality a substitute for the splendor of the imperial court of Constantinople. Similarly, *Gillion de Trazegnies* (ca. 1450–60) follows the itineraries for crossing the Mediterranean from eastern and western Italy (with Genoese and Venetian merchants) to the Near East and gives an accurate representation of Christian sites of pilgrimage in medieval Syria and travel from Jaffa to Jerusalem, as well as the logistics of travel across the desert to Cairo (provisions, merchants, use of fixers; Morrison and Stahuljak 2015).

Awareness of language difference and the necessity of language study were widespread, not just among educated clergymen, but even among the general population, from those who went among the people—the mendicant orders—to different levels of the aristocracy and, after the fourteenth century, the bourgeoisie, who read (or were read to) about overseas travel and pilgrimage. Regardless of the genre or type of document by which we label texts and narratives—guides, travel reports, or romances—they described similar itineraries and prepared for comparable situations, just as they prescribed and demonstrated linguistic proficiency as a major solution.

There is, however, one set of writings that has escaped the attention of historians of language study and crusade historians precisely on the point of language learning. Crusade treatises, written after the 1291 fall of Acre, were manuals of foreign language acquisition in governmental policy. They laid out foreign language learning and training of fixers as a matter of a (re)conquest strategy of the Holy Land and are pivotal for understanding the interaction of the practice and theory of foreign language acquisition in the European Middle Ages. They were practical and not merely theoretical treatises. Although today we see the loss of Acre as a critical and terminal event, it is important to note that in medieval minds, the loss of the Kingdom of Jerusalem and of Acre was temporary. It is for this reason that crusade treatises, as well as their strategies and taxonomy, not only were pieces of political theory, but were intended for use as manuals. What they have to say about language learning was to be put into practice.

Crusade Treatises (1291–1330)

The loss of the Latin Kingdom of Jerusalem in medieval Syria had begun with the conquest of Jerusalem by Sultan Saladin (r. 1174–93) in 1187. It was slowed down at three different moments: in 1192, with the partial reconquest of the domains by Richard I the Lionheart; during the 1204 peace between sultan Al-Malik and the Latin king of Jerusalem Amalric II; and at the retaking of Jerusalem, by treaty, by Emperor Frederic II Barbarossa in 1229. But in 1244, Jerusalem returned again to Muslim rule, while the Frankish kingdom, still called the Kingdom of Jerusalem, with its new capital in Saint John of Acre, was being progressively reduced to smaller strips of land. The fall of Acre on May 28, 1291, marked the loss of the last Christian foothold in Asia Minor. Between 1291 and 1336, almost thirty treatises were written in favor of "the recovery of the Holy Land" (Lat. *recuperatio Terre Sancte*, Fr. *recorrement / recourement de la Terre Sainte*).[6] The year 1336 was when Benedict XII canceled the crusade by Philip VI of France, precipitating the outbreak of the Hundred Years' War between the Kingdoms of England and France. Even before 1291, and since the 1244 loss of Jerusalem, the recovery of the Holy Land had preoccupied Christian thinkers with some frequency. It can be traced distinctly back to the disastrous final major crusade of Louis IX crusade to Tunis in 1270. Thus the ideas that were so clearly articulated between 1291 and 1336 had already surfaced around 1270 at the Second Council of Lyon (1274), held during the pontificate of Gregory X (1272–76). Gregory X was very favorable to crusading, a position likely boosted by his stay in 1270–71 in Acre (Paviot 2008, 12).

Three major goals of papal policy were determined in Lyon in 1274: aid to and maintenance of the Holy Land, which included the collection of tenths and the interdiction of commerce with Muslims; universal peace among Christians and reform of the church; and union with the Greeks and alliance with the Mongols (Paviot 2008, 14). Centered along these three axes, crusading treatises written approximately between 1291 (the fall of Acre) and 1336 (the Hundred Years' War) constitute a distinct genre. They abandoned the earlier spiritual rhetoric and theologico-juridical justification of the crusading movement, in circulation since the twelfth century, and focused instead on the practical strategies of recovery of the Holy Land.[7]

The categories that this cluster of crusading treatises deployed are practical, concerning preferred trajectory (by sea, by land, by land and by sea); preferred departing and landing points (Constantinople or Alexandria or a port along the coast of Syria); logistical support and supply routes (Cyprus; Rhodes; Armenia); numbers of troops and types of military contingents (knights/cavalry; archers and crossbowman; infantry); types of military commands; spiritual leadership and the preliminary preaching with the crusade; the size of naval forces and maritime blockades; budget; climate and topography; local populations and religions; the maintenance and control of occupied lands; and, not the least, the intellectual and moral (or psychological) qualities required of the leader and his army for successful conquest, conversion, and permanent occupation. Few treatises include all these elements; instead they mix and match categories according to the fluctuating political-historical conditions, the addressee, and the author's viewpoint and experience. There is nevertheless one constant: almost all, whether long or short treatises, put on the same footing material logistics (human and nonhuman resources) with intellectual and psychological (moral) preparation. Troop and fleet numbers, coordination and negotiation of military movements across kingdoms and territories, climate conditions affecting troops and their battle readiness are treated as resources (the terms often used are *commodity, staple,* "mercimonia," whether human or material; Llull 1981, 281). Equally important is the leadership of the crusade, the psychological and intellectual qualities of the "capitaneus." A limited number of treatises add to this discussion another agent, presented as critical to conversion and occupation: the fixer.

Descriptions of the leader and the fixer demonstrate the vital importance of human agency, since they act as interfaces that bring together the material and human resources, as nodal points whose moral fortitude and shrewd intellect alone palliate an otherwise uncontrollable volatility of physical, geographical, climatic, and human elements. More importantly, treatises show that invasion and conquest, "recuperatio," may rest on a leader, but maintenance and permanent occupation, "conservatio," "custodia," rest on fixers. It is important to note here that language concerns and human agency dominate the treatises that strategize the reconquest by land route (as opposed to the sea route) and that advocate for reconquest in total independence of any allies, by reliance on crusaders' own resources. Fidentius of Padua encapsulates this approach when he describes the conditions of the "via per terram": "Pilgrims of Christ must have guides with them, who are called pilots, who lead them by good and straight paths, who provide them with necessities during the crossing. . . . They should also have with them interpreters who know different languages, because they will have to cross different lands that have different spoken languages (vernaculars) and different written languages" (Debent peregrini Cristi secum habere ductores, quos pedotas vocant, qui ducant eos per vias bonas et rectas, qui procurent eis necessaria in via. . . . Habeant etiam secum interpretes qui sciant diversas linguas, quia oportet eos transire per diversas provintias que habent diversa ydiomata et diversas litteras; Fidentius of Padua 2008, 149). Without guides and interpreters, fixers, the passage by land would be impracticable. Again, invasion and conquest, "recuperatio," may rest on a leader, but maintenance and permanent occupation, "conservatio," "custodia," rest on fixers. Military conquest, without the knowledge of foreign languages to enable permanent colonization, would not suffice.

Of some thirty treatises written between 1291 and 1336, I focus on those that theorize the centrality of language education and human agency to medieval political and legal thought and governmental policy: in addition to Fidentius of Padua's *The Book of the Recovery of the Holy Land* (*Liber recuperationis Terre Sancte*; March 1290–January 1291), I study William of Adam's *How to Defeat the Saracens* (*De modo Sarracenos extirpandi*; ca. 1314–18); Riccoldo of Monte Croce's "Appeal to the Eastern Nations" ("Libellus ad nationes orientales"; before October 1320); and *Directory for the Making of the Passage across the Sea* (*Directorium ad passagium faciendum*; ca. 1332) by a Dominican known as Pseudo-Brocardus or Brocardus. I pay special attention to Pierre Dubois's *The Recovery of the Holy Land* (*De recuperatione Terre Sancte*; June 1305–July 1307) and several works by Ramon Llull that cover a considerable length of the period under examination, from 1292 to 1311, among them *The Book of the End* (*Liber de fine*; 1305) and *A Contemporary Life* (*Vita coaetanea*; 1311). I also include *Opus tripartitum* (ca. 1274), of Humbert of Romans, as an important early precursor of their ideas. Beyond the factual information and a taxonomy of the treatises, often characterized by a certain dryness, and the interest that these treatises stimulate in foreign language acquisition policies of the Latin Middle Ages, the fixer apparatus allows us to unravel a whole universe of language learning and lived experience.

Foreign Language Acquisition (Humbert of Romans, Pierre Dubois, Ramon Llull)

Humbert of Romans (1190/1200–1277), master general of the Order of the Preachers, the Dominican order (1254–63), was the first to ground the unity of the "schismatic" Greeks with Latin Christians, and the rees-tablishment of the Latin Empire of Constantinople, in foreign language acquisition. There are two versions of his *Opus tripartitum* (ca. 1272–74), one written by Humbert for the Second Council of Lyon in 1274, and the other summarized and redacted by the Curia.[8] Humbert dedicates the length of the second, and middle, part of his tripartite work to the "rec-onciliation" (reconciliatio) and "to the accomplishment of the business of reuniting the Greeks with the Latins" (ad consummandum negotium reductionis Graecorum ad unitatem cum Latinis). The seventeenth article of the second section proposes nine ways "that would be useful and indis-pensable to the execution and accomplishment of this matter" (Quae sint utilia & necessaria ad istius negotii executionem & consummationem). The first among the indispensable tools is "the knowledge of the Greek language" (scientia Graecae linguae; Humbert of Romans 1690, 220). The redacted version explains succinctly that language has to be learned (*sci-entia*) and practiced (*peritia*) because interpreters are insufficient: "But in the Roman Curia scarcely can one find someone who knows how to read the letters they [the Greeks] sent, and legates sent to them [the Greeks] ought to have interpreters, because it is unclear whether they understand [the Greeks] or are being deceived by them [the Greeks]" (Sed vix in curia Romana invenitur, qui sciat legere literas ab eis missas, et legatos ad eos missos oportet habere interpretes, de quibus nesciatur utrum intelligant aut decipiantur; Humbert of Romans 1968, 7:194). Humbert harks back to the Pentecost, when the apostles were infused with the knowledge of tongues. Had it not been that "God had given to the preachers in the early church varieties of languages, nations speaking an unknown language would not have been converted" (dominus dedisset in primitiva Ecclesia genera linguarum praedicatoribus, non fuissent conversae nationes lin-guae ignotae; Humbert of Romans 1690, 220). Instead of using interpret-ers, apostles spoke the languages of others, becoming their own fixers. But after the Pentecost, the church must train its fixers:

> Whence just as after God ceased to instill knowledge through the Holy Spirit, the church applied a treatment in order that from study would be gained what could not be obtained from infusion [of the Spirit], so

it seems that in the church study should have and should always thrive for the purpose of learning diverse languages, succeeding among people of an unknown tongue, and among others learning the Greek language, just as it was in the time of Augustine and Jerome.

(Unde sicut postquam Dominus cessavit infundere scientiam per Spiritum Sanctum, Ecclesia apposuit curam, ut ex studio haberetur, quod jam non habebatur ex infusione, ita videtur, quod in Ecclesia semper debuisset, & deberet vigere studium, ad addiscendum diversas linguas, ad proficiendum inter gentes ignotae linguae, & inter alias ad linguam Graecam addiscendam, sicut tempore Augustini & Hieronymi fiebat.) (Humbert of Romans 1690, 220)

Just as the Pentecostal knowledge of languages enabled the Christianization of the many nations of "unknown languages" at the time of the first church, so the acquisition of Greek in Humbert's time will bring about reunification of the Christian Church. Humbert regrets that, in contrast to the church's beginnings, and severed from the Pentecostal gift of languages, "ex infusione," in his day those who know and read Greek are few and far between: "Alas! What sorrow! Thus, there are few among the Latins, who know [the Greek] language well, so that one can scarcely even in the Roman Curia find someone who knows how to read the letters that the Greeks occasionally send" (Nunc autem proh dolor! ita pauci sunt inter Latinos, qui sciant hujusmodi linguam, quod vix in curia etiam Romana invenitur quandoque, qui literas, quas Graeci mittunt interdum, sciant legere; Humbert of Romans 1690, 220). If Greek were taught well, so that there were "many good and wise men who knew this language well" (boni viri et prudentes multi qui scirent bene hanc linguam), they then could "quickly read [through the Greek scriptures], see on what they rely, and debate with the wisest among them" (transcurrere & videre quibus innituntur, & conferre cum sapientibus eorum; Humbert of Romans 1690, 220). For all the above reasons "it is important to have interpreters who either fully understand this [Greek] language or, if they know it, faithfully interpret it" (oportet habere interpretes . . . utrum plene intelligant illam linguam, vel si sciant eam, utrum fideliter interpretentur; Humbert of Romans 1690, 220). The church must make its fixers to be the new apostles.

The argument remains the same into the fourteenth century: the pope should with each legate "send two or more experienced persons highly skilled in every branch of knowledge. They would outdo the experts of that country in disputing, advising, discussing, and in every other way" (simul mitteret cum ipso peritissimos in qualibet scienia duo vel plures, qui peritiores de illa terra, disputando, consulendo, conferendo, et modis omnibus superarent), because, to begin with, they would be "well grounded in Greek and Latin" (in greco et latino bene fondati; P. Dubois 1956 / P. Dubois 1977, sec. 62). The main point seems to be that knowledge and practice of languages will bring about the unity of the church, "because the diversity of peoples is gathered into a single faith through a plurality of languages" (videtur scientia seu peritia linguae graecae, quia per genera linguarum diversitas gentium in unitate fidei congregatur; Humbert of Romans 1968, 7:194). For Humbert, language acquisition was the key to the integrity of the church and European and Christian territory. The goal was not to impose one language, but to acquire knowledge of languages spoken in the territories projected for reunification—foreign language is the vehicle to the territorial unity as much as to the unity of faith. Foreign language acquisition would thus substitute for the infusion of the tongues of the Pentecost.

Two other authors for whom foreign language acquisition held a central place in the project of the "recuperatio Terre Sancte" wrote in the period between 1274 and 1336: Pierre Dubois (ca. 1250/55–1320?) and Ramon Llull (1232/23–1315/16). Dubois was a French civil lawyer and advocate for royal ecclesiastical cases in the bailiwick of Coutances. He wrote his theoretical treatise *The Recovery of the Holy Land* (*De recuperatione Terre Sancte*) between June 1305 and July 1307.[9] It is divided into two parts, part 1 addressed to the English king Edward I, and part 2, to the French king Philip IV.[10] Ramon Llull is one of most prolific authors of the medieval period, a Dominican theologian and missionary who, in his two hundred works in Catalan, Arabic, and Latin, returned repeatedly to the subject of the recovery of the Holy Land between 1292 and 1311, first in a two-part *Liber de passagio* (*The Book of Passage*; 1292), composed of "Quomodo Terra Sancta recuperari potest" (How to reconquer the Holy Land) and "Tractatus de modo convertendi infideles" (Treatise on how to convert the unbelievers), which could be read and seemed to have circulated independently. He continued his advocacy in *Liber de fine* (*The Book of the End*; 1305), addressed to pope Clement V; *Liber natalis pueri parvuli Christi Iesu* (The book of birth of the small child Jesus Christ; 1306–7), addressed to Philip IV; *Liber de acquisitione Terrae Sanctae* (*The book of conquest of the Holy Land*; 1309); and his autobiography, *A Contemporary Life* (*Vita coaetanea*; 1311).[11]

Both Dubois and Llull were proponents of the reconquest of Jerusalem via a land route, a strategy that depended on fixers. For Dubois, the point of departure is a new Latin Kingdom of Constantinople and from there a land route (P. Dubois 1956 / P. Dubois 1977, sec. 117). In *De fine*, Llull discusses four different sea and land routes—via Constantinople, Alexandria, Cyprus to Armenia, Tunis—only to give preference to a departure from a fifth location, "Spain, that is, in Andalusia" (Hispania, uidelicet in Andalusia; Llull 1981, 276).[12] Unlike Fidentius of Padua, neither Dubois nor Llull intimated that the training of fixers was directly necessary for military advance or occupation. Rather, each author discussed foreign language acquisition within a global approach to conquest and occupation; language learning was central to the second phase of the conquest: occupation. Llull understood that in order for the occupation to take hold, the lands had to be permanently settled (Llull 1927, 268; Llull 1927, 269). The main means of maintenance (and, likewise in Llull's case, preparation for conquest) were conversion and multiplication of population numbers. Christians must imitate the primitive church: "Catholic faith began with preaching and multiplied with purity, blood, and sweat. From which it follows that its expansion consists in the force of holiness, martyrdom, and labor" (Fides catholica incepti cum praedicatione, et multiplicata fuit cum sanctitate, sanguine et labore. Vnde sequitur, quod sua multiplicatio consistit in potentia sanctitatis, martyrii et laboris; Llull 1981, 254; also Llull 1927, 278).

The objectives of conversion, multiplication, and maintenance can be achieved only by preaching in a foreign language by those "who will learn the Arabic language precisely in order to convert unbelievers" (qui linguam ibidem discerent arabicam pro conuertendis infidelibus; Llull 2010, III.17). By the impetus of the Dominicans and the Franciscans, this thirteenth-century opinion that nonbelievers can be converted through disputation if preached to in their language was widespread. The Franciscan William of Tripoli, in the *Treatise on the State of the Saracens* (*Tractatus de statu Saracenorum*, ca. 1271–73), dedicated to Pope Gregory X, claims that even a simple word of God suffices: "And so with a simple word of God, without philosophical arguments or military arms, just as simple sheep seek the baptism of Christ and pass over into God's fold" (Et sic simplici sermone Dei, sine philosophicis argumentis sive militaribus armis, sicut oves simplices petunt batismum Christi et transeunt in ovile Dei; William of Tripoli 1883, 597–98; see also William of Tripoli 2011). "Disputatio infidelium," disputation of errors, is on the same footing as "land and sea battles" (modus bellandi per terram et per mare); for Llull, there is no distinction between the "two swords: one spiritual and the other physical" (duo gladii: unus spiritualis et alius corporalis; Llull 1954, 100), even if the spiritual sword should always be the first choice and the physical sword should serve only as reinforcement for the conversion work done in a foreign language: "if those Saracens knew our manner of belief, many would join our faith" (si ipsi Sarraceni scirent nostrum modum credendi, multi ad fidem nostram venirent; Llull 1954, 97).[13]

Pierre Dubois's approach is unique in its exclusive focus on the mainte-nance rather than merely the recovery of the Holy Land. Recovery alone is not enough, since when crusader armies "return home, those same Saracens, fiercer than ever and in greater numbers, will return at once on the departure of (the) troops. . . . They will slay those who remain and once more possess themselves of that delectable land" (ad propria cito reversuros, ipsi Sarraceni statim post recessum ferociores et in majori multitudine redibunt, ut interficiant superstites et dulcedine terre potian-tur; P. Dubois 1956 / P. Dubois 1977, sec. 2). Just like with Llull, a stable and durable "conservatio," that is, permanent occupation and systematic colonization by resettlement, is the ultimate objective: people are called on to inhabit and populate the land (terram populandam et inhabitandam; P. Dubois 1956 / P. Dubois 1977, sec. 18). But how to achieve that "a suf-ficient number of people may be induced to journey thither and remain there" (tanta multitudo ducatur illuc et duret; P. Dubois 1956 / P. Dubois 1977, sec. 2) as "inhabitants" (habitatores; P. Dubois 1956 / P. Dubois 1977, sec. 57)? Dubois's answer comes exactly halfway through part 1: "I can-not see how this can come to pass unless provision is made for learning languages" (Quod non vido posse contingere, nisi facta provisione no-tionis linguarum, modo prescripto seu meliori; P. Dubois 1956 / P. Dubois 1977, sec. 63). As with Humbert, colonization does not mean imposition of one language foreign to the occupied, but knowledge and practice of languages of the occupied. There will be confessors for each inhabitant, "experienced with [their] own language and well educated" (de sua lingua peritum ibi et bene litteratum; P. Dubois 1956 / P. Dubois 1977, sec. 57). Both powers—the temporal, the head of the (reconquered) Kingdom of Jerusalem; and the spiritual, the Roman pontiff—should strive "to have many very trustworthy and experienced secretaries, acquainted with the language and writings of the Arabs and other idioms of the world" (habere secretarios multos fideles, peritos, qui linguas Arabum, scripturas eorum, et alia mondi ydiomata cognoscerent; P. Dubois 1956 / P. Dubois 1977, sec. 59). How else shall the pope, Dubois asks, "who does not know their languages, who cannot understand them speaking nor they him, draw these [eastern peoples] into unity and obedience to the Roman Church? How shall he remove errors from their hearts unless through wise and faithful interpreters who must first understand the language of both and expound their mutual wills?" (qui linguas horum non novit, qui ipsos loquentes intelligere non potest nec ipsi eum, eos attrahet ad unitatem et obedienciam ecclesie romane? Quomodo amovebit errores a cordibus

eorum, nisi per aliquois interpretes prudentes, fideles, qui prius utriusque linguam intelligant, mutuas voluntates explicent; P. Dubois 1956 /
P. Dubois 1977, sec. 59). Dubois believes that foreign language acquisition
is the key to European temporal dominion and Christian spiritual unification. Foreign language acquisition is the key to dominion. The historical
justification for it, similar to Humbert's argument (Humbert of Romans
1690, 220), lies in the fact that "the omnipotent Lord in a miraculous manner gave to the preachers whom He chose and sent through the whole
world a knowledge of all languages and the ability to speak them, just as
if they had been natives of the several regions" (Deus omnipotens miracu-
lose dedit predicatoribus quos elegit et misit per universum orbem noticiam omnium linguarum, et potestatem loquendi secundum eas ac si nati
fuissent de singulis regionibus; P. Dubois 1956 / P. Dubois 1977, sec. 64;
also sec. 63). We find the same comparison as in Humbert; fixers must be
like the apostles at Pentecost: "How could the blessed Paul and the other
apostles . . . who knew only Hebrew, the lettered language and the maternal around Jerusalem, preach and teach the Gospel of God intelligibly
to all barbarian nations, except God himself had granted them the usage
of all languages?" (Quomodo potuisset beatus Paulus et alii apostoli . . .
tam litteratam quam maternam partium Jerusalem cognoscentes, omnibus
barbaris nationibus Euvangelium Dei predicare intelligibiliter et docere,
nisi Deus ipse exercitium omnium linguarum dedisset eisdem?; P. Dubois
1956 / P. Dubois 1977, sec. 117).

Languages and Liberal Arts Education (Dubois and Llull)

If speaking foreign languages is key to European and Christian dominion
of lands overseas, Dubois is nevertheless keenly aware that the need for
foreign language speakers cannot be remedied quickly. Fixers may be like
the apostles but the Holy Spirit will not infuse them instantly with the
gift of languages at Pentecost: "There are no interpreters prepared for this
task, nor can they be found for all the money in the world unless provided
far in advance" (nec tales interpretes parati sunt, nec inveniri possent pro
omnibus mondi thesauris, nisi de longe provisi; P. Dubois 1956 / P. Dubois
1977, sec. 59). Unlike making apostles, making fixers is a long-term project
and investment that may not yield results for over a generation, "after the
example of Moses, who did not see the Land of Promise but only, as it is
written, labored for its conquest from without" (ad instar Moysi qui Terram promissionis non vidit, et tantum, prout scriptum est, et ultra super
ejus conquestu laboravit; P. Dubois 1956 / P. Dubois 1977, sec. 59).

For the next forty-eight articles (or almost the entire second half of part 1), Dubois discusses what this long-term comprehensive project of making fixers, the new apostles, should include: the establishment of schools, the curriculum of study and training, and the missions to which the students would be ultimately dedicated: "In every province, according to the local facilities available for this purpose and the size of the population . . . there should be established . . . two or more schools for boys and about the same number for girls" (Videlicet quod in qualibet provincia, secundum locorum facultates in hoc applicandas, populorum multitudines . . . statuantur duo vel plura studia puerorum et fere totidem puellarum; P. Dubois 1956 / P. Dubois 1977, sec. 60). The merger of the Templars' and Hospitallers' orders and the confiscation of their property would finance the entire project of education and the transportation of supplies and human resources to overseas (P. Dubois 1956 / P. Dubois 1977, sec. 60, sec. 15).[14] The technology that Dubois proposes is the systematic education of an equal number of children of both sexes (P. Dubois 1956 / P. Dubois 1977, sec. 61; also sec. 71). This education would start at the age of four or five or six (P. Dubois 1956 / P. Dubois 1977, sec. 60, sec. 71) and would be completed by the age of thirty (P. Dubois 1956 / P. Dubois 1977, sec. 76). Between the age of ten and twelve, pupils would have covered grammar and the articles of faith, at which point they would begin the study of logic and, at the age of fourteen, natural science (P. Dubois 1956 / P. Dubois 1977, sec. 71, sec. 72). At the end of the curriculum, they would embark on the study of "moral sciences, namely monostica [dealing with virtues relevant to one's life], ethics, rhetoric, and politics" (morales sciencias, videlicet monosticam, ethicam, rhetoricam et politicam; P. Dubois 1956 / P. Dubois 1977, sec. 73). At this point, and according to the thirteenth-century university structure, students would choose their specialty, as preachers, doctors, or lawyers and judges. Those who "proved to be rather slow in learning" (in addiscendo fuerint rudiores; P. Dubois 1956 / P. Dubois 1977, sec. 74) would specialize in medicine and surgery (human and veterinary); others, "more promising and teachable" (bene dispositi magisque dociles; P. Dubois 1956 / P. Dubois 1977, sec. 62), would specialize in civil, canon, and divine law; astronomy; mathematical and natural sciences; theology and philosophy; and medicine. Finally, students more physically gifted (robustiores) would train in military art and handicrafts useful in warfare (P. Dubois 1956 / P. Dubois 1977, sec. 84).

Students would be taught three languages: first Latin, then either Greek or Arabic, and another literary idiom (in lingua latina . . . in lingua greca, alii in arabica, et sic de aliis ydiomatibus litteratis; P. Dubois 1956 /

P. Dubois 1977, sec. 61). Dubois here introduces another hierarchy for more and less gifted students. More brilliant, "sapientiores" students would be trained in the three "lettered languages" (in linguis . . . litteratis), some also in Chaldean (Persian); the rest, "for whom less study of the lettered and mother [vernacular] tongues would be sufficient" (quibus sufficiet minus studere in litteratis et maternis), would train to serve as "speech interpreters for the unlearned" (ad non litteratos . . . interpretes sermonum; P. Dubois 1956 / P. Dubois 1977, sec. 83). Of the different lettered idioms (vernaculars), French, "gallicum," is the most common one "among us Latins" (apud Latinos), and so even those who are not gifted for languages should learn it (P. Dubois 1956 / P. Dubois 1977, sec. 83). According to Dubois's method and curriculum, the students' education would take up to twenty-six years, not surprisingly that the investment may exceed the lifetime of its investor. But the ends justify the means, "so that eventually with the help of these youths, trained to speak and write the languages of all peoples, the Roman Church, and the Catholic princes as well, may through them communicate with all men and draw them to the Catholic faith and into unity with its head" (ut demum per istos, in loquendo et scribendo secundum linguas omnium instructos, communicare possit per ipsos ecclesia romana ac etiam principes catholici cum omnibus hominibus, ipsos ad fidem catholicam et unitatem ejus capitis attrahendo; P. Dubois 1956 / P. Dubois 1977, sec. 61).

Girls education is narrower. They would be taught Latin grammar, logic, one foreign language, surgery, and medicine (P. Dubois 1956 / P. Dubois 1977, sec. 85). Women "of noble birth and others of exceptional skill who are attractive in face and figure . . . may then conveniently be married off to the greater princes, clergy and other wealthy easterners" (nobiles et alie prudentiores, apte corporibus et formis . . . ut convenienter possint majoribus principibus, clericics, et aliis ditioribus Orientalibus in uxores dari) and "Saracen chiefs" (majoribus Saracenis; P. Dubois 1956 / P. Dubois 1977, sec. 61, sec. 69). Women's knowledge of medicine and surgery would impress and influence their husbands and children to adhere to the Roman faith, because they would admire these women for their knowledge (P. Dubois 1956 / P. Dubois 1977, sec. 61). Especially other women would admire their relative emancipation and monogamy, which could induce them to convert, according to merchant reports (P. Dubois 1956 / P. Dubois 1977, sec. 69). Dubois here echoes and, by suggesting marriage with Muslims as a means to conversion, much expands on Humbert of Romans, who recommended marriage with Greek Christians (Humbert of Romans 1968, 7:194), so that Christianity can return to its previous state under Emperor Constantin's heirs who "peacefully ruled over the Eastern and Western Empire" (pacifice imperabant Orienti scilicet & Occidenti; Humbert of Romans 1968, 7:195).[15]

Ramon Llull is much less elaborate. He recommends the foundation of least three monasteries, in Rome, Paris, and Toledo (Llull 1927, 271), if not "four monasteries in suitable and pleasant places" (quattuor monasteria in locis comptentibus et amoenis; Llull 1981, 252) "throughout the world" (per mundum; Llull 2010, IV.19), in Rome, in Paris, "in Spain near the Saracens; or Genoa or Venice, because they go among Saracens and Tartars more than other men; and others in Prussia, Hungary, Caffa, Armenia, Taurus, and several other suitable places" (in Yspania propter Sarracenos; aliud Janue, aliud Venicie, quia vadunt plus inter Sarracenos et Tartaros quam alii homines, et alius in Pruscia; alius in Ungaria, aliud in Capha; aliud in Herminia; aliud Taurus et in pluribus aliis locis comptentibus; Llull 1954, 102–3). There, chosen religious and lay men could "learn the languages of different nations, so that they could preach the Gospel to all the unbelievers in accordance with the Lord's command" (diuersarum gentium idiomata addiscentes, possent uniuersis infidelibus praedicare euangelia iuxta Domini mandatum; Llull 2010, IX.35), and "study different types of languages so as to know how to preach the doctrine of Gospel to every creature" (studentes in diuersis linguarum generibus, quod omni creaturae scirent doctrinam euangelicam praedicare; Llull 2010, XI.44).

When it comes to the curriculum Llull is likewise less specific than Dubois. What truly interests him is the number of languages to be taught: in 1292, he suggests "different languages, that is Arabic, Persian, Koman, Chaldean, and other schismatic languages" (diversas linguas . . . scilicet arabicam liguam [sic], persescam, comanicam et guscam et alias linguas sismaticas; Llull 1954, 96). In 1294, he specifically focuses on the "idioms/ dialects of the Greeks" (ydiomata Grecorum; Llull 1954, 100). By 1305, he assigns one language to each of the four monasteries: "so that in one monastery Arab language were taught, in another Hebrew, in the third the language of the schismatics, and in the fourth Tartar or a pagan language" (quod in uno lingua saracenica doceretur, in alio iudaica, in tertio schismatica et in quarto tartarica seu paganica; Llull 1981, 253). Students would have "the knowledge of speaking, reading and comprehending Arabic and other barbaric and different languages" (scientiam ad loquendum, legendum et intelligendum linguam arabicam et alias barbaras et diuersas; Llull 1981, 283). In addition, these students, without exception male, would be "learned and wise in theology and philosophy, possessing necessary arguments" (scientes et sapientes in theologia et philosophia, habentes rationes necessarias; Llull 1954, 100, 96). The monasteries would be well endowed (Llull 1981, 252; Llull 1927, 271), and the education would take place in pairs, "and thus educated, let them be sent on the mission two by two, and when two are sent off, let another two be accepted" (et sic instructi mitterentus bini et, quando missi essent duo, quod alii duo essent recepti; Llull 1927, 271). "Vigorous men" (Ualentes homines) would be taught by "poor men, who would come willingly for gain and would provide training in the said languages" (homines pauperes, qui libenter uenirent causa lucri, et informarent praedictis lingatgiis; Llull 1981, 253). This hands-on pedagogy stems from Llull's direct experience of learning Arabic with a Muslim slave whom he had bought for that purpose in Mallorca (Llull 2010, II.11).

Human Agency: From Interpreters to Fixers (Riccoldo of Monte Croce, Roger Bacon, Pierre Dubois)

But why do Dubois and Llull insist on such a broad-based liberal arts education when it is clear that language should be the primary focus of education, as at once the biggest obstacle to and the best vehicle for European dominion across the Mediterranean? The point is that liberal arts are intended to enable agency in interpreters and make them into fixers. According to the Dominican Riccoldo of Monte Croce, "the first rule to know" in any engagement with "foreign peoples" (exter[is] nation[ibus]) is that

> it is not advantageous under any circumstances to preach or to dispute with foreigners concerning faith through an interpreter, for ordinary interpreters inasmuch as they know sufficiently well languages for selling and buying and common living conditions, they do not know how to translate the faith and the secrets of the faith with proper and appropriate words, and they're ashamed to say "I don't understand" or "I don't know how to say it" and therefore modify words and mistranslate. . . . Therefore brothers [monks] must learn the language well as it behooved me among Arabs to learn not only the language but also dialectics.

> (Prima regula est quia scire oportet quod nullo modo expedit predicare vel disputare cum extraneis de fide per interpretem, nam interpretes communes quantumcumque bene sciant linguas et sufficienter quantum ad vendendum et emendum et ad communiter convivendum, nesciunt tamen fidem et ea que sunt intima fidei exprimere per verba propria et convenientia, et verecundantur dicere "Ego non intelligo," vel "Nescio dicere," et ideo pervertunt verba et dicunt alia pro aliis. . . .

Unde oportet quot fratres bene discant linguam, et oportuit me inter
arabes non solum discere linguam sed etiam dyalecticam.)[16]

This is a drastic change from the start of his mission (1288–1302), when
Riccoldo and the brothers "were preaching to them through an interpreter
of Arabic" (an predicabamus eis per turchimannum in lingua arabica).[17]

Riccoldo's hard-won experience during the late thirteenth century
teaches that linguistic skills alone are not enough. Llull had exactly the
same experience with interpreters: "And because they haven't addition-
ally learned these languages, they can do little among them. . . . Likewise,
when they dispute among them through interpreters, they can barely do
anything with these interpreters, because they do not grasp the merits
of Christian faith nor do they have an adequate vocabulary of our faith"
(Et quia istic lingatgia non addiscunt, inter illos facere pauca possunt. . . .
Similiter quando per interpretes disputant penes illos, quasi nihil faciunt cum praedictis, eo quia interpretes non apprehendunt uirtutem fidei
christianae, neque sufficientiam uocabulorum nostrae fidei ipsi habent;
Llull 1981, 254).

It is the liberal arts education, the one so stubbornly advocated for
by Dubois, and to a lesser extent by Llull, that makes all the difference
between an "interpres," the one who "nescit," and a "fixer," the one who
"scit," that is who has full agency to debate and dispute with the power to
convert.[18] The difference between interpreters and fixers is this agency,
which, in fixers, exceeds by far their linguistic skills: they must know how
"to respond so reasonably to the objections of the barbarians that they de-
stroy their erroneous opinions; they must be able to convince them with
incontrovertible arguments and draw them to the truth of the Christian
faith" (respondere tam rationabiliter sciant ad objecta barbarorum, quod
eorum opiniones erroneas destruant; per inconvincibiles rationes eos
moveant et attrahant ad veritatem professionis christiane; P. Dubois 1956 /
P. Dubois 1977, sec. 59). Highly skilled in every branch of knowledge, "they
would outdo the experts of that country in disputing, advising, discussing
and in every other way, so that there would be no one who could withstand
the wisdom of the Roman Church" (peritissimos in qualibet sciencia duos
vel plures, qui peritiores de illa terra, disputando, consulendo, conferendo,
et modis omnibus superarent; ut non esset qui posset sapiencie romane
ecclesie resistere; P. Dubois 1956 / P. Dubois 1977, sec. 62). For all intents
and purposes, a fixer is not actually "translating," but producing an "original" of equal value in both languages. He is translating thought, spirit, into
words, but he is not translating from one language into another; he is the
agent of his thought translated.

A fixer furthermore must be acquainted with the customs of the foreign regions, a sort of cultural translation that is implied in language education in Dubois and Llull, but is explicated in Roger Bacon, a Franciscan, who advocated language learning of sacred languages as much as of the vernacular French:

> Knowledge of the regions of the world is most necessary to the commonwealth of believers and conversion of nonbelievers and to counter nonbelievers and Antichrist and others. For, on account of various advantages to the commonwealth, and on account of the preaching of the faith, men are sent to various regions of the world; for these uses it is rather necessary that they be knowledgeable so that they may know the customs of foreign places and that they may know where to choose moderate places through which they might pass. . . . They indeed undertake untold perils, because they do not know when they entered the regions of the faithful, when of the schismatics, when of the Saracens, when of the Tartars, when of tyrants, when of peaceful men, when of Barbarians, when of men of reason. Because of this, either to seek the conversion of nonbelievers or for other church matters, it is necessary to know the rituals and foundations of each race [natio]. . . . Indeed so many of the Christians have been prevented from the greatest of business, because they did not know the regional differences. Consequently and henceforth, a substantial need arises for the knowledge of the places of the world, because it is necessary that the church know very well the situations and conditions of the ten tribes of the Jews.

> (Cognitio locorum mundi valde necessaria est reipublicae fidelium et conversioni infidelium et ad obviandum infidelibus et Antichristo, et aliis. Nam propter diversas utilitates reipublicae, et propter preaedicationem fidei mittuntur homines ad loca mundi diversa; in quibus occupationibus valde necessarium est proficiscentibus ut scirent complexiones locorum externorum, quatenus scirent eligere loca temperata per quae transirent. . . . Receperunt etiam pericula infinita, eo quod nesciverunt quando intraverunt regiones fidelium, quando schismaticorum, quando Saracenorum, quando Tartarorum, quando tyrannorum, quando hominum pacificorum, quando barbarorum, quando hominum rationabilium. . . . Et ideo, sive pro conversione infidelium proficiscatur, aut pro aliis Ecclesiae negotiis, necesse est ut sciat ritus et conditiones omnium nationum. . . . Quamplurimi enim a negotiis Christianorum maximis sunt frustrati, eo quod regionum distinctiones nesciverunt. Deinde non

modica necessitas sciendi loca mundi oritur ex hoc, quod oportet Ec-
clesiam optime scire situm et conditiones decem tribuum Iudaeorum.)[19]

Bacon drew this idea from the insights gained by his fellow Franciscan
William of Rubruck, who spent two years on a mission to the Mongols,
from 1253 to 1255 (see chapter 2). One must know "positions, and motivations and causes of different sects" (positiones eorum et motiva et causas
diversarum sectarum; Riccoldo of Monte Croce 1967, 169). There is a direct link between war and linguistic and cultural information; fixers should
become "familiar enemies" (domestici inimicis; Brocardus 1869, 439).

Just like language is not enough, intellect by itself cannot suffice. The
ultimate feature that characterizes fixers is agency, which exceeds by far
their linguistic skills:

> The fifth rule is that it is not enough for the preacher on the mission to
> be gifted with intellect, that is, that he may know a language to express
> himself, to understand the scriptures, to unite sects and motivations, to
> discern wisely with what and from what he ought to begin. But above
> all, it is necessary to know what he may be in disposition [affect, tem-
> perament], that is, how much is he fervent and steadfast, for he ought
> to be moved by the sole love of God and the salvation of souls.

> (Quinta regula est quia non sufficit predicatori qui mittitur esse illumi-
> natum intellectu, scilicet quod sciat linguam per se proferre, scripturas
> intelligere, sectas et motiva colligere, discrete discernere cum quibus et
> a quibus debet incipere, sed summopere scire oportet qualis esse debeat
> in affectu, scilicet quam fervidus et constans quod solo Dei amore et
> animarum salute moveri debeat.) (Riccoldo of Monte Croce 1967, 170)

A fixer is a man "moved," driven, motivated—an agent. Neither a mere interpreter nor a monolingual teacher, a fixer is a man of theory and practice:
"Nor does knowledge of one subject coupled with practical experience in
another suffice unless the two are correlated" (Nec bene sufficit sciencia
in uno cum experiencia alterius, nisi duo conjungantur; P. Dubois 1956 /
P. Dubois 1977, sec. 80). In short, the goal is to create fixers with full
agency, just like God gave "the knowledge of all languages and wisdom
in preaching to His apostles and disciples who were to preach the gospel
to all people" (apostolis suis et discipulis euvangelim omnibus populis
predicaturis noticiam dedit omnium linguarum et sapientie predicandi;
P. Dubois 1956 / P. Dubois 1977, sec. 63). Fixers are the apostles of this age.

Indoctrination and Loyalty

These treatises also tell us about the place of education in the larger task of the creation of agents and subjects. Fixers are not entirely free agents; they need to be loyal. Education thus serves as indoctrination. It begins at a tender age to create disciplined, learned, and loyal subjects by the age of thirty, who will act "through love of their native land" (propter terre natalis affectionem; P. Dubois 1956 / P. Dubois 1977, sec. 61), "studied in childhood and repeated in formal lectures. . . . They will from childhood be amply disposed to understand, carry off, and commit to memory sermons . . . and the manner of preaching will be so familiar to them as to become second nature" (in puericia cognita, repetita solempniter . . . sufficiente ex tunc a puericia disponet eos ad intelligendum, reportandum ac memorie commendandum . . . ita quod predicandi modus sic assuefactus erit eis quasi naturalis; P. Dubois 1956 / P. Dubois 1977, sec. 76). Here, the role of women in indoctrination is quintessential as they are the closest to children; not only would wives convert men and their children, but they would arrange marriages of other girls from schools with clerics and prelates of other religions (P. Dubois 1956 / P. Dubois 1977, sec. 61).

In his *Directory for the Making of the Passage across the Sea*, a Dominican known as Brocardus holds very similar opinions when it comes to the reunification with the Greeks. His strategy is twofold: on the one hand, destruction of schismatic persons and books by fire or expulsion, and on the other, education and "indoctrination in Latin customs and letters" (latinis moribus et litteris imbuendum; Brocardus 1869, 374). "Imbuo" means to soak, but also to suffuse, permeate, infiltrate, that is inculcate, indoctrinate. The success of this policy would be assured through the indoctrination of future generations: "Therefore I say suffuse Greek children with our letters, so that even as they grow in knowledge and age, they may see and understand by themselves in our books the things by which their errors are disproved by true arguments and scriptural testimony, and sound faith and church doctrine are confirmed" (et ideo dico Grecorum pueros nostris litteris imbuendos, ut saltem cum adoleverint sciencia et etate in nostris libris illa videant et intelligant per seipsos, quibus ipsorum errores racionibus veridicis ac Scripturarum testimoniis confutantur, et sana fides pariter et doctrina Ecclesie roborantur; Brocardus 1869, 471; see also 374, 488–89).

Such recommendations are based, perhaps, on the observations of the mechanisms and efficiency of the Mamluk state. Already in 1291, Fidentius remarked that young slaves, "whether sons of pagans or Christians" (sive filii Paganorum sive Christianorum), are turned into Saracens by the

Mamluk sultans (facit eos fieri Sarracenos). This "making of Saracens" is an inculcation, for they are "bene docti" in the arts of battle and chivalry (Fidentius of Padua 2008, 142). Some thirty years later, William of Adam specifies that the young male slaves are "fully trained in arms and military matters according to their custom" (in armis et rebus bellicis, secundum morem eorum plenius eruditi). William connects the depletion of Christianity to the child slave trade (conducted by Christian merchants for the Mamluks) and children's subsequent indoctrination (William of Adam 2012, 30/31). Llull suggests over and over again that the power of indoctrination by books can work on the captives, who convert willy-nilly: "And that those captives, whether they want to or not, learn those books for as long as they are imprisoned" (Et illi capti, uelint aut nolint, dum capti erunt, addiscant istos libros), before being sent back as instruments in the spreading of faith to "Saracen kings and other princes from regions that they came from" (regibus Saracenis et aliis principibus, de quorum regionibus ipsi erunt"; Llull 1981, 283; Llull 1954, 104).

The ultimate goal of indoctrination is to create perfectly loyal subjects. The treatises present a method for the training of people, men and women, who will possess linguistic skills and intellectual capacities that will make them independent, albeit devoted, agents: "devout, intelligent, and educated" (deuoti, sapientes et litterati; Llull 1975, 70; also Llull 1981, 253; Llull 1927, 271); "holy and devout" (sanctos et devotos; Llull 1954, 96); "devout and capable" (deuoti et apti; Llull 2010, IX.35); "devout and of a spirited mind" (deuoti et intellectu uigentes; Llull 2010, XI.44). Well educated, able, bright, and, most importantly, devout and devoted—the learning of foreign languages and cultures goes hand in hand with the inculcation of psychological (moral) qualities. The quality that is prized above all: loyalty. At no point could autonomy of agency take precedence over obedience in well-trained Christian subjects, "because true obedience contains in itself the high virtue of humility" (car vraie obedience contient en lui la haute vertu d'umilité), which is itself "the foundation of all other virtues" (le fondement de toutes les autres vertus; Mézières 2008, 131). Obedience was humility, the root of all virtues and the foundation of ethics, and it was intended to command and steer even the greatest autonomy. If in the Christian ethos obedience was a virtue, disobedience was a sin. Thus, just like obedience, disobedience had a much greater semantic field than our modern term "insubordination." Obedience was fundamentally about loyalty, while disobedience, far beyond insubordination, was a road to rebellion, inconstancy, and apostasy, in short a betrayal of allegiance, whether to one's lord or to the church. Loyalty was structured around obedience and allegiance; it was a virtue before which agency was to bow.

Almost without exception writers agree that there should be "one head by which [all the Christians] are directed, united, and disciplined" (unum capud per quod dirrigantur, uniantur et corrigantur [omnes Christiani]; Fidentius of Padua 2008, 127). This leader should be "superior in force; honest in life; illustrious in wisdom; equitable in justice; strongly upright; lavishly munificent; attentive to frugality; gentle in conduct; steadily stable" (potencia excelsus; vita honestus; sapientia conspicuus; justicia equus; probitate animosus; largitate copiosus; diligentia sollicitus; conversatione mansuetus; stabilitate firmus; Fidentius of Padua 2008, 127). His example would foster the quality of loyalty in the subordinate ranks, he "whom all Christians obey loyaly and faithfully" (cui omnes Cristiani obedient fideliter et devote; Fidentius of Padua 2008, 166). The Christian conquerors would be "loyal men" (hominibus fidelibus; Brocardus 1869, 478): ship captains should be "loyal in all" (fideles in omnibus; Fidentius of Padua 2008, 145); the commander of the crusade, "loyal, honest, stern, and good-hearted" (fidelis et probus et astrictus et boni cordis; *Informationes Massilie* 1872, 247); members of the military-religious order, "the lord's army," "more loyal than those who are not of the order" (fideliores erunt domino bellatori, quam alii, de ordine qui non essent; Llull 1981, 284); the treasurer "most knowledgeable, loyal, and shrewd" (sapientissimo et fideli, subtili; Llull 1981, 284); spies, "loyal . . . and discreet who will make inquiries into the loyalty of subordinates and equally of captains" (exploratores fideles . . . et secretos, qui de fidelitate subditorum inquirant et etiam praeceptorum; Llull 1981, 285); and messengers, "loyal and official," who "will faithfully examine all the clergy" (fideles nuntios et legales, qui inuestigarent per clerum fideliter uniuersum; Llull 1981, 253). For Dubois, the pope should strive "to have many very trustworthy and experienced secretaries" (habere secretarios multos fideles, peritos), "wise and loyal interpreters" (interpretes prudentes, fideles; P. Dubois 1956 / P. Dubois 1977, sec. 59), just as the king (Charles) should be surrounded by "some prudent men, experienced and loyal to him" (aliquos prudentes, expertos, sibique fideles; P. Dubois 1956 / P. Dubois 1977, sec. 117). Loyalty means obedience (obedienciam atque fidelitatem; Brocardus 1869, 473). According to the authors of "Memoria" (before 1289–1308), the sole path to reconquest is collective obedience: "The business of war or the signal of attack can be neither well managed, nor perfectly conducted, nor led to a good end, specifically in this feat if not through obedient men" (negocium guerre seu bellicum non potest bene tractari nec deduci perfectualiter nec ad bonum finem, specialiter in facto isto nisi per gentes obedientie; "Memoria" 2008, 249). This means that the treatises do not follow a logic of material logistics supplanted by allegory of virtues, rather that loyalty is less an ideal to which all Christians should strive, and more a necessity. Loyalty is a fact of behavior as material as the number of troops. Indoctrination is a creation of loyal, that is, obedient subjects.

By contrast, hired interpreters are free agents whose minds or translation cannot be controlled—they are untrustworthy—and therefore they cannot be used for the purposes of conversion and conquest:

> Foreign interpreters of their languages will not suffice, since it would be dangerous to trust them, and such persons could not be found adequate in number or prudence for the administration of an empire. Men of a foreign land, barbarians in the eyes of the French, as are all those who understand the language of the Greeks, would be readily influenced and bribed to betray and deceive those whom they in their turn would regard as barbarians in that country. (P. Dubois 1956, sec. 117)

> (Nec sufficient extranei linguarum interpretes, quoniam de ipsis confidere periculosum erit, et quoniam tales ad sufficienciam inveniri non possent ad regimen Imperii, numero et prudencia sufficientes. Homines extranei, quoad Gallicos barbari, sicut sunt omnet qui linguam Grecorum noverunt de facili moverentur et corrumperentur, ut proderent et deciperent quos sibi terreque illi Barbaros reputarent.) (P. Dubois 1977, sec. 117)

Likewise, local Christian populations cannot be trusted, neither Armenians, nor Greeks, nor any other Eastern Christians: "Christians who live in the Holy Land . . . are for their part many and different, and for this reason also less capable to fight against the unbelievers" (Cristiani habitantes in Terra Sancta, ut dictum est, ita sunt ad invicem varii et diversi, ideo etiam ad bellandum contra Infideles sunt minus apti; Fidentius of Padua 2008, 64).[20] The faith of the new converts from Islam to Christianity, "Baptizati neophiti," is questionable, although they are immensely useful as informants (Brocardus 1869, 494–95). Generally, one could trust the descendants of crusaders, "the courageous Syrian knights and nobles, descendants of valiant knights who had conquered the Holy Land, knew the language of Saracens, the ways of the Sultan, and the ebbs of the river Nile" (les vaillans chevaliers anciens et preudommes de Surrie qui estoient extrais des vaillans chevaliers qui avoient conquis la Terre Sainte . . . savoient le langaige des Sarrasins, les condicions du soudant et de la croissance d'un flun du Nil).[21] But it is hard to shake off the idea that their loyalty is suspect. In a historically remarked example, Louis IX's councillors mistrusted them, bringing about Louis's defeat at Damietta in 1248: "Sire, you believe these old knights who speak Arabic? They are half Arab; do not believe them" (Monseigneur, creez vous ces vieulx chevaliers qui parles le sarrasin? Ilz sont moitié Sarrasins, ne les creez pas; Mézières 2008, 141). This is the danger that looms: since the First Crusade, it had been remarked that religious, linguistic, and cultural barriers quickly become permeable (Fulcher of Chartres 1969, 271). The local fixers are distrusted because of their double profile.

This sheds new light on the disciplinary and security measures implemented through linguistic and liberal arts training that writers propose in order to control the overseas settlements. Schools and education can be only "on this side of the Mediterranean" (citra mare Mediterraneum; P. Dubois 1956 / P. Dubois 1977 sec. 14; similarly, in Llull), and preferably in Paris: "In this way, all the kings of Egypt, Acre, and the emperors of Constantinople . . . would be conceived, born, nourished and educated in France" (Ut omnes reges Egipti, Acon, et imperatores Constantinopolitani . . . sic facerent in Francia generati, nati, nutriti et eruditi).[22] Dealing with the perceived disloyalty and treachery of the Greeks, Brocardus also advocates that preachers and confessors come from the Christian mainland (Brocardus 1869, 475–76). After all, the reunification of Greeks, or simple conquest, means that the throne of Constantinople will go to a Latin (French) king. The writers of "Memoria" likewise insist on the necessity of perpetual renewal from the mainland center; "the secular ones would wish to return to their own [nation/region] after two or three years" (seculares post duos vel tres annos vellent redire ad propria), but since new arrivals are often ignorant of the overseas war, continuity has to be maintained by a permanent military-religious order: "Those religious men, who are subjugated by obedience, would die in war throughout the time of their own life" (religiosi illi, qui sunt astricti per obedientiam, morarentur in guerra per spacium vite sue; "Memoria" 2008, 250).

Colonizers having been imported from the mainland center, the prevention of their assimilation by early indoctrination is supplemented by one final technique proposed by Dubois: simultaneously coercing the natives to adopt the Western lifestyle and epistemology.[23] Uniform education from the mainland center would counter assimilation and institutionalize a society of the Holy Land, a society that would be mixed "by peoples from many lands" (per habitatores diversarum regionum), who would be coerced "to abandon the peculiar customs and mode of life of any of the peoples newly migrating thither, and substitute a mode of procedure beyond all others easy, less cumbersome, less wasteful and shorter, and which the inhabitants of the Holy Land . . . would find easier above all others to comprehend, to remember and to be trained in" (expediens

videtur proprias cujuslibet populorum de novo supervenientium consue-
tudines et ritus vivendi reicere, verisimiliter modum procedendi super
omnes facilem minus laboriosum, magis de facili concipere, retinere, et
in eo se exercitare; P. Dubois 1956 / P. Dubois 1977, sec. 90). This would
be made possible through the common education curriculum in French
and through the application of a single law, abandoning "the law, custom,
or statute of one's native land" (lex vel consuetudo seu statutum terre sue
natalis; P. Dubois 1956 / P. Dubois 1977, sec. 90; translation modified).
On the one hand, education would produce exemplary subjects of Latin
Christian culture, whose degree of indoctrination would be such that they
could not be acculturated to the local conditions, and, on the other, all
others arriving in the new colonies would be coerced to adopt to Western
Christian lifestyle and epistemology.

The Economy of Foreign Language Acquisition

As we briefly saw earlier, foreign language acquisition is a matter of economy. In the absence of a Pentecostal infusion of tongues, learning the
language of the overseas populations is an investment that exceeds a single generation (P. Dubois 1956 / P. Dubois 1977, sec. 59). Llull spent his
entire life promoting this risky but high-yield investment. A surprising
notion that the most suitable candidates for foreign language learning are
those who wish to die is the trait unifying Llull's entire work dedicated to
foreign language acquisition in the mission of preaching and conversion:
"strong, educated men, wishing to suffer death for Christ, would learn
and understand various languages of unbelievers, so that subsequently
throughout the entire world they would go preach the Gospel" (ualentes
homines litterati, pro Christo desiderantes mortem pati, diuersas linguas
infidelium addiscerent et audirent, ut per consequens per uniuersum mundum irent euangelium praedicatum; Llull 1981, 250). Llull selects students,
"saintly and religious men, wishing to die for Christ, [to] learn the idioms
of unbelievers" (addiscentes [ydiomata infidelium] viri sancti et religiosi, desiderantes mori propter Christum; Llull 1954, 102; also 103), and
asks for "devout men, instructed in diverse languages, who would then
go preach the Gospel across the world . . . wishing to die for Christ as did
the apostles" (homines sapientes, devoti, in variis linguis et postea irent
praedicaturi Evangelium per totum mundum . . . desiderantes mori pro
Christo sicut faciebant Apostoli; Llull 1927, 3:271). Students of foreign
languages should be willing to die while preaching in a foreign language;
they must be ready for translation martyrdom; Llull says explicitly that
the expansion of the Catholic faith needs its "martyres" (Llull 1981, 254).

Translation martyrdom operates in a strange economy, for Llull proposes investing in the training of interpreters only so that they can die on the job. This economy has to be thought of as an *imitatio Christi*; the sacrifice of one fixer brings about the salvation of many: "such devout schoolteachers who ... want ... to die purposefully for that most good son of God, our Lord Jesus Christ, who did not fear to suffer death for them" (tales deuotos homines litterators, qui ... uellent ... mori finaliter pro illo Benignissimo Dei Filio, nostro Domino Iesu Christo, qui mortem pati non metuit pro eisdem; Llull 1981, 253). It is an economy that through translation exchanges the individual freedom to die for collective salvation, because through conversion in translation a fixer puts himself to death for many others, not only for Christ. What looks like a sacrifice and like a renunciation of a calculable, commercial yield to investment ultimately includes profitability and surplus of one to many. It is thus that the investment for which Llull calls—namely, the training of fixer-missionaries who will die in translation and that seemed to be a pure loss—turns out to produce a surplus that is not directly proportional to investment. Translation martyrdom is then not simply a sacrifice for God but is a part of an economy of surplus and profitability, which it cannot escape.

But there is more to the economy of foreign language acquisition, as Llull conveys. Even though he believes that conversion by spirit is always preferable to conversion by sword, there is an economic coercion that occupies a median ground between faith and war:

> Dominion that began in good understanding is stronger than that begun in conflict, for to rule over unbelievers by disputation and concordance for the honor of God and with indispensable arguments is more important than so much fighting against unbelievers, alienating them with the physical sword, seizing their land from them, and killing them. But in converting them and restituting to them their property, harmony and love matter, and thus this concordance is the inclination, the reason on account of which dominion achieves its ends having found the middle ground.

> (Principium inceptum in concordantia est fortius quam in contrarietate, sed principare contra infideles disputando et concordando in dignitatibus Dei et in rationibus necesariis plus importat quam bellare tantum contra infideles contrariando eis cum gladio corporali et ab eis auferendo terras quas possident et ipsos interficiendo, sed convertendo et dimittendo eis bona que possident, [sic] importat concordantia [sic]

et amorem, et sic talis concordantia est dispositio, ratione cujus prin-
cipium transit per medium ad suum finem.) (Llull 1954, 109)

Speaking a foreign language induces concordance and love, and it predis-
poses unbelievers favorably. It dissipates errors without having to dispos-
sess; rather the restitution of property incites the unbelievers to conversion. Unbelievers are thus doubly invested, with faith and with property,
leading them to accept the accomplishment of Christian dominion. Conversion is possession.

In Dubois, speaking a foreign language is similarly meant to eliminate
errors and nurture love among the occupiers and occupied: without it, "it
will be difficult to dwell in a land whose lettered language and all of whose
spoken dialects are unfamiliar to all Frenchmen. It will also be difficult
to seek the friendship and alliance of the natives" (in terra cujus omnes
Gallici literas et omnia laicorum ydiomata ignorant, difficilimum erit
habere, dilectionem et confederationem Latinos, querere; P. Dubois 1956 /
P. Dubois 1977, sec. 117). But Dubois does not turn love and harmony
through language into his ultimate goal. Besides making it "difficult to seek
the friendship and alliance of the natives," Dubois says that it would also
be difficult "to rule them if they are subjugated, and to mingle with them."
He goes on: "A good prince ought not to aim at the destruction of a whole
people; if this be his intention his cause does not deserve to prosper, nor
would he be able to realize his purpose. How, then, should one attempt to
gain the love of the survivors?" (et ipsos, si subjugarentur, regere, et cum
ipsis conversari. Nec tendere debet bonus princeps ad totum populum pe-
rimendum; si ad hoc tenderet, non bene sibi contingere deberet, nec hoc
facere posset; Quomodo ergo superstitum dilectio queretur?; P. Dubois
1956 / P. Dubois 1977, sec. 117). In the space of one sentence the desire for
friendship and love with the natives is transformed into rule over them and
the subjugation of those that have survived the violence. The engagement
with the natives is commendable only until it eliminates its own necessity
having achieved their defeat and submission. The question of how to gain
the love of the survivors turns into "How should they be governed by those
who understand them no better than they understand the twittering birds
of the air, the roaring beasts, and the hissing serpents?" (quomodo regentur
per illos qui ipsos non intelligent plusquam aves celi garulantes et feras mu-
gientes ac serpentes sibilantes?; P. Dubois 1956 / P. Dubois 1977, sec. 117).

As we discover, language is a means to world domination, spiritual as
well as economic, that will be achieved through education: "If the Catholic
sect were ... to simulate study in all favorable localities, the result ought to

be that this commonwealth would in the course of time obtain dominion over the whole world" (si secta catholicorum . . . studium suscitet in omnibus loci ad hoc aptis, sequi deberet hic effectus quod hec respublica mondi monarchiam, ex nunc in posterum augendo; P. Dubois 1956 / P. Dubois 1977, sec. 70). But the ultimate purpose of domination is to provide "valuable commodities, abundant in those regions but rare and highly prized among us . . . in adequate amounts at a reasonable price, once the world were made Catholic" (res preciosas, in partibus illis habundantes, nobis deficientes et apud nos carissimas, satis pro modico nobis communicari, mondo catholicorum ordinato; P. Dubois 1956 / P. Dubois 1977, sec. 63). Ever a pragmatist, Dubois would like to "regulate the purchase price and transportation charges" (de bonis nostris reportari mandarique precia rerum emptarum) resulting in "moderate prices" (pro preciis moderatis; P. Dubois 1956 / P. Dubois 1977, sec. 67). Furthermore, "the economic advantages resulting from the proposed foundation will be of great benefit to the communities of those [eastern] lands. They will export their products and thereby profit much more than if those goods were faithfully devoted to the poor which would rarely if ever happen" (Hujus vero provisionis erunt, et ab ipsa per eamque procedent commoda temporalia, que plus longe proderunt communitatibus regionum, de quarum bonis fient impense, quam prodessent hujusmodi bona si etiam fideliter, quod vis aut nunquam contingeret, pauperibus erogarentur; P. Dubois 1956 / P. Dubois 1977, sec. 67). This is then a commercial mission, with the goal of exploitation. Foreign language is a medium to love and concordance with an economic purpose; learning a language in order to have gain is the ultimate goal of settlement: "And many Christians who will hear of the good start to this good matter will open their hearts to piety and others to greed for gain. And thus Christians will forever proliferate" (Et moult Crestiens, qui orront le bon commencement de ceste bone oeuvre, esmouvront leurs cuers a devocion et les autres pour couvoitise de gaaignier. Et ainsi multeplieront tous jours les Crestiens; de Villaret et al. 2008, 228. See also Bratianu 1942, 360). When all these projects have been accomplished, Christian monopoly will have been created: "Catholics of the same mind will be in possession of the whole Mediterranean coast, from the west all the way to the east on the north side, and the greater part touching the Land of Promise on the south" (Catholici concordes possidebunt totam ripam maris Mediterranei, ab ejus occidente usque ad orientem versus septentrionem, et meliorem partem tangentem Terram Promissionis versus meridiem; P. Dubois 1956 / P. Dubois 1977, sec. 105). Consequently, a Catholic monopoly will essentially amount to a punitive measure for non-Catholics, Arabs, and Eastern Christians, who will not be able to prosper materially.

Colonization and Language

Fixers not only are like apostles; they actually replace them: they are the new apostles. The model profile of such a new apostle includes being a man born in Christian Europe, and reading, speaking, and writing languages of non-Christians or schismatics, being familiar with their customs and ways, in full control of his cognitive capacity and endowed with agency and subjectivity. But this extraordinary agency means that he also has to be made loyal and obedient. Long-term education and indoctrination would give these new apostles knowledge, wisdom, and full agency but also make them loyal, linguistically and epistemologically. Education would prepare them to die productively for faith, in an *imitatio Christi*. Because there is no Pentecost, the only path toward world domination is a long-term investment in fixers; there is no instant solution. From the outset, fixers are about economy, and a truly Christian one: they are an investment that will multiply in returns, whether in the form of converts or of goods.

Such a linguistic deployment of strategies for economic domination of newly conquered territories and of disciplinary control of native populations seems to correspond to the rule over the modern colonies from the mainland center. However, there is one significant difference: whether the aim is colonization or conversion, writers intend to achieve it by means of the language of the people that they wish to subjugate and convert. In other words, if the (re)conquest of the so-called Holy Land is to be interpreted as a pathway to colonization, the goal of these treatises is never to impose the language of the conqueror, contrary to the case of modern imperial nation-states.[24] Quite to the contrary, the goal is to create conditions for learning and mastery of the territories to be occupied. The occupiers do not impose their language, but learn the language of the occupied. The acquisition of foreign languages is a means to control of the conquered territories, to conversion, and ultimately to assimilation within one true faith (regardless of the language in which this faith is spoken). This also means that the onus of responsibility is on the colonizer and the preacher. Faced with the problem of the loyalty of fixers, modern empires will instead impose their languages on the colonized. They will engage in the mode of possession fully: not only will they own the resources, but they will also aim to own the spirit of the people in the language of the colonizer. When Dubois wanted world domination by imposition of Western episteme and Christian laws in local languages, the modern empire will achieve the imposition of its episteme also through the imposition of its own language.

The Economy of Translation

MISSIONARIES TO THE MONGOL EMPIRE,
PILGRIMS TO THE HOLY LAND,
AND THE GIFT OF LANGUAGES
(THIRTEENTH TO FIFTEENTH CENTURIES)

There is an apostolic economy of fixers: one for many. Fixers are an investment without whom the maintenance and occupation of the overseas lands—and the gain that this will bring to Christians—will not be possible: "It is in every way advisable and necessary to procure far in advance men fluent and well-trained in languages. Such training cannot be bought with gold, silver, or precious stones. Therefore it is desirable to make provision for this before necessity arises" (Hoc exercitium et notionem linguarum habentes, modis omnibus opportet et expedit diu ante providere; hoc enim est, quod pro auro, argento, et gemmis tunc sufficienter reperiri non posset. Idcirco . . . hoc expedit, antequam veniat neccessitas, procurare; P. Dubois 1956 / P. Dubois 1977, sec. 117). Because it takes a long time to make a fixer, fixers are more precious than the most precious metals or stones. There is no ready supply of fixers; they cannot be bought but only invested in, their skills, knowledge, and, above all, their loyalty cultivated over a long period of time. Such insistence on a long-term investment in fixers, one that may well exceed the lifetime of rulers and popes who would initiate such a project, has as the ultimate goal "the recovery of the Holy Land," an unimpeded supply chain, property, gain, and monopoly, in short an early form of colonization. Training fixers is part of this larger commercial and exploitation structure in the Mediterranean referred to with the term "negotium,"[1] that is, "enterprise," "business," "undertaking." The same term was used occasionally to reference crusading.[2] The use of "negotium" clearly indicates that for many writers of crusade treatises a (re)conquest of the Holy Land was not a purely military affair, but also a matter of economic strategy.

One of the immediate results of the 1291 fall of Acre was the renewal of the papal ban on trade with Muslims. The idea that merchants hurt Christian stability and security in the Near East and Europe by supplying raw materials, arms, and slaves to Muslims was not new; the Fourth

Lateran Council (1215), and the First and Second Councils of Lyon (1245 and 1274) pronounced excommunication against those who engaged in commerce with Muslims (Schein 1991, 40–41, 50, 79–83). Indeed, certain writers endorsed naval blockades, a form of economic embargo that was a precondition to any military engagement. Marino Sanudo Torsello (ca. 1270–after 1343), for example, says that part 4 of his 1323 *Book of the Secrets of the Faithful of the Cross* (*Liber secretorum fidelium crucis super Terrae Sanctae recuperatione et conservatione*) "shows how essential it is that a new means of [commercial] sanctions be found and considered thoroughly and by showing just how this can be drawn tight so that scarcely anything is carried to the lands subject to the Sultan" (Qvarta pars continet qvomodo necesse est nouum modum prohibitionis inuenire magis solito exquisitum: ostendendo etiam qualiter potest distringi, quod per mare Mediterraneum ad partes Soldano subiectas minime transfretetur; Sanudo 2011, 56 / Sanudo 1611, 27). Already Fidentius of Padua in 1291 ascertained that Egypt was a revolving door of trade between the Mediterranean Sea and the Indian Ocean and that there was reciprocal trade between Europe and Egypt. Christians fed Egypt both with the goods originating in Europe and with merchandise that they transported across the Mediterranean: wood, iron, slaves, oil, honey, gold, silver, copper, tin, lead, mercury, coral, amber, wool, and so on. Likewise, the Europeans craved flax, cinnamon, linen, silk, pepper, and precious stones (Fidentius of Padua 2008, 140–42). This reciprocity of trade disadvantaged Christians: "the Catalan, Pisan, Venetian, and other maritime merchants, and above all the Genoese, supply the Saracens with necessary goods. . . . [They are] ministers of hell, false Christians" (ministrantur necessaria Sarracenis per mercatores Catalanso, Pisanos, Venetos et aliorum maritimos mercatores et maxime Ianuenses . . . ministros inferni, falsos Christianos).[3] From each trade, the Mamluk sultan benefited: "all the aforesaid are brought to that land through our Mediterranean sea, and the Sultan exacts a heavy tribute on them in Alexandria" (omnia praedicta ad ipsas terras per nostrum mare feruntur, de quibus Soldanus percipit in Alexandria magna tributa; Sanudo 2011, 52 / Sanudo 1611, 24). This is why sanctions had to be stringent and absolute: "all trade and all access to the Saracens subject to the Sultan should be prohibited" (sine distinctione omnis mercatio et omnis accesio ad Saracenos Soldano subiectos prohiberi debeat; Sanudo 2011, 56 / Sanudo 1611, 27).

Pilgrimage was seen as a subset of these commercial relations, and it required a special papal dispensation. This official, public, and mutually beneficial Christian-Muslim trade was important enough to draw severe criticism. After 1291, there were persistent calls for the renewal and reinforcement of the papal ban on pilgrimage, namely by writers of crusading treatises, who strongly opposed an integrated Christian-Muslim economy.[4] In the writings of Fidentius of Padua, William of Adam, and Marino Sanudo, pilgrims, unlike wood or slaves, are not considered merchandise transported across the sea, but commercial agents on the same footing as the merchants:

> For the sultan exacts and receives about thirty-five pennies of Tours from each pilgrim, and since innumerable pilgrims flow to Jerusalem from various regions of the world, what I say will be clear when this tribute is multiplied. Evil is concealed under the piety of those pilgrims, therefore their devotion leads to disobedience and their zeal indiscriminately produces injustice. (William of Adam 2012, 38–39)

> (Soldanus enim circa triginta quinque turonensium grossos exigit et recipit a quolibet peregrino, et cum de diversis mundi partibus in Ierusalem confluant innumerabiles peregrini, uidebitur id quod dico cum multiplicatum fuerit hoc tributum. Ergo sub peregrinorum istorum pietate celatur iniquitas, eorumque deuotio inobedientiam parit, eorumque feruor indiscrete iniustitiam operatur.)

The pilgrims' payments finance the sultan's wars against Christians: "You may know that not only Latin Christians, that is the Italians, French, Spanish, English, Germans, thus go to Jerusalem, but also Christians from overseas, that is Greeks, Georgians, Armenians, and many others, from whom the sultan collects great tribute. And with that money that the sultan receives from the Christians, he can wage war against them" (Et scias quod non solum Cristiani qui vocantur Latini, videlicet Ytalici, Gallici, Hyspani, Anglici, Theotonici et hujusmodi vadunt in Jerusalem, sed vadunt Cristiani ultramarini, videlicet Greci, Georgiani, Armeni et multi alii a quibus soldanus accipit tributum magnum. Et cume ista pecunia quam soldanus accipit a Cristianis, potest soldanus pugnare contra Cristianos; Fidentius of Padua 2008, 95). Pilgrims are as responsible as the merchants for making the Egyptian economy thrive, the flow of their money and the supply of the raw materials making the military reconquest of the Holy Land impossible: "It is a great evil and loss to the Christians, because they go to Jerusalem against the sentence of excommunication and pay huge sums of money to Saracens, with which money Saracens wage war on Christians. Likewise God and the church condemn the Latins who transport iron, arms, wood, and other embargoed products and thus give the Saracen tools with which they cut the Christians' throats and kill them"

(Et quod est valde malum et magnum dispendium Cristianis, faciunt quia vadunt in Jerusalem contra latam sententiam excommunicationis et magnam pecuniam Saracenis solvunt, cum qua pecunia Saraceni Cristianos impugnant. Sunt etiam quidam Latini a Deo et ab Ecclesia maledicti, qui Saracenis deferunt ferrum, arma, ligna et cetera prohibita, et dant Saracenis instrumenta cum quibus Cristianos jugulant et occidunt; Fidentius of Padua 2008, 63). An economic strategy of sanctions must include the cessation of all pilgrim (and merchant) traffic—not just to enable a reconquest of the Holy Land, but also to stop the Muslim war against the Christians. William of Adam's lament on the treachery of pilgrims "who go to Jerusalem [and] also greatly assist the prince of Babylon at the expense of the Holy Land" (qui uadunt in Ierusalem magnum adiutorium dant principi Babilonis in dispendium Terre Sancte; William of Adam 2012, 38/39) makes this clear.

Translation between languages was an integral part of the medieval economy of exchange between Latin Christians and Muslims. It played such an important role that we can speak of an economy of translation, one that was enabled by multiple fixers working for merchants and pilgrims. This economy of translation is the focus of this chapter: the contractual economy that very quickly gets overwhelmed by what exceeds the contracted exchange of goods and products, where translation appears less as a product or outcome, but more as a process of commensuration and relationality. The focus on translation as economy likewise enables a reconsideration of the economy of gift exchange and the structural relationality of gift economy. We can observe this with thirteenth-century Franciscan missionaries and fourteenth- and fifteenth-century European pilgrims who resort to local fixers who turn out to be far from the ideal of a Christian- and European-born, educated, intelligent, agentive, and loyal fixer, the apostolic profile of fixers developed in crusade treatises (see chapter 1). Translation seems to operate within a gift economy, as can be seen in the experiences of two Franciscan missionaries to the Mongols in the second half of the thirteenth century, John of Plano Carpini in the *History of the Mongols* (*Ystoria Mongalorum*; 1245–47) and William of Rubruck in his *Journey* (*Itinerarium*; 1253–55).[5] They had no trained loyal fixers—their missions took place just as the Dominican language schools were being instituted—and all subsequently deplored the poor linguistic skills of their hired local fixers and the mutual lack of trust. As monks— especially as Franciscans, who made a vow of poverty—they could not pay for the services received: "I further explained, by way of apology, that I was a monk and neither owned nor accepted nor handled gold or silver or anything of value, with the sole exception of the books and the liturgical items with which we worshipped God, so that we were bringing no gifts for him or his master: as one who had relinquished his own belongings, I could not be the bearer of what belonged to others" (Excusavi etiam me quia monachus eram, non habens neque recipiens neque tractans aurum vel argentum vel aliquid preciosum, solis libris et capella in qua serviebamus Deo exceptis, unde nullum exennium afferebamus ei nec domino suo. Qui enim popria dimiseram, non poteram esse portitor alienorum; Rubruck 2009, 115 / Rubruck 1929, 200–201). Thus, more often than not, missionaries depended on the kindness of strangers and their gifts in order to communicate their message and preach to non-Christian populations. As Franciscan monks, bound by their vow of poverty, they wished not to reciprocate yet found themselves coerced into an exchange, however small, of food and clothing. By 1330s, almost one hundred year after the first Dominican circular on language schools (1236), the Dominican (and Llull's and Dubois's) project of systematic foreign language acquisition had failed, perhaps linked to the loss of the Latin Christian foothold in Asia Minor after the fall of Acre. As a result, instead of loyal and obedient Christian fixers, trained in Europe, "on this side of the Mediterranean" (P. Dubois 1956 / P. Dubois 1977, sec. 14), Christian pilgrimage fueled a full-blown translation market overseas and filled the sultan's coffers with tolls and tributes. Indeed, pilgrimage developed into a veritable tourist industry, a genuine economy with its own rules that the pilgrims documented in evaluating ceaselessly the price-performance (price-quality) ratio between itinerary, services, and money. Over seventy-five pilgrimage accounts record the emergence of a translation market, and some are especially rich in information (e.g., Giorgio Gucci, Georges Lengherand, and Felix Fabri).[6] However, even though the pilgrims paid for the services of their local fixers—interpreters and guides—they found that, for all the money in the world, they could not extricate themselves from a gift economy that bound them to a non-Christian other. Like the missionaries, despite themselves, the pilgrims too had to exchange gifts with their non-Christian fixers and live to tell the stories of gift exchange, gift and countergift, reciprocity and indebtedness.[7]

The Gift of Translation: Missionary Travel (Carpini and Rubruck)

Latin Christian missionaries to the Mongols use a variety of terms to describe gift giving: "munera" (Carpini 1929, 1:68; Rubruck 1929, 259), "donaria" (Carpini 1929, 1:105), "xennia" (Benedict the Pole 1929, 139), "munusculum" (Rubruck 1929, 190), and "exennium" (for "xennium," Rubruck 1929, 196). The Franciscan William of Rubruck, Louis IX's envoy to the Mongols (April 1253–June 1255), could not have been more explicit about the gift exchange into which the Franciscan brothers entered by obligation: "They admittedly take away nothing by force, but when they see something they ask for it in a highly persistent and impudent fashion. If a man gives it to them, it is wasted because they feel no gratitude; for they regard themselves as the masters of the world, and think that nobody should deny them anything. If he fails to give, and later has need of their services, they serve him with an ill will" (Verum est quod nichil auferunt vi, sed importune valde et impudenter petunt quod vident, et si dat eis homo perdit, quia sunt ingrati. Reputant enim se dominos mundi, et videtur eis quod nichil debeat eis negari ab aliquo; si non dat et postea indigeat servitio eorum, male ministrant ei; Rubruck 2009, 98 / Rubruck 1929, 189). A gift is an exchange for a service, yet it is neither truly a gift, nor is it exchanged for its symbolical equivalent. A gift is a coercion, an imposition in a circulation; at the limit of being taken, a gift must be ceded. If it is offered, it is a pure loss, because either its gesture or its value is forgotten. But if it is retained, the refusal to "give" is remembered, and the service is poor. There is then an exchange, coerced and reciprocated with a service, but a man cannot subtract himself from it; he must enter into this circulation. The missionaries thus express the logic of the economic circle of gift exchange.

The first diplomatic contacts between the Mongol khans and the West were established only after the Mongol invasion of Poland, Silesia, Moravia, and Hungary and incursion into Dalmatia in pursuit of King Bela IV in 1241–42. The early reports that started trickling in during the 1220s to the West about the rise and gradual advancement of the Mongols had largely been ignored. The Rus and the Cumans were attacked in 1222–23, and the Georgians as well. They were under attack in 1237 again. The last, and furthest, Mongol advance into the West of 1241–42 by the forces of Batu, Chinggis Khan's grandson, ended with a sudden retreat of Mongol forces in the spring of 1242 to the Volga, attributed to the death of Great Khan Ögödei and the forthcoming election of the new qaghan (Güyük, enthroned only in August 1246 and died in April 1248). The new pope, Innocent IV, who inherited the throne from Gregory IX after eighteen months of vacancy in June 1243, sent the first mission led by the Franciscan John of Plano Carpini.

Carpini's mission started in Lyon in April 1245 and returned there in November 1247. He began writing his Ystoria Mongalorum on the return voyage but finished it only once he returned. Avidity for information about the Mongols from those Carpini encountered in Poland, Bohemia, Germany, Liège, and Champagne led to an incomplete version, not authorized by Carpini and known as the "Tartar Relation" (Carpini 1980, 72 / Carpini 1929, 1:130). Another, brief, version of the mission was dictated in October 1247 by Brother Benedict the Pole (Benedictus Polonus), Carpini's "companion in our tribulations and interpreter" (nostre tribulationis socius et interpres; Carpini 1980, 4 / Carpini 1929, 1:28).[8]

Taking up over two-thirds of the official version of his report to the pope, Carpini provides a systematic and methodical description of the land, the population, their beliefs and customs, the Mongol court, and its military strategy and its army's organization. Carpini's mission was launched for the specific purpose of information gathering (Carpini 1980, 4 / Carpini 1929, 1:28), so that "if by chance they made a sudden attack they would not find the Christian people unprepared" (ne forte subito irruentes invenirent eos impreparatos; Carpini 1980, 3 / Carpini 1929, 1:28). Carpini considered a Mongol invasion all but certain (Carpini 1980, 45 / Carpini 1929, 1:95). The last third of Carpini's report (chapter 9) relates the actual voyage across Bohemia and Poland to Kyiv and to Batu's encampment on the lower Volga, from where they were sent to Qaraqorum, the Mongol capital, where they stayed between July and November 1246. It is in this section that a link between translation and gift giving organizes the narrative of the mission.

Even before Carpini and his companions leave Kyiv, we are introduced to the notion that their travel can proceed only by engaging in gift exchange. Unidentified gifts are offered in exchange for horses and guides: "We had to give the captain presents, so as to make him disposed to give us pack-horses and an escort" (Quare oportuit nos millenario munera dare, ut ipsum haberemus propicium ad dandum nobis equos subducticios et conductum; Carpini 1980, 52 / Carpini 1929, 1:104). The trip across the Asian continent is punctuated by a scansion of gifts at each juncture, gifts that Carpini feels were "extort[ed] from us" (a nobis munera extorquere) by various officials: "he was unwilling to be of service to us in any way, unless we promised him presents" (nisi munera promisissemus eidem, nullo modo conducere nos volebat). Hindered in their movement, unable to proceed into Mongol territory without a guide, "we promised to make some offering. When we gave him what seemed good to us he would not accept it unless we gave more; and so we had to increase it in accordance with his desire, and other things he took from us by cunning, stealth and knavery" (promisimus ei aliqua donaria dare. Et cum daremus ei ea que nobis videbantur, nolebat recipere, nisi plura daremus eidem. Unde oportuit nos addere secundum voluntatem ipsius; et quedam nobis subdole et furtive et malitiose subtraxit; Carpini 1980, 53 / Carpini 1929, 1:105). The same request for a gift in exchange for a service—further advance on the journey—is repeated at the first frontier crossing (Carpini 1980, 54 / Carpini 1929, 1:106). Then twice more, from Correnza, who was commander of frontier forces, and from Batu, commander of all Western Mongol forces, gifts are demanded, to which a very similar answer is given: "I gave the same answer as I had given to Correnza, namely that the Lord Pope had not sent any presents, but we wished to honour him as well as we could from among those things which, by the grace of God and the Lord Pope, we had with us for our needs" (Cui respondimus ut prius Corenze dixeramus, scilicet quod dominus Papa non miserat munera, sed nos de hiis que habebamus, de gratia Dei et domini Pape pro expensis, ipsum, sicut possumus, volumus honorare; Carpini 1980, 56 / Carpini 1929, 1:109). It is clear from the earlier gift giving at Correnza's that the friars make an offering from "our daily needs" (ad victum nostrum; Carpini 1980, 54 / Carpini 1929, 1:106), from "food" (cibariis; Carpini 1980, 53 / Carpini 1929, 1:105).

In the beginning, gifts were used to "purchase" travel. Gifts at Correnza's and at Batu's are an exchange; on both occasions, Carpini says that "gifts [were] offered and accepted" (datis muneribus et acceptis; Carpini 1980, 56 / Carpini 1929, 1:109; also Carpini 1980, 54 / Carpini 1929, 1:107). In return, gifts opened the gates of *yurtas* for an audience in which the missionaries expected to communicate their message. Unfortunately at Correnza's, "our interpreter whom we had brought from Kyiv was not competent to translate the letter, and there was no one else at hand capable of doing it" (noster interpres quem de Kyovia, dato precio, duxeramus, non erat sufficiens... nec ad hoc aliquis alius ydoneus habebatur; Carpini 1980, 55 / Carpini 1929, 1:107). Continuing on their mission, they repeated the same process of gift giving at Batu's: the friars "delivered the letter and asked to be given interpreters capable of translating it. . . . We carefully translated the letter with them into Ruthenian, Saracenic [i.e., Persian] and Tartar characters" (litteras obtulimus et rogavimus ut darentur nobis interpretes, qui litteras valerent transferre. . . . Et diligenter transtulimus eas cum ipsis in littera ruthenica, sarracenica et in littera Tartarorum; Carpini 1980, 56 / Carpini 1929, 1:109). The narrative is patterned on the exchange of gifts and translation: for each gift given, there is a translation, that is, the possibility of communication. Once Batu decides to send them onward as envoys to Qaraqorum for the inauguration of the next Great Khan, Güyük, gift giving fades away from the narrative, as emissaries are now under the khan's protection. At their arrival, highlighting the scarcity of food and the importance of gift giving, Güyük provides the envoys with "a tent and provisions, such as it is the custom for the Tartars to give, though they treated us better than other envoys" (tentorium et expensas,

quales Tartari solent dare, nobis tamen melius quam aliis nunciis facien-
bant; Carpini 1980, 61 / Carpini 1929, 1:116).[9]

A similar situation occurs on the mission of the Franciscan William of
Rubruck to the Mongols (April 1253–June 1255), who was quick to understand the relationship between gift giving and service providing, especially
when it came to "translation services." His trajectory—from Constantinople to the camp of Scacatai, the nearest Mongol commander, to the camp
of Sartaq, Batu's son, then Batu's headquarters, and finally to Möngke's
court—is strewn with numerous examples of demands for gifts in order
either to continue the voyage or to obtain an audience to deliver the message. At Scacatai's camp, his interpreter "asked for some garment or other,
since he was going to pass on our message to his master" (Poscebat etiam
vestimentum aliquod, quia dicturus erat verbum nostrum ante dominum
suum; Rubruck 2009, 100 / Rubruck 1929, 190). "Our guide," who takes
them to Sartaq, "wanted me to visit every commander with a present,
and for this we did not have sufficient stores" (Volebat enim dux noster
quod ad quemlibet capitaneum ingrederer cum exennio, et ad hoc non
sufficiebant expense). The gifts consist of food: "Each day there were eight
of us eating our bread (not counting those who fell in with us, all of whom
wanted to eat with us)" (Cotidie enim eramus octo persone comedentes
panem nostrum [exceptis supervenientibus qui omnes volebant comedere
nobiscum]; Rubruck 2009, 108 / Rubruck 1929, 196). Indeed, food giving
and meal sharing is the token gesture to which Rubruck resorts repeatedly (Rubruck 2009, 100 / Rubruck 1929, 190), though at Sartaq's court
clothes and books are taken from him (Rubruck 2009, 119 / Rubruck 1929,
204). But whenever he is able, Rubruck refuses to engage in gift exchange,
"saying by way of apology that I was a monk and that it was not in keeping
with our Order to own gold, silver or expensive garments, and that for this
reason I had nothing of that kind to present to him; but would he accept
some of our food for a blessing. At this he ordered it to be accepted" (ex-
cusans me quia monachus eram, nec erat Ordinis nostri possidere aurum
vel argentum vel vestes preciosas; unde non habebam aliquid talium quod
possem ei dare, sed de cibis nostris acciperet pro benedictione. Tunc fecit
recipi; Rubruck 2009, 101 / Rubruck 1929, 190; also Rubruck 2009, 115 /
Rubruck 1929, 200–201).

At this point, Carpini's and Rubruck's trajectories reveal several things.
First, they resist gift exchange as Franciscans bound by the vow of poverty:
"I was a monk . . . ; I could not be the bearer of what belonged to others"
(Excusavi etiam me quia monachus eram . . . non poteram esse portitor
alienorum; Rubruck 2009, 115 / Rubruck 1929, 200–201). At the same time,
they do participate, unwillingly, in the gift exchange since a refusal threat-

ens their mission, as happened to the Dominican Ascelin at the camp of Baichu (May-July 1247), recorded by Simon of Saint-Quentin: "How can you, bringing letters from your lord and with regard to modesty, want to appear before our lord empty-handed, that which no man coming here has done to him?" (Quomodo potestis pre verecundia ante dominum nostrum velle comparere manibus vacuis, porrigendo litteras domini vestri, quod nullus hominum hunc veniens fecit ei?).[10] They are also trying to avoid the fate of a failed mission of another Dominican, Andrew of Longjumeau. He carried sumptuous gifts and a letter from Louis IX (January 1249–51) that were misinterpreted at the Mongol court as a gesture of submission.[11]

Thus, gifts are appropriated from Carpini and Rubruck, enforcing on them the gift exchange. They learn to function in this economy of give and take. Their gifts enable and facilitate their travel; they bring them into audience with the rulers and earn them the services of interpreters. But it is at this critical point that they face a different problem: the interpreters provided are unable to translate their official letters and, at other times, their missionary message. Both Carpini and Rubruck are forced to receive the gift of translation, no matter how resistant they are to gift exchange with non-Christians. This gift of translation definitively puts them in the circle of gift exchange.

Carpini and Rubruck start their missions with a hired interpreter at their side. Carpini is explicit about purchasing his services, "our paid interpreter whom we had brought from Kyiv" (noster interpres quem de Kyovia, dato precio, duxeramus; Carpini 1980, 55 / Carpini 1929, 1:107). Rubruck retained the services of "dragoman Homodei" (homo Dei turgemanus; Rubruck 2009, 69 / Rubruck 1929, 170). But these interpreters both turn out to be incompetent, overwhelmed by events. Carpini's interpreter "was not competent to translate for them the letter" (non erat sufficiens ut per eum littere possent interpretari; Carpini 1980, 55 / Carpini 1929, 1:107), and Rubruck's Homodei "was neither intelligent nor articulate" (nullius erat ingenii nec alienius eloquentie; Rubruck 2009, 101 / Rubruck 1929, 191), "incapable" (non valens; Rubruck 2009, 156 / Rubruck 1929, 232), "inadequate" (non erat sufficiens; Rubruck 2009, 227 / Rubruck 1929, 290), "not up to the task" (defficiebat michi; Rubruck 2009, 167 / Rubruck 1929, 240). This puts both emissaries into a singular situation, where translation becomes not an individual, (pre)paid service, but often a collective, multilingual effort between Latin, Greek, Russian, Turkish, Persian, and Tartar, translated "sentence by sentence" (per singulas orationes; Carpini 1980, 67 / Carpini 1929, 1:123–24) or "word by word" (de verbo ad verbum; Saint-Quentin 1965, 106). Because of incompetent interpreters, the emissaries were obliged, and often relieved, to receive translation as a gift.[12] In Carpini's case, he depended for translation on the kindness of strangers, facilitated perhaps by Benedict the Pole's knowledge of Slavic languages:

> At Batu's yurta we came across the son of Duke Jerozlaus; he was accompanied by a knight from Russia called Sangor, who was a Coman by nationality but is now a Christian, like the other Russian who was our interpreter with Batu and came from the Susdal district. At the court of the Emperor of the Tartars we met Duke Jerozlaus . . . and one of his knights, by name Temer. This latter acted as our interpreter with Güyük Khan . . . both in translating the Emperor's letter to the Lord Pope and in speaking and replying. (Carpini 1980, 70)

> (Apud Bati invenimus filium ducis Ierozlay, qui habebat secum militem unum de Ruscia qui vocatur Sangor, qui fuit natione Comanus sed nunc est christianus, ut alter Ruthenus qui apud Bati noster fuit interpres, de terra susdaliensi. Apud Imperatorem Tartarorum invenimus ducem Ierozlaum . . . et militem suum qui vocatur Temer, qui fuit interpres noster apud Cuyuccam . . . tam in translatione litterarum Imperatoris ad dominum Papam, quam in verbis dicendis et respondendis.) (Carpini 1929, 1:128)

Here, the gift of translation is offered by someone who happens accidentally to be present at the same place and time.

Rubruck's ability to communicate hinges even more on such chance encounters and fortuitous coincidences. Rubruck carried a letter from Louis IX, and early on in his journey, because of an Armenian mistranslation at Sartaq's court that he attributed to "a more forceful rendering just as it suited [the Armenians] who loathe Saracens bitterly" (gravius fuissent interpretati, secundum placitum eorum; Rubruck 2009, 171 / Rubruck 1929, 243), he was represented as an envoy seeking a Mongol alliance, though it appears that his main mission was to provide pastoral care to German captives and their offspring whose existence had been discovered by the Dominican Longjumeau.[13] Under the pain of death, Rubruck was advised against openly identifying himself as other than envoy and was greeted at the Mongol court with amazement, "mirabantur": "Why have you come, seeing that you did not come to make peace?" (Quare venistis, ex quo non venistis facere pacem?; Rubruck 2009, 172 / Rubruck 1929, 244).

As a Franciscan, Rubruck refused keeping gifts, which he gave to his interpreter, Homodei: "they were amazed beyond measure that we were unwilling to accept gold or silver or expensive garments" (Et mirabantur supra modem quia nolebamus recipere aurum vel argentum vel vestes preciosas; Rubruck 2009, 42 / Rubruck 1929, 222). But he did accept the gift of translation, which for him was the most precious of gifts, enabling him to communicate and preach, and to understand the world around him. A woman from Metz in Lorraine, who had been captured in Hungary, connected Rubruck with "a master goldsmith, called William" (magister aurifaber, Willelmus nomine), who had "a young man whom he had fostered and treated as a son, and who was an excellent interpreter" (quemdam iuvenem quem nutrierat quem habebat pro filio, qui erat optimus interpres; Rubruck 2009, 183 / Rubruck 1929, 253). When Rubruck reached Qaraqorum he was invited to William's lodging. William's wife, born in Hungary of a Lorrainer, knew French and Coman, and there he met "Basil, the son of an Englishman, who had been born in Hungary and who knows these same languages" (Basilium nomine, filium Anglici, qui natus erat in Hungaria, et scit predicta ydeomata; Rubruck 2009, 212 / Rubruck 1929, 278). Carpini likewise relied for information on a familiar and familial network, "a number of Russians and Hungarians knowing Latin and French, and Russian clerics and others, who had been among the Tartars, some for thirty years, through wars and other happenings, and who knew about them, for they knew the language and had lived with them continually some twenty years, others ten, some more, some less. With the help of these men we were able to gain a thorough knowledge of everything" (Rutenos plures Ungaros et scientes latinum et gallicum et clericos Rutenos, et alios qui fuerant cum eis, aliqui qui XXX annis, in bellis et aliis factis et sciebant omnia facta eorum, quia sciebant linguam et cum eis assidue morabantur, aliqui XX, aliqui X, aliqui plus, aliqui minus, a quibus poteramus perscrutari omnia; Carpini 1980, 66 / Carpini 1929, 1:122–23).

These networks of linguistic affinity functioned on the basis of person-to-person interaction, rather than institutional interaction, and they did not correspond to ethnic lines. They were all the more welcome as they appeared to compensate for the linguistic and cultural isolation that the friars experienced during their journey; Rubruck points out that they always had the worst horses and were treated poorly, going hungry and thirsty (chapters 21; 22). These stories also reveal that the monks were not communicating because they wanted to but because they needed to obtain something through communication. Rubruck repeatedly blamed his interpreter for his failure to convert Mongols because Homodei refused to translate: "whenever I wanted to do some preaching to them my interpreter would say: 'Do not make me preach, since I do not know how to express these things.' He was right. Later, when I acquired some little knowledge of the language, I noticed that when I said one thing he would say something totally different, depending on what came into his head. After that, I realized the danger of speaking through him, and chose rather to say nothing" (quando volebam eis dicere aliquod verbum edificationis, interpres meus dicebat: "Non faciatis me predicare, quia nescio talia verba dicere." Et verum dicebat. Ego enim percepi postea, quando incepi aliquantulum intelligere idioma, quod quando dicebam unum, ipse totum aliud dicebat secundum quod ei occurrebat. Tunc videns periculum loquendi per ipsum, elegi magis tacere; Rubruck 2009, 108 / Rubruck 1929, 196). It is on the basis of Rubruck's experience that Roger Bacon advocated for the training of fixers in matters of language, doctrine, culture, and agency (see chapter 1)—language alone was not enough in the real world. Rubruck even resorted to the performative power of prayer in his own language since "I was unable to do anything else, since to speak in doctrinal terms through an interpreter like this was a great risk—in fact an impossibility, as he was ignorant of them" (Aliud non poteram facere, quia loqui verba doctrine per interpretem talem erat magnum periculum immo impossibilite, quia ipse nesciebat; Rubruck 2009, 167 / Rubruck 1929, 240). In counterpoint, fortuitous encounters, these gifts of translation, provided by total strangers who were living among Mongols yet seemed familiar because of language affinity and shared Christian upbringing with the missionaries, seemed to open wide the communication, to the point that Rubruck acquired knowledge of some Tartar and Mongol languages and toward the end of his journey began to state openly his missionary purpose and even requested the permission to return to the Mongol court to continue his missionary activity (Rubruck 2009, 238 / Rubruck 1929, 299).

The essential link between gifts and translation is highlighted in the very last sentence of Rubruck's *Itinerarium*, "For they listen to what an ambassador has to say and always ask whether he wishes to say more; though he would have need of a good interpreter—several interpreters, in fact—and plentiful supplies" (Audiunt enim quecumque nuncius vult dicere et semper querunt si vult dicere plura, sed oporteret quod haberet bonum interpretem, immo plures interpretes et copiosas expensas; Rubruck 2009, 278 / Rubruck 1929, 332). A successful mission needed to have plenty of food and objects to offer and be staffed with loyal, well-trained fixers, the new apostles: they would perform much beyond the linguistic function, disputing the errors and winning doctrinal arguments, that would lead to conversion of non-Christians. Having fixers would free missionaries of exchange, where translation is bartered for gifts, and protect them from "bad translation": "Had I been possessed of a good fixer, this would have given me an opportunity of sowing much good seed" (Unde si habuissem bonum interpretem, habebam oportunitatem seminandi multa bona; Rubruck 2009, 141–42 / Rubruck 1929, 222; translation modified). Alternatively, a missionary could learn the language and be his own fixer, as the Dominican Riccoldo of Monte Croce would do, "as it behooved me among Arabs to learn not only the language but also dialectics" (et oportuit me inter arabes non solum discere linguam sed etiam dyalecticam),[14] and as Rubruck attempted to do late in the game.

Several conclusions can be reached. First, the friars did not wish to participate in the economy of the gift exchange, from which they insisted on being excluded as Franciscans. Rather they wanted to be transmitters of a divine message, offering a gift without any condition, that is, without the obligation to give and to receive. But they were faced with the necessity of gift exchange, for it is impossible to give freely and without reciprocity; for instance, the khan reciprocated with money. They assumed that because they were envoys, their message would be heard, but to have an audience to deliver this message, they first had to offer a gift. In other words, missionaries were forced into an understanding that communication—even if their message is divine—is an exchange. Having a (divine) message to deliver does not exempt them from making a gift that gives them the right to speak.

Second, the friars tried to avoid participating in the circle of exchange because the papal message, the message of divine truth that Carpini carries, or the royal message that Rubruck delivers, "urging [the khan] to be a friend to all Christians, to exalt the Cross, and to be the enemy of all who are enemies to the Cross" (monetabis eum ut esset amicus omnium christianorum et exaltaret crucem et esset inimicus omnium inimicorum crucis; Rubruck 2009, 171 / Rubruck 1929, 243), got caught up in the economy of exchange. The gifts that enabled the delivery of the message at the same time turned the message into an object of exchange that was possibly seen as an act of submission to the Great Khan. The divine message should be outside the gift exchange; it should be an inalienable object that would not need a translation but whose performative power—the power of prayer—would make it immediately accessible. Rubruck preached: "What is written here is the belief a man should have concerning God, and a prayer in which God is asked for whatever a man needs. So believe firmly what is written here, even if you cannot understand it" (Hic scriptum est illud quod homo credere debet de Deo, et oratio in qua petitur a Deo quidquid est necessarium homini; unde credite firmiter quod hic scriptum est, quamvis non possitis intelligere; Rubruck 2009, 167 / Rubruck 1929, 240). Conversely, the need for translation underlined the fact that divine Christian truth was inextricably entangled in a system of exchange, that a message could not avoid the necessity of translation no matter how divine, that its very translation turned it into an object of exchange. Divine truth was not immanent; it was a part of an exchange. The divine message became no more than monetary payment with which the khan reciprocated.

Finally, the friars found out that the word of God was not universal, that there was cultural difference. This message Güyük Khan's return stated clearly: "But you men of the West believe that you alone are Christians and despise others. But how can you know to whom God deigns to confer His grace?" (Sed vos homines occidentis solos vos christianos esse creditis et alios despicitis. Sed quomodo scire potestis, cui Deus suam gratiam conferre dignetur; Benedict the Pole 1980, 83 / Benedict the Pole 1929, 143). The missionaries were inscribed not in universality, but in cultural specificity; they discovered that they themselves were indigenous to their own culture rather than universal to all humanity. Specific to their culture, they therefore also had to engage in gift exchange with others.[15] The missionaries discovered their own particularity and the particularity of their truth, and that, when translated, "truth" enters into an exchange. Most importantly, missionary narratives highlight the necessity of a long-term investment into making of fixers, who will perform more than just the linguistic (see chapter 1).[16]

The Translation Market: Pilgrim Travel (Frescobaldi, Gucci, Fabri, Breydenbach, Lengherand, von Harff)

In contrast to the thirteenth-century missions to Central and East Asia, before 1323, the year of the Franciscan Simon Fitzsimon's pilgrimage, few narratives of pilgrimage to the Near East spoke in personal tones and touched on interpreters, guides, or communication issues (Fitzsimon 1960). Previous accounts were cut-and-dried guides, impersonal descriptions of sites, known as *descriptiones Terrae Sanctae* (descriptions of the Holy Land), such as the often copied work by Burchard of Mount Sion.[17] But between Jacob of Verona's 1335 voyage and Arnold von Harff's 1496–99 travels, there exist more than seventy-five known pilgrim travel accounts written in Latin, French, Italian, German, and English.[18] They are filled with personal information and pilgrims' emotions and opinions, and they provide empirical, situational evidence on translation activity and fixers.[19] There is one possible explanation for this phenomenon in pilgrim accounts after 1300: the loss of Acre in May 1291 made visits to pilgrimage sites and communication more problematic.[20]

Before the final fall of the Kingdom of Jerusalem and Acre in 1291, communication was relatively unproblematic in medieval Syria by virtue of the Frankish presence. Pilgrims were protected and could count on assistance (military protection, guides) to some degree. Most often, pilgrims would land in Acre, the capital of the kingdom. Although throughout the period before the fall of Acre ships could disembark passengers in Jaffa and sometimes in various other ports along the Syrian coast, it was only after the fall of Acre and in the course of the fourteenth century (around 1335) that the pilgrimage to the Holy Land became a matter of organized visits, and by the fifteenth century it developed into routine group tourism. This development also contributed to the regulation of translation by contracts; however, the contractual economy failed to undo or eliminate the fundamental link between translation and gift giving.

In the fourteenth and fifteenth centuries the standard, "most common, and most traveled pilgrim route on pilgrim galleys," "reputed much safer and busier" (cum galeis peregrinorum, quod est commune passagium et usitatum; multo tutiorem et magis frequentatam), was between Venice and Jaffa. Throughout the fifteenth century, some rare pilgrims still continued to travel from Genoa, Marseille, or Barcelona, because Venetian pilgrim galleys were overpopulated: they had tight quarters, and diseases circulated easily among pilgrims of so many different nations.[21] The monopoly of the Venetians over the pilgrim trade relied on their alliance with the Franciscans. Robert d'Anjou, king of Naples (and titular king of Sicily and Jerusalem) and Count of Provence, and Queen Sancia of Majorca, both greatly influenced by the Franciscans, purchased territory on Mount Sion from the sultan of Egypt and transferred ownership to the Franciscan Friars; this took place between 1335 and 1337, as recorded in the deeds of purchase and in Franciscan annals. Soon thereafter, the Franciscans were given permission to build a monastery in Mount Sion,[22] and by 1380, reception and guidance on the ground in Syria were provided by the Franciscan order.[23] In 1342, Pope Clement VI had declared the Franciscans the official custodians of the Holy Places. The mercantile-missionary alliance between the Venetians and the Franciscans contributed to the standardization of pilgrimage routes, on sea and land, and their legislation (Newett 1907, 26–28). This shift also led to a tidal change in a dominant language of the Mediterranean, from French (crusaders) to Italian (merchants). Finally, the mercantile-missionary alliance made pilgrimage accessible to increasing numbers of lay people, who formed the largest contingent of visitors in the fifteenth century (Bourel 1997).

Venetian administrative records indicate that there was a whole system in place intended to secure at the starting point, in Venice, all the provisions and services that pilgrims needed to get to the Holy Land: *tolomaci* (guides and interpreters, that is, fixers) in Piazza San Marco and Rialto connected pilgrims with inn owners, ship captains, and money changers.[24] Often, such connections were made through affiliation networks. Germans Felix Fabri and Arnold von Harff stayed at an inn in Venice where "the entire household, the landlord and the landlady, and all the manservants and maidservants, were of the German nation and speech, and no word of Italian was to be heard in the house, which was a very great comfort to us; for it is very distressing to live with people without being able to converse with them" (Omnis autem domus, hospes et hospita et cuncti famuli et ancillae erant de lingua alemanica, nec audiebatur in domo illa verbum italicum, de quo singulare solatium habuimus, quia valde poenale est convivere hominibus, cum quibus locutione conversari non potest).[25]

By the fifteenth century, some Venetian captains (*padrone* or *patronus*) were offering pilgrimage packages on a trip that resembled a group tour to the Holy Land. In 1420, an anonymous French pilgrim tells us that "as much for the safe-conduct as for the entry fee, for transportation of luggage and the sights of the pilgrimage, food and animal expenses, everything from the moment of disembarking until the return to the galley, one should count per head at least 15 ducats" (tant que pour leur saufconduit que pour entrée, et pour porter [leur bagaige] et veoir les pellerinaiges, leurs despences de bouches et l'asne que chevauchent, par tout dès la descendue jusques au remonter en la galée, fault du mains pour teste XV ducas; "Un pèlerinage en Terre Sainte" 1905, 80). By 1480, we learn from Santo Brasca, secretary to the Duke of Milan, that the contract with the ship's captain was all inclusive, from and to Venice with visits to Holy Land sites, much like today's cruises: "One should make a contract with the galley's captain, who usually asks between 50 and 60 ducats. For this sum, he is required to provide round-trip transportation, food (except during stopovers at ports of call), animals for land transportation in the Holy Land, and payment of all tributes and tolls" (far laccodio col patrono el quale e solito prendere de .50. tre .60. ducati. E sopra questo lui e obligato dare el nolo, fare le spese abarie [?] in landare e tornare excepto in terra pagha le calvacature. In terra sancta e cosi pagbare tuti li dati et [sic] tributi).[26] Another pilgrim traveling the same year confirms the costs:

> And whenever the said ship captain moors in a port, one has to live at one's expense beyond the given amount of 55 ducats. And sometimes, he remains in port for four, six, twelve, or fifteen days, depending on the wind without which he cannot sail on. Moreover, because this ship captain provides only two meals a day, one must make in Venice provisions of things that one could not obtain aboard the ship. And if one falls sick and has no supplies, one is treated very poorly.

(Et touttefoys que le dict patron arrive à ung port, il fault que chascun vive à ses despens propres oultre la dicte somme de cinquante cinq ducatz. Et aulcunes foys, il sejourne à ung port quatre, six, douze ou quinze jours, selon la disposition du vent sans lequel il ne peult aller avant. Et oultre, pour ce que le dict patron ne faict que deux repas le jour, chascun fait garnyson, à Venise, de plusieurs choses qu'on ne pourroit avoir au navire. Et quant on est mallade, qui n'a aulcune provision est tres mal traicté.)[27]

In 1483, Bernhard von Breydenbach, deacon of the Mainz cathedral, says that the return trip cost forty-two ducats per person (Wiryme solten geben ye fur eyn person .xlii. ducaten bis gen jherusalem vn her wyder; Breydenbach 2010, 54–56; for Latin, see Breydenbach 1486, 8). The ship's captain had his own secretary, scribe, or clerk, "escrivain de leur nef" (Caumont 1858, 118), "l'escripvain de la galée" ("Un pèlerinage en Terre Sainte" 1905, 80; Le voyage 1882, 57), "scribanu[s]" (Fabri 1896, 7:139 / Fabri 2000–2006, 1:164), who made contact with the sultan's representatives on land and in turn issued safe-conducts for pilgrims. On land, pilgrims were herded as a group, in the company of "the aforementioned friars of Mount Sion, with the ship's captain, dragomans, officers, and guards" (lesdits frères du Mont de Sion avec les patrons des gallées, les truchemans et oficiers et gardes d'illec). These "lead the pilgrims on all the pilgrimages" (mainent les pellerins par tous les pélerinages qui s'enssuivent; Lengherand 1861, 117–18), meaning Jerusalem and the nearby sites. The pilgrims were often disappointed by the minimal amount of time allowed for visits, between eight and ten days, while the ships waited in Jaffa: "I was by no means satisfied with my first pilgrimage, because it was exceeding short and hurried, and we ran round the holy places without understanding and feeling what they were. Besides this, we were not permitted to visit some of the holy places, both within Jerusalem and without" (Nequaquam enim contentus fui de peregrinatione prima, quia nimis festina fuit et brevis, et per loca sancta cucurrimus absque intellectu et sine affectu. Non etima dabatur nobis tempus visitandi quaedam alia loca sancta tam in Jerusalem, quam extra; Fabri 1896, 7:48 / Fabri 1843–49, 1:61). Only those pilgrims who wished to continue to Mount Sinai were authorized to remain in Jerusalem; they would return later by way of Cairo and Alexandria, and the contracts stipulated that the ship's captain reimburse a part of the sum prepaid for their round-trip, usually about ten ducats (Fabri 1896, 7:89 / Fabri 1843–49, 1:91).

The Franciscans on Mount Sion were the anchor of pilgrimage tour operations in the Holy Land. They provided lodging and occasionally acted as guides.[28] As pilgrims became more numerous, the arrival procedure apparently underwent a change. By 1418, the year of the Lord of Caumont's journey, the pilgrims were greeted by Franciscans in Jaffa: "I remained in the galley without descending for two days, when came to me one of the Friars Minor of those who guard the Holy Sepulcher, consolation for the Christians and who brought the safe-conduct from the Sultan of Baby-lon. . . . Then I left the ship" (je demouray en la nef sans saillir en terre deux jours, que furent venus devers moy ung des frères Meneurs de ceulx qui gardent le saint Sépulcre, . . . consols pour les crestiens; lesquels me portarent sauf conduit du Soudain de Babiloyne. . . . Alors je sailli hors de la nef).[29] By 1420, the Franciscans attained such a degree of organization that they communicated with and provided for pilgrims arriving from most Christian countries:

> When the custodian of Mount Sion learns of the pilgrims' arrival, he im-mediately comes to see them to find out who they are. . . . He separates the pilgrims according to nations and sends for a brother belonging to each; then he assigns to each nation one brother who gives them con-fession, leads and guides them during all the visits, and announces and informs them of the sites and what indulgences they bring.

> (Mais quant le gardien du mont de Syon scet la venue des pelerins, il les vient tantost veoir, et savoir quelz gens ilz sont. . . . Et lors il fait audit hospital venir de chascune nacion ung frere, et fait les nacions desdis pellerins chascune mettre à part et leur baille cedit frere pour les confesser, qui les menra et conduira par tous les voyaiges, et pour leur dire et declairier que c'est et les indulgences.) ("Un pèlerinage en Terre Sainte" 1905, 82)

By 1461, the pilgrimages attain such frequency and numbers that upon arrival to Jerusalem, the custodian must give a sermon of guidance. In his account, Bishop Rochechouart provides an abbreviated version: "Third, of the dangers that we could be accustomed to befalling us in the pilgrimage, that is, that we all travel together, protect our purses, and hide the wine, which is highly valued by the Saracens. Fourth, that for injuries inflicted on us we reward them with favors, and much else that is not written in this book" (Tercio, de periculis que in peregrinacione nos contingere solent, videlicet quod omnes simul ambularemus, bursas custodiremus, vinum occultaremus, quod multum diligunt Sarraceni. Quarto, quod pro illatis nobis injuriis gratias retribueremus, et multa alis que non sunt scripta in libro hoc).[30]

Alongside the Franciscans, the pilgrims were greeted in Jaffa by local Muslim officials, the dragomans of Gaza or Jerusalem, who performed a registration procedure of persons and possessions: "Nanchardin, at the time the great dragoman of Jerusalem, asked each one of us his first and last name, nickname, age, and had those, together with our physiognomy, scars or other marks on the face, height and bearing, written down and a double sent to the great dragoman of Cairo" ([Nanchardin lors grant truchement de Ihersualem] demanda à chascun de nous son propre nom et son surnom et son eaige et les feist tous mettre en escript, ensemble les philozommnie et aucuns seignes de blesseures ou autrement s'il estoit au visaige, et la haulteur et la fachon de nous tous: et de toutes ces choses il envoye le double au grand truchement du Caire).[31] After such formalities pilgrims were given "each a seal [or a certificate] to keep on them wherever they went" (chascun une bullette que fault porter avec soy où qu'ilz voisent), and led to Ramallah and then Jerusalem ("Un pèlerinage en Terre Sainte" 1905, 80; see also Barbatre 1972–73, 128). The sultan's officials in Jerusalem and Gaza, who were Muslim Arabs, often did not speak a foreign language (well), so they employed subsidiary interpreters: in 1461, "this [dragoman] did not know well Italian, so he had two or three mercenaries who knew Italian and German" (Iste plene non noverat linguam italicam, sed habebat duos vel tres latrunculos qui noverant italicum et theutonicum; Rochechouart 1893, 237–38). In Felix Fabri's case, the dragoman "knew the Italian tongue and some bad broken German which he had learned from the pilgrims" (scivit enim lingam [sic] italicam et corruptum malum teutonicum, quod didicerat a peregrinis; Fabri 1896, 9:106 / Fabri 1843–49, 2:109).

In Egypt, pilgrims were led to the sultan's grand dragoman in Cairo. The case of the great dragomans in Cairo was different since the post was occupied by Christian renegades, most often Italians (there are records of French- and Spanish-speaking great dragomans in Cairo), and there could be up to four, presumably for different languages.[32] One of the first missions to the sultan, in 1303–4 by Angelo di Spoleto to comfort the captives from Acre and Tripoli, records the language barrier and the excellent preparation by the sultan's court: "And Emir, interpreter of the Latin or French language, questioned the brothers" (Et Ammiratus interpres lingua Latina seu Gallica interrogavit fratres; Angelo di Spoleto 1906–27, 70).

The sultan's officials collected the tribute and fees, issued safe-conducts for pilgrims, and organized travel provisions, guides, and interpreters, but they did not accompany pilgrims beyond Jerusalem and Cairo into the desert. As Lionardo Frescobaldi explained in 1384, "The grand interpreter of the Sultan . . . is in charge of all the interpreters of the sultan" (al gran

turcimanno del Soldano, il quale è sopra tutti e turcimani del Soldano;
Frescobaldi 1944, 44 / Frescobaldi 1948, 77). The service was provided
instead by local fixers, "the lower dragomans" (Trutschelmannus/Calinus
minor; Fabri 1896, 9:105 / Fabri 1843–49, 2:108), hired on the spot. These
were the true, multifunctional fixers, "dragomans—that is to say, protec-
tors, conductors, or guardians of the Christian pilgrims" (Trutschelmanni,
i.e. defensores et ductores, sive provisores Christianorum peregrinorum;
Fabri 1896, 9:105 / Fabri 1843–49, 2:108). "They have the duty to help the
foreigners, to speak for them and to accompany them in the city, for which
they receive from them rewards" (Habent enim de extraneis onera de
eos adjuvando, pro eis loquendo ac eos per civitatem associando, unde et
emolumenta ab eis recipiunt; Adorno 1978, 208).

But "few good and loyal interpreters could be found on the spot"
(Trucemanni et interpretes pauci comperiuntur, unde fideles et boni paucissimi; Adorno 1978, 210). This could be remedied by hiring a dragoman
in Venice, albeit a more costly option. The Dominican Felix Fabri's fellow
traveler Bernhard von Breydenbach, in the first printed pilgrim guide, also
considered to be the first illustrated travel book, *Pilgrimage in the Holy
Land (Peregrinatio in Terram Sanctam)*, written in 1485 and published in
1486, provides a sample of a Venetian transportation contract, concluded
at the time of his travel in 1483–84, in which it is specified that "if the pilgrims, as is customary, wanted to take a 'dolmetscher' in Venice, that is,
an expert in the languages of the lands to which they are going, the ship's
captain is obliged to sustain him with food and drink until the Holy Land
and then back until Venice, and the patron can't and shouldn't ask for a
payment for the 'dolmetscher'" (Item ob die pilgran eynen dolmetzen
venedig zu ynen nemen wur den so soll der patron dem selben dolmetzen
kost geben zu dem heiligen lande vnd widervmb bis gen venedig).[33] The
pilgrims are responsible for all costs associated with their fixer, and Breydenbach is clear that a separate contract is to be concluded with the fixer
and indicates that such a hire was customary: "After the pilgrims have
disembarked in Jaffa, they themselves will provide the fixer whom they
brought with them, without any damage to the ship's captain, with everything that they had brought with them, in everything that concerns food,
dues, fees, safe-conducts, and provisions . . . which the pilgrims would
have taken care of with the fixer with a written contract" (und so die pilgram gen japha kommen an das land was dan der dolmetsch verzeret vnd
vnkoften haben wurdt mit zollen vnd esel gelt sollen die pilgram die den
dolmetschen mit ynen furen vssrichten vn ezalen on des patron schaden.
Wie aber die pilgram mit dem dolmetschen vberkommen das hatt eyn
eygene verschribung).[34]

This was the case of the German knight Arnold von Harff, who traveled in the Near East and Egypt between 1496 and 1499, and hired his fixer in Venice. Von Harff provides the most thorough description of a pilgrim's fixer and their contract:

> Item, they [the German merchants] helped me to find a dragoman, that is a guide knowing many languages. He was called Master Vyncent, a Spaniard; he was a renegade Christian, but I did not know this. He knew many languages such as Latin, Lombard, Spanish, Wendish, Greek, Turkish and excellent Arabic. . . . I had to give him four ducats a month, as well as food and drink, and a hundred ducats as a gift. In return he was to take me from Venice to Cairo, further to St. Catherine's and through all the heathen lands to Jerusalem. Item, as soon as I had made my contract with him, he went to buy everything which would be necessary for us in the ship.

> (Item van stunt an hulffen sij mir an eynen trutzselman, dat is eyn geleytzman kunnende vil spraichen, her hiesch myschier Vyncent eyn hyspaneoler, he was eyn verlueckener kryst, des wyst ich auer nyet. Hee kunt gar vyllerleye spraiche, as latijn lumbartz hyspanioils wyndichs greex turcks ind guet arabs. . . . Ich moist ime geuen des maentz vier ducaeten, dar zoe essen ind dryncken ind hundert ducaeten zo eyner schenckonge, des suyldt he mich voerent van Venedich bys zo Alkayr, voert zo sijnt Katrijnen ind durch alle heydensche landen bys zo Jherusalem. Item doe ich dit verdynckenysse mit ime gemaich hatte gynck hee ind kuefft mir alles wes wir noitturfftich in dem schyff waeren.)[35]

Von Harff's fixer was "a renegade Christian," and there are records of Muslims,[36] Jews,[37] Christians of the girdle,[38] renegade Christians,[39] or Greek Christians acting as dragomans.[40] The summary of this variety can be gathered from the journals of the three Florentines who traveled together in 1384, Giorgio Gucci, Lionardo Frescobaldi, and Simone Sigoli: "From Alexandria to Cairo is the well known Said, who had accompanied Poggibonsi; then in Cairo, Simon of Candia; in Sinai, Fra Giovanni of Candia; on the journey to Sinai, Ali, the traitor; in Jerusalem, Friars and pious women; in Damascus, as in Alexandria, the turcomans and Florentine merchants of the firm of Portinari and others."[41]

How much did a fixer cost? In the 1340s, an anonymous Englishman and the Franciscan Niccolò da Poggibonsi are among the first to report the cost of tribute and cost of fixers: "On entering and leaving five dirhems a head are paid to the said port and two dirhems to the fixer" (All'entrata et all'uscita si paga al detto porto [di Jaffa] V drame per testa et due drame allo 'nterpreto).[42] By the time of his travel in 1392–93, Thomas Brygg in his budget mentions expenses per person paid to each of the six different "drugemanni" and four "great dragomans" (*magnis drugemmanis*) between Alexandria, Cairo, the desert, the monastery of Saint Catherine, the river Jordan, and Beirut (from a few grosso up to six ducats; Brygg 1884, 387–88). As the cost of paying fixers became more prominent, certain merchants and travelers accompanied the expense with a justification. Already around 1340, the Florentine banker-merchant Francesco Balducci Pegolotti, in his *La pratica della mercatura*, counsels that no cost be spared in hiring an interpreter, "and you want to take a dragoman, without trying to save in choosing between the bad and the good, because in the long run the good one doesn't cost you as much as the greedy one" (E vuolsi fornire . . . di turcimanni, e non si vuole guardare a rispiarmo dal cattivo al buono, chè il buono non costa quello d'ingordo che l'uomo non sene megliori via più; Pegolotti 1970, 21). In 1470–71, 130 years later, aristocrat and diplomat Anselme Adorno from Bruges makes the exact same remark: "Dragomans and interpreters are few, and even rarer loyal and good ones. I advise that you spare no expense, if you find a good and loyal one, for he will spare you many dangers" (Trucemanni et interpretes pauci comperiuntur, unde fideles et boni paucissimi. Nullo igitur precio, bono ac fideli aliquo quovis in loco invento, quo plura evadatis pericula, dimitti consulo; Adorno 1978, 210).

An Economy of Translation: "Robberies" and "Courtesies" (Frescobaldi, Gucci, and Sigoli)

Pilgrimage, including the whole system of fixers put in place to serve the pilgrims, was an economic system intended to be regulated by contracts.[43] Upon embarking in Venice, the pilgrims could have the impression that they contracted an all-inclusive package that protected them from want during the sea voyage and dispensed them from any further financial dealings with the ship's captain or the Mamluk authorities. But the journey's labors, the emotional price, and the extra costs began immediately, with the disputes over the quality of ships' berths and food served.

> But worst of all were the extortions on the part of Venetian ship captains: Tuesday, the 8th [of August], we spent the whole day in Ramla and were told that we would not enter Jaffa or board the galley unless each pilgrim paid to the ship captain two ducats less a quarter. And

so it was that each paid in full to the captain, over and above the price concluded in Venice etc., which made several unhappy, while others were threatened with being imprisoned by the Saracens, etc. (Barbatre 1972–73, 152; see also *Le voyage* 1882, 101)

(Le mardi VIIIe nous fusmes toute journee a Rame et nous fust dict que nous ne entresrions point en Jaffe n'en gallee se chacun pelerin ne payet au patron deux ducas ung quarte mains, et force fust que chacun appointast a luy oultre le pris fait a Venize etc. dont plusieurs furent mal contens, aulcuns furent menassés d'estre mis en prison par les Sarrazins etc.)

Even worse were the captains who seemed to work in collusion with Arab Muslim officials. An anonymous pilgrim traveling in 1480 tells a long story of the dispute with the ship's captain regarding the visit to the river Jordan, made dangerous on account of Arabs who were said to be lying in wait to rob them. The pilgrims insisted that as part of their contract, the ship's captain had to ensure their visit under escort, but he refused to be paid out of the contractual price (*Le voyage* 1882, 86–88). Finally, according to the abbreviated version of another pilgrim, the guardian of Mount Sion took them there protected "with the great force of various Muslim armed men" (avecquez grant renffort de gens d'armes sarrazins et mores; Barbatre 1972–73, 146).

The best examples of the complex economic machinery of the pilgrim translation market are to be found in the contracts drafted locally for the crossing of the desert, between Jerusalem and Cairo via Saint Catherine's monastery on Mount Sinai. This desert crossing was regulated by contracts that stipulated the exact amount of remittance and what the contract covered. Many pilgrims thus included detailed descriptions of provisions and budgets outlining all the expenses, from provisions to services.[44] The Dominican priest Felix Fabri and Bernhard von Breydenbach, deacon of the Mainz cathedral, were fellow pilgrims in 1483, and both their accounts include a "copy" of the contract they made with the sultan's dragoman for the crossing of the desert. They emphasize the written nature of the contract, which was sealed by the sultan's officials. After presenting the articles of the contract, they immediately turn their attention to the contract's lack of validity:

These were the articles of the contract which we made, and we had many disputes and much trouble before we could be of one mind. (Fabri 1896, 9:96)

(Hi sunt articuli conventionis, quos composuimus, et multa litiga et difficultates habuimus, antequam concordes fieri possemus.) (Fabri 1843–49, 2:101)

[The great dragoman of Jerusalem] was hard upon the pilgrims, ever hurrying them from place to place, and exacted money from them grievously. Moreover, he did not keep his contracts well, and broke many of his promises, yet he protected us tolerably faithfully, and took pains to succour us when we called upon him for help. (Fabri 1896, 9:105–6)

([Major Trutschelmannus de Jerusalem] peregrini durus in continua ductione et gravis in pecuniarum mulctatione, et non satis bene tenuit compactata et in multis promissis cessit; satis fideliter tamen nos defendit, et in quibus eum invocavimus, diligenter adjuvit.) (Fabri 1843–49, 2:109)[45]

This contract, recorded in writing, was registered at the chancellery with seals from the governor and from the great dragoman of Jerusalem. Then, as is customary among these pagans, it was not respected. For the seal of the contract we paid two ducats.

(Item disser vertrag ward beschrieben vnnd mit deß obersten amptmans zu Jherusalem vnd deß grossern Calyns sygeln yn der kantzelly versygelet vnd bewaret. Noch dan ward eß vns gehalten als gewonlich von den heyden geschicht. Fur denselben versygelten brieff gaben wir zwen ducaten.) (Breydenbach 2010, 539)

There are numerous testimonials of similar extortions in addition to contracts: "Hereupon a great dispute arose between us and the dragoman. We wished for him to provide the additional camels at his own expense, according to what was set down in the fifth article of our covenant ... but he refused to do this, saying that we had a great deal of useless baggage" (Exo hoc autem ortum est magnum litigium inter nos et Trutschelmannum. Nos volebamus, quod ipse expensis suis residuos camelos disponeret, prout in V. articulo conventionis nostrae expressum erat. . . . Ipse vero noluit hoc facere dicens, multam suppellectilem inutilem [nos] habere; Fabri 1896, 10:487 / Fabri 1843–49, 2:405). Georges Lengherand, burgomaster (mayor) of Mons in Hainaut had the same experience during his pilgrimage in 1485–86: "although we had warned our dragoman Calix not to take the job of guiding us without respecting the conditions stated in our contract [drawn with the great dragoman of Jerusalem], we nevertheless had to be subjected to it. So it was for us twelve remaining pilgrims to continue our way that we drew four gold ducats" (avions très bien averty ce truceman Calix de non prendre la charge de nous mener pour l'autre sinon aux condicions déclarées en nostre pact [avec le principal truceman de Jhérusalem], sy nous failly passer par là. Ce fut que nous douze pélerins demourez pour tirer oultre ensemble tirames quattre ducas d'or; Lengherand 1861, 149). Fabri signals petty breaches of the contract that add insult to injury: "We suffered during this part of our pilgrimage from the abominable nuisance that our servants, for whom we had paid much money, and hired them at a great price to wait upon us, were unfaithful to us, and stole from us whatever they could" (Hoc enim detestabile malum in hac peregrinatione sustinuimus, quod famuli nostri, quos grandi conduximus pretio et excessiva pecunia emimus, pro nostro famulatu erant nobis infideles et furabantur omnia, quae poterant; Fabri 1896, 10:507 / Fabri 1843–49, 2:420).

The complexity of relations between pilgrims and their fixers, and the psychological, emotional, and financial cost of hiring fixers, are especially well illustrated in the narratives written by three Florentines, Lionardo Frescobaldi, Giorgio Gucci, and Simone Sigoli, who traveled together in a group of twelve pilgrims in 1384.[46] The account of one of these pilgrims, Giorgio Gucci, contains a detailed budget of shared expenses, from the start to the end of the pilgrimage in medieval Syria and Egypt: "In Alexandria, we made a purse and lived in common as far as Damascus" (In Alessandria facemmo borsa, e andammo a comuni ispese insino in Domasco; Gucci 1948, 149 / Gucci 1862, 420). The purse was renewed six times for a total of fifty-four ducats per head. Gucci divided the expense budget into the following categories:

1) "which money was solely for toll and to toll only can it be applied" (i quali denari solo per propi passaggi e solo a' passaggi si possono appiccare);

2) "the money paid or spent solely for guides, that is, the dragoman who guided us from one place to another" (tutti i danari pagati e ispesi solo per guide, cioè in turcimanni che ci guidavano); this section also includes "courtesy" (cortesia) paid to their fixers;

3) "expenses that the local vernacular calls *mangerie*, that is, robberies" (le quali spese secondo il volgare di là si chiamano mangerie, cioè ruberie);

4) "expenses for the hiring of ships, asses, mules and camels" (spese di noli di navilio, d'asini, muli e cammelli);

5) "food expenses, and expenses incurred for supplies" (ispese di bocca, e ispese fatte che ad opera di bocca s'appartengono);

6) "expenses incurred for supplies of things and utensils for the desert,"
including lodgings (spese che si appartengono a fornimenti di nostre
cose et di nostre masserizie per lo diserto).[47]

This detailed travel budget is of great historical interest. The last item is
particularly complex, for as the pilgrimage drew to its close, that is, as the
pilgrims neared Jerusalem and Damascus, Gucci recorded complex transactions of reimbursement of debts for services and purchases by other
people on behalf of the pilgrims, as well as the resale of unused supplies
and provisions from which each pilgrim was reimbursed at the end of the
journey. But it is the first three items that are of the greatest interest here
as they reveal a complex economy of translation and relationality in which
pilgrims were entangled with their fixers.

Tolls, and also safe-conducts, are fees and tributes paid to the sultan's
officers. "The money paid or spent solely for guides" refers to contracts
concluded with pilgrims' fixers. But two new terms come to populate this
contractual space, "cortesia" and "mangerie." That these payments constitute a separate category, rather than appearing as a part of expenses, registers the degree of the pilgrims' surprise, but also refusal of engagement
with their fixers. For them, these payments exceed the contract and their
commitment to a transactional, market economy of translation, because
they verge into an imbricated economy of relation. But in precarious situations, translation and the ability to communicate are not a transaction, but
a relation. In that sense, the additional payments of *cortesia* and *mangerie*
are a form of commensuration that fixers perform in a cycle of relationality.

For Gucci and the Florentine pilgrims, "mangerie, that is, robberies"
(mangerie, cioè ruberie), were an extorsion, "and yet they must be paid,
though properly they are extorted" (e pure si convengono pagare, posto
che sieno come danari tolti; Gucci 1948, 151 / Gucci 1862, 424). "Mangerie" is a word from the lingua franca, "mangiaria" or "mangearia," that
means extortions or exactions.[48] It seems to refer specifically to the desert
Bedouins, whom the pilgrims call Arabs, seeking nourishment. The blame
for the taking or offering of food from the pilgrims' reserves was always
laid at the feet of pilgrims' fixers, who guided the pilgrims in the "proper"
conduct. Frescobaldi, Gucci's companion, reports that their fixer directed
them: "Have no fear of them, they are Arabs, who come so that you give
them some biscuits. And so it was, for having given to each one a bit of
biscuit, they departed without doing anything out of the ordinary" (Non
ne abbiate paura, e'sono Arabi, che vengono perchè voi diate loro del biscotto. E così fu, chè dato che noi avemo a ciascuno un pezzo di biscoto
si partirono sanza fare alcuna novità; translation modified; Frescobaldi

1948, 56 / Frescobaldi 1944, 98). It is interesting to see the resentment and displacement of blame onto fixers, when the pilgrims were advised of this in Cairo and prepared for it: "We carried with us more biscuits than we thought we would need, to give them to the caloyers of Mount Sinai and to the Arabs, that they should not treat us roughly, because we were advised by those who had done the journey" (Portamo più biscotto, che non pensavamo ci bisognasse per darne a Calori del monte Sinai e agli Arabi, acciò che non ci facessino villania, perocchè ne fummo avvisati da chi avea fatto il cammino; Frescobaldi 1948, 52 / Frescobaldi 1944, 88). One hundred years later, such extortions still most often ended up in theft or gift of food: "Sometimes some of them travelled with us for three days at a time—men whom no one knew, and no one understood how they had found us out. We asked Calinus to drive these unknown people away from us . . . but he advised us—nay, begged us—not to refuse bread and water to any such people whom we might meet, saying that we should be safer if we did so" (Et quandeque aliqui tribus diebus proficisceban-tur nobiscum, quos nemo novit, et unde aut quando invenerint, nemo scivit. Unde ideo Calinum rogavimus, ut illos nobis ignotos repelleret, qui dixit . . . suasit tamen, imo petivit nos, quatenus sic occurentibus non denegaremus panem et aquam, et securiores essemus; Fabri 1896, 10:506 / Fabri 1843–49, 2:419–20). Oftentimes food was openly stolen by those who traveled with the pilgrims: "In sooth, those watches [at night] were more needed by us on account of our own servants, the camel-drivers and ass-drivers, than on account of strangers. These men stole our biscuits, eggs, and everything they could. . . . We often caught them in the act of stealing, whereat they did not blush, but rather mocked at us" (verumta-men ista vigilia et custodia erat nobis magis necessaria propter nostros famulos, camelarios et asinarios, quam propter alienos: furabantur enim nobis paximatios, ova et quaecumque poterant. . . . Saepe reperimus eos in facto furti, nec deprehensi erubuerunt, sed potius nos deriserunt; Fabri 1896, 10:490 / Fabri 1843–49, 2:407).

Anger and violence characterize the accounts of the Florentines and Fabri, even though they traveled one hundred years apart.[49] But other pilgrims express either contempt or resignation. In 1420, the anonymous pilgrim tells us that "by harassment, one has to throw them a piece of bread for dogs, which they eat and leave as promptly" (par ennuy leur fault getter une piece de pain à chiens, qu'ilz menguent et tantost s'en vont; "Un pèlerinage en Terre Sainte" 1905, 86). In 1486, Georges Lengherand spoke of "some Arabs, people who are almost naked, . . . and to whom we had to give biscuits, fresh drinking water, and money for courtesy; and then they left" (aucuns Arabes qui sont gens quasi tous nudz, . . . ausquelz nous failly donner du bescuit, de l'eauwe fresche à boire . . . et de l'argent pour courtoisie; et puis s'en allèrent; Lengherand 1861, 152).

The gift of food describes well the meaning of the word "mangerie" (It. "mangiare," to eat). Either food or money for food is received or taken. All pilgrims, no matter when they traveled, resented them, likely for a very simple reason: the cycle of nourishment points to everyone's precarious survival in the desert, and the hierarchy implicit in the "client–hired help" dynamic makes place for equality of the human condition in the face of danger.

But what of the "robberies"? Pilgrims constantly complain of minor extortions by the sultan's officials: "Every hour, new officials appeared, not only the real ones but also those impersonating them, to whom it seemed opportune to extort money from Christians as if they were enemies" (Qualibet hora . . . novi semper officiales, non solum veri verum etiam ficti creverunt. . . . Visum est eis a christianis veluti ab hostibus pecunias extorquendas esse; Adorno 1978, 174). But the most egregious cases are those in which fixers seem to exploit the situation, either by threatening to abandon the pilgrims in the middle of the desert (and in collusion with others), or by threatening "not to continue on the way so as to extort some money from us" (ut pecunais aliquas a nobis extorquerent, nolle amplius nobiscum profisisci; Adorno 1978, 316), or by otherwise exploiting their position of seemingly absolute power over the life and death of pilgrims and ultimate control over the accomplishment of their pilgrimage vows.[50] Pilgrims report many dramatic situations that go far beyond the theft of food and rise to the level of robberies:

> Pretending to be officials of the grand interpreter of the Arabs, they said they wished to check our receipts and safe-conducts and right away began to push our camels out of the straight route, and to take clothes, mantles, hats, wax and many other things, pilfering by force, and in the end forced us to ransom ourselves for about XV ducats and gave us back the greater part of the things wrested from us: and plainly we saw that these robberies proceeded from our interpreter who guided us, and by the owners of the camels we had hired, because one day before one of the three with the said camels departed from us pretending to go ahead to reconnoitre the way, because already he had drawn us somewhat from the straight way; and our interpreter and the other cameleers following him lost sight of him, and together we lost him and the right way. (Gucci 1948, 121)

> (Faciendo vista d'essere uficiali del gran turcimanno degli Arabi dissono volere vedere les nostre bullette del salvo condotto, e subito cominci-

arono a volgiere i nostri cammelli della diritta via, e torre panni et man-
telli e capelli e cera e più altre cose per forza rubandoci, e finalmente
ci feciono rimedire circa di XV ducati e renderonci la maggiore parte
delle cose tolte; e chiaro vedemmo che queste ruberie procedettero dal
nostro turcimanno che ci guidava, e da quelli di cui erano i camelli che
manammo con noi, perchè uno di innanzi l'uno de'tre ch'era co'detti
cammelli si parti da noi facendo vista d'andare a provedere la via, perchè
già della diritta via alquanto ci avea tratti; e il nostro turcimanno e gli
altri camellieri seguendo costui, il perdemmo di veduta, e a uno tratto
perdemmo costui e la diritta via.) (Gucci 1862, 348)[51]

Robbery is a serious theft of something other than food. Georges Lengherand's account a few year later does not appear any different: "Having
arrived there, we were 'composed' and reduced to giving to the dragoman
of Gaza, who led us there, three medins per pilgrim. And in order for us
to 'compose' a larger amount, our dragoman even wanted to return to
Gaza and abandon us right there" (Nous illec arrivez fusmes composez
et constrains de donner au truceman dudit Gazera qui nous avoit conduit
jusque illec, pour chascun pellerin trois medins, et pour parvenir à plus
grande composicion nostre truceman mesmes s'en volt retourner audit
Gazera et nous là endroit habandonner; Lengherand 1861, 150). Although
instead of "robberies" Lengherand uses another term, "composicions"—
compromises, accommodations—the meaning of theft is clear: "all the
mangeries, great and small accommodations" (touttes mengeries, composicions grandes et petites).[52] There are also limit cases, where pilgrims
seem to have a hard time distinguishing between extortion and down-
payment: "Sabathytanco, the chief Calinus, came and exacted from each
pilgrim five ducats, in part payment of the sum contracted for, saying that
he had not enough money in hand to begin to make preparations for taking us across the desert. So, lest he should thereafter say that we had been
the cause of a long delay, we gave him the money, every man five ducats" (Venit Sabathytanco, Calinus major, et exegit a quolibet peregrino
quinque ducatos in defalcationem conscripti pretii, dicens, se non habere
in promptu tantum, ut dispositionem facere inciperet pro nostra per de-
sertum ductione. Ne ergo in posterum diceret, nos fuisse causam tantae
tardationis, tradidimus sibi pecuniam, quilibet V ducatos; Fabri 1896, 9:132 /
Fabri 1843–49, 2:129).

Rare are the pilgrims who attempt to understand the fixers' motivations, renouncing understanding of this custom, which they qualify as
continual harassment and extortion. An anonymous French pilgrim traveling in 1383 complained that "the last day of the month of February I was

in Guini and paid 12 dirhem, and still I was forced to pay 9 dirhem; I don't know why" (Le darrenier jour du mois dessus dit [de fevrier] fuz a Guini, et paiai xii. derans, et si me fist on paier par force ix. derans, je ne sçay pour quoy; "Journal d'un pèlerin français" 1895, 459). The Dominican Fabri is notable for his irregular but consistent efforts to present another point of view: "For the Arabs say that they are the lords of all wildernesses and waste places, and therefore they take no heed of safe-conducts, but extort toll from all who pass through the desert" (Dicunt enim Arabes, se esse dominos omnium solitudinum et desertorum, et ideo de salvo conductu non curant, sed pedagia a transeuntibus per eremos exigunt; Fabri 1896, 9:64 / Fabri 1843–49, 2:77–78).[53] His statement indicates that there is a system of Arab (Bedouin) rule in the desert parallel to that of Mamluks in population centers, representing the sultan. Together they make one larger economy. This allows us to understand the position of fixers better. Fixers are not the sole and final destination of moneys and food gifts, which they would keep, but payments and foods are in circulation within this large desert-urban economy of the Mamluk state.

Pilgrims seem to grasp only fragments of this longer and larger cycle. Here is the explanation that Gucci provides of the dramatic scene of robbery in the desert and the "collusion" of the pilgrims' fixer with the Bedouins: "And this robbery we thought was for a camel, which they had worn out on the way to St. Catherine's in the desert, and which they said was our fault for making such long days; and in this fashion they wished the fine. The money stolen from us went in part, as we understood, to the said interpreter, part to the cameleers and part to our robbers" (E questa ruberia pensiamo nascesse per uno camello, ch'eglino allo andare a Santa Caterina per lo diserto straccarono, che dissono fu alle nostre cagioni per fare troppe grandi giornate; et per quello modo vollono menda. Èbbene parte, dei detti danari rubati, secondo che comprendemmo, il detto turcimanno, e parte i cammellieri, e parte quelli che ci rubarono; Gucci 1948, 121 / Gucci 1862, 349). The loot is split in three parts and herein likely lies the answer: fixers in the desert are protecting the lives of the pilgrims just as much as theirs. They too participate in an economy, not only as takers or receivers of payments and food stuffs, the way pilgrims see them; they are in an economy of relation, made less to enrich themselves or to despoil the pilgrims, then to flow through them as they connect the urban and desert economies of the Mamluk sultanate.

Georges Lengherand records a situation that allows us to comprehend the difficulty of the fixers' position: "Having arrived, we found the church full of sultan's armed men, so many that our trip to Hebron was interrupted. We had to take another path, and our dragoman was 'composed' of eight ducats by them" (Mais nous là arrivez, trouvames l'église plaine de gens d'armes du Soudam [sic] tellement que à ceste cause nostre voyage dudit Ebron en fut rompu, et nous failly prendre aultre train, et fut nostre trucheman composé de eulx de huit ducas; Lengherand 1861, 145). Fixers themselves have to pay tributes, extortions, and *mangeries* both to the sultan's men and to the Bedouins of the desert. Fixers participate in the circulation of moneys, whereby they pass on the earnings as much as they mediate conflict. In fact, they pass on the moneys because they mediate tensions and negotiate mobilities across spaces organized by different rules. The contract that the pilgrim-clients conclude with their fixers opens the possibility of movement; but at each threshold of parallel rule, the tributes—whether as moneys or as food stuffs—are to be given or taken. This does not mean "renewed"; each rule being a new one, the gesture is renewed, but the receiver is different. This resembles missionary travel to the Mongols.

In other words, what the pilgrims experience as extortions, in excess and breach of contract, is part of a relational economy in which few get to keep the bounty they supposedly take, but everyone gets to safeguard their life. Niccolò da Poggibonsi conveys this threat of death that weighs over fixers and over their clients. When their fixer is kidnapped, the pilgrims fear for their lives: "We proceeded thus in tribulation, without a shepherd, for we had been deprived of our interpreter, who was our guide, without whom we could not but experience evil" (Andando così tribolati, sanza pastore; chè ci era stato tolto lo nostro interpito ciò era guidatore nostro, chez sanza lui non potavamo altro che male arrivare; Poggibonsi 1945b, 102 / Poggibonsi 1945a, 120). When after two days they find him again, albeit worse for wear, they seem to understand that ransom is the price to pay for the safeguard of all their lives:

And when we had come to know that he was our interpreter, all of us made a reverence to God for the grace that he had given us . . . , and we gave him well to eat, for he had great need of it; and he told us how those Saracens had taken from him his sword and bow, because he would not agree to our being ransomed from them; and therefore had they done me this. And we consoled him saying that everything that had been taken from him would be made good by us. (Poggibonsi 1945b, 102)

(Quando l'avemo conosciuto, che egli era lo nostro interpito, tutti facemo riverencia a Dio della grazia ch'egli chi aveva fatta . . . , e demogli bene da mangiare, però che n'avea grande bisogno; e disseci come quelli Saracini gli avevano tolta la spada e l'arco, perchè non volle aconsentire

che noi ci ricomperassimo da loro: e però m'ànno fatto questo. E noi lo
confortamo, e dicemo che ogni cosa che gli era stato tolto gli ricomper-
remo.) (Poggibonsi 1945a, 121)

Felix Fabri, whom we saw engage with the perspective of fixers and
Bedouins, never accepted the exaction of additional tolls, continuing to
see them as robberies: "our camel-drivers played us false, and some of
them helped the Arabs to steal things from off the camels" (ad haec dis-
simulaverunt nostri ductores et quidam de nestris camelariis eos detrahere
spolia juverunt). Still, he reports the double bind of the fixer, who takes
only so he can give:

> We ran up, forcibly tore the sacks of biscuits out of their hands, and
> showed them a bold and fierce countenance. When they saw this, they
> ceased their violence, and turned upon Calinus, with whom they wran-
> gled most bitterly. I suppose that they fell upon him because he had
> suffered us to resist them. . . . Calinus warned us that we must not be
> so headstrong, but must collect some sum amongst us, to which each
> pilgrim should give somewhat, one or two medins. (Fabri 1896, 10:537;
> translation modified)

> (Accurrimus nos et saccos paximatiorum de manibus eorum evulsimus
> vi et eis durum et audacem vultum ostendimus. Hoc autem cum vidis-
> sent, cessaverunt a violentia et in Calinum conversi cum eo durissime
> litigaverunt, puto, quod eum invaserint, quia nos eis resistere permis-
> erit. . . . Calinus autem hortabatur nos, ne tenaces essemus, sed inter
> nos taxam poneremus, qua quilibet peregrinus aliquid daret, madinum
> vel duos.) (Fabri 1843–49, 2:443–44)

Fixers did not (only) take for themselves; robberies were part of a circulation that interrogates the notion of property that could be regulated
transactionally with contracts. Thus, the veil of "double language" ("du-
plici lingua"; Adorno 1978, 302) may in reality amount to the inextricable
position of an interface, the fixer, that protects his life as much as that of
his clients (e.g., Fabri 1896, 9:155; Adorno 1978, 177, 239, 240). Fixers commensurate, thanks to the double language, the parallel system of the city
and the desert: between the two, they are the third term, *commensuration*.
Having agency is always suspect. The accusation of duplicity denotes the
condition of all circulation and communication, the protection of all lives.
Duplicity appears to be the condition of commensuration of disparate

value of two or more units, and this commensuration of differences creates relationality, whether peaceful or conflictual.

A Relational Economy of Translation:
A New Anthropology of Gift Exchange

These extortions, whether they be "mangerie, cioè roberie" in Gucci's description or Lengherand's "composicion," are distinct from another term we saw featured prominently in Gucci's budget. Pilgrims often mention gifts, in coins, that they offer throughout their travels, especially to their dragomans and camel and ass drivers. They call it "courtoisie" (Middle French), "cortesia" or "curtusiae" (Latin), "cortesia" (Italian), or "curtesy" (Middle English):[54] "Item, at Saint Catherine's, courtesy is due to the dragoman. . . . Item, courtesy is also due to the ass and camel drivers" (Item, quant on est à Sainte Katerine fault au trussemant donner la courtoisie. . . . Item, aussy fault donner la courtoisie aux asniers et chamelliers).[55]

In Gucci's budget, courtesy appears in the itemized list of "the money paid or spent solely for guides, that is, the interpreter who guided us from one place to another."[56] Of the thirteen payments made to eight fixers, Gucci speaks of four extra disbursements "per cortesia" (Gucci 1948, 150–51 / Gucci 1862, 422–24). Each time, he proceeds in the same fashion: he presents the official, contractual expense, for example: "To Saetto, interpreter, and his son, who guided us from Alexandria to Cairo, V ducats" (A Saetto turcimanno e ad uno suo figliuolo, che ci guidò da Alessandria al Cairo, ducati V), followed by the description of the courtesy offered: "To the same, for their expenses from Alexandria to Cairo, and from our kindness, in all II ducats" (A loro medesimi per lor ispese da Alessandria al Cairo, e per cortesia che facemmo loro, in tutto ducati II). Another Arab Muslim, whom Gucci does not name, and friar Giovanni, a monk of the monastery of Saint Catherine, receive money "per cortesia." To the fourth fixer, Ali, who guided the Florentines from Cairo to Jerusalem for thirty-six days, each pilgrim paid four ducats for a total of forty-eight ducats. To this were paid four extra ducats to cover Ali's expenses. But "to the same in Gaza, through kindness and by force, for he took them from us, VIII ducats" (A lui medesimo in Gazera, tra per cortesia e per forza, che ce gli tolse, ducati VIII). The ambiguity of that position is also shown by Adorno, who recounts that, in the desert, pilgrims were saved "as much by friendship as by the effects of corruption" (partim amicicia, partim corruptione; Adorno 1978, 240).

One hundred years later, burgomaster Lengherand will report the same practice, "each pilgrim having paid several courtesies to the great dragoman himself as to the assistants and servants" (après avoir payet par chascun de nous pélerins pluiseurs courtoisies tant au grand trucheman mesmes comme à ses commis et serviteurs; Lengherand 1861, 182; see also Barbatre 1972–73, 129). The pilgrims are clear: there is a contract, and there are supplements, but these extra payments qualify as "courtesies." The pilgrims engage in a relational economy, abandoning the transactional and contractual interaction with their fixers. But why do courtesies differ from robberies? Why are they somehow more acceptable, why do the pilgrims seemingly willingly engage in them? Why so much anger and violence around "mangerie, cioè rubberie," but gestures bordering on kindness with "courtesy"?

Unlike "mangerie," "courtoisie" has not yet been identified in the lingua franca, although it should be, since situational evidence from travel accounts indicates that the word was likely understood and even used by both Bedouins and Muslim Arabic speakers in their relations with European travelers in order to claim and encourage the dispensation of gift money, "which are called in their language *courtesies*" (dat heyscht *kortesije* in yerre spraiche; von Harff 1946, 134–35 / von Harff 1860, 116; my emphasis). While the practice seems to correspond to the eastern notion of "bakshish," gift or money offered in excess of the cost or price and that incorporates the notion of gratitude, it was likely linked to the majority presence of French-speaking nobility in medieval Syria and the dissemination of the ideal of *courtoisie* in the lands from which the pilgrims hailed. *Courtoisie* emerged distinctly in twelfth-century northwestern Francophone Europe as part of the courtly code of social conduct that accompanied chivalry, and it spread rapidly throughout the Western Christian world (Bumke 2000, 307–11). One of the most important manifestations of *courtoisie* was *largesse*, liberality or generosity.[57] By the fourteenth century, *courtoisie* was also adopted by the urban bourgeois class, and, by the fifteenth century, it had become for nobles and nonnobles alike more a convention of behavior, in the narrower sense of etiquette, than a lifestyle emanating from an ideal.[58] It is in this sense of convention and largesse that we should understand the term "courtesy" in fourteenth- and fifteenth-century pilgrimage narratives. In these accounts, courtesy seems always to be monetized, unlike the extortions that are most often taken in the form of food and the robberies committed in the form of stolen objects. Pilgrims nevertheless seem to reject courtesy as somehow symbolic of their relations with fixers. Rather, for them, courtesy constitutes a payment, divorced from any symbolism, just as the contractual disbursement of money does. But there is one difference: the payment of courtesy is not in the written contract, but one is still, as it were, bound to make it.

Insights from anthropology offer a possible interpretation, wherein gifts are interpreted as both courtesy and ritual; they are a kindness, *and* they are an obligation, *and* they are a custom. For the pilgrims, courtesy is a payment, whose value is measured in ducats. Unlike extortions, which are "over and above" the contract and subject to permanent disagreement, courtesy is regulated by a secret or tacit contract that both sides accept—both parties share in the same understanding and expectation of it. Sometime a bit of pressure serves to convey this tie that binds, the fact that relationality is based in the circulation of objects, as we saw in Ali's case, "per cortesia et per forza," or Adorno's, "partim amicicia, partim corruptione." In 1499, Arnold von Harff explains that courtesy is a payment, a "secret present," that reinforces the contract:

> They gave me this letter as a certificate concerning these things. But anyone who does not give also secret presents, which are called in their language *courtesies*, by the way and share his provisions with him [the *mokarij*, the camel and ass drivers], will have to suffer insults and hardships. But if you produce ten or twelve ducats, and give them as *courtesies*, then they stand loyally by you, as happened often to me on the journey. For often, when the wild Arabs charged at us in the wilderness with loud cries, as if they would strike us dead, demanding *courtesies*, which are tributes or presents, then my *mokarij* stood by me faithfully ready to answer with blows or battle, for he was himself a wild Arab. (von Harff 1946, 134–35; my emphasis)

> (Desen brieff gaeuen sij mir zo getzuge dat deme also geschien suldt. Aber wer yen nyet heymliche schenckonge, dat heyscht *kortesije* in yerre spraiche, off dem wege en gheyfft ind sijner perfanden yen mit deylt, der moyss vil smaeheyt ind armoytz van yen lijden. Aber der neyt an en suyt tzien ader tswelff ducaeten ind gheyfft die vss vur *kortesije*, dem staynt sij gar trulichen bij, as mir duckmaell vnder wegen geschach. Want gar ducke die wilde Araben vns in der woestenijen an ranten gar mit eynem groyssen geschrey als weulten sij vns gar zo doyt geslagen hauen, begerende van vnss *kortesije*, dat is tribuyt ader schenckonge, dae inne mijn mokarij gar getruwelich mir bij stunt mich zo verantworden mit slay ind kijuen, want er selbs eyn wyldt Araben was.) (von Harff 1860, 116; my emphasis)

Fabri reports, "If, however, [the pilgrims] chose to graciously bestow a *courtesy* or a small present upon them, [they] should have them at [their] service" (Si autem eos *curtusia* vel aliquibus *bibalibus* honorare vellemus, paratos eos haberemus etiam ad descendendum nobiscum ad mare et ad defendendum; Fabri 1896, 9:155 / Fabri 1843–49, 2:147; my emphasis; translation modified). There are two things of interest here: first, "curtusia vel aliquibus bibalibus" confirms the idea of bakshish. "Bibalibus," from Lat. *bibale, bibalis* (n.), literally means "(small change) for a drink." Second, the report confirms the earlier analysis of "robberies": small change smooths the way out of double economies of rule and puts the pilgrims into a circulation, where the money that is changing hands is also a path to their unfettered mobility.

Von Harff explained that without courtesies, pilgrims "have to suffer insults and hardships." Courtesy, a form of enforced and tacitly contractual "graciousness," ensures, precisely, good treatment. In other words, the quality of the pilgrim's treatment is not included in the contract and delivery of the service:

> I am weary of writing about the petty tricks wherewith they [our camel drivers] plagued us almost every morning when the beasts were being loaded; for they purposely used to leave a bed, a basket, or a bag. . . . They did this with the intent that the pilgrim to whom the thing which was left behind belonged might be forced to beg them to take it; whereat they . . . would ask him for money or bread, and would pretend that they would leave it behind unless he paid them. (Fabri 1896, 10:492)

> (Taedet me profecto scribere nequitias eorum, quibus nos quasi omni mane in oneratione bestiarum turbabant, cum industria enim aliquid jacere permittebant, vel lectulum, aut sportam, aut aecum, scientes nos oculum habere ad illa. Hoc autem ideo faciebant, ut peregrinus ille, cui derelicta res erat, cogeretus eos petere accipere, et ipsi petebant vice versa eum pro denariis vel panibus, et simulabant, se rem velle dimittere, nisi dato pretio.) (Fabri 1843–49, 2:408)

Taken at face value, the delivery of a service should be unrelated to harassment in a translation economy that is thought of purely as a market; but the pilgrims' experiences show that service and the quality of its delivery were bound up into one. The pilgrims' experience, and the term they choose to describe it, elucidate the fact that a market economy does not function without a gift. If there is a courtesy, then the pilgrim is well treated by the service provider; if there is no courtesy, then the pilgrim is poorly treated by the same. "Courtesy," so to speak, buys courtesy.

It would not be accurate, however, to give too much credit to this distinction between the quality of delivery and the simple delivery of the fixer's services. For, without courtesy, the contract is constantly on the verge of being broken. This impending threat is in itself the reason why the pilgrims feel mistreated and harassed. The distinction is less between a good and a poor service than between a service and no service at all, as we witnessed with the threats of fixers to turn back and abandon their clients. In other words, the purely commercial rapport of selling and buying a service does not secure the delivery of the service. The contract does not suffice for its delivery, but it is courtesy that activates the fulfillment of the official, contractual service that has been purchased. Courtesy is a payment that guarantees the fulfillment of an already signed contract. It is an endorsement, a countersignature to the contract, an insurance, as it were. Courtesy is a tacit acknowledgment of the type of economy that pilgrims are engaged in, and this kind of acknowledgment makes the service possible: translation is not a transaction; translation is a relational economy that requires commensuration.

This then is the case not of an official and a shadow economy, but an economy in which courtesy actually underwrites the market. Von Harff specified that courtesy is a "secret present." Von Harff's agreement with his fixer obliged him "to give him four ducats a month, as well as food and drink, and a hundred ducats as a gift." The hundred ducats were agreed not as payment for the service but as a "gift." Similarly, on his second pilgrimage in 1483, Fabri asks for the ass driver who served him in 1480. In the crowd, he calls out his name, Cassa:

> As soon as he saw me he recognized me, and I him, and he ran to kiss me after the fashion of the Saracens, and greeted me with a most joyous countenance, rejoicing and marvelling much at my return; and he laughed and said much to me which I did not understand. Now, I had brought with me from Ulm two iron stirrups, which I presented to him, and which he received with many thanks. He led me to where his own asses stood amongst the herd, and gave me his best beast. My lords and the other pilgrims wondered to see the Saracen treat me with such friendship, for pilgrims often suffer great annoyance from their ass-drivers, in being struck by them and thrown from their asses and having their property stolen, from all which troubles I was free, for as in my former pilgrimage, so now this man served me most loyally. (Fabri 1896, 7:242; translation modified)

> (Ut me vidit, agnovit me, et ego eum, et ruit more Sarracenorum in osculum meum, et aletissimo vultu me suscepit, plurimum gaudens et admirans de reditu meo, et multa cum risu loquebatur mihi, quae ego

non intellexi. Duxeram autem de Ulma mecum duas strepas ferreas, quas sibi propinavi, quas cum multa graulatione suscepit: duxit ergo me in gregem ad asinos suos, et optimam bestima mihi assignavit. Et mirabantur Domini et nobiles de tanta Sarraceni ad me amicitia, cum frequenter peregrini multas molestias patiantur a suis asinariis, percussiones et dejectiones de asinis et furta: a quibus omnibus fui liber: et sicut in priori peregrinatione, ita et in illa fidelissime mihi servivit.) (Fabri 1843–49, 1:208)

Like von Harff, Fabri suggests that his gift spares him numerous difficulties. It could be argued, from Fabri's account, that the gift of stirrups creates a bond of friendship. Indeed, courtesy has to do with affect, but not in the most commonly accepted meaning of creating an affective bond. Rather, pilgrims link "courtesy" consistently to life-and-death situations, situations of survival in which the pilgrim translation market functions. A pilgrim engages in courtesy, becomes courteous, because he feels that his life may come under threat, not because he is on friendly terms with his fixer.

Pilgrims' accounts are filled with descriptions of potentially fatal situations in the desert of Sinai, often brought on by their interpreters. Adorno could not be more explicit: "They invent always something new to damage the purses, or if purses are empty, their bodies, or both. The Franks do not enjoy a single moment of security and tranquility, but are always ravaged by fear and apprehension of being killed" (Adversum Francos novi semper aliquid figmenti inveniunt ut vel bursis, vel, si burse vacue sint, corporibus, vel utrique noceant. Nullum sane securum a curaque quietum momentum Francis est, sed timoribus vehementibus atque curis ne trucidentur semper; Adorno 1978, 350). We have already observed the situations of violence (the Florentine pilgrims; Fabri) and disorientation (Poggibonsi). Admittedly, things did not change much from the early days of fourteenth-century pilgrim travel. The Franciscan Antonio de Reboldi's 1330 *Journey to Mount Sinai* (*Itinerarium ad Montem Sinai*) was in reality a sequence of episodes of ever "greater danger" (majus periculum): "we endured outwardly many hardships of the strenuous journey, and inwardly the fear of our death in the hands of those Arabs, who served as our guides" (multa substinuimus adversa exterius laboris viae, et interius timoris mortis nobis intentatae ab illis Arabis, qui nos ducebant), "we endured many tribulations and hardships" (plures tribulationes et angustias substinuimus; Reboldi 1906–27, 3:340, 337). Pilgrims were harassed constantly, and all the actors—from Mamluk officials to fixers to Bedouins—exploited their powerless status. So, to be courteous, to give courtesy, was really a means to save one's own life. If pilgrims participated in the relational economy, they were fine, like Fabri or von Harff; if they refused, they were harassed or were playing with their lives: "Arabs persecute the Franks inhumanly and often kill them if they have nothing to give them" (Francosque ultra humanum modum vexare atque sepissime nichil habentes quod dent trucidare; Adorno 1978, 240). In such conditions, the "gift" is a recognition of the powerful status of the receiver, in whose hands the giver places his life: "The life of travelers is in their hands" (Stat enim vita sic itinerantium in manibus illorum; Adorno 1978, 214). It is also a recognition of pilgrims' own precarious state of dependency.

An analysis of the relational economy of translation, via the apparatus of fixers, reveals that life and payment need commensuration. How does giving and taking a gift change our perception of the gift economy? Classical interpretation of anthropology is that the gift is offered in order to dominate, to indebt the receiver. To receive the gift is to become indebted. But what emerges from the fixer apparatus is that to receive or take a gift gives rights to the receiver over the giver; in giving, the giver gives over his rights to the receiver who is charged with protecting his life. The giver establishes a privileged, albeit provisional, relationship with the receiver; it is not the one who receives that is indebted, but the one who gives who is always in debt for his life to the receiver charged with protecting it. To give therefore is not to indebt the receiver; rather, to give is to become a debtor. The gift giver is the debtor, the gift receiver his creditor. The giver owes his life to the receiver. Courtesy is then not a gift to establish a gift exchange, but a monetized endorsement of a base contract to spare one's life. It is, as it were, a credit on one's life. As such, despite the pilgrims' reticence, it is symbolic of a bond, necessary and unavoidable, that ties the pilgrim and the fixer, a bond of indebtedness because one's life was protected and saved, regardless of the cost.

That courtesy does not establish an enduring affective bond in the most commonly accepted meaning of "friendship" or "caring" is confirmed by Fabri: "It often happens that when pilgrims are about to leave the infidels, they give one another ill-names, and abuse one another—albeit, they may have been good friends while ashore" (Frequenter enim contingit, quod in recessu peregrinorum a paganis male se salutant, et quam boni amici fuerint per terram sibi ipsis antedicunt). At the end of the perilous journey, pilgrims and locals participate in verbal abuse of each other, behavior that highlights the contingent nature of their bond; they even come to a pitched battle: "wherefore not many years ago, at the port of Joppa, the pilgrims were angered by the Saracens, and the Saracens by the pilgrims, till they both ranged themselves in battle array, and fought with one another" (Unde non sunt multi anni elapsi, quod peregrini concitati a Sarraceni et Sarraceni contra ipsos in portu Joppe acies ordinaverunt ad invicem et congressionem fecerunt cum eis; Fabri 1896, 9:98–99 / Fabri 1843–49, 1:103). Pilgrims understood well the notion of enforced and tacit generosity given the Western medieval practice of gift giving and hospitality, largesse and charity (alms), but the situations of life and death that turned the giver into a debtor, the dependency to which the pilgrims acquiesced by giving courtesy, were not tolerated beyond the duration of the dangerous crossing of the desert. It is from this perspective that we can understand why pilgrims label their fixers as "thieves," "liars," and "duplicitous." *Theft* and *lies* refer to this contingency, the precarity of their life and dependency on another that pilgrims would prefer to eschew. These epithets measure the pilgrims' discomfort at their utter dependency on their fixers, and their desire to neutralize relationality and to reduce translation to a contractual market.

Although pilgrims, much as missionaries who stubbornly avoided gift exchange, refuse the symbolism of courtesy, they occasionally do talk about money symbolically. There are at least two, if not three, purses into which the pilgrims regularly reach: Santo Brasca speaks of two purses, one containing money, and the other "filled full with patience" (bien piena de patientia), while canon Casola talks about three purses, "a sack of patience, a sack of money, and a sack of faith" (uno sacho de patientia, uno sacho de dinari, et uno sacho de fede).[59] Arnold von Harff writes the most complex allegory of the three purses: the first two are made of human skin, where the first contains carefulness and wisdom, the second, patience and humility. The third, an actual purse, is made of deer skin, filled "with all kinds of gold below, which is current in the country of your pilgrimage, each according to his rank, and white [silver] money upon it, which is current in the district through which you travel." If the first two are tied tightly with straps that signify seeing and hearing, and are bound close to the heart, the third strap means silence and ties the money purse "by the navel, so that they may not be stolen" (by den nauel vff dat sij dir nyet gestoellen en werden; von Harff 1946, 307 / von Harff 1860, 260).[60] Pilgrims relate to non-Christians from only one of the three, the money purse: "My experience proved that it helped matters greatly to shake one of the three sacks I had carried with me—I mean that of the money" (Io provai che a executere uno di quelli tre sachi haveva portato con mi, me haveva giovato, dico quello de li denari; Casola 1907, 337 / Casola 1855, 108). Pilgrims had to keep "purses continually open, for we were obliged to pay to escape from these harassments" (Sic ergo bursas continue apertas habuimus, quod necesse fuit ad redimendum nos a vexationibus; Fabri

1896, 10:625 / Fabri 1843–49, 2:508; translation modified), "because a full purse and a generous hand served to greatly appease in that pilgrimage" (quod bursa plena et manus larga magnam deservit pacem in peregrinatione illa; Fabri 1843–49, 1:4–5).

As the only mode of relationality to non-Christians, and sometimes Eastern Christians, courtesy remains a monetized, contingent bond, given with a large hand from the deer-skin purse. The other two purses, faith (or wisdom) and patience (or humility), made of human skin, are self- and identity-centered, nonrelational, and kept private among those of the same faith. Pilgrims are willing to engage in courtesy for a good translation that will save their lives. For them, a translation that kills is always a bad translation, and a small courtesy, even to a non-Christian, that can be counted in moneys, is ultimately a means to an end, a small price to pay to save one's own life. The allegory of the purses, of the Christian double economy that keeps relationality in the sphere of belonging to the same faith, while exacting a transactional and contractual relationship with all others, will take us into the next chapter. Purses, containers of different values, moral or monetary, are linked to faith: Christian faith, faith in God, and fidelity. Fidelity, or rather loyalty, is to be kept untainted by the circulation of moneys. That is, ethics and economy should be separated, loyalty and transactionality kept distinct, and terms of commensuration kept under constant watch. Knights and merchants, honor versus trade: such is a crude division of labor that we will pursue in the next chapter.

PART II

Disciplinary Realities: Authorship, Genre, and Literary History

* 3 *

The Ethics of Translation

LOYALTY, COMMENSURATION, AND
LITERARY FORMS IN THE FOURTEENTH CENTURY
(MACHAUT, FROISSART, MÉZIÈRES)

In July 1390, French and Genoese forces began the siege of the city of Mahdia, a haven for corsairs disrupting Genoese trade in the Mediterranean, located in present-day Tunisia. The siege lasted for almost ten weeks. Fourteenth-century chronicler Jean Froissart reports that during the siege, fixers, or perhaps the one and the same "drug(e)man," intervened on three separate occasions, each time from the Arab side.[1] The translation occurred between Arabic and Genoese Italian: the fixer "knew how to speak a good and fluent Genoese language" (moult bien et bel le langaige jennevois parler sçavoit; Froissart 1867–77, 14:232).[2] In Froissart's account, the Arabs have the capacity to translate from and to Genoese because of the closeness that the war had created and the geographic proximity between them: "we and the Genoese have been at war and in conflict, and the Genoese are our neighbors" (nous et les Jennevois nous sommes guerroiés et hustinés . . . et les Jennevois nous sont voisins; Froissart 1867–77, 14:232). But there is no Arabic-French translation because the French host is "from faraway nations" (de moult loingtaines nations; Froissart 1867–77, 14:232). At one point during the conflict, the Arabs send their fixer to propose a judicial combat between two parties of ten, which the fixer begins to justify to the host on theological grounds. A French knight stops him before he can continue for long: "Hey ho, dragoman, do not speak a word more of this matter for it is not up to you to speak or debate our law" (Ha! a! drugman . . . ne parles plus avant de ceste matière; car à toy n'en appartient point de parler, ne à disputer nostre loy; Froissart 1867–77, 14:244). The French knight's interdiction to speak is a refusal to engage in a religious-juridical debate. It maintains a state of hostile confrontation, keeping the opponent at a physical and affective distance that defines the relations between the French and the Arabs at the siege of Mahdia. More importantly, it strips the agency from the Arab fixer: "It is not up to you to speak or debate our law." The order reduces the fixer to the sole linguistic function of interpreter; an interpreter is not an interlocutor.

The Arabs sent a fixer to the Christian host—but the French wanted nothing more than an interpreter who would deliver the message, and they rejected the agency of the fixer. Significantly, the fidelity of the translation of the message did not even come up. The French disputed not the fidelity or the competence of the fixer's translation, but his right and ability to be an agent—a subject in a religious-juridical debate—because of his appurtenance or allegiance. The conjunction of the fixer's agency and his appurtenance to Islam—and not the combination of the fidelity of his translation and his religious appurtenance—bring up the specter of loyalty of persons. It is as if denying the fixer his agency, his loyalty would be better controlled and, in this case, even eliminated as a factor. In this chapter, focused on fourteenth-century French and Latin sources, we will see that loyalty of persons (ethics), defined separately from the fidelity or competency of their translation (deontology), is the driver of social exchange and discursive production on past events and phenomena. We will follow the competing claims of loyalty and truthfulness throughout the communication and exchange networks, from the fixers on the ground, to the fixers in princely courts, to the secretaries who consign and interpret events in writing. We will find that fixers, in exercising their agency (see chapter 1), commensurate between two warring or competing sides. It is their work of commensuration, the ternary nature of "translation" (see the introduction), that will again and again place loyalty at the center of attention of all the participants in the communicative process. Rulers and writers did not question the faithfulness of the translation of content or the adequacy of linguistic competence; rather, they confronted problems of the loyalty of knights and messengers, a social category that differed from fixers who served missionaries and pilgrims (see chapter 2). Regardless, the same general claim holds: in medieval minds, it was not their translation that was suspect, but the personal loyalty of fixers who commensurated. Having agency is always suspect, but it was par for the course for medieval communication. As Nicole Oresme explained, there would be no communication without commensuration (see the introduction). We therefore have to see distrust as a norm in medieval communication, rather than as a signal of an exceptional or irregular situation. Put differently, it is not the fact of someone's distrust that should focus our scholarly attention, but understanding how loyalty, and concerns surrounding the performance of commensuration, organized medieval social relations and discursive productions. Moreover, understanding the centrality of personal loyalty to European medieval ethos, sociality, and discursive practices obliges us, as scholars, to reexamine medieval writing of all genres and forms, which we have thus far evaluated through modern notions of fidelity between text and event.

To bring these points to the fore, I focus on discursive productions on two key events that strongly marked fourteenth-century European political and historical consciousness: the brief Western capture of the Egyptian city of Alexandria (1365) and the Christian defeat of the French-Burgundian and Hungarian armies by the Ottomans at Nicopolis (1396). The events were narrated by two near contemporaries respectively, Guillaume de Machaut, in his verse history *The Taking of Alexandria* (*La Prise d'Alixandre*), and Jean Froissart, in his prose *Chronicles* (*Chroniques*). Philip of Mézières was their contemporary and wrote about both events in his prose works, *A Letter of Lament and Consolation* (*Une epistre lamentable et consolatoire*), *The Life of Saint Peter Thomas* (*Vita Sancti Petri*), and *Chivalry of the Order of the Passion* (*La chevalerie de l'Ordre de la Passion*). These works are of interest because their writers took on an agentive role in the world, as intermediaries to kings and their publics, exercising their agency in government, state affairs, and memorial politics. All three, Guillaume de Machaut (ca. 1300–1377), Philip of Mézières (ca. 1327–1405), and Jean Froissart (1337–1404?), are held as the fourteenth-century's greatest writers in the French language (Mézières also wrote profusely in Latin). Machaut, secretary, poet, and musician, wrote ten long narrative poems, among them the verse history *The Taking of Alexandria*; about a hundred lyric poems (many set to music); and a mass.[3] Froissart, secretary, historian, and poet, wrote the *Chronicles*, spanning fourteenth-century events in Europe and the Mediterranean; a long Arthurian verse romance, *Meliador*; and a number of lyric poems and longer narrative *dits*.[4] Mézières, mercenary, chancellor of the Kingdom of Cyprus (1360–69), and scholar, wrote, in addition to the allegorical treatises and a *vita* mentioned above, two devotional treatises and several other allegorical treatises.[5] They were emissaries, personal secretaries to great lords, and government officials— that is, intermediaries by virtue of their professional positions. It is not surprising then that intermediation and commensuration were central to their writing. What is more, their multifunctional positionality may have influenced them to present themselves as fixers in their works. In this first part of the chapter, fixers are thus analyzed in two ways: in view of the critical role that Machaut's, Mézières's, and Froissart's east-west fixers operating in the Mediterranean, between Christians and Muslims, played in the historical turn of events; and in light of the discursive construction of those events by Machaut, Mézières, and Froissart as fixers, commensurating critical contemporary events for their audiences. The role that different multilingual fixers had in the preparation and aftermath of events at Alexandria and Nicopolis, and Machaut's, Mézières's, and Froissart's use of fixers and their own presentation as fixers, bring forth medieval notions of loyalty and truthfulness, not as grounded in a subject and his *vita* (and his allegiance or religious appurtenance), but as constructed in commensuration. Froissart and Mézières especially articulate the work of commensuration in the terms of "moien" (intermediary, medium) and "moiener" (mediate). Again, at stake are not fidelity of translation or linguistic competence, but claims to loyalty and truthfulness by those who commensurate, and how their claims are established and countered, that is, made functional or rendered inoperative in the process of commensuration. I then extend the analysis to the truth claims and commensuration by these writers who position themselves as fixers.

In the second part of this chapter, I apply the conclusions on fixers' loyalty and commensuration to our current understanding of literary forms and genres. Since the entire European medieval system is built on personal loyalty, and not fidelity of translation, the relation of fact and fiction that turns around the modern criterion of fidelity between text and event now seems less central to medieval literary history. Seeing personal loyalty in its structuring force of medieval society and relationality ultimately provides us with a different way of assessing medieval writing of the period, no longer separating prose versus verse (form) and chronicle versus allegory (genre)—based, precisely, on the parameter of fidelity of text to event—but seeing each as an equal element of a construction of fidelity to an event in and through the commensuration and personal loyalty of the fixer. Despite the harsh critical judgment passed on Machaut's verse history in favor of Mézières's and Froissart's prose writings, each writer lodges the truthfulness of his narrative in similar terms, regardless of the status of verse or prose. Similarly, viewed through the lens of fixers, allegory appears as a historical discourse. The final aim of this chapter is thus to reconsider Machaut's verse, Machaut's and Mézières's allegories, and Froissart's prose histories side by side, within their larger historical and historiographical context, and to use the fixer apparatus to reassess the value judgment of literary history based on form (verse vs. prose) and genre (allegory vs. chronicle) that modern scholarship has until now adopted in the study of European medieval writing.

Guillaume de Machaut and the Raid of Alexandria (1365)

The one late medieval expedition that appears to have drawn ideas directly from the crusade treatises studied in chapter 1 is Peter I's raid on

Alexandria in 1365 (Leopold 2000, 191). Peter I of Lusignan was king of Cyprus and titular king of Jerusalem (r. 1359–69); Jerusalem had been lost to Saladin in 1187, and Peter ruled only over Cyprus, the dominion of the Lusignan family since 1197.[6] The raid on Alexandria began as a crusade "for the recovery of the Holy Land" declared at the court of Pope Urban V in Avignon during a truce (1360–69) in the Hundred Years' War between France and England (Edbury 1991; Edbury 2001). Peter's advisers, Peter Thomas, papal legate in Cyprus, and Philip of Mézières, chancellor of Cyprus, staunch and fervent proponents of "the recovery of the Holy Land," played a large role in the proclamation of the crusade. King John II of France and Peter took the cross on March 31, 1363. The crusading tradition demanded that a French king lead the crusade. However, when John II died in April 1364, Peter became the new crusade leader, set to lead a preliminary expedition to be followed by the main crusading army. By the time of John's death, Peter had already been recruiting the participants at the royal court of England and in western Plantagenet-controlled France, but without much support from Edward III of England.[7] He attended the coronation of Charles V of France in Reims on May 19, 1364, where Guillaume de Machaut is said to have met him.[8] The new French king declined to support the crusade, and Peter then lobbied for support at a summit in Krakow called by the Holy Roman emperor, Charles IV of Bohemia, where the king of Poland and the king of Hungary pledged their support. He arrived in Venice in November 1364 and set out in June 1365 with a hired Venetian fleet for the crusader armies' rendezvous at Rhodes. None of the Western princes arrived or sent contingents, leaving Peter with his own Cypriot fleet, the knights of Saint John of Rhodes, and an international band of mercenaries, altogether about ten thousand troops.[9] On October 9, 1365, the fleet reached Alexandria, which it entered on October 10, raping, murdering, and pillaging. Since the city gates were burned or destroyed and the army was unable to bring down a key bridge linking Alexandria to Cairo, whence the Muslim reinforcements were going to arrive, the crusaders insisted on withdrawing despite Peter's opposition. The army abandoned the city and set sail from Alexandria back to Cyprus on October 16.

Medieval accounts, including fourteenth-century Philip of Mézières's *Life of Saint Peter Thomas* and al-Nuwayri al-İskandarāni's *Book of Knowledge*, and fifteenth-century Leontios Makhairas's *Recital*, agree with this schematic version of events.[10] Peter's spectacular raid on Alexandria and his no less stunning murder in 1369 by his Cypriot nobles resonated throughout the Christian world.[11] Here are the terms in which Froissart lamented Peter's death: "If the noble king of Cyprus, Peter of Lusignan, had lived, he who was such a courageous man of high deeds, who conquered the strong cities of Alexandria and Adalia, he would have kept the sultan [of Egypt] and the Turks so busy that since the time of Godfrey of Bouillon they would not have had as much to do as they would have had to" (se le noble roy de Cyppre Pierre de Lusegnan qui fut si vaillant homme et de si haulte emprinse, et qui conquist les puissantes cités d'Alexandrie et de Sathalie, euist vescu, il euist tant donné à faire au souldan et aux Turs, que depuis le temps Godeffroy de Buillon ils n'eurent autant à faire comme ils eussent eu).[12] Philip of Mézières spoke in similar terms of the "very courageous king Peter who had many victories against the Saracens and Turks" (tres vaillant roy Pierre qui fu tres victorieux contre les Sarrasins et les Turs; Mézières 2008, 182; also Mézières 2008, 102, 212).[13]

Guillaume de Machaut's *Taking of Alexandria* (ca. 1369–77) is an important account of the 1365 raid of Alexandria, and its preparations and consequences.[14] From the outset, Machaut presents Peter's preliminary expedition both as an effort to reconquer Jerusalem, Peter's heritage (Machaut 2002, line 308), and as a *passagium* either to Egypt (Machaut 2002, lines 1730–32; also line 1763) or to Syria (Machaut 2002, lines 1604–6). Peter's grand design since childhood had been "to conquer and occupy the promised land with all its surrounding territories" (de promission la terre / . . . avoir et conquerre / avec tout le pais dentour; Machaut 2002, lines 3491–93). Alexandria was to be the foothold to the recovery of the "promised land." But even though Machaut presents Peter as a God-anointed defender of Christianity, an Eastern hero of a Western crusade, the one who directs the actual raid is Perceval of Coulonges (or Couloigne), the king's chamberlain and captain (Contamine 2004).

Machaut gives an exceptional prominence to this fixer when he stages a scene to show the determining role played by Perceval in the decision process about the target of the attack. Opting for an imagined conversation between Peter and Perceval, rather than a detached account of events, Machaut presents the decision to target Alexandria, first, as a matter of private counsel and, second, as a last-minute decision on the eve of the departure.[15] The exclusive focus on Perceval's advice and experience serves to highlight his role as fixer. At the same time, Machaut takes care to justify the secrecy surrounding the decision process as well as the withholding of information about the final destination from the crusade participants; in his conversation with Perceval, Peter underscores the importance of misleading his men in order to mislead his enemy (Machaut 2002, lines 2077–80). For Machaut this enhances the dramatic effect of surprise (Machaut 2002, lines 2092–95). Only when he is on the high seas does Peter make his announcement that Alexandria is the final destination; the dramatic effect is yet increased as the crusaders are trapped in the ships and have no choice but to accept, despite their fears (Machaut 2002, lines 2121–22).

Both the target of the military expedition and the attack plan are based on Perceval's local knowledge, for he has been "many times in Cairo, in Alexandria, in Syria and Egypt" (maintes fois as estet au quaire / en alixandre et en surie / et en egypte; Machaut 2002, lines 1976–78): "Sire, it is true that I was a prisoner for a long time in Alexandria. But I was able to disport myself through the city as I wished. I will give you an accurate account of the city and the customs" (Sire jay este vraiement / en alixandre longuement / prisonniers. Mais je mesbatoie / par mi la ville ou je voloie / si vous diray la verite / dou pais et de la cite; Machaut 2002, lines 1997–2002). Although the inhabitants are "a hundred thousand" (cent mille hommes en une place; Machaut 2002, line 2013), they are "of a weak constitution and worth nothing as soldiers and so they flee like goats, . . . they are of quite poor disposition" (de foible marrien / quen armes il ne valent rien / eins sen fuient comme chevriaus / . . . / il sont de trop povre couvine; Machaut 2002, lines 2015–19). The city will fall, says Perceval, through an old port. Perceval bases his advice not only on the topographical knowledge "de la cite," but also on the cultural knowledge "dou pais" that he acquired during his imprisonment. The people of Alexandria are superstitious enough that they do nothing to fortify the city despite the prophecy (divination) that "the city of Alexandria will be laid waste through the Old Port, destroyed, captured, burned, set afire, and undone. And I tell you that this is supposed to happen on a Friday" (que par ce viez port la cite / dalixandre sera gastee / destruite prise arse et brulee / et desconfite et si vous di / que ciert en jour de venredi; Machaut 2002, lines 2025, 2031–38). This tells us that Perceval is familiar with the Friday prayer and perhaps has knowledge of the role of fate in Islam. Not only does Peter's last-minute momentous decision—the final target of the attack—rest on the opinion of one informant, but Perceval devises the attack plan, the landing in the Old Port that must take place on a Friday. Only an insider can circumvent the obstacles of an otherwise impregnable city (Machaut 2002, lines 2600–2605).

After the first failed attack on the city, Perceval proposes to attack the Customs Gate, "smaller than the others" (mendre des autres; Machaut 2002, line 2772), that "does not seem to me so strong" (ne me samble pas si forte; Machaut 2002, line 2788). Familiarity with the place—its topography and culture—and familiarity with the sovereign are intertwined in the figure of Perceval the fixer. The intimacy between Perceval and Peter, which allows Perceval to influence privately the king's decisions, is replicated in his familiarity with the city of Alexandria and Islam; in fact, this familiarity is the base for his intimate counsel to the king. Both are acquired: Perceval was a French, not a Cypriot knight. Perceval's case doubly shows that the local is constructed: to be local is not determined either by one's being born there or by one's being born into the language. In other words, Machaut deploys the notion of acquired familiarity with the place, and not the notion of geographic origin (birth). The fixer is not the one who knows both the inside and the outside; rather, the fixer is inside on both (or all) sides. This, of course, is the cause of a prevailing ambivalence about where he really belongs, or where his loyalty lies, if anywhere.

Distrust and suspicion are integral to the intermediary position, the third space of the fixer. In *The Old Pilgrim's Dream* (*Le songe du Vieil Pelerin*, 1389), Mézières stated that there is no such thing as "loyal spies" (loyalles espies): "The craft of this shrewd spy . . . is a game of chess, for he who succeeds in better deceiving and does so most slyly, checkmates his companion" (Le mestier de ceste espie subtille . . . est un jeu des esches que qui scet le mieulx trayre et le plus subtilement, il matte son compaignon).[16] And there hovers a shadow of doubt over Perceval. We know that he is French and not Cypriot. He also says that he was a prisoner in Alexandria, yet he was allowed "to disport himself freely" through the city. If he was allowed to walk freely, this raises the question of exactly what kind of prisoner he was; perhaps it even raises the specter of a double spy, who acts "in order to obtain your mercy and by force of corruption" (pour avoir ta grace et par force de corrupcion; Mézières 1969, 2:405).

This shadow of doubt results from Machaut's dramatic staging of Perceval's last-minute intervention, for "Machaut's version of Pierre's strategic decision is a pleasing fiction. That the king embarked with no idea of a destination and was swayed by the testimony of Perceval of Coulonges is an epic touch in the tradition of the *chanson de geste*, yet another characterization of the noble king who relies . . . on his trusted counselor."[17] Though the timing of the decision-making process may be historically inaccurate and thus skews our perception of Perceval's loyal counsel, Perceval's figure and role are historically true. That is, in rejecting Machaut's staging, the "epic touch," as it were, we should not reject the historical information contained in Machaut's chosen dramatic procedure. We can take it as proof that Peter relied on informants (merchants, envoys, former prisoners) in order to plan for the crusade. Although Perceval may not have personally contributed the information, may never have been a prisoner in Alexandria, and most likely did not counsel the king at the last minute, his figure stands for the pivotal role of local and insider information provided by fixers in the process of strategic attack planning. The secrecy and the timing of the decision point moreover to one particular historical personage in Peter's entourage, Philip of Mézières. Mézières was one of Peter's two top advisers, along with Peter Thomas, the papal legate.

In *The Taking of Alexandria*, Peter Thomas appears under his name, "messires s. thomas" (my lord St Thomas; Machaut 2002, line 3513). But Mézières is completely occulted in favor of Perceval (B. Palmer 2002, 17–20; Hardy 2011, cxxi). Parallels between Machaut's *The Taking of Alexandria* and Mézières's biography of Peter Thomas, *The Life of Saint Peter Thomas*, written in 1366 after the sudden death of Peter Thomas, establish Mézières as a possible written source for Machaut: Peter's crusading desire from a young age (Mézières 1954, 96, 102), the description of his capture of Antalya (Mézières 1954, 97), Urban V's declaration of the crusade (Mézières 1954, 105), the description of Peter's journey through the European courts in 1363–64 (Mézières 1954, 105–6), the departure of the crusade without any European great lords (Mézières 1954, 120–21), the journey to Rhodes (Mézières 1954, 125), the last-minute revelation of the final target (Mézières 1954, 128–29), the sequence of attacks (Mézières 1954, 130–33), the military council, Peter Thomas's impassioned speech, and the decision to abandon Alexandria (Mézières 1954, 133). We can only speculate on whether Machaut knew or used Mézières's biography, although the sheer number of parallels seems fairly determining. Thus Perceval, who was a historical person, embodies not necessarily a written source, but the actual presence of another historical person, Philip of Mézières, whose role was that of a "trusted counselor." Mézières was a fascinating figure to writers, and at least one more (nameless) portrait of him exists in Geoffrey Chaucer's portrait of the Knight in the "General Prologue" to the *Canterbury Tales* (Elst 2009). The "puzzling omission" of Mézières is not an omission, then.[18] Machaut only indirectly acknowledges using some written sources (Machaut 2002, lines 7983–84); he definitely privileged the immediacy and the truth claims of eyewitnesses. Since Mézières was a textual source, this presented several problems. Neither Perceval nor Mézières was ever a prisoner in Alexandria; but Perceval, a more obscure figure of a knight, can certainly embody better than the illustrious chancellor of Cyprus the multitude of fixers and informants who actively participated in Peter's strategic decision. The personification of many in one character can be likened to other situations in *The Taking of Alexandria* where Machaut negotiates a multitude of details "that are not included here, for the tale would be too long were all of these [details] mentioned, and the man who would want to write them all down could bore the reader" (qui ne sont pas ci contenues / car trop longue chose seroit / qui toutes les y meteroit / et anuier porroit au lire / qui toutes les vorroit escrire; Machaut 2002, lines 7164–68; also lines 4777–78, 6817–18).

Again, it is Machaut's staging that in Perceval's case seems to raise questions, and not necessarily Perceval's loyalty per se. Machaut's treatment of Perceval the fixer also describes the dependence of the historian on his own fixers and his need to ascertain their loyalty. Machaut clearly states his preference for eyewitness accounts given by Jean of Reims (Machaut 2002, lines 5937–42) and Gautier of Conflans (Machaut 2002, lines 7977–84, 8017–18, 8213, 8433–34, 8825–26). Thus, Perceval of Coulonges is a fixer to Peter in the same way that Jean of Reims and Gautier of Conflans are fixers to Machaut. Machaut says of Perceval that he belongs to "les nostres" (ours; Machaut 2002, line 4807), "chevaliers de France" (knights of France; Machaut 2002, line 2421), the ancient homeland of Peter's Lusignan family, thereby effectively erasing any difference between the French and Cypriot knights. By assimilating Cyprus to France, Machaut creates fixers of unquestionable loyalty both to Peter I and to himself, thus erecting a historical narrative of unquestionable truthfulness. In addition, Machaut repeatedly asserts his truthfulness: "it is not right that I lie to you" (nest pas raisons que je vous mente; Machaut 2002, line 1535); "I will never lie to you about anything" (ja ne vous en mentiray; Machaut 2002, line 7976; also lines 1294, 3087, 3143). As proof, he advances his reliance on eyewitness testimony in the construction of the historical narrative: "this Jean of whom I speak, taught, instructed, and informed me, and provided me my material. For he was a witness to everything" (cils jehans dont je vous parole / maprent et menseingne et mescole / et mamenistre ma matiere / car il vit toute la maniere; Machaut 2002, lines 5937–40), "as I was informed by the man who was there and witnessed it" (einsi comme cils le ma dit / qui y estoit et qui la vit; Machaut 2002, lines 7977–78). Moreover, Machaut inserts integrally three letters into his work (Machaut 2002, lines 7489–90; lines 7491–528).[19] The preference for oral eyewitness testimony reflects the nature of the event. The event is recent enough for the historian to have direct access to eyewitnesses, superseding the written testimony (but not firsthand documents such as letters). And the event is controversial enough that eyewitness testimony is perceived as more reliable because more interactive. The engagement of a historian with an eyewitness permits the kind of questioning, a "fair inquiry" (juste enqueste; Froissart 1991–98, 1:1), that cannot be brought to bear on a written source. Perceval's figure and role are therefore historically true in that they represent several key issues in Machaut's treatment of a contemporary event: the nature of insider information and interaction with fixers, loyalty and commensuration of truth claims, all paramount to the successful conduct of a military campaign as much as to the retelling of that campaign. In the process, we can observe the commensuration of information by Peter's and Machaut's fixers.

Jean Froissart and the Battle of Nicopolis (1396)

Written by Machaut's younger contemporary Jean Froissart (1337–1404?), *Chronicles* is a vast prose history of Europe and the Mediterranean, with the focus on the Hundred Years' War between the Kingdoms of France and England, covering the events from circa 1325 to 1400.[20] Although fixers are omnipresent in it—after all it was wartime, and all wars need their mediators and interpreters—they come to full light in Froissart's writing on the events that took place at the Battle of Nicopolis (1396). Froissart uses fixers to defend and restore chivalry, and shield it from any disloyalty or disobedience. Much like Machaut's, Froissart's goal is to position the chivalric class as free of all blame and suspicion of disloyalty. But this proves to be particularly challenging when knights who act as fixers pass between the West and the East.[21]

After 1393, under the mounting threat of Ottoman advances in southeast Europe, King Sigismond of Hungary appealed for Western help in defense of Christianity on the eastern front. A large force including the closest members of King Charles VI's entourage, among them Philippe of Artois, Count of Eu and Constable of France, and Boucicaut, Marshal of France, left in the spring of 1396 and joined the Hungarian forces in Buda in Hungary. The Burgundian-French contingent was led by John the Fearless (r. 1404–19), then Count of Nevers and future Duke of Burgundy, son of the then ruling Duke Philip the Bold. The battle against Sultan Bayezid I's Ottoman forces took place on September 25, 1396 (Mézières 2008, 101n2). Many contemporary observers accused the French-Burgundian forces of disorder and excess, and "pride" (orgueil);[22] their contingent reportedly formed an avant-garde that rushed into battle headlong without the support of the Hungarian main army.[23] More than three hundred nobles and knights perished in the battle and the subsequent massacre ordered by Bayezid as vengeance for earlier Christian exactions against Turkish prisoners. However, the Count of Nevers and twenty, or at most twenty-three, other nobles, among them Marshal Boucicaut, who were taken prisoner in the battle, were saved thanks to the intervention of a Turkish-speaking knight, Jacques de Heilly de Créquy.

Jacques de Heilly was from a cadet branch of the Créquy family, an important Burgundian noble family.[24] He had served for more than three years as a mercenary in the army of Murad I, Bayezid's father (Froissart

1867–77, 15:334). This was not entirely unusual. In the late fourteenth century, Christian knights chose to travel to foreign courts to test and improve their prowess and acquire glory and riches. Philip of Mézières was "in his time mercenary in Lombardy to learn the arms and in service to the noble king of Sicily, Andrew, brother of Louis, brave king of Hungary" (en son temps soudoyer en Lombardie pour aprendre le fait d'armes et au service du noble roy de Sicile, Andrieu, frere du vaillant Loys, roy de Hongrie).[25] Others traveled to Muslim courts with the hopes of going to war against Muslim enemies of those courts. The most famous among them was Marshal Boucicaut (1366–1425?). In his youth, he had spent three months at the court of Murad I.[26]

Because Heilly "could speak a bit of Turkish" (sçavoit ung petit parler turc; Froissart 1867–77, 15:319), he was asked to confirm the identities of the highly prized captives to Bayezid. The noblest Christian prisoners had already been identified by the sultan's interpreters, "an order was given to make inquiries and requests to find out which of the Christian lords were the greatest, and they were thoroughly interrogated by the king's interpreters and shielded to the side from killing" (on avoit enquis et demandé par ordonnance lesquels des seigneurs crestiens estoient les plus grans, et furent bien examinés des lattiniers du roy, et furent mis d'un lés pour les sauver de non occire; Froissart 1867–77, 15:324–25). Heilly himself had to confirm their identities: "Go to them, make them out, and size them up and certify their identities and their names to the Emir, for he will decide on your word" (Alés par devers euls, et les advisés et regardés bien et rapportés la certaineté de euls à l'Amourath et de leurs noms; car sur vostre parole il aura advis; Froissart 1867–77, 15:325). This double procedure—first Turkish interpreters, then French informants—is confirmed in Marshal Boucicaut's biography that tells that Bayezid "learned from good dragomans and through confirmed information that the Count of Nevers was the son of the son of the king of France and his first cousin" (sceut par bons truchimens et par certaine informacion que le conte de Nevers estoit fils de filz de roy de France et cousin germain; Lalande 1985, 114), although the writer did not name Heilly. Later, still on account of his linguistic skills and familiarity, Heilly became a messenger, shuttling between Sultan Bayezid and Duke Philip the Bold, the Count of Nevers's father, "because he knew the routes, the ways, and the passages" (pour tant que il sçavoit les voyes, les chemins et les passages; Froissart 1867–77, 16:36). Philip the Bold ransomed John and the nobles at the exorbitant amount of two hundred thousand ducats; John returned to Dijon in Burgundy in February and arrived in Paris in March 1398.

Froissart highlights Heilly's familiarity with the Ottomans and foreign-
ness at home among the French, who at first do not recognize him on his
return from Nicopolis "because he had frequented and pursued the faraway
lands overseas, in search of adventure, much more than the nearby lands of
his birth" (car il avoit trop plus poursuivy et hanté les parties de oultre-mer
et loingtaines, quérant les aventures, que les prouchaines de sa nation; Froissart 1867–77, 15:333).[27] Heilly's acquaintance among the Ottomans was so
extensive that, after the battle, he had "such good fortune on his side that he
was recognized by the men and guards of Emir Pasha's body and household"
(si bonne adventure pour luy que il fut recongneu des gens et serviteurs du
corps et del hostel de l'Amourath-Bacquin; Froissart 1867–77, 15:324) and
"by the emir whom he had served" (recongneu de l'Amourath auquel il avoit
servy; Froissart 1867–77, 15:325). Heilly then served as the sultan's personal
informant on Burgundian matters (par espécial messire Jacques de Helly
l'avoit infourmé; Froissart 1867–77, 16:39). The sultan so greatly appreciated
his mediation services that he reportedly credited Heilly with a colossal sum
of twenty thousand out of two hundred thousand ducats agreed on for the
ransom of Christian captives (Froissart 1867–77, 16:42).

Countering the notion of a disloyal fixer that this staggering reward
would imply, Froissart reports that, when Heilly first brought the news of
John of Nevers to the court, Duke Philip the Bold attached him immediately to the ducal household; "he made him one of his knights with 200
livres of yearly income, which he gave him in fiefdom for life" (le retint de
ses chevalliers parmy deux cens livres de revenue par an, dont il le doua
et fiefva à le tenir tout son vivant; Froissart 1867–77, 15:336). Philip later
charged Heilly with bringing the estate of the Count of Nevers from Burgundy to Venice for his return from Turkey: "and lord of Hangest and my
lord Jacques de Heilly were independent and executors of all those things
and orders" (et furent souverains et conduiseurs de toutes ces choses et
ordonnances le sire de Hangiers et messire Jacques de Helly; Froissart
1867–77, 16:57). In other words, Heilly had full agency to commensurate.
And it was by virtue of his agency, and autonomy, that both the sultan and
the duke paid for his service. For all his perceived maneuvering (or rather,
commensurating) and cultural subtlety, Heilly remains clear of suspicion;
his agency in negotiations created a third space, and he could be doubly
paid for loyal services to both sides. Without understanding the fixer's
position as a third, autonomous space, we might find this double payment
compromising Heilly's loyalty, when this is not the case.

In Froissart's account where he is a central figure, Heilly is, nevertheless, tainted with one thing that threatens chivalry overall and requires a

defense: the chivalric fixer is just a placeholder, a movable chess piece in a larger play of commensuration where chivalric prowess is superseded by other prerogatives and measured in money. Heilly in fact owed his survival not to chance, but to a calculated surrender thanks to his cultural knowledge: "When he saw the defeat as inevitable, he thought he would save himself" (Quant il vey que la desconfiture tourneroit sur euls, si eut advis de soy saulver; Froissart 1867–77, 15:319). Heilly sells himself (and another squire) up for ransom even before any other noble prisoners are taken. He is likewise the first, in Froissart's account, to alert the duke to the possibility of ransom; "he was verily hoping that King Bayezid will put them up for ransom within a year or two at most, because he greatly coveted to acquire gold and wealth, and he knew this from experience, because he had lived and dealt with them in Turkey and served the emir" (il espéroit bien que le roy Basaach dedens ung an ou deux au plus tard les metteroit à finance, car il convoittoit or et richesses à avoir par devers luy trop grandement, et ce sçavoit-il de sentement, car il avoit demouré et conversé en Turquie aveuc euls et servy l'Amourath; Froissart 1867–77, 15:334). And, while the ransom is negotiated, he counsels the duke on the gifts that the sultan most covets from the West: rich tapestries from Arras, white cloth from Reims, and gyrfalcons (white falcons) (Froissart 1867–77, 15:337). The ransom and the gifts are the measure of commensuration of the two sides in conflict; it is the role of the fixer to provide the third space for communication, commutation, and commensuration (see the introduction). But that knights could be fixers was a problem for these writers describing interreligious conflicts and the superior value of Christian chivalry. Knights should not commensurate; only merchants can.

Commensuration: "Moyenner" and "Monneyer" (Froissart and Mézières)

Heilly is the first to suggest the possibility of ransom—a commercial transaction—as a way to mediate and commensurate the conflict between the duke and the sultan. Yet he keeps the role of an honorable fixer; his agency does not taint him. Knights get the noble part, because the Italian merchants are the ones doing the dirty work. This is true in both Machaut and Froissart. In *The Taking of Alexandria*, after the raid, Venetians expedite an embassy to liberate Christian prisoners in Alexandria that the sultan arrested after the raid and to resume trading privileges (Machaut 2002, lines 3831–38). The commercial motives of King Peter's peace negotiations with the sultan of Egypt are made explicit by Machaut: "that this treaty and agreement be published throughout the land . . . so that trade will flow since, so help me God, it seems to be a problem in every court when buying and selling are not conducted" (que ceste pais et ceste acorde / soit publie par la terre . . . par quoy marcheandise queure / quavis mest se dieux me sequeure / que cest deffaus en toute court / quant marcheandise ne court; Machaut 2002, lines 5780–81, 5789–92). This resonates in the *Chronicles* with the words of the Duke of Burgundy's main counselor and creditor in the affair of Nicopolis, a Lombard merchant, Dino Rapondi, who recommends the involvement of the merchants of Venice and Genoa of the Aegean archipelago, "because, as you know, trade goes and travels everywhere, and the world is governed and supplied by its prescription" (car, ainsi que vous sçavés, marchandise va et court partout, et se gouverne et estoffe le monde par celle ordonnance; Froissart 1867–77, 15:356). If we are to trust the words of the merchants, no door is ever so tightly shut as to not be pried open by trade circulation and negotiation. There is no doubt that, just like Machaut in Peter's case of attenuating the commercial fallout of the Alexandria raid, Froissart found the figure of Heilly most useful to honorably, chivalrously present what in essence became a commercial transaction in the aftermath of the Nicopolis battle. The commercial proposition, laid bare, would have been contrary to chivalric prowess, the main through theme of the *Chronicles*.

Another work dedicated to Nicopolis, Philip of Mézières's *A Letter of Lament and Consolation* (1397), is explicit about the separation line between chivalry and trade in the negotiation with the Ottomans: "to reclaim our prisoners" (recouvrer nos prisonniers) can be done either by "way of negotiation" (la voie de traittié) or by "way of exploit" (la voie de fait; Mézières 2008, 171). In negotiations, Mézières gives the same counsel as Froissart's Rapondi, charging the merchants: "Although the principal negotiators are not French, but Venetians or Italian merchants could at first show the treaty in a more favorable light for Bayezid than for the king or his royal lineage, for there are merchants who have more contacts with the Turks for their trade than they do with the French" (Encores que les traicteurs principaux ne soient pas François, mais soient Veniciens ou marchans d'Italie qui pourront monstrer d'enprime le traictié plus a la faveur de Baxeth que la faveur du roy ou de sa royalle lignee, car il y a des marchans qui ont plus grant accointance pour leurs marchandises aus Turs qu'ilz n'ont avec les Françoiz; Mézières 2008, 174–75). But Mézières, on account of his experience in the East, does not believe that Turks can set "a good, moderate, and acceptable ransom" (bonne rançon, moienne et supportable; Mézières 2008, 174), or, for that matter, keep to the agreement, "often they do not remain truthful to the Christians unless it is to their great profit" (souvent ils ne tiennent pas verité aus crestiens se ce n'est a leur tres grant prouffit; Mézières 2008, 172). Mézières projected that the (ransom) negotiations would fail, and the only resolution possible would be by "way of exploit and good war" (la voie de fait et faire bonne guerre; Mézières 2008, 183), that is by way of chivalry.

It is the nature of mercantile circulation to seek resolution, compromise, and middle ground, in short to commensurate: "There is no such thing that cannot be appeased and *mediated* with gold and silver" (Il n'est chose qui ne s'appaise et *moyenne* par or et par argent; Froissart 1867–77, 15:356; my emphasis), says Froissart's Rapondi. The verb "moyenner" or "moiener" means to mediate, moderate, find or split the middle, while the noun "moyen" or "moien" has several principal significations, "middle," "intermediary," and "means," bringing us to the idea of the one who is in the middle and also the medium and instrument in a negotiation. "Moyenner" also resonates fortuitously with "monneier," money changer, the person who converts the value, Rapondi's role being to supply and advance the money for ransom. Rapondi's statement comes early in the description of the negotiations for liberation of the captives, but Froissart lets the implications of "moyenner-monneier" do the work silently, without further elaboration on monetary mediation.

Mézières, on the other hand, illuminates the richness of this term and the resonance between "moien" and "monnoie." Mézières's *Letter* is addressed to Duke Philip in the wake of the Nicopolis disaster in an attempt to revive Mézières's proposals for the chivalric Order of the Passion (1367), a new religious-military order, "the design of a small, dedicated, self-sustaining, standing fighting unit, a flexible and efficient . . . nucleus of a larger army" (Blumenfeld-Kosinski and Petkov 2011a, 10), distinguished by the willingness of its members to die, to be the new sacrifice, "offering to God a pleasing sacrifice of Christians without number" (offrant a Dieu un plaisant sacrifice de crestiens sans nombre; Mézières 2008, 144). The order's coat of arms is "the murdered lamb" (l'Aingnelet occis; Mézières 2008, 144) and its name "the chivalry of the Crucifix" (chevalerie du Crucefix; Mézières 2008, 209). This universal, rather than national, order (Mézières 2008, 145, 186), "a new generation of Christian soldiers" (une nouvelle generacion de combatans crestiens; Mézières 2008, 134, 136), is to be composed of "the middle class of Christianity" (moien estat de la crestienté; Mézières 2008, 142), that is "of the middle class of knights, some lords, noble squires, bourgeois, and merchants" (les chevaliers moiens, aucuns barons, escuiers nobles, bourgoiz et marchans; Mézières 2008, 136). Moreover, Mézières clearly elects the Duke of Burgundy as the leader of the crusade—his son's captivity is the duke's singular "wound," which elects him to this very position. The duke holds here a pivotal—

intermediary and instrumental—role in leading the kings of England and France on a crusade, "by means of high courage, prudence, experience and wisdom of the very powerful and very noble Philip of France, Duke of Burgundy" (par le moien de la haute vaillance, prudence, experience et sapience du tres poissant et tres noble prince Philippe de France, duc de Bourgoingne; Mézières 2008, 185). The duke is the middle estate in a princely hierarchy, neither king nor lesser nobility, and he is the medium, "par le moien." This middle, intermediary estate of the new chivalric order is thus the medium and the means by which will be recovered the prisoners and the Holy Land, and the shame of Christian faith and Christianity avenged: "The proverb says that 'the middle estate [or ground] is the most safe.' ... All extremes are perilous; virtue is to be found in the middle" (Il se dit en proverbe que "le moien estat est le plus seür." ... Toute extremité est perileuse: ou milieu est trouvee la vertu; Mézières 2008, 143)[28]—the "middle ground," the intermediary state, the third space.

Having identified the middle agent, the "moien" cadences with stunning frequency and regularity Mézières's *Letter*, whether to mean "medium, instrument" (par le moien du sacrifice de la chevalerie, Mézières 2008, 192, 201; par le moien de sa chevalerie, Mézières 2008, 220) or to designate "the negotiators or intermediaries of the treaty" (ceulx qui seront moien du traictié; Mézières 2008, 174, 175), that is fixers. Mézières also assigns this double role to Jesus Christ, who "was the medium between God and man, and reconciled man to God" (Jhesu Crist fu moien entre Dieu et l'omme et le reconsilia a Dieu; Mézières 2008, 143). Mézières relies on the near homology of "medium" and "money": "Jesus Christ paid the money with which he was redeemed, that is his precious blood" (Jhesu Crist ... paia la monnoye dont il fu racheté, c'est assavoir son precieux sang; Mézières 2008, 143). Mézières could have avoided using the term "monnoye" here, since blood is the exchange value for the coins paid for the betrayal of Christ, yet, he monetizes blood to indicate that it was a payment; blood commensurates for sins of humanity. Blood is the money for the medium. Money is the preferred medium of commensuration for intermediaries, even if they are Christ himself. The same pairing of "moien-monnoye" resonates later in the text, at the recovery of prisoners "by means of money" (par le moien de monnoye; Mézières 2008, 175). It is for this reason that only "by some good ransom, moderate (median) and acceptable, our lords will be ransomed" (par aucune bonne rançon, moienne et supportable, messeigneurs pourront estre rançonné; Mézières 2008, 174).

Throughout, Mézières makes a clear-cut distinction between "exploit" and "negotiation"; the chivalric class is the means and the merchants the intermediary; the former are French, the latter Venetian or Italian: "the principal negotiators are not French, but Venetians or Italian merchants." Chivalry is the tool to victory, but its job is not to negotiate and make money deals with the Turks. Indeed, writers of crusade treatises found the merchants to be generally corrupt, ready to strike any deal for profit, and they called them "falsi Christiani," an accusation repeated by Mézières: "false Christians, secretly or publicly in alliance with the enemies of the faith would sell their father for money" (faulx crestiens, aliez secretement ou publiquement aux ennemis de la foy vendroient leur pere pour argent; Mézières 2008, 175). A knight does not negotiate and commensurate; a knight is not a fixer, in Mézières's view. The exchange of chivalry for a commercial transaction clearly bothers Froissart as well. It is perhaps in order to recover the taint of using knights, like Heilly, as fixers in negotiating the ransom that Froissart stages the departure from Bursa where the sultan invites the Christian nobles to attack him again: "I thus wish that, when you will have returned over there and it will so please you, you gather your forces and come against me" (ainchois vueil que, quant tu seras retourné par delà, et il te vendra à plaisance, que tu assambles ta puissance et viengnes encontre moy; Froissart 1867–77, 16:47).[29]

In Machaut and Froissart, chivalry had to be shielded from negotiation (moiener) that would essentially amount to a commercial transaction (monnoye) with the enemy. Mézières's militant treatise, which makes no other claims to an accurate portrayal of historical events beyond the exactitude of his personal experience in the East, reveals this ideological dimension of chivalric Western historiography: "One has to come to the way of exploit that has to be ready in case negotiation fails" (Or fault venir a la voye de fait qui doit estre preste ou cas que la traictié faudra; Mézières 2008, 183). All three writers essentialize the chivalric class and in the process compromise their narratives in different ways. Mézières makes his chivalry militant and intransigent, made up of a chivalric middle (*moien*) class, the easiest to make obedient and loyal. By refusing to negotiate a treaty (*monnoye*), while insisting on the knights as means (*moien*) to be used only in war, Mézières manages to sidestep the actual question of chivalric loyalty in matters of negotiation: an armed confrontation seems less compromising than a diplomatic commensuration. Machaut and Froissart describe actual events that make fixers of the chivalric class look disloyal, only to reaffirm their loyalty and replace them in compromising roles with merchants, who take on the "dirty," transactional work. Knights are judged by their loyalty, and merchants according to their in-network power, and each obeys to their code. It appears that in Machaut and Froissart the function of fixers between the East and the West is to save the honor of Christian chivalry. In Mézières, the honor of chivalry that never negotiates, while paradoxically occupying the position of "moien," will be redeemed by a war waged to death, "by means of the sacrifice of chivalry" (par le moien du sacrefice de la chevalerie; Mézières 2008, 192). Ultimately, what these writerly efforts show, time and again, is that, just as are the merchants, the knightly class is as tainted by suspicion and distrust when occupying the role of fixers. However, in the chivalric regime of truth, chivalry is redeemed by the merchants, who take the taint of transactionality. Commensuration is not a chivalric enterprise, and the loyalty of fixers is not judged by who pays them.

Commensuration: Writers as Fixers

Both Froissart and Machaut lay equal claims to the truthfulness of their histories. Machaut defends himself from any accusation of undue influence from a patron or lord: "I do not write this for a benefit or profit or out of promise" (ne le di pour avantage / pour promesse ne pour avoir; Machaut 2002, lines 7990–91). His authorial remonstrations that he is telling the truth—"I will never lie about anything" (ja nen mentiray; Machaut 2002, line 1294 and line 3087), "because I do not lie" (pour ce que je ne mente; Machaut 2002, line 3143)—are made on the grounds that he is reporting "as I was informed by the man who was there and witnessed it" (einsi comme cils le ma dit / qui y estoit et qui la vit; Machaut 2002, lines 7977–78). Machaut is not any more or less insistent on the truth and eye witnessing than twelfth-century verse romances of antiquity such as Benoît de Saint-Maure's *The Romance of Troy* or twelfth-century verse histories such as Jordan Fantosme's *Chronicle*. More importantly, Machaut's claims are no different from Froissart's assurances in the *Chronicles:*

> And all that is written is true. One cannot say that I have biased the noble history on account of the favor received from count Guy de Blois. . . . Indeed not, for I do not wish to tell anything except the truth and stay on the cusp without coloring one or the other [side]. And the noble and gentle lord and count, who had me write and compose the history, would not have wanted me to write it differently than true.

> (Et tout ce qui est escript est veritable. On ne dye pas que je aye la noble hystoire corrompu par la faveur que je aye eu au conte Guy de Blois. . . . Nennil vrayement, car je ne vueil parler fors que de la verité et aler parmy le trenchant sans coulourer l'un ne l'autre et aussy le gentil sire et

conte, qui l'istoire me fist mettre sus et edifier, ne le voulsist point que je feisse aultrement que vraye.) (Froissart 1869–75, 13:223–24)

Just like with knights of whom they write and who serve as fixers, Machaut's and Froissart's truthfulness is important because both writers also position themselves as fixers.

Machaut declares that he was one of the three persons present when Gautier told his story: "my lord Gautier de Conflans told me—not just me, I was the third" (ce me dit messires gautiers / de confflans, non pas seul, moy tiers; Machaut 2002, lines 8017–18). This is no doubt a double self-reflexive moment for Machaut the fixer; indeed, Machaut is the third fixer in the historical line of transmission of information on the raid on Alexandria and on Peter's life and death: first, from Perceval of Coulonges (and the multiple informants that he represents) to Peter I; second, from Jean of Reims and Gautier of Conflans to Machaut; and, third, from Machaut to his audience. Machaut sees himself as the third party to those who witnessed the events: "this is just as Gautier told me; I don't say anything different in my *dit*" (si comme gautiers le ma dit / autrement ne di je en mon dit; Machaut 2002, lines 8433–34; also lines 8825–26; translation modified). As the one who receives the eyewitness testimony, Machaut fills a role that has been not so much to consign it to written memory as to disclose it: "I don't wish it kept secret" (pas ne vueil qui soit enclose; Machaut 2002, line 7410). Indeed, Machaut's insistence on faithful transmission without surplus—"I don't say anything different in my *dit*"—makes him as loyal a fixer as Perceval. He reinforces it furthermore with the refusal of any allegiance or affiliation that might compromise him:

> I'm not speaking out of envy or hatred, or because of kin loyalty, since I am not a member of his lineage, nor do I say this out of promise or for a benefit or profit that another or I might gain thereby. Instead I say it because it is true, just as he recounted it to me.

> (Je ne le di pas par envie / par haine ne par lingnie / car pas ne sui de son linage / ne ne le di pour avantage / pour promesse ne pour avoir / que je n'autre en doie avoir / einsois le di pour verite / si comme il le ma recite.) (Machaut 2002, lines 7987–94)

This allows us to reread the statement that "it is not right that I lie to you" (nest pas raisons que je vous mente; Machaut 2002, line 1535) as "there is no reason to lie." It is because "neither love nor hatred nor friendship would be able to persuade me to twist the facts into some lie" (quamour haine namite / ne me puissent ad ce mouvoir / que mensonge face dou voir; Machaut 2002, lines 8384–86) that Machaut the fixer can disclose truthfully everything his own audience needs to know: "I will not pass [it] over in silence for I must speak the truth here" (je ne vous celeray point / car ci doy dire verite; Machaut 2002, lines 8382–83). At different levels of this history, one loyalty reinforces the other(s), creating indeed the chain of loyalty along the line of "les nostres," those who are French of France, the ancient homeland of Peter's Lusignan family. Perceval, Philip, Jean, Gautier, and Guillaume all act as fixers in a chain of information flow, and their loyalties mutually question and reinforce each other in the network of its transmission. It is a question of loyalty between persons, and not of translational fidelity to a text.

Machaut's stated preference for eyewitness accounts by Jean of Reims and Gautier of Conflans over the written sources (as we saw, he never acknowledges Philip of Mézières's *Vita Sancti Petri*) also resembles Froissart's supersession in later redactions of book 1 of his *Chronicles* of Jean le Bel's prose narrative by "the true information that I received from valiant men, knights, and squires" (la vraie information que je ay eu des vaillans honmes, chevaliers et esquiers; Froissart 1972, 35).[30] Throughout his chronicle and in its different versions, Froissart used various strategies to establish his truthfulness and, even, neutrality. To begin with, he chose prose over verse. In the first version of his *Chronicles*, he acknowledged an initial verse version, not preserved: "I undertook boldly to compose in verse and rhyme the above-mentioned wars and to bring to England the composed book, as I did" (Si emprins je assez hardiment ... à dittier et à rimer les guerres dessus dittes et porter en Angleterre le livre tout compilé, si comme je fis). In his own judgment, this book did not do justice to the events: "It is possible that this book is not fairly analytical and organized as such a thing demands. For the deeds of arms must be faithfully attributed and assigned" (Or puet estre que cest livre n'est mie examiné ne ordonné si justement que telle chose le requiert. Car fais d'armes ... doivent estre donnez et loyaument departis; Froissart 1869–75, 1.2:210).[31] With time, he increasingly relied on oral testimonies of war protagonists and eyewitnesses. The first versions of book 1 of *Chronicles* contained in the manuscript of Amiens (ca. 1377–81?), and manuscripts A and B (before 1391?) combine his predecessor Jean le Bel's prose *Chronicle* (for the years 1325–50), which Froissart "translated," and Froissart's "fair inquiry" of eyewitnesses. But the last version of book 1 in the manuscript of Rome (ca. 1396–1400?) definitively supersedes le Bel's written source, no longer mentioned in the prologue; testimonies appear as the exclusive source for the historian Froissart, "the true information that I obtained from the valiant men, knights, and squires" (Froissart 1972, 35; also Froissart 1869–75, 1.2:1). Always concerned with rendering his due to the readers, Froissart collected the testimonies himself, "in order to "discharge my duty to you, as is right" (moy acquitter envers tous, ainsi que drois est; Froissart 1869–75, 1.2:210). Thus it was the true testimonies, and not the prose, that founded the truthfulness of historiographic writing: "to write in prose and organize according to the true information" (mettre en prose et ordonner selonch la vraie information; Froissart 1972, 35). And while the responsibility to be truthful in the early manuscript of Amiens rested primarily with the witnesses, "such people are fair investigators and reporters of endeavors and . . . they would not dare lie because of their honor" (tels gens sont juste inquisiteur et raporteur des besoingnes et . . . pour leur honeur il n'en oseroient mentir; Froissart 1991–98, 1:1; also Froissart 1869–75, 1.2:1), and in the last redaction of Rome, Froissart inscribed himself in the collective obligation to truthfulness: "One should absolutely not lie about it" (Nullement on n'en doit mentir; Froissart 1972, 35). And he tasked himself with actively seeking out information in the world: "I didn't at all want to rest from the pursuit of my subject matter and from knowing the truth of the distant lands, but without dispatching there anyone else than myself" (je ne voloie mie sejourner de non poursuivir ma matiere, et pour savoir la verité des lointaines marches, sans ce que je y envoiasse autre personne que moy; Froissart 1869–75, 12:2). He set out to the Gascon court of Count Gaston de Foix, where "I could not fail to be fairly informed, better than anywhere else in the world, of all the news" (je ne povoie mieulx ou monde escheir pour etre informé justement de toutes nouvelles; Froissart 1869–75, 12:2). Finally, Froissart attempted to provide accounts of war events from all parties involved in the conflict, "from whichever side he may be" (douquel costet qu'il soit; Froissart 1991–98, 1:1), "from whichever land they may be" (de quel pays qu'il soient; Froissart 1869–75, 1.2:2), "from whichever land or nation they may be" (de quel païs et nation que il soient; Froissart 1972, 35). These were a method and form unique to medieval historiography.[32] Froissart ostensibly did this without altering the testimonies collected. He proclaimed in the opening prologue to the *Chronicles* to "memorably [record] . . . by fair inquiry" (notablement registré . . . par juste enqueste; Froissart 1991–98, 1:1) testimonies of the participants in the war, "without inventing or taking sides, without tainting one more than the other" (sans faire fait, ne porter partie, ne coulourer plus l'un que l'autre; Froissart 1869–75, 1.2:1). But he took responsibility for their translation into the narrative, and their ordering (ordonnance)—his "neutral" historiographic writing was a feat of commensuration.

While Machaut inscribed his own performance in the chain of "French" knights, "les nostres," transforming himself into a chivalrous fixer, Froissart adopted a different method, which likewise landed him in the chivalrous camp. In book 1 Froissart first implicitly compared himself and his own historiographic endeavor to a brave knight, a "preu." Like the brave knight's physical effort and endurance, "in great pain, sweat, toil, care, wake, laboring day and night without rest" (en grant painne, en sueur, en labeur, en soing, en villier, en travillier jour et nuis sans sejour; Froissart 1869–75, 2:4), Froissart composed the book in "much pain and labor" (mout de paine et de traveil) and "intellectual toil... and privation of my body" (le labeur de ma teste et... l'exil de mon corps; Froissart 1991–98, 1:1). In book 4, he drew an explicit comparison between a writer and a knight: "Just like a gentle knight or squire who loves the arms takes nourishment and perfection from them by persevering and pursuing them, so do I practice and take pleasure in toiling and in laboring on this subject matter" (Car ainsi comme le gentil chevallier ou escuier qui ayme les armes, en persévérant et continuant, il s'i nourrist et parfait, ainsi en labourant et ouvrant sur ceste matière je me habilite et délite; Froissart 1867–77, 14:3). In short, he upheld his historiographic commensuration as a feat of (chivalric) prowess.

Philip of Mézières was perhaps the most important writer-fixer of the three. We saw his role in the comparison of his *Life of Saint Peter Thomas* and Machaut's verse history. In *Chivalry of the Order of the Passion* (1367–68), in a manuscript held in Paris, Bibliothèque de l'Arsenal, MS 2251, Mézières describes briefly his time with Peter and the conquest of Alexandria, to position himself doubly as a fixer:

For the king, and in his absence, a special messenger of his royal magnanimity, for this same cause for fifteen years or thereabouts without pause, only went from the East to the West, from the South to the North, to Pope Urban and Pope Gregory, to the above-mentioned kings and a few others, to great princes and communes of Catholic Christianity, asking for full assistance in continuing the holy divine battle against the enemies of the faith.

(pour celle mesme cause, ... avec le dit roy et sans sa presence, especial messagier de sa magnanimite royale, par XV. ans ou environ continuelement ne fist autre chose que d'aler d'orient en occident, de midi

en septentrion, a pape Urbain et a pape Grigoire, aux roys dessus diz
et a pluseurs autres, aux grans princes et communes de la crestiente
Catholique, en demandant par tout aide pour continuer la sainte bataille
de dieu encontre les anemis de la foy.) (Arsenal, MS 2251, fol. 17v)

Although he was chancellor of Cyprus, Mézières seems to have spent
more time elsewhere as Peter's fixer. His eyewitness experience of "about
25 years that he lived and dealt with the Turks and Saracens, while in the
service . . . of three kings of Cyprus, one after another" (Mézières 2008,
172), is complemented with firsthand sources: "Several old knights who
had been present at the above-narrated events told me this story" (Ceste
histoire me raconterent . . . pluseurs anciens chevaliers qui avoient esté
presens a tout ce que dit est dessus; Mézières 2008, 182). Mézières argues for the establishment of the new chivalric Order of the Passion, a
sacrificial "chivalry of Crucifix" (la chevalerie du Crucifix; Arsenal, MS
2251, fol. 7) in a form of allegory, "parabole" (Arsenal, MS 2251, fol. 7, 7v).
Mézières, "Old Writer" (Vieil escripvain) is the same as Burning Desire,
"Ardant Desir"; he is a messenger-fixer before the head queen of "Divine
Providence" (Providence divine; Arsenal, MS 2251, fol. 9v).[33] In the course
of this dream-letter-parable-allegory, Mézières recounts again his experience in the East, from his mercenary days in Lombardy (fol. 12v), to his
service to Peter I (fol. 16), followed by a brief description of conquest of
Alexandria (fols. 16v–17v). Just like Froissart, Mézières took to the road
and worked tirelessly on his embassy, "messagerie": "your unworthy messenger Burning Desire, in toil and dangers without number to the body
and to the soul, sometime sad, another time cheerful, once consoled,
hundred times disconsolate, once honored and many times played a fool,
several times robbed and shipwrecked, suffering a thousand tribulations
in body and his soul castigated, as it is plainly obvious" (vostre indigne
messagier Ardant Desir a grant traveil et perilz sans nombre et du corps
et de l'ame, une foiz triste, l'autre foiz en joye, une foiz conforté et cent
foiz desconforté, l'une foiz honnouré et pluseurs foiz degabé, aucune foiz
desrobé et aucune foiz en mer naufragé, souffrant et de mille tribulacions
en corps et en esperit flagellé, comme il appert assez; Arsenal, MS 2251,
fol. 17v). His book of the Order of Passion is the message, "the book of
his mission," "livre de la legacion" (Arsenal, MS 2251, fol. 18v), a hybrid
of autobiography and spiritual-military treatise occupying a first third of
the manuscript (Arsenal, MS 2251, fols. 1–43). The last two-thirds are full
of practical advice on "the form and practice of forming and instituting
the new chivalric Order of the Passion of Jesus Christ" (la forme et la

pratique de la composicion et declaracion de la nouvelle chevalerie de la passion de jhesu crist; fol. 92) and the foundation of the order (fol. 44–112), followed by a list of nobles who have signed up for the venture (fols. 113–14v).[34] In the end, Mézières's experience as a fixer and witness grounds his truth claim.

In short, Machaut, Froissart, and Mézières all lay a claim to loyalty and truthfulness and in similar ways. Yet, each fixer writes in a different form: Machaut composes a verse history (with some elements of allegory), Froissart a prose history, and Mézières a prose allegorical treatise. All three use eyewitness accounts, either their own or firsthand witness accounts, regardless of the form. Despite their claims to commensurate events and accounts faithfully, literary history has not treated them in the same way. The reason lies in the very form and genre of their narratives as modern scholarship has defined them: verse and allegory are not perceived as compatible with eye witnessing and historical narrative, while prose is. In fact, the use of allegory and verse to convey historical events, especially events reported by eyewitnesses, do not seem such an outlier as our previous understanding of the literary history of genres would seem to suggest.

Verse, Prose, Allegory: Commensurability and Literary History

The most important factor in the determination of literary history of the European Middle Ages that verse and allegory are not compatible with historical narrative, while prose is, has precisely been Froissart's preference for prose over verse, since this choice concords with our modern sensibility that attributes prose to a historic and verse to a poetic exercise, or prose to truthfulness and verse to fables. Froissart forcefully rejected the use of verse in history writing, following in the footsteps of his predecessor Jean le Bel (1290?–1369?), whose Chronicle Froissart used as a base for a portion of book 1 (years 1325–50) of his Chronicles. Le Bel vehemently criticized rhymed chronicles: "in these verse histories one finds great many errors" (en ces hystoires rimées treuve on grand plenté de bourdes). Hyperbole of rhyme has the effect of discrediting the narrative and, by implication, its narrator: "by such outsized words . . . their true deeds will be less credible" (par telles parolles si desmesurées . . . leurs vrais fais en seroient mains creus; Le Bel 1904, 3, 1–2). Le Bel's refutation of verse, via Froissart, as an inappropriate hyperbolic vehicle of historical representation has struck a cord with critics and lent authority to the affiliation of prose with truthfulness:

Several *jongleurs* and singers have sung and rhymed the wars of Brittany there. Their songs and artificial rhymes corrupted the exact and true history, which displeased greatly my lord Jean le Bel, who started to write down the wars in a prose chronicle, and myself, sir Jean Froissart, I have faithfully and exactly continued it to the best of my ability. For their artificial rhymes and songs do not come close in anything to the true matter.

(Pluiseur gongleour et enchanteour en place ont chanté et rimet les guerres de Bretaigne et coromput, par leurs chançons et rimes controuvees, le juste et vraie histoire, dont trop en desplaist à monseigneur Jehan le Biel qui le coummencha à mettre en prose et en cronique et à moy, sire Jehan Froissart, qui loyaument et justement l'ay poursuiwi à mon pooir. Car leurs rimmez et leurs canchons controuvees n'ataindent en riens la vraie matere.) (Froissart 1991–98, 2:96)

Froissart's devaluation of verse in favor of prose is thought to illustrate the general movement toward prose as the language of truth that began in the early thirteenth-century vernacular histories and continued with prosifications of verse romances and *chansons de geste* in the fourteenth and fifteenth century.[35] If le Bel set the course, it is nevertheless Froissart's active pursuit of eyewitness testimonies of the war collected on all sides of the conflict, exceptional for his time, that has undoubtedly contributed to his reputation as a neutral, balanced historiographer—Froissart commensurated well between many pieces of information.[36] As a result, critics have readily accepted and taken as authoritative Froissart's institution of prose as more truthful than verse. To write about war with equanimity is a feat in itself, but the feeling of Froissart's success—and Machaut's failure in the same effort—is helped by our sensibilities that associate more readily prose and truthfulness. Closer to our modern sensibility, prose alone established Froissart, and not Machaut, as the preeminent historian of contemporary events of the fourteenth century.[37] Ways of establishing fidelity to the event—eyewitness testimonies—were dismissed in favor of form.

The confusing status of verse has been aggravated further by two facts in Machaut's case. *The Taking of Alexandria* is said to be the only history in Machaut's poetic corpus.[38] This exceptional existence of a history in an otherwise unified poetic corpus is complicated by Machaut's unhesitant use of allegory and myth. His verse history of recent controversial events—the raid of Alexandria and the murder of a king—opens with a 259-line historical-mythological prologue, where Machaut deploys the topos of the Nine Worthies to link the ancient pagan and Jewish past— Hector, Alexander, Julius Caesar, Joshua, David, Judas Maccabeus—to the Christian past—Arthur, Charlemagne, and Godfrey of Bouillon. The topos was popularized in 1312–13 with *The Vows of the Peacock* (*Les vœux du paon*) by Jacques de Longuyon.[39] The Nine Worthies represent the narrative axis of universal history, just as they encompass along the east-west axis, the geography of the known world, from India and Persia to the Near East and England. The last in line, Godfrey of Bouillon, the first ruler of the Latin Kingdom of Jerusalem conquered in 1099 in the First Crusade (and who famously refused the title of "king"), is positioned as Peter's predecessor. Peter is ordained by God Mars as the tenth Worthy, born of the union, the "conjunction," of Mars and Venus.[40] Throughout, Peter is situated in the lineage of mythological or historical heroes: Aeneas, Jason, Achilles, Hector, Salomon, Julius Caesar, Saint Louis (Hardy 2011, xciii). Machaut's verse history is thus a mixture of different, and more and less distant pasts: Greco-Roman myths and history (e.g., Battle of Pharsalus), those of the Old Testament, and recent crusading experience. Seemingly out of place in this narrative of most recent events, almost jarring, the prologue sets up the recent history of the raid of Alexandria as both continuation and transformation of a hero and king-crusader, from the pagan council of gods to *imitatio Christi*.[41]

Yet, the late fourteenth-century audiences did not seem to have a problem with verse or allegory as historical forms. *The Taking of Alexandria* was not a lone verse history; it was followed by *The Life of Bertrand du Guesclin* (*La vie de Bertrand du Guesclin*) by Cuvelier (ca. 1381), *The Life of the Black Prince* (*La vie du Prince Noir*) by Chandos Herald (ca. 1385), and the anonymous *Geste des ducs de Bourgogne* (*The Epic of the Dukes of Burgundy*, early fifteenth century). It was contemporary to the intense activity of reworkings of the epic (including the cycle of the crusades) and versification of chronicles, such as Jean d'Outremeuse's *Geste de Liege* (*The Epic of Liège*, ca. 1370). A similar relationship of verse form and historical content was seen in the alliterative revival in England, especially in poems in the tradition of William Langland's *Piers Plowman* (ca. 1360–87), like *Richard the Redeless* and *Mum and the Soothsegger*. These verse histories all dealt with contemporary political events and figures. Machaut's verse history continued to be valued well into the second half of the fifteenth century, at the height of the vast prosification movement at the court of Philip the Good, Duke of Burgundy. Machaut's authoritative manuscript A (Paris, BnF, MS fr. 1584, ca. 1372–77), produced under his direction in Paris and Reims, was purchased by Louis of Gruuthuse (Durand and Giovannoni 2012, 209). Louis was a Flemish-Burgundian noble with a stellar career at the courts of Philip the Good (1396–1467) and his son, Charles the Bold (1433–77), Dukes of Burgundy (see chapter 5).[42]

It seems that ancient history and mythology served the purpose of integrating a recent experience into a larger historical continuity of reception and consciousness. That is, they performed a commensuration of a recent event in historical time. Indeed, one of the questions that these methods of deploying allegory and repurposing myth may be an answer to is the difficult question for historiographers of how to transform experience into history, how recent events, unprecedented or controversial, can become a matter of authoritative, or at the very least, credible reception. The grand narratives of mythology do not possess any ontological integrity, but they do carry instead the potential for their own recycling and repurposing. It would seem that allegory and myth in *The Taking of Alexandria* liberate the historical events from controversy and enable reflection at the meta-historical level. They also function as a form of a *longue durée* along which the recent events become only the latest transformation. Likewise, it can be argued that verse, as an ancient form, serves to distance the immediacy of events and facilitates engagement with controversial, disputed, and unprecedented facts.[43] The prose medium vehicles its content as truth; verse enables reflection and meditation. What for us is a cognitive dissonance is really the way in which grand narratives, in verse and mythology, help commensurate the new outsized or unprecedented experience.

Rereading *The Taking of Alexandria* through the lens of fixers furthermore resituates the work's significance for its readership. Crusading is not simply the subject of Machaut's verse history; it is in fact the context from which this verse history emerges. Reading *The Taking of Alexandria* alongside crusade proposals shows that Machaut in many ways does not do anything extraordinary in verse. When Machaut chose to write his history, the conquest of Alexandria had already had a long past as an event in abeyance, since the mid-thirteenth century. If the event of Peter's raid, however brief, had great resonance in Europe, it was not simply because it was sensational but also because it was the accomplishment of a one-hundred-year-old projection. I need only mention some of the treatises of crusades whose objective was Alexandria and that preceded Machaut's composition: "The Council of King Charles II of Anjou" ("Le conseil du roi Charles II d'Anjou," 1292?), Hayton's *Flower of Histories of the East* (*La fleur des histoires d'Orient*, 1307), Foulques de Villaret's "Information and Guidance" ("Informatio et instructio," 1306) and "How the Holy Land Can Be Recovered by Christians" ("Coment la Terre Sainte puet estre recouvree par les Crestiens," 1307–8), the anonymous "The Project of the Paths of Babylon" ("La Devise des chemins de Babylone," before

1308), Marino Sanudo Torsello's *The Book of the Secrets of the Faithful of the Cross* (*Liber secretorum fidelis crucis*, 1307–21), William of Adam's *How to Defeat the Saracens* (*De modo Sarracenos extirpandi*, 1317), and Roger de Stanegrave's *The Charbuncle of Arms of the Precious Conquest of the Promised Holy Land* (*L'Escarboucle d'armes de la conquête précieuse de la Terre Sainte de promission*, 1320–32).[44] These make Machaut's verse history a far less "anachronistic" genre, because they reinscribe it squarely within the crusade debate of the best strategy for the reconquest of Jerusalem and the Holy Land: Alexandria and the sea route, or Constantinople and the land route. Moreover, Machaut actually contributes to the debate in unexpected ways. While some, but by no means all, crusade treatises consider the purpose and role of fixers, Machaut's history actually shows not only the necessity of having fixers in the conduct of war, but their pivotal role in its success. And while crusade treatises generally treat the problem of logistics, against all expectations, Machaut's verse history integrates linguistics and fixers as an absolute and fundamental element of crusading logistics. In fact, Louis of Gruuthuse's interest in Machaut may possibly be attributed to the ongoing interest in Alexandria throughout the fifteenth century, notably in Emmanuel Piloti's treatise, wherein "the city of Alexandria . . . is the mouth itself that feeds meats and life to Cairo and the rest of the land of Egypt" (la cité d'Alexandrie . . . est la bouche propre qui donne lez viandes et la vie au Cayre et aussi au reste du pays d'Egipte). Even if Jerusalem were reconquered, the sultan of Egypt would always be able to rescue Syria from Cairo. "And because of this, Christian lords, the Christian force must wait to conquer Cairo, which is the head, and deliver it the blow; then, swiftly, it will have all its members without opposition" (Et pour tant, seigneurs crestiens, la puissance de crestiens doit attendre de conquester le Cayre, qui est la teste, et li donner le cop: pourquoy subbitement se aura tous les membres, sans nulles contradictions; Piloti 1958, 116–17, 118). Piloti's treatise was translated into French in 1441, and its French manuscript likely belonged to Philip the Good, Duke of Burgundy, and is kept today in Brussels (KBR, MS 15701).[45]

Perhaps the most relevant of the treatises that preceded *The Taking of Alexandria* is a little-known crusade treatise by Roger of Stanegrave, *The Charbuncle of Arms of the Precious Conquest of the Promised Holy Land* (1320–32), written in Anglo-Norman and dedicated to Edward III of England.[46] The sole manuscript, a part of a codex on the Orient (Carpini, Hayton, descriptions of the Holy Land, fragments of Marco Polo), was badly damaged in the Cotton library fire of 1731, and Stanegrave's verse treatise is legible only in fragments. Stanegrave's work is an allegorical "carbuncle of arms" (escaboucle d'armes) in which he narrates his real experience as a prisoner of the sultan in Cairo for thirty-four years (Stanegrave 2008, lines 302–12, 327). Stanegrave's proposal was well received at the English court. On his liberation from captivity in 1318, Stanegrave presented his case to Edward II and called for a crusade in Egypt. Edward responded by intervening twice, in 1318 and 1320, with the pope and the master of the Hospitallers, seeking their help on behalf of Stanegrave.[47] One can imagine that, after his favorable reception, Stanegrave wrote down all his insider information that had stirred the usually unresponsive Edward II to action. In 1332 he presented the book to his son, Edward III, the new king of England (r. 1327–77), while preparations for a joint French-English crusade were in progress.

The allegory of the carbuncle carries the empirical details of his experience and his insider knowledge on how to attack Alexandria. Stanegrave recommends the conquest of Alexandria via Rhodes (Stanegrave 2008, lines 314–15, 349, 354–61), and especially a surprise attack after having misled the enemy, who has spies, into believing that the fleet is going to Tripoli (Stanegrave 2008, line 354). By virtue of his thirty-four-year-long captivity in Cairo, Stanegrave is the quintessential fixer, the ultimate insider (Stanegrave 2008, lines 302–12). His experience allows him to spare humiliation and waste of noble effort: "for this reason I made this present book following the place and the manner of the said passage" (pur ceo ay fait y cestui presente [livere] ensuivant en quel lieu et coment le dit passage; Stanegrave 2008, line 313). In the interplay of the practical with the allegorical and mythological, Stanegrave calls for a new Arthur or Charlemagne (Stanegrave 2008, line 336), takes as models Roland and Oliver (Stanegrave 2008, lines 335–36) and Tristan and Lancelot (Stanegrave 2008, lines 335–36, 377), and refers repeatedly to Merlin's prophecies (Stanegrave 2008, lines 295, 348–49; Stahuljak 2017). In short, the *Escarboucle* is an empirical narrative and a logistics manual couched in an allegorical-mythical narrative. In other words, Stanegrave's treatise is a quintessential example of combining allegory and fixer narratives. Such an accretion of history lessons and their allegorical transformations reinscribes Machaut completely within the crusade debate and may explain Machaut's mythological-historical "anomaly" as being in the spirit of the times. To this, we can add Mézières's allegorical treatise *Chivalry of the Order of the Passion* as another proof of real-life fixers in an allegory. Rather than emphasizing the truth of form (verse vs. prose), we can see allegory as a tool of commensuration of the magnitude of an event with the historical narrative. In turn, seeing verse, prose, and allegory through the lens of fixers allows us to see the ways in which they may have been commensurable in their own time instead of irreconcilable in modern literary history (see also chapter 5).

Fixers, Loyalty, and Literary History

The delineation between verse and prose cannot be maintained as the deciding factor in literary criticism and history. Put differently, verse is at the core of the problems that make Machaut appear suspect in his reporting of the events, just as, conversely, it is Froissart's use of prose that prevents us from getting suspicious of his reporting and displacement of tricky mediations from knights to merchants. Each writer uses his medium to commensurate in the eyewitness testimonies of recent events.

The figure of the fixer thus provides us with a different perspective on medieval history writing, where form and genre are not opposed but inform each other. This is particularly timely and in the spirit of the period because the writers and their audiences were not preoccupied with the fidelity of translation, but with their own truthfulness and allegiance to chivalry and Christianity. Fidelity of translation implies a focus on form (verse vs. prose) or on genre (chronicle vs. allegory), but it is the loyalty of persons, and their commensuration, that is under scrutiny in the medieval period. Such an analysis of fixers—where personal loyalty and commensuration bridge the divide between verse and prose, and between allegory and chronicle—gives due status to verse history and allegory in both literary and historical research. The fixer paradigm gives us a way to commensurate verse, prose, and allegory.

Machaut, Froissart, and Mézières bring out another crucial dimension of translation in the European Middle Ages. They record and embody the emergence of writers as fixers in the world, who are no longer translators confined to their study, but are active intermediaries to kings or publics, in state politics or in memorial politics of the fourteenth century. This emergence of translators as fixers in the world, in text and image, is the subject of the next chapter.

Fixer Literature

In the fourteenth century, we saw writers take an agentive role in the world as intermediaries to kings and publics, and be active in the affairs of the government and state, and in memorial politics. Machaut, Mézières, and Froissart stepped out of their study into the world, they abandoned the role of translators enclosed within walls, and, by venturing outside, they became fixers. This movement from interior to exterior is also a move from written to oral, from passive to active. It transforms the translator—who was a maker of objects of knowledge and an end point in a binary relationship of transmission from and to the patron—into a fixer who is part of a chain of transmission and an interface in a larger network. This chapter, the continuation of questions asked in the previous chapter, takes the historical figure of the fixer and the apparatus of the fixer to task in addressing two broad concerns relevant to translation in the European Middle Ages: primacy of translation (translation as originary and not derivative of an earlier "original") and translation as process (and not product or object). Here, "fixers" are analyzed as linguistic and cultural agents who traffic in translations and as state agents who act as international powerbrokers or as a fixer state. In short, this chapter expands from the historical, descriptive analysis of the fixer to a conceptual use of the fixer paradigm to understand the social, cultural, and artistic phenomena of the late medieval western Europe, and our modern scholarly narratives about them.

From the modern perspective, translation often appears to be an invisible and undervalued process, tangible only in the object it produces, beholden to the greatness of the original, handmaiden to creative genius. But in the medieval world, translation is pivotal and primary. In contradistinction to modern translation, late medieval translation presents itself as the primary text and takes precedence over any notion of "original." The primacy of translation is embodied in the vogue of pseudotranslation that attains its apex at the court of the Dukes of Burgundy in the fifteenth century: many new and updated older narratives were labeled as translations alongside actual translations of older works. This literature of pseudotranslations and translations—that I call "fixer literature"—was commissioned by the Burgundian dukes, by their entourage of counselors who offered manuscripts as gifts to the dukes, and by the noble and bourgeois Burgundian elites. Medieval illuminators put the phenomenon of translation on display when they pictured the translator in the frontispieces of these secular luxury manuscripts. In fact, they developed distinct compositions to represent translation. Evidence indicates that the Burgundian involvement in a new crusade across the Mediterranean Sea (*outremer*), its imperial ambitions on the European continent, and its position as a fixer state, on the one hand, between England and France and, on the other, between the eastern Mediterranean and western Europe, led to an artistic formula for representation of translation in frontispieces as primary and as a process. Artists showed the translator as an agent active in a larger network in the world, that is as a fixer, outside of an exclusive binary relation in which he would be only at the command of a patron. The fixer apparatus on display in manuscript illumination renders visible the translation process, the "making of" translation as a total social phenomenon.

Fixers were the focal point of literary and manuscript production, and of social and political history in fifteenth-century Burgundy. Zooming in, fixers were characters or actors of major importance in narratives, where interlingual communication was seen and portrayed as a strategic component of any expansion or crusade. This literature was used to explore possible scenarios both for a Burgundian crusade across the Mediterranean Sea in medieval Syria (*outremer*) and for Burgundian imperial expansion on the European continent. At an intermediate level, writers presented and enacted themselves as agents of (socio-cultural) translation, as interpreters of the world; even writers of new works presented their output as translations. Translation and communication seemed to have an aura of prestige that no "original" rivaled. Zooming out, ducal counselors acted as fixers when they commissioned (pseudo)translations for the duke in view of the political and economic interests of the duchy. Ducal advisers were thus not acting in separate roles of political counselors, on the one hand, and of literary advisers, on the other. Quite the opposite, literature was a policy and a politics. Burgundy itself, at a level of a state formation, was not a kingdom but an independent duchy—a fixer state—that flourished in the conflicts of larger kingdoms, until its final transformation into a world empire: the Valois Burgundian dukes, after the conclusion of their dynastic alliance with the Habsburgs in 1477, gave birth to the Habsburg Spanish dynasty, and Burgundian Netherlands became central to the Spanish Empire for many decades after becoming part of it.

This chapter thus uses the fixer apparatus to provide a paradigmatic reading of the political, social, and art histories in the pivotal moment of the late fifteenth century. Through the lens of fixers, this chapter argues for a reevaluation of Burgundian politics, and of artistic and literary production that is more in line with the high appreciation of southern Netherlandish painting, sometimes referred to as the Northern Renaissance (Wijsman 2010d; Wijsman 2009). Fixers and translation as organizing principles of Burgundian cultural and political life go against the notion that Burgundy embodied "the waning of the Middle Ages," the dying embers in contrast to the renewal of the Renaissance.[1] Rather, the Burgundian example shows the vitality of translation and of fixers in the long Middle Ages; the Middle Ages were waning only if we measure them against the modern notions of state centralization, nation (and nation-state), authorship, and individuality. If, however, we adopt the fixer paradigm and translation as process, we will come to understand the extraordinary transformation of the Valois Burgundian dukes into the Valois-Habsburg Spanish kings and emperors, ruling over the largest world empire and creating the base for the long cross-pollination of Netherlandish and Spanish (and even Portuguese) arts, science, and trade for over two hundred years, from the early 1500s until the Wars of the Spanish Succession in the early 1700s.

The Making of Burgundy: The Hundred Years' War and the Crusades

By 1435, the Hundred Years' War was drawing to a close: in that year, Duke Philip the Good (r. 1419–67) signed the Arras peace treaty with King Charles VII of France (r. 1422/1429–14), thereby abandoning the English alliance that he had forged in the aftermath of the assassination of his father, John the Fearless, which the entourage of the Dauphin, the future Charles VII, had orchestrated in 1419. In exchange, the duke was exempted from homage to the French crown, thus reaffirming the autonomy of the duchy, which had been given in 1363 by King John II of France to his fourth and youngest son, Philip the Bold, as an *apanage*.[2] Burgundian dukes remained vassals to French kings only nominally, since the duchy's territory had never been absorbed into the royal domains when John II first inherited the duchy in 1361. The 1435 peace with France coincided with the Burgundian expansion and unification of the Low Countries. The construction of the Burgundian Low Countries, also known as the

Burgundian Netherlands, began in 1384 with the death of Louis of Male, Count of Flanders. His daughter, Margaret of Flanders, married in 1369 Philip the Bold, who thus inherited the counties of Flanders, Rethel, Nevers, Artois, and Franche-Comté, and the cities of Antwerp and Mechelen.[3] After a long protracted fight that had begun in 1419, Philip's grandson, Philip the Good, gradually but forcibly also annexed the territories of Hainaut, Holland, and Zeeland from his cousin, Jacqueline de Bavière, in 1428 (taking office in 1433). He also purchased Namur in 1429 and inherited both Brabant and Limbourg in 1430.[4] Thus around 1435, at the same time that the Duke of Burgundy reasserted his independence from the French crown as a consequence of the Hundred Years' War, he grew bigger and more powerful than ever. Then Philip conquered Luxembourg in 1443 (and was recognized by the Estates of Luxembourg in 1451; Blockmans and Prevenier 1999, 104–5). All these acquisitions were the result of childless and bankrupt dynasties, and they were carved out of the border regions of France and the Holy Roman Empire. They increased the duke's original southern possessions of the Duchy of Burgundy and the County of Burgundy (Stein 2017, 2). Nevertheless, the sprawling Burgundian possessions had one potentially fatal flaw: the territories of the Burgundian Low Countries, known as "the lands here" (les pays par deçà), and the Duchy of Burgundy, whose capital was Dijon, "the lands there" (les pays par-delà), were noncontiguous (Bousmanne and Delcourt 2011, 40; Cockshaw 1974).

As peace returned to the West after the appeasement of the Hundred Years' War in 1435, the duke set his sights on enhancing his European stature and brandishing his international image. The pillar of his strategy was his Mediterranean policy, which was intended ultimately to lead to a new crusade. Christian princes upheld a general commitment to reconquering Jerusalem ever since the fall of Acre in 1291, which had been the last Christian foothold in Asia Minor. But the Burgundian crusading project moreover had direct roots in the trauma of the Battle of Nicopolis experienced by Philip the Good's father, John the Fearless, who during the lifetime of his own father, Duke Philip the Bold, was Count John of Nevers. The defeat of the French-Burgundian forces by the Ottomans and John of Nevers's dramatic capture by Sultan Bayezid I took place in September 1396 at Nicopolis, three months after John's son Philip was born (see chapter 3). More than three hundred nobles and knights perished in the battle and the subsequent massacre ordered by Bayezid. Only twenty, or at most twenty-three, nobles survived along with the Count of Nevers, who returned to Burgundy and France in 1398 after months of ransom negotiations. In his *Letter of Lament and Consolation* (*Une epistre lamentable et consolatoire*, 1397), Philip of Mézières instituted Philip the Good's grandfather and the first Valois Duke of Burgundy, Philip the Bold, as the leader of a new crusade to avenge Nicopolis. Similarly, in the final book (4) of his *Chronicles* (ca. 1396–1400), Mézières's contemporary Jean Froissart, chronicler and secretary, cast the future return of the Burgundians to the east as an invitation from the sultan himself to John of Nevers: "I thus wish that, when you will have returned over there and it will so please you, you gather your forces and come against me" (Ainchois vueil que, quant tu seras retourné par delà, et il te vendra à plaisance, que tu assambles ta puissance et viengnes encontre moy; Froissart 1867–77, 16:47).

Philip's third marriage, to Isabel of Portugal, and the support of a Portuguese crusade against the Kingdom of Morocco may have been the initial motivation for the construction of the Burgundian naval fleet, initiated in 1438.[5] But, in response to papal encouragements, Philip expanded the plans to the eastern Mediterranean, sending a fleet of seven ships from his Atlantic port of Sluis (present-day Holland) to provide military support to the Knights Hospitaller of Rhodes: "He made the Moors fear his sails, and with his anchors he terrified pagan lands; he saved Rhodes and lifted its siege; he built the church of Nazareth; in the holy city of Jerusalem and in the Holy Land, he created many generous benefices; he provided great aid and reinforcements on the borders with pagans; he always remained loyal to the Holy See of Rome" (fit aux Mores redoubter ses voiles, et par ses ancres trembler les terres payennes; sauva Rhodes et la délivra de son obsession; édifia l'église de Nazaret; en la sainte cité de Hiérusalem et en la Terre-Sainte fit de moult beaux bénéfices; fit de grans secours et prestances sur les frontières des payens; adhéroit tousjours au Saint-Siége de Rome).[6] In 1444, Philip named his chamberlain and counselor, Waleran de Wavrin, "commander of the army and fleet of the Levant" (Naber 1987, 284). Aiming to position himself as the defender of Christianity, the duke reinforced his tactics around 1450.[7] His first public commitment to a crusade was made at the chapter of the chivalric Order of the Golden Fleece (Ordre de la Toison d'or) held in May 1451 in Mons; it was spearheaded by Bishop Jean Germain, the chancellor of the duke's order. The duke proposed to take the cross and lead a new crusade to the East. His plan was received without enthusiasm by the European rulers, and it was especially discouraged by both the French king Charles VII, who preferred to direct his resources toward evicting the last of the English from the Continent, and the king of Aragon, who denied the duke the leadership of the crusade, claiming it for himself because he was titular king of Jerusalem. But when in 1453 Constantinople fell to the Ottoman Turks, Pope Nicolas V (1447–55) launched another call for a crusade. Philip the Good, the son of John the Fearless, responded to the call by taking the cross in 1454 at the famed Feast of the Pheasant (Le Banquet du faisan), held in Lille on February 17, 1454.

The Feast of the Pheasant, a sumptuous illustration of the duke's crusading project and the apex of the Burgundian enactment of its own importance and wealth, was organized around Saint Andrew, the patron saint of Burgundy.[8] Saint Andrew, one of the first disciples of Christ with his brother Peter (Simon), was an Eastern saint whose cult took hold late, in fifteenth-century Burgundy. In the early fifteenth century, John the Fearless had adopted the cross of Saint Andrew, a cross in the shape of an X (for Christ) on which Saint Andrew is said to have been crucified. It became the sign that distinguished the Burgundians from the Armagnacs in their struggle for control over the French royal throne in the early fifteenth century. When John's grandson, Charles the Bold, established a professional army in 1473, its soldiers wore the Saint Andrew's cross. It was John's son and Charles's father, Philip the Good, who proclaimed Saint Andrew, who had evangelized a number of eastern lands, the patron saint of Burgundy and of his new chivalric Order of the Golden Fleece.[9] Duke Philip founded the order in Bruges in 1430, on the occasion of his marriage to Isabel of Portugal. It was to become the most successful and coveted of numerous similar princely initiatives, rivaled only by the Order of the Garter (founded by King Edward III of England, ca. 1348) and the Order of the Collar (founded by the Count of Savoy, Amédée VI, in 1363–64; Pastoureau 1996). The rationale offered for the order's foundation was to honor the "knights of old" (anchiens chevaliers), to encourage those "who at present are strong and vigorous of body" (qui de présent sont puissants et de force de corps), and to legitimize the aspirations to membership of knights and noblemen. But the order was also established "to pay due respect to God and to defend the holy Christian faith" (pour le respect dû à Dieu et pour la défense de la sainte foi chrétienne; De Smedt 2000, 1–2).

Crusades were an important part of the ducal library. Between 1363 and 1477, during the reigns of four Valois dukes, Alexander the Great, a major crusading and imperial figure in the European Middle Ages, was the subject of about thirty works—historical, didactic, and romance—appearing in sixty-six manuscripts.[10] The ducal library also contained about a dozen manuscripts of crusading treatises (e.g., Pseudo-Brocardus, Hayton, Marino Sanudo, Ghillbert de Lannoy, Bertrandon de la Broquière; see appendix A, section 1). The inventory of John the Fearless's library from 1420 indicates that he owned the original of Mézières's *Letter of Lament and Consolation*, with the arms of Philip the Bold (KBR, MS 10486; Contamine and Paviot 2008, 75–82; Doutrepont 1906, 74–76). And the library inventory completed in 1469, after Philip the Good's death in

1467, contained an entire section dedicated to the lands overseas: "*Ou-tremer, medicine, and astrology*" (Oultremer, medecines et astrologie; seventy-four items).[11]

The build-up of the library, just like that of the fleet and the army; the creation of the Order of the Golden Fleece; the declaration of the patron saint; and the taking of the crusading vows at the Feast of the Pheasant—all converged toward the realization of the long-term crusading project of Philip the Good. However, Burgundian internal problems—the Ghent wars (1449–53) and dissensions and conflict between Duke Philip and his own son Charles (1457–February 1464)—obstructed any serious action. Finally, in 1463–64, a crusade was mounted, but the new French king Louis XI (r. 1461–83) did not grant leave to the duke, his vassal, under the pretext of formally reestablishing peace with England and requiring his assistance. To keep the crusade promise made to Pope Pius II (1458–64), the duke appointed as commander his bastard son, Anthony, the Great Bastard of Burgundy, but Pius's death in August 1464 canceled the crusade. The duke died in June 1467, a month before his seventy-first birthday, leaving his crusading dream unfulfilled. With Charles the Bold's ascension to the duchy (r. 1467–77), the crusading dreams progressively receded into the past as Charles became increasingly embroiled in a prolonged conflict, first, with Louis XI of France (1472) and, then, with the Swiss confederacy and the Duke of Lorraine (1474–77). Charles died in 1477 at the siege of Nancy in Lorraine, while trying to unite his noncontiguous territories, the lands "here and there."

Burgundy, a Fixer State

The balance of power that the Burgundians held in the later phase of the Hundred Years' War between France and England, between 1418 and 1435, crystalized their position as fixers. At least two generations of Valois Burgundian dukes thought of themselves as powerbrokers; Georges Chastellain, Burgundy's official historiographer, declared that Philip the Good "held the key to the preservation of France and, in his hand, the peace in the West" (tenoit le salut de France en sa clef et la tranquillité d'Occident en sa main; Chastellain 1865, 217; Thiry 1995, 752). The original autonomy of the Duke of Burgundy, vassal only in name to the king of France, did not come into play during Philip the Bold's lifetime, but the ascension of his son John the Fearless, at Philip's death in 1404, brought out the fragility of the Kingdom of France and the unique potential of the Burgundian position. While King Charles VI of France was increasingly incapacitated by his bouts of madness, his cousin, John the Fearless, and brother, Louis of Orleans, fought to fill the power vacuum. John had Louis assassinated in 1406, starting a civil war that by 1420 brought the French Kingdom north of the Loire river under the English rule and threatened its outright fall: John did not join Charles VI at the Battle of Agincourt (1415), which the French tragically lost, and he watched the English conquer Normandy and Rouen (1417–19) without intervening while he himself occupied Paris (1418; Vaughan 1969). Philip the Good decisively shifted the balance of power in the Hundred Years' War by formally switching the Burgundian allegiance to the English, in the wake of the 1419 assassination of his father John by the party of the Dauphin, Charles VI's son. The 1420 Treaty of Troyes disinherited the Dauphin and gave the English king the city of Paris and the throne of France. Burgundians became kingmakers. In 1430, they captured, and sold to the English, Joan of Arc, who had defeated the English at the siege of Orleans in May 1429 and in June had led the Dauphin to be crowned as Charles VII of France at Reims. Despite Joan's death in 1431 and French setbacks, Orleans was the turning point from which the English never recovered, causing irreparable divisions in their management of war and resources. In 1435, Philip restored the balance of power on the Continent by signing the Treaty of Arras with the king of France.

In this role of fixer, the court of Burgundy played host to knights from all the Christian nations: "Travelers from all of Christianity traveled to his domain; they came there to combat in battle and find renown, . . . and of the multitude that appeared before him over time, not one was refused. He was arrayed with knights from across the world, the exquisite body of this kingdom, and, among a thousand others, the most remarkable ones; no one on earth was in better or as good company" (De toute chrestienté les voyageurs se rendoient en sa maison; y vinrent faire armes et los quérir de toutes nations; . . . et de multitude qui y sont comparus en divers temps, oncques un n'en partit à refus. Avoit le parement des chevaliers du monde emprès luy, les corps exquis de ce royaume, et entre mille autres d'ailleurs les plus voyables; n'avoit mieux accompagné de luy, ne si bien en la terre"; Chastellain 1865, 217; Thiry 1995, 751). Moreover, ever since the ransom and return of John of Nevers from Ottoman captivity, the court was also teeming with Turks, Arabs, and Greeks (Paviot 2003, 273–90). In 1461, Duke Philip adopted a title, which Burgundian chroniclers used to describe him, of "le Grand Duc du Ponant," the Great Duke of the West.[12] Identifying the duchy with the West appears to situate it at the opposite extreme of the Mediterranean and the East, as if embodying a western essence. But this title was discerned by ambassadors from Trebizond, Persia, and (present-day) Armenia, Georgia, and Iraq, who arrived at Philip the Good's court in May 1461 on the way to the coronation of

Louis XI of France in August in Reims. It was thus the Levant that named the Ponant, and the East that was designating the West and reflecting its stature in East-West relationships. The duchy may have not been elevated to a kingdom, but it was the compulsory passage in dealing with European kingdoms, the ducal fixer brokering relationships with other western kingdoms. The duke's historiographer Chastellain said it succinctly: "East and West, in the heaven's vault, everything swelled his sails; everything aspired and yielded to him" (Orient et Occident, à la croisure du ciel, tout souffloit dans ses voiles; tout aspiroit et tournoit en ses acquiescences"; Chastellain 1865, 226; Thiry 1995, 757).

Over several decades of the Hundred Years' War, the Valois Burgundians were kingmakers but held no royal title themselves. And yet, "by his appearance alone, he was imperial; he deserved a crown, by sheer grace of nature" (son semblant seulement le jugeoit empereur; et valoit de porter couronne, seulement sur les grâces de nature; Chastellain 1865, 220; Thiry 1995, 753). The turn to the Mediterranean after 1440 and the germination of crusade plans for the recovery of the Kingdom of Jerusalem through an intense diplomatic activity with the papacy and the Christian East— Rhodes, Cyprus, and the Near East—were one aspect of ducal royal ambitions. After the Hundred Years' War and the unification of the Burgundian Low Countries, Philip also began to pursue a royal crown from the Holy Roman emperor Frederick III in 1447 by trying to elevate Frisia into a kingdom; this was possible as Frisia had been part of the Holy Roman Empire. A royal title within the empire would have been the stepping stone to the imperial title, the ultimate goal. But the emperor would not let Philip include all his territories into the new kingdom; the plan was dropped in 1448.[13] The duke kept the dream of a title alive in later negotiations. In 1463, the emperor again offered a crown, and even the office of imperial vicar, in exchange for a marriage between Philip's granddaughter Mary (Charles's daughter, b. 1457) and Emperor Frederick's son Maximilian (b. 1459), Archduke of Austria, but Philip declined to bring the Valois Low Countries so close to the orbit of the empire.[14] After Philip's death and under Charles the Bold, a Burgundy-Habsburg alliance through a marriage of Charles's daughter Mary and the emperor's son Maximilian was resurrected again in 1472–73. With Charles's plans to conquer Lorraine and unite the noncontiguous Burgundian territories, which resulted in his premature death in 1477, the alliance was part of the effort to reactualize the imperial Lotharingia of the Carolingian era that in the ninth century, under Lothair, stretched from Frisia and the North Sea to Provence and Lombardy and down into the Italian peninsula.

Burgundy, a Translation Zone

A fixer state whose court gathered knights from all corners of the known world was a translation zone. Burgundy was already predisposed to translation, because translation was first and foremost a matter of daily governance. French was the official language of the Burgundian court but was also native to much of the southern Netherlands. Netherlandish was native to Brabant, Flanders, and Holland. The linguistic complexity of the ducal domains required regular translation and bilingual officers. The ruling class was often bilingual (Armstrong 1983). The manuscript of *Privileges and Statutes of Ghent and Flanders from 1241 to 1453* (*Collectio statutorum, privilegiorum et documentorum urbes Flandriae et inprimis Gandavum concernentium*, Vienna, ÖNB, Cod. 2583) is a striking example of the trilingualism of the Burgundian Netherlands that the management of the duchy required: the statutes were written in French and Netherlandish, occasionally using Latin as a language of intermediation.

Beyond the practical administration of a complex, noncontiguous state, Burgundians understood well the political impact of translation in the vernacular. The Burgundian translation movement was characterized by commissions of works updated into prose Middle French either from earlier Old French verse (prosification) or from Latin (translation), although new narratives were also being composed in Middle French.[15] The ability to build cultural capital by sponsoring a translation movement projected the ability to reign, and doubly so: with an autonomous, local book production of narratives and manuscripts, and with the types of stories told in new or readapted (refurbished) narratives. Although Philip the Good's pursuit of the royal and imperial titles was ultimately unsuccessful, it is in the context of his ambitions that he began to commission works promoting Burgundy to its ancient status of kingdom and employing exclusively writers and translators as well as scribal and artistic workshops of the Burgundian Netherlands, especially in Flanders and Brabant. Prior to this shift, until the early 1440s, the Dukes of Burgundy purveyed themselves of manuscripts in Paris, copying works of French writers and using Parisian workshops of bookmakers and sellers, that is book agents (*libraires*; Rouse and Rouse 2000, 1:14). But by the middle of the fifteenth century, the Burgundian Netherlands became well established as the preeminent site for manuscript illumination of secular and devotional books in Europe. In March 1446, in a meeting in Lille, Philip commissioned three translations from Jean Wauquelin established in Mons, Hainaut: *Chronicles of Hainaut* (*Chroniques de Hainaut*), *Girart of Roussillon* (*Girart de Roussillon*), and *Deeds and Conquests of Alexander the Great* (*Faits et conquêtes d'Alexandre le Grand*).[16] These three would be the backbone of the ducal library produced locally.

The first to be completed, the *Chronicles* is a history of the County of Hainaut, the centerpiece of Burgundian expansion in 1433 (Brussels, KBR, MSS 9242–44; Cockshaw 2000b). Wauquelin translated the *Chronicles* from a Latin history written by Jacques de Guise in the second half of the fourteenth century, *Historical Annals of the Noble Princes of Hainaut* (*Annales histoire illustrium principum Hannonie*).[17] According to Wauquelin's translation, Guise wished to reassemble the "history of the kingdom of the Belgians or of the principality of Hainaut, which are the same and very ancient" (histoire du regne de Belges ou de la princie de Haynnau, que pour une meiseme cose ont et tiennent moult d'anchiens; KBR, MS 9242, fol. 6). In the ancient—pre-Roman—times, Hainaut was a large territory of "noble Belgium" (la noble Belge; KBR, MS 9242, fol. 5v), incorporating most of the Burgundian Low Countries and spreading into the territory of the Holy German Empire. By Wauquelin's time, it was ruled "in the year 1446 of the incarnation of our lord Jesus Chris, by my most feared lord, prince by grace of my most feared lady, Madam Marguerite of Bavaria" (l'an de l'incarnacion nostre seigneur Ihesu Crist 1446, princes mon dit tresredoubte signeur de par ma tresredoutee dame, madame Margherite de Baviere; KBR, MS 9242, fol. 1v).

The second commissioned translation to be completed, *Girart of Roussillon* is a prose epic translated from an anonymous late eleventh- or early twelfth-century Latin chronicle and a twelfth-century French decasyllabic *chanson de geste* (Vienna, ÖNB, Cod. 2549).[18] It retells the deeds of Girart, the first historical Duke of (southern) Burgundy who "was lord of all Burgundy, and not only of the whole of Burgundy, but of Auvergne, Gascony, Avignon, Limousin, Auxerre, Tournay, Nevers, and a major portion of Spain and Germany; his lordship extended from the Rhine River to the city of Bayonne in Spain, but without duchies and counties like Flanders and others, of which we will speak henceforth" (fut seigneur de toute la seignorie de Bourgoigne, et non mie seulement de toute Bourgoigne, mais de Auvergne, de Gascoigne, d'Avignon, de Lymosin, d'Ausserre, de Tournerre, de Nevers et de la plus grant partie de toute le province d'Espaigne et d'Almaigne; car sa seignorie duroit depuis la rivière du Rhin jusques à la cité de Bayonne qui siet en Espaigne, sans les autres duchiés et contés comme Flandres et autres dont nous parlerons cy après). Wauquelin affirmed that the duke was now lord over some, albeit not all, of Girart's territories (Wauquelin 1880, 2–3). The historical Girart at once validated the claim of the Valois Dukes of Burgundy to autonomy from the French crown and legitimized their ducal title; the literary Girart valiantly fought to maintain his lands and title against Charles the Bald, until reconciliation and submission to the king, much like Philip did against the French kings Charles VI and Charles VII between 1419 and 1435.[19]

Burgundian archives indicate that in the 1446 meeting in Mons, the duke wished to discuss with Wauquelin "the matters related to the translation of several histories of the lands ruled by my said lord" (aucunes affaires touchant la translacion de plusieurs histoires des pais de mondit seigneur; LDB-V 2015, 23), that is, southern Burgundian possessions, "the lands there" (les pays par-delà), the origin of the duchy and evidence of the ancient status of Kingdom of Burgundy (*Girart*), and Hainaut, "the lands here" (les pays par deça), the centerpiece of northern expansion into Burgundian Netherlands (*Chronicles of Hainaut*). In Wauquelin's day, Hainaut and southern Burgundy were noncontiguous, united only by the same ruler, the Duke of Burgundy. This is where the translation of *The Deeds and Conquests of Alexander the Great* (fig. 4.1) plays a role, clarifying the three ducal commissions not as separate acts, but as a coherent and contiguous trilogy of commissions.

The noncontiguous Hainaut and southern Burgundy are given territorial cohesion within the imperial framework of *The Deeds and Conquests of Alexander the Great*. This work was copied last and was a compilation of prosifications of verse Alexander romances written by Alexandre de Paris and Lambert Le Tort and translations mainly from the anonymous Latin *Historia de preliis Alexandri Magni* (*The Wars of Alexander the Great*).[20] Wauquelin's prose compilation thus tells the legendary story of "the deeds and conquests of that mighty and feared emperor Alexander. Now, it is universally recognized that his prowess won him lordship and kingship over all the earth, both East and West" (les fais et les conquestes du trespuissant et tresredoubtet empereur Alixandre lequel comme la commune fame et renomee tesmongnent fu roy et seigneur par sa proesce de toute la terre d'Orient et d'Occident).[21] The all-encompassing vault of East and West that we saw earlier in Chastellain's ducal legend is here put to work. Jean Wauquelin's *Deeds and Conquests of Alexander* justify the Burgundian present—the simultaneous rule over the Burgundian Netherlands (*les pays par deça*) and the Duchy of Burgundy (*les pays par-delà*)—with an imperial past, the most glorious of all. In the prologue to book 2, which retells Alexander's conquests in the (marvelous) East, Wauquelin inserts his already completed translation of the *Chronicles of Hainaut* to create a narrative of a contiguous Burgundy.[22] According to the *Chronicles of Hainaut*, Alexander was "lord of the whole of France and all neighboring lands" (seigneur de Franche et de toutes les marces adjacentes) and

FIGURE 4.1: Master of Wauquelin's Alexander and Master of Girart de Roussillon-Dreux, *Jean Wauquelin Presenting a Book to Duke Philip*. From *Faits et conquêtes d'Alexandre le Grand*, Bruges, 1448–49. Paris, BnF, MS fr. 9342, f. 5r. Photograph: Bibliothèque nationale de France.

of "Picardy and Artois and especially Hainaut, Flanders, Brabant, Liège, Hesbaye and several other neighbouring lands," lands under the present-day rule of Philip the Good. These territories were known in Alexander's time under the name of "Forest Carbonniere," where maiden Lirope, who received them from Alexander, reigned.[23] Thus, in a few folios, between 127 and 131, Wauquelin established Alexander as the Lord of the West and the East, from the Burgundian Low Countries to India. The explicit return to the *Chronicles of Hainaut*, the first translation in the commission trilogy, elucidates the larger framework; with the insertion of Alexander's conquest of the West, Wauquelin made the world of West and East into one, "his prowess won him lordship and kingship over all the earth, both East and West." Not only were these lands part of a large East-West Empire, such as the duke may have been aspiring to in his crusading ambitions, but Wauquelin indirectly addressed the genealogical connection between an imperial Burgundy and Alexander's empire.[24]

The trilogy thus proposed the unity of two noncontiguous territories—southern Burgundy (*Girart of Roussillon*) and Hainaut (*Chronicles of Hainaut*)—within an Alexandrine imperial framework (*Deeds and Conquests of Alexander the Great*). Wauquelin's methods, imperial in scope, were translation and prosification. The trilogy also reconstructed the ancient Carolingian Kingdom of Lotharingia. In this frame, Burgundian Lotharingia stretched, uninterrupted, from the North Sea to the Italian Peninsula and the Mediterranean. This was consistent with Burgundian imperial policy, begun under Philip the Good and enacted under Charles the Bold, to unite the Low Countries and the Duchy of Burgundy into a continuous territory inclusive of Lorraine and Liège, the very efforts that will culminate with Charles's death at the siege of Nancy in 1477.

Translation and Empire in Burgundian Libraries

In the second half of the fifteenth century, the court of Burgundy was a vast translation zone that instrumentalized translation to promote its own political interests as a subject matter. These first three commissions were cultural capital of an ambitious duke, looking to raise the stature of the duchy to a royal and imperial title. Wauquelin, translator and valet to the duke, and his scribe Jacotin du Bois, were paid in April 1448 for the three works produced in record time, just when in 1447 Philip began to seek the path to the imperial title through the Holy Roman Emperor Frederic. Dynasty building through stimulating translation but also new cultural production ran through the veins of the Valois Dukes of Burgundy. Philip the Bold, the first of the Valois Dukes of Burgundy, shared the love of the letters with his brothers, King Charles V of France and Duke John of Berry. John II of France, their father, initiated the translation of Latin classics into the French vernacular with Pierre Bersuire's translation of Titus-Livy in 1354–56 (Rychner 1963; Tesnière 2000). His son, Charles V, employed translators from Latin into French for some of the most revered and widely circulated medieval works: Jean Corbechon (Bartholomeus Anglicus, *On the Properties of Things* [*Livre des propriétés des choses*], 1372), Denis Foulechat (John of Salisbury, *Policraticus*, 1372), Raoul de Presle (Saint Augustine, *The City of God* [*La cité de Dieu*], 1371–75), Nicole Oresme (Aristotle, *Nichomachean Ethics, Politics, Economics* [*Ethiques, politiques, yconomiques*], 1370–74), Simon de Hesdin (Valerius Maximus, *Memorable Doings and Sayings* [*Faits et dits mémorables*], 1375),[25] and Nicolas de Gonesse (Valerius Maximus, *Memorable Doings and Sayings*, 1401); and Laurent de Premierfait translated for John of Berry (Boccaccio, *On the Fates of Illustrious Men and Women* [*Des cas des nobles hommes et femmes*], first version 1400, second version 1409). John of Berry's library had about three hundred volumes at his death in 1416 while Charles V's and Charles VI's library had 827 volumes when it was spoliated by the English Duke of Bedford in 1424–25.[26] When Philip the Bold's grandson, Philip the Good, succeeded at the head of the duchy after the assassination of John the Fearless, according to the 1420 inventory, the ducal library had 248 volumes (Doutrepont 1906; Falmagne and van den Abeele 2016). At the time of Philip the Good's death, the library had grown to almost nine hundred titles, some of them consisting of several volumes, according to the 1467–69 inventory.[27] In 1477, the year of Charles the Bold's premature death at the siege of Nancy, the library had almost one thousand volumes (Charles added about eighty-five volumes; Bousmanne and Delcourt 2011, 104; Falmagne and van den Abeele 2016, 272–77).

David Aubert, Philip's "escripvain" or secretary, described the extent of the literary and translation activity at the court of Burgundy in the dedicatory prologue to a universal history, the *Abbreviated History of Emperors*, or *Chronicle of Baudouin d'Avesnes* (*Histoire abrégée des empereurs*, or *Chronique dite de Baudouin d'Avesnes*),[28] that he copied for Philip in 1462:

> And to inform you, this truly renowned and truly virtuous prince has been accustomed for a long time to have daily readings of ancient histories performed. And in order to be appointed with a library without comparison to any other, he has since an early age employed several translators, principal secretaries, skilled readers, illuminators, and writers, working diligently in great numbers in different provinces.

(Et pour vous avertir icelluy tresrenommé et tres vertueux prince a des long temps acoustumé de journellement faire devant luy lire les anciennes histoires. Et pour estre garny d'une librairie non pareille a toutes autres, il a des son jenne eage eu a ses gaiges plusieurs translatteurs, grans clers, expers orateurs, ystoriens et escripvains et en diverses contrees en groz nombre dilligamment labourans.) (Paris, Bibliothèque de l'Arsenal, MS 5089, fol. Q.)

Indeed, after Wauquelin (1445/46–52), Jean Miélot (1448–69) and David Aubert (1458–69) were commonly associated with Philip's commissions, until his death in 1467 (Wijsman 2010b; Cockshaw 2000a). By 1460, Raoul Lefèvre, another writer in the ducal entourage, called the duke "the father of writers" (pere des escripvains; Pinkernell 1971, 125, edition of Paris, Arsenal, MS 5067, fol. C). After his initial commission trilogy, the duke continued to pursue the sponsorship of translation and local manuscript production. Aubert conveys this whirlwind of activity, in which politics and literature coincide:

He is today the Christian prince without any doubt the best appointed with an original and rich library, as can be seen clearly. And as much as this is a small thing in comparison to his most excellent and most noble magnificence, nevertheless this should be remembered forever in order for all others to imitate his high virtues in which he has invested all his time. And especially, with his wisdom and conduct, he has held Christianity in great peace, on account of his humility and goodness, and he has refused great lordships that were offered to him, not wanting to usurp another. To conclude, he is today the most honored prince, the most loved, the most feared, and the most renowned of all monarchs in the world.

(Au jourdhuy cest le prince de la chretienté sans reservation aucune qui est le mieulx garny de autentique et riche librairie comme tout ce peoult plainement apparoir. Et combien que au regard de sa tresexcellente et tresnoble magnificence ce soit petit de chose, touteffois en doit il estre perpetuelle memoire a celle fin que tous autres se mirent cy apres en ses haultes vertus ou il a tout son temps habondé et par especial par son sens et conduitte il a tenu la chretienté en grant paix, par son humilité et debonnaireté il a refusé les grandes seignouries quy luy estoient presentees non veuillant usurper lautruy. Et en conclusion cest pour le jourdhuy le plus honnouré prince, le plus amé, le plus redoubté et le plus renommé de toute la monarcie du monde.) (Paris, Bibliothèque de l'Arsenal, MS 5089, fols. Q-Qv)

Writing in 1462, while Philip's hope for a royal and imperial title was still alive, Aubert transformed ducal political ambitions into a peacemaking mission. The duke is portrayed as a fixer who has brokered and maintained peace in the Christian realm, in part by refusing titles offered to him. The duke's historiographer Chastellain reported that the duke refused the imperial title three times in his lifetime.[29] Aubert makes a clear connection between book collecting and peacemaking, inviting all readers and listeners to hold the duke as a model. The magnificence of the ducal library is a substitute for imperial ambition and war. Aubert seems to suggest that great rulers should "make libraries, not war." Similarly, Vasco da Lucena, in his 1468 translation of *The Deeds of Alexander the Great* (*Les fais du grand Alexandre*), dedicated to Charles the Bold, called Philip "the Alexander of our time, for he revealed himself so valiant in conquests, more magnanimous in the refusal of principalities, kingdoms, and empires than Alexander ever showed himself in conquering them" (Alexandre du nostre [temps], car il se monstra si vaillant en conquester, plus magnanime en refuser principautez, royaumes et empires que Alexandre ne se monstra oncques en yceulx conquerant; Paris, BnF, MS fr. 2254, fol. 1v). If peace is what characterizes the duke's politics, then culture raises him to the highest status. In Aubert's 1462 description, the duke's rich library is greater than any king's. It is the size of the library that makes Philip more king than all kings by title; its abundance makes him king of kings, "the most honored prince, the most loved, the most feared, and the most renowned of all monarchs in the world." Aubert reiterates his praise in 1463, in a similar, albeit shorter, description in his copy of the *History of the Three Sons of Kings* (*Histoire des trois fils de rois*, or *Chronique de Naples*, or *Chronique royale*): "Although he is the prince the best appointed with the most rich and noble library in the world, he is most inclined and desirous to enlarge it daily, as is the case" (Et nonobstant que ce soit le prince sur tous autres garny de la plus riche et noble librairie du monde, si est il moult enclin et desirant de chascun jour l'accroistre, comme il fait).[30] The library is an imperial institution, an empire of books.

Philip's 1446 series of commissions were the large imperial-like framework that assimilated into one whole (Alexander) the noncontiguous Duchy of Burgundy (Roussillon) and the Burgundian Netherlands (Hainaut) of the second half of the fifteenth century. Philip was indeed especially active in commissioning translations and prosifications of epics and histories. The later commissions of Roman history and imperial histories of Charlemagne projected the aura of empire onto Burgundy (e.g., *Croniques et conquestes de Charlemagne*), while contemporary histories of northwestern Europe burnished its role of a fixer state. The *History of Charles Martel* (*Histoire de Charles Martel*, Brussels, KBR MSS 6–9) serves as a good example of translations that nourished the imperial ambition of Philip the Good and his son Charles the Bold. From 1463–65, David Aubert translated the beginnings of the Carolingian Empire into this new compilation—Charles had it illuminated after Philip's death by Loyset Liédet in 1472. Charles the Bold also completed the illumination of Jean Miélot's translation of *Romuléon*, a manuscript that accompanied Charles on his military campaigns but also shaped it: "Its broad and richly populated narrative presented a distilled and apparently authoritative account of the past that was focused on the triumphs and tribulations of secular leaders as they deployed warfare, diplomacy and other means to strengthen the power of the city of Rome and extend its territorial empire" (McKendrick 2012, 82–83). Charles wished to emulate Caesar, as well as Hannibal, featured prominently in the *Romuléon*, great military leaders, alongside stories of Trajan, Hadrian, and Constantine, who expanded the Roman Empire.

The translation zone also included the ducal entourage of counselors who commissioned prosifications and translations of romance material as well as some new literary compositions.[31] Among them, Jean V de Créquy and Jean de Wavrin were two of Philip's most prominent literary counselors and were also his political advisers.

Jean V de Créquy (ca. 1395/1400–1472) had been chamberlain to Philip the Good since 1426, his military commander and ambassador, knight of the Order of the Golden Fleece (inducted in 1430). His commissions were imbricated with Philip's. He commissioned the first volume of the *Chronicles and Conquests of Charlemagne* (*Croniques et conquestes de Charlemaine*) before 1458, but volumes 2 and 3 were commissioned directly by Philip and completed in 1458 by Aubert (KBR, MSS 9066–68).[32] Raoul Lefèvre, most likely Créquy's chaplain,[33] wrote the *History of Jason* about 1460, consecrating Jason as the founding figure of the ducal Order of the Golden Fleece. Another of Créquy's scribes, Isidore du Ny, is thought to have copied for Philip the *Flower of Histories* (*Fleur des histoires*), Jean Mansel's universal history (Gil 1998, 75, 74). Créquy was later either protector or patron to Vasco de Lucena, translator of Quintus-Curtius's *Deeds of Alexander the Great* for Charles the Bold (Willard 1996, 60; Gil 1998, 71, 72). Créquy also ordered the prosification of at least four, if not five, romances (*Florent and Octavian, Blancandin and the Lady-Proud-in-Love* [*Blanchandin et l'Orgueilleuse d'amour*], *Beuve de Hantone, Gilles de*

Chin, and possibly the *History of the Three Sons of Kings*). He also ordered the prosification of the epic *Renaut de Montauban*. All these works have plots that take place wholly or partially in the lands of the Mediterranean (Gil 1998; Wijsman 2010c, 310–15). Philip's copies of the epic *Renaut de Montauban* seem to be based on Créquy's commission of the prose work (Paris, Arsenal, MSS 5072–75; and Munich, BSB, Cod. Gall. 7), while the above-listed romances are also part of Philip's library. Finally, it is possible that Créquy commissioned the short version of *The Romance of Gillion de Trazegnies* (*Roman de Gillion de Trazegnies*; Stahuljak 2015, 85–89).

Jean, Bastard of Wavrin (ca. 1394/1400–ca. 1472/1475), was a military commander who retired from service after the 1435 Treaty of Arras and became the duke's chamberlain sometime before 1462. He is best known as the writer of the six-volume *Chronicles of England* (*Chroniques d'Angleterre*; 1445, updated in 1469–71),[34] which he wrote at the instigation of his nephew, Waleran de Wavrin, on his return from the east where Waleran had been in charge of the duke's naval expeditions in the Mediterranean from 1444 to 1446.[35] Wavrin's book commissions are remarkable for their cohesion: among thirty-two manuscripts (eight of those are probable attributions), sixteen manuscripts (in fifteen volumes)[36] transport the reader to the Mediterranean basin, especially the lands under attack by the Muslims (Spain, Greece, the Near East).[37] They are divided between local chivalric heroes, tied to the regions of Flanders, Artois, and Hainaut (*Gillion de Trazegnies*, *Gilles de Chin*, *Chastelain de Coucy*, *Le roman du Comte d'Artois*, *Les seigneurs de Gavre*, *Gérard de Nevers*, *Jean d'Avesnes*, Antoine de la Sale's *Jean de Saintré*), chivalric heroes of Greek, Roman, or Trojan antiquity (*Roman de Florimont*, Raoul Lefèvre's *Histoire de Jason*, *Roman de Thèbes*, *Histoire de Troie*, *Apollonius de Tyr*, *Roman de Florent et Octavien*, *Romuléon*),[38] and chivalric heroes fighting or living among Muslims (Philippe Camus's *Histoire d'Olivier de Castille et Arthus d'Algarbe*, *Paris et Vienne*).[39] The works he commissioned all came from the same workshop and are easily recognizable thanks to the work of one illuminator, known as the Master of Wavrin.[40] Most of these commissions by Créquy and Wavrin found their place in Philip's library (see appendix A, section 2).[41]

The library is an empire of books; the library is also an empire that rises from books. Or to put it correctly in the Burgundian case: the library is an empire of translations and an empire made in translation. Based on past experiences of Philip's successful politics of northern expansion, the duchy could aim for territorial cohesion and contiguity, while maintaining its potential for a royal and imperial crown of its own making somewhere in Europe or across the sea. In the imperial model of *translatio* (see introduction), the acquisition of an imperial title was more important than the identity of a lineage to a geographic site; such an idea of unity of place and time is grounded in a nation-state model and, as the Burgundian case demonstrates, erroneously applied to medieval state making. The translations created and carried forward this expansionist imperial policy, while ducal counselors served as a kind of interface between centripetal and centrifugal policy dissemination: they provided the duke with translations and works that promoted the subject matter of Burgundian expansionist imperial interests, while simultaneously disseminating it outwardly. They also drove forward the vision to establish the empire beyond the ancestral "lands there" (*les pays par-delà*), the Duchy of Burgundy, and the more recent historical "lands here" (*les pays par deça*), the Burgundian Low Countries. Beyond the fact that libraries promoted imperial interests by their subject matter, the commissions also cultivated the notion of the primacy of translation.

The Primacy of Translation (Prologues and Frontispieces)

Under John II and Charles V of France, translators' prologues started to be placed at the head of translations. Prologues written by Pierre Bersuire, Raoul de Presle, Nicole Oresme, and Simon de Hesdin became a model in the later Middle Ages.[42] Bersuire, Presle, and Hesdin—just like Jean de Vignay (ca. 1280 to the mid-fourteenth century) a few decades before when he was translating in the 1330s for the Valois Philip VI of France and his wife, Jeanne de Bourgogne (Evdokimova 2014; Brun 2010, 59)—used their prologues to explain the merits of translation, "for the benefit and service of your kingdom, your people and the whole Christianity" (pour le profit et utilité de votre royaume, de votre peuple et de toute crestienté; Laborde 1909, 66. See also Oresme 2013), and to signal the difficulty of rendering Latin: "for reasons of brevity and oddity of the discourse, the difficulty of Latin, and the surprising style of the book, it is therefore my intent to translate it sentence by sentence and to render the hard Latin into a clear and understandable Romance [French] language" (les causes si sont la brieve et estrange maniere de parler, la difficulté du latin et le merveilleus stille du livre et pour ce est mon entente de translater le de sentence a sentence et de faire de fort latin cler et entendable romant; Hesdin, n.d., 3. See also Laborde 1909, 67). The labor of reconciling Latin and French was hardly commensurable: Jean de Vignay favored literal translation, while Presle and Hesdin rejected it. Bersuire resorted to a glossary inserted between his prologue and translation. In other words, most translators' prefaces remained linked to the specific circumstance of the commission and their translation from Latin, "I did not write a prologue at the beginning of this book, . . . nevertheless, by way of a short preface, I must state a few principles essential to the book's meaning" (je ne ay pas fait a ce commencement le prologue de ce livre . . . toutefois, par maniere de un petit proheme, il me faut faire aucune declaracions neccessaires pour l'entendement de ce livre; Hesdin, n.d., 1). Unique among them, Oresme also discussed the task, the methodology, and the larger cultural import of translation (see the introduction; Lusignan 1987, 163). Regardless of their scope, all the translators' prologues are a precious source of information for the history of translation and the constitution and evolution of translation practices. But even more important is the fact that their very emergence and frontal position in manuscripts marks translation as a central force of cultural production. Translation partly owes this position to the fact that it is recognized as physical and manual labor, for the labor of translators and illuminators was as material as that of peasants: "you will eat your hands' labor" (Le labour de tes mains mengeras; Vignay in Brun 2010, 83. See also Laborde 1909, 66).

In 1332, when Vignay finished his translation of Vincent of Beauvais's *Mirror of History* (*Speculum historiale*), he inserted a prologue ahead of the translated text (Cavagna 2014. See Brun 2010, 83–85, for an edition of the prologue). In 1455, the Flemish painter William Vrelant illuminated an early fourteenth-century manuscript of Vignay's translation, *Miroir historial*. Vrelant painted first the translator, Jean de Vignay, translating alone surrounded by books (Paris, BnF, MS fr. 308, fol. 1), and then the author, Vincent of Beauvais, reading alone without any books (fol. 2). To illuminate *The Mirror of History*, Vrelant followed the suggestion given by the Valois translators of Charles V of France and participated in the making of the Burgundian model of translation that gives absolute primacy to translation, superseding the original.

The translation into French of Valerius Maximus's *Facta et dicta memorabilia*, written during Emperor Tiberius's reign (first century BCE), was commissioned in 1375 by Charles V from Simon de Hesdin (d. 1383), but it was completed only in 1401 by Nicolas de Gonesse by order of Duke John of Berry. *Memorable Doings and Sayings* (*Faits et dits mémorables des Romains*) is a collection of moral tales from Rome and the ancient world. The particularity of the French text is that it is tripartite: the translation of the Latin text *sensu stricto* is indicated with the rubric "acteur"; the commentary (*glossa*) of the translator is demarcated under the rubric "translateur"; additional examples appear under the rubric of "additions du translateur." This is a quintessential example of the medieval practice of a translator as compiler and interpreter (see also chapter 5).[43] The frontispiece of the first manuscript offered to Charles V presents the writer and the translator as isolated figures working on the order of the king (Paris, BnF, MS fr. 9749, fol. 1, ca. 1378–80). The manuscript frontispiece of this incomplete translation follows chronological order, from left to right, from Valerius to Hesdin in the two top images, to the presentation scene by Hesdin to Charles spread over two frames. Very quickly, however, there is a reversal in the order of the presentation of the relationship between the translation and the original. One manuscript (Paris, BnF, MSS fr. 45–46; ca. 1401–10), contemporary to the first complete copy for Duke John of Berry (Paris, BnF, MS fr. 282, ca. 1401), reverses the chronological order used in Charles V's copy of Hesdin's incomplete translation (MS 9749), placing the translation first, followed by the Latin original.[44]

The copy of *Memorable Doings and Sayings* produced for the Burgundian noble Louis of Gruuthuse (Paris, BnF, MSS fr. 288–89, ca. 1470–80) was painted by the Master of Margaret of York, known to work under the influence of Lieven van Lathem, visible in the characterization of space and people and colors schemes. He was the most employed of Louis's artists, with twenty known commissions, and would have worked closely with Louis. He divides the frontispiece into two separate illuminations: the presentation of the book to Charles V by Simon de Hesdin in the frontispiece (MS 288, fol. 1) and the translation by Simon de Hesdin (MS 288, fol. 4), placed in the small miniature at the head of the first chapter.[45] The two images encircle the translator's "proheme" where Hesdin explains his method of work. One could argue thereby that the Master of Margaret of York's choice both highlights and isolates the work of the translator; but by placing the presentation of Hesdin's translation before Valerius's writing, he insists on the primacy of translation.

The frontispiece of the copy produced for the Van Borssele family (Louis of Gruuthuse's wife came from the family) and painted by the Rambures Master after 1472 takes up Lieven van Lathem's composition in Louis of Gruuthuse's copy of the *History of Jason* (Paris, BnF, MS fr. 331, fol. 1).[46] The Rambures Master paints a mirror image of the composition from van Lathem's frontispiece (Paris, Arsenal, MS 5196, fol. 1).[47] He shows the moment when Simon de Hesdin presents the book to Charles V. A pillar separates Simon from the king, unlike the open view of the hall in MS 331. This same pillar is painted over the book being presented to the king. This has the double effect of separating the book from its translator and of hiding the book and placing the translator in the center of our gaze as he is framed by two pillars in the image. The Rambures Master's variation of the composition, making the translator central to the process, emphasizes the transmission of the book: that is the moment of the passage from the hands of the translator to the hands of the patron. The Rambures Master's framing of the translator in the center and the overpainting of the book also has the effect of insulating the translator, perhaps to further highlight the translator's isolation and how the product of his work is somehow overshadowed by his presence but also independent of him.

The *Chronicles of Hainaut*, in many ways the foundational work of the Burgundian Netherlands, was made in this tradition, textually and visually: it opens with Jean Wauquelin's "Translator's Prologue" (Brussels, KBR, MS 9242, fols. 1–2) and is followed by Jacques de Guise's "Author's Prologue" (MS 9242, fols. 2–14).[48] According to Wauquelin's fairly accurate translation of the "Author's Prologue," Guise wished to recompose the "history of the kingdom of the Belgians or of the principality of Hainaut, which are the same and very ancient." What surprised Guise was not that "the laws, the books and the histories of the kingdom of the Belgians are or have been forgotten, dispersed, dismembered, and destroyed" (les lois, les livres et les histoires du regne de Belges . . . sont ou ont este mis en oubly, espars, despechies et anichilleis), but that any records survived at all: "one can be amazed that anything could be found about it, given the destruction that Julius Cesar had wrought" (chose a esmerveillier que riens en a poet estre trouvet, consideree la destruction qui fu faite par Julius Cesar; fol. 6). The history of Hainaut was dispersed across many written and oral sources,

> in the books of the Treveri, deeds of the Romans, lands of the Tungri, kingdoms of Germanias, deeds of the Bretons, and charters of the Morini, but also in the writings of the Saxons, records of the people of Sens, deeds of the Albanians, charters of the Austrasians, sayings of the Hostilians [?], expressions of the Lotharingians, books of the people of Liège, histories of the French, deeds of the Celts and Burgundians, legends of the Hungarians, Rhaetians, and Menapians, inscriptions of Wandals and Huns, and records of Flems and Brabantians.

> (ens es livres des Treveriens, ens es fais des Romains, ens es terres des Tongriens, ens es regnes des Germanies, ens es gestes des Bretons, ens es chartres de Moriniens, . . . mais ossy ens es escriptures des Saxons, ens es registres des Senonensiens, ens es fais des Albaniens, ens es cartres des Austrasiens, ens es dis des Hostiliens, ens es parlers des Lorrains, ens es livres des Liegois, ens es histores des Franchois, et ens es besongnes des Celtes et Borguignons, et ens es legendes des Hongres, Retiens et Menapiens, ens es rescription des Wandeles et des Huns, ens es registres des Flamens et Brabenchons.) (fol. 6)

The fragmentation of memory and the dispersed state of the historical record were the reasons why there existed in the past "some arguments that the history of the Belgians is not authentic" (Aulcuns argumens que l'istore des Belges n'est point autentique; fol. 7), which were claims that Guise set out to refute. Comparing the dispersion of Hainaut's people and historical records with the story of Israel, Guise inscribed his Latin compilation in the Judeo-Christian tradition, moreover finding in the Old Testament the prefiguration of the glory of the Kingdom of the Belgians (fols. 4v–5v). The author's prologue is an explanation of why and how a written compilation, a gathering of historical writings, serves to build a community, which Wauquelin renders as "le communité." Israelites, and Christians after them, reassembled the fragmented writings after the dispersal of its peoples: "How those who gather scattered writings of one region show their desire for its welfare and salvation" (Comment cheulx qui recoellent les escritures esparses apartenant a une region monstrent signe que il desirent le bien d'icelle et le salut; fol. 3), "how those who recorded the advent and birth of laws and who wrote genealogies aspired to the salvation of the community" (Comment cheulx qui ont escript la venue ou naissence des loys et les histores des lignies ont desiret le salut de le communité; fol. 3v). The notion of the common good, "le commun bien," also appears, as men who exposed themselves to danger, either bodily or "by composing entertaining books" (en composant livres agreables; fol. 4), contributing to "the salvation of the people" (le salut du peuple; fol. 4). The author's prologue thus explains that a compilation by "those who gather" is community building, or more precisely, community rebuilding.

Similarly, Wauquelin's translator's prologue states his determination to "take, expound, and translate from Latin into our common maternal language the beginning and advent of the noble princes of the said land of Hainaut" (mettre, exposer et translater de latin en nostre comun langage maternel le commenchement et venue des nobles princes du dit pays de Haynnau; fol. 1v). Wauquelin's translation is aligned with de Guise's emphasis on the creation of community and articulated around translation in the shared maternal tongue. Since Wauquelin's prologue precedes de Guise's, the linguistic community of translation is the ground on which Wauquelin's—and Burgundian—community is built. For what makes a community is the gathering of writings into the same, commonly held language by virtue of translation. In comparison, Wauquelin states in *Girart of Roussillon* his motivation of unification by language "to put, compose, and organize in writing in our maternal language that we call Wallon or French" (de mectre, composer et ordonner par escript, en notre langaige maternel que nous disons wallet ou françoys; Wauquelin 1880, 2).

Wauquelin has dropped the word "comun" and instead specifies the shared language as French. In *Alexander*, he specifies neither that the language is shared (*Chronicles*) nor that it is French (*Girart*): "to put in writing in the maternal language" (mectre par escript, en langaige maternel; MS 9342, fol. 5v). In book 2 of *Alexander*, Wauquelin declares writing "in our maternal language" (en nostre langage maternel; MS 9342, fol. 127), the possessive "our" recreating the commonality of the implied mother tongue of the prologue. Thus, the compilation—Wauquelin's translation—of historical fragments into one whole—is an act of the collection of a community, in translation. At the same time, a translational community of the present speaks clearly to a supersession of something that would be an "original." Translation into the common maternal language (French) is the latest instance of the collection into a community that therefore supersedes the previous community (the Belgians). It is the very fact of precedence—in a sequence of fragmentation and forgetting, then recollecting and remembering—that makes the original merely a previous translation, an antecedent but not an original, that precedes and that the latest translation supersedes.

The primacy of translation sheds another light on the prominence of translators in the frontispieces to the duke's initial translation trilogy, *Chronicles of Hainaut, Girart of Roussillon,* and *Deeds and Conquests of Alexander the Great.* All three feature the presentation of the book by the translator to the duke: the duke in a stately posture, wearing the collar of the Order of the Golden Fleece, surrounded by his cabinet, Chancellor Rolin and Bishop Chevrot, head of ducal council, and in the company of the young Count of Charolais, the future Duke Charles the Bold, and other knights of the Order of the Golden Fleece, and the translator prominently presenting his translation.[49] Illuminations reflect the textual order. In his half-page frontispiece to the *Chronicles of Hainaut*, Roger van der Weyden—along with Willem Vrelant and a group of artists—painted Wauquelin presenting his translation to the duke at the head of a translator's prologue (MS 9242, fol. 1, 1447–48), and anonymous Bruges artists followed with a one-column miniature of the first writer, Jacques de Guise (fol. 2).[50]

That translation superseded the "original"—that is, the antecedent—is made abundantly clear in a set of manuscripts illuminated by Jean le Tavernier (Audenarde, active 1450–62) in the mid-1450s. Tavernier illuminated many translations of Jean Miélot, a writer who translated many works for Philip and his most intimate circle (few of his works were disseminated beyond one or two copies). In 1455, a year after the Feast of the Pheasant, Miélot translated Pseudo-Brocardus's (William of Adam's) crusade treatise *Directory for the Making of the Passage across the Sea.*[51] A "translator's prologue" precedes the original "author's prologue" in this luxury copy (Paris, BnF, MS fr. 9087), which also contains Burchard of Mount Sion's *Description of the Holy Land* (ca. 1280–84) and Bertrandon de la Broquière's travel report *Voyage in the Land of Outremer* (1432–33) (after 1455). The volume opens with the translator's prologue by Miélot (fols. 1–1v), whom Jean le Tavernier paints presenting the treatise to the duke in the intimacy of his room (fol. 1).[52] The author's prologue begins on fol. 2, where le Tavernier paints Pseudo-Brocardus / William of Adam presenting his Latin treatise to Philip VI of France, who in the early 1330s was mounting a crusade, canceled in 1336. In le Tavernier's rendition, the frontispiece with Philip the Good precedes that of Philip VI. The duke comes before the king and, more importantly, the translation precedes and supersedes the original. The margins of both folio 1 and folio 2 bear the arms of Burgundy, while the illumination with the French king Philip VI (fol. 2) is inscribed with the ducal motto, "Autre naray." The French crusading project is overridden by the Burgundian one. The Paris luxury copy reproduces the 1455 paper manuscript, held in Brussels (KBR, MS 9095), likely containing Miélot's autograph translation (Bousmanne and Delcourt 2011, 225; LDB-V 2015, 113–18) and likewise illuminated by le Tavernier. The frontispiece shows Miélot translating in his scriptorium (fol. 1), alone and surrounded by his books. The next image shows Pseudo-Brocardus / William of Adam presenting his treatise to Philip VI (fol. 2), while the last image imagines Philip VI's departure on a crusade (fol. 9). Although le Tavernier does not copy the compositions between the paper and luxury parchment copies, the illumination sequence remains the same: in both manuscripts the translation comes first. The artist, who often collaborated with Miélot,[53] renders translation as primary and originary. Le Tavernier's visual rhetoric posits translation as a supersession of the original.

Pseudotranslation

The originary status of translation in the Burgundian multilingual context explains why some fifteenth-century Burgundian works stage themselves as translations regardless of whether they were actually new works or prosifications and translations or earlier ones. They seem to abandon their "originality" for the "artifice" of translation. Pseudotranslations abounded at the court of Burgundy, especially among the works commissioned by the duke's counselors. The Burgundian prose romances from the library of Jean de Wavrin and Jean de Créquy almost uniformly present themselves as translations, although they are not: either they are new works, or they are prosifications of older Old French verse works, all masquerading as translations.

In Wavrin's collection, the *History of the Lords of Gavre* (1456), a new work, identifies in the prologue its source as Italian: "I wanted to transpose this present history from the Italian to the French language" (ay volu transmuer ceste presente histoire de langaige ytalyen en langue franchoise). Curiously, the epilogue presents an alternative translation genealogy: "This history was translated from Greek to Latin, and from Latin to Flemish; after that, it was translated into the French language, the last day of March in the year 1456" (Ceste histoire a esté translatee de grec en latin, et du latin en flamenc; depuis a esté translatee en langaige franchois, le desrain jour de mars l'an mil .CCCC.LVI; Stuip 1993, 1, 220). The *Romance of the Count of Artois* (ca. 1453–60) is also a new composition, but its writer presents it as a compilation of several books, thus implicitly a translation or at best a prosification. He portrays himself as a simple compiler and transmitter: "for in this short work I must claim to be a writer who writes only what he has found in other tomes, the content of which follows" (car en ceste petite oeuvre je ne doy estre reputté que l'escripvain qui escript ce qu'il a trouvé ez aultrez volumez dont la substance s'ensieult).[54] Wavrin's short version of *Gillion de Trazegnies* (1450–60) presents itself as a translation from Italian. Although the *Gillion* romance is a new work, the anonymous writer stages his work as a translation: "Seeing my desire to know the truth, the abbot thereupon had one of the monks bring a small book in parchment, written in Italian, in very ancient and obscure writing. Having read and understood thoroughly the matter that seemed beautiful and poignant to hear, I took the pains and labor to translate the content of the said little book into our French language" (L'abbé voyant en moy le desir de savoir la verité par l'un de ses religieux me fist apporter ung petit livre en parchemin escript d'une tres anchienne lettre et obtuse en langue ytalyenne. Alors que je ai leu et bien entendu la matere quy me sembla estre bien belle et pitoyable a oir, je pris la painne et labeur de transmuer le contenu du dy livret en langue franchoise; Brussels, KBR, MS 9629, fol. 1v). Wavrin's copy of *Paris and Vienne* (Brussles, KBR ms, 9632–33), written in 1432 by Pierre de la Cépède, identifies the story as a translation from Catalan to Provençal to French: "But among others, I was in possession of a book written in the Provençal language, which was derived from another book written in Catalan. . . . So I undertook for you a translation of the history from the Provençal language into French" (Mais entre les autres ay tenu ung livre escript en langage provenceaulx, qui fut exgtrait d'un autre livre escript en langage catallain . . . sy ay entreprins à vous extraire l'istoire du langage provenceal en françois; De Crécy and Brown-

Grant 2015, 127). Wavrin's *History of Olivier de Castille and Artus of Algarve* is also a new work, composed by Philippe Camus (ca. 1430–60) for Jean II de Croÿ, another high noble in the entourage of Duke Philip, and copied by David Aubert, the duke's writer. However, Camus also claimed that his work is a translation from Latin to French: "I, Philip Camus, undertook the translation of this present history from Latin to French at the request and command of my most feared lord, messire Jean de Croÿ, lord of Chimay" (je Philippe Camus . . . ay empris de translater ceste presente hystoire de latin en franchoys a la requeste et commandement de montresredoubte seigneur, monseigneur Jehan de Croy, seigneur de Chimay).[55] The prologue to the *Chronicles and Conquests of Charlemagne* (1458 and before), commissioned by Créquy for the Duke of Burgundy and copied by David Aubert, is both a translation and a prosification: "my most feared lord . . . charged me to diligently investigate and explore several tomes in Latin as in French, . . . to take and extract from them what was useful to my subject, in order to collect them into one book" (mon dit tres-redoubte seigneur . . . m'a chargie de curieusement enquerir et viseter pluseurs volumes tant en latin comme en francois . . . et en tirer et extraire ce qui servoit a mon pourpos, pour les assembler en ung liure; Guiette 1940–51, 1:14).

When it comes to prosification, three of the works from Créquy's library admit to their status of prosifications: *Blancandin* (1450–60), declaring, "I transposed from rhyme to prose" (ay transmué de rime en prose)[56]; *Florent and Octavian* (before May 1, 1454), declaring, "according to what I found in a rhymed book whose name of the author I do not know" (selonc ce que j'ay trouve en ung liure mys en rime dont je ne scay le nom de l'aucteur")[57]; and *Gilles de Chin* (before 1467–68), declaring, "I wanted to transpose from rhyme to prose this present treatise" (ay voulu transmuer de rime en prose cest present traictiet).[58] Others, like the *History of Jason* and *History of the Three Sons of Kings* (1454–63), remain silent on the issue. David Aubert simply indicates that the *History of the Three Sons of Kings* was a copy: "this present tome was copied and its layout organized" (a cestuy present volume esté grossé et ordonné; Palumbo 2001, 82). The *History of Jason* alludes to a sea of stories in which the writer—implicitly, the translator—found his: "The galley of my mind drifting back then in the deep sea of many old histories" (La galee de mon engin flotant naguieres en la parfondeur des mers de pluseurs vielles histoires; Pinkernell 1971, 125, edition of Paris, Arsenal, MS 5067, fol. C).

Wavrin's library presents an even more interesting case of prosifications that pass themselves off as translations. The cycle of *Jean d'Avesnes* (1464–68) claims to be a translation "from Latin to French" (de latin en françoys; Quéruel 1997, 41, 12), but in reality *Jean d'Avesnes*, the first part of the cycle, is a prosification of the short fourteenth-century *Dit of the Plum Tree* (*Dit du prunier*); *The Daughter of the Count of Ponthieu* takes up an earlier prose narrative from the thirteenth century; and *Saladin*, the last work in the cycle, is a rewriting of a set of epics from the Second Crusade Cycle. The cycle's prologue makes an explicit reference to several stories composing the cycle, "an ancient book in Latin that contained several histories" (ung ancien livre en latin qui contenoit pluiseurs hystoirez; Quéruel 1997, 41), implying that all three stories were translated from a Latin source. *Gérard de Nevers* (ca. 1451–64) is a prose version of the thirteenth-century verse *Roman de la Violette*, written by Gerbert de Montreuil (1227–29), but it claims to be a translation from Provençal: "I have inserted and introduced myself to transform in writing this little book that had previously been in the Provençal language and very difficult to understand" (je . . . me suis ingeré et avanchyé de moy traveillier par escript ce petit livret lequel par avant estoit en langage prouvençal et mout dificile a entendre; Marchal 2013, 2). Finally, the *Romance of Florimont* is a 1418 prosification of Aimon de Varennes's verse romance from 1188 that pretends to be a translation from Latin to French (Timelli et al. 2014, 259–66). The story's translator, an anonymous Picard, purportedly found the Latin translation of *Florimont* in a library in Thessalonica: among "several tomes of books that were shown to me I chose a small manuscript, translated from Greek to Latin" (pluiseurs volumes de liures qui me furent monstre choisy ung petit livre escryt, translate du grec en latin; Paris, BnF, MS fr. 12566, fol. 1v), which he then decided "to translate from Latin into French" (de translater de latin en franchois; fol. 2r).[59]

A narratological study of much of this material has established "the seeming repetitiveness of these romance prologues in setting out the author's role as simply a transmitter of texts rather than as a creator" (Brown-Grant 2012, 363). This strategy is thought to have liberated writers from tradition and authority and to have provided a greater creative freedom for the author as well as interpretive freedom for the reader/listener. But if that was the case, it is then important to assert the prestige of translations at the court of Burgundy. Translation was valued, central, and primary; it was seen as the fixer's job. This prevailing artifice indicates that writers collectively and, by common agreement, bought into the symbolic power of translation.

Pseudotranslations and Fixer Literature

This kind of analysis of acts of pseudotranslation can be complemented with the ways these same romances portray translation in their plots.[60] As we saw, Créquy and Wavrin commissioned many stories, presented mostly as pseudotranslation, whose chivalric heroes, often of local origins, were active in global, Mediterranean contexts (the Muslim lands or Byzantium) or across non-Christian Europe (pagan Germany, Muslim Spain): Jean d'Avesnes, Gilles de Chin, Gerard de Nevers, Gillion de Trazegnies, Louis of Gavre, Count of Artois, Paris, Blancandin, Florimont, and Oliver of Castille. In their fight against "infidels"—Muslims and pagans, in order to protect Christianity, sometimes without recompense and sometimes ascending to royalty—these heroes seem to follow a similar script: they become fixers, acculturate successfully, then use their military skills to promote the Christian viewpoint and/or their royal or imperial ambition. In other words, pseudotranslations were filled with fixers.

In the cycle of *Jean d'Avesnes*, *The Daughter of the Count of Ponthieu* and *Saladin* show how and why medieval people became fixers. Jean d'Avesnes was a pseudohistorical figure based on Jean I, whom Louis IX made Count of Hainaut in 1246 (Quéruel 1997, 25–26). In the cycle, Jean d'Avesnes's granddaughter is the nameless daughter of the Count of Ponthieu. Ponthieu was acquired by Philip in 1435 with the Treaty of Arras between France and Burgundy. The daughter's granddaughter is the mother of Saladin, the revered and feared historical sultan who wrested the control of Jerusalem from the Latins in 1187. Genealogically, Saladin is the daughter's great-grandson, and Jean d'Avesnes is his ancestor, even though the dates for Jean I (1246) and Saladin (1187) do not match chronologically. Victim of a mass rape, the daughter is abandoned on the sea by her own husband and father, captured by merchants, and then offered as gift to the sultan of Almaria. For about seven and a half years, she lives with the sultan, and bears a son and a daughter; and "she, who had a bright mind, exerted herself until she spoke the language of the land" (et elle, qui estoit de vif engin, fist tant qu'elle sceust parler le langaige du pays; Brunel 1923, 98). In the end, this female fixer, thanks to her fluent French, Arabic, and presumably Italian, saves herself and the lives of her family (her captive father, husband and son) and returns to Christianity via Brindisi.[61]

In *Saladin*, the continuation of *The Daughter of the Count of Ponthieu*, the new Count of Ponthieu, Jean, is made captive on his pilgrimage to Jerusalem. Saladin treats him kindly and offers him his life in exchange for his service as a fixer in France: "And you will help guide me in France, where I committed to cross over just as you have come over here" (Et me aiderés a conduire en France ou j'ay devocion d'aler ainsi que vous estez venus par deçà). Jean accepts to be Saladin's guide to save his life, but he also cautions him: "By God, Saracen, this the count replied, if you want to spare me death, I leave it up to you, but you would not be very wise to place trust in me, for I could not love you" (Par Dieu, Sarrasin, se lui respondi le conte, se de la mort me voulés respiter, je m'en rapporte a vous, mais d'avoir en moy fiance ne ferés vous mye grand sens, car aymer ne vous pourroye). When Saladin decides to return to France, this time as conqueror rather than curious visitor, Jean effectively exploits Saladin's trust to stall his expedition by suggesting England as the military point of entry to France. He then chooses the most difficult mountain pass as entryway into England, while secretly alerting the English king of Saladin's arrival. But Saladin "did not want to trust his word" (ne se volut mie du tout fier en sa parolle) and sends an appropriately named character, Espiet (Spied), on a reconnaissance mission, until he is convinced "that this act is manifest treason" (qu'en ce fait a traÿson evidente; Crist 1972, 57–58, 122).

For the daughter of the Count of Ponthieu and Jean of Ponthieu, learning to pass in a hostile environment is an exercise in the art of survival. Survivor of a mass rape, saved from slavery or concubinage through conversion to Islam and marriage to the sultan, the daughter of the Count of Ponthieu tells the story of how fixers become what they are: the circumstances of their language acquisition, their survival strategies, and their life choices calibrated on chances of survival. The daughter's conversion is not merely "a strategic position" (Kinoshita 2006, 176); it is a strategy for survival. So is Jean's acceptance to become a fixer, attested by a carefully calculated public oath. Both stories turn on and exploit the issue of loyalty.[62] While the daughter easily calms the sultan of Almeria's mistrust at each turn, Sultan Saladin, her great-grandchild, is more circumspect. The duality of fixers is exploited, and—although the particular happy endings work to Christian advantage in these romances—they are a cautionary tale for the Christian audience: a fixer, the one who knows (a language, a culture, a topography, etc.), may always be lying as the daughter and Jean do. This is the duplicity, necessary to commensuration, of which all the fixers were suspected, in the eyes of pilgrims (chapter 2).

Other Créquy and Wavrin books explore these issues. Blancandin may be the fixer with the most languages under his belt, much like the narrative's first thirteenth-century verse version. The short prose version of the manuscript that belonged to Philip mentions French, Greek, and Arabic, in addition to his native Frisian (Brussels, KBR, MSS 3576–77). Another manuscript that belonged to Créquy adds German to the list: "He could speak several languages and especially the German language" (Il sçavoit parler pluseurs langaiges et par especial la langue thioise).[63] Blancandin exploits his linguistic skills and cultural disguise. He survives all his adventures only thanks to a combination of linguistic skills and cultural knowledge as well as his ability to pass in disguise—he passes for a local wherever destiny brings him. Blancandin "thought to himself that he will blacken the skin of his face or make it the color of the people of the land. He took and picked the herbs for that purpose, which he rubbed on his face and hands so that no one could recognize him" (pensa en lui mesme qu'il se feroit le visaige noir ou de la couleur telle que pour le tempz avoient les gens d'icelui paÿs. Il prist et cueilla herbes qui a ce servoient, dont il se frota le visaige et les mains affin que de nulz ne fust reongneu). Blancandin passes easily, since later "the provost did not recognize Blancandin at that moment, because his face was blackened and deformed, but thought that he was a Saracen like others" (le prevost a ceste heure ne congneut point Blanchandin pour ce qu'il estoit noirchis et deffigurés, mais cuidoit qu'il fust sarrasin comme les aultres; Greco 2002, 200, 219). Another of Créquy's major commissions, *Florent and Octavian*, retains issues of interlingual communication that were already present in the original fourteenth-century *chanson de geste* (Marchal 2016, 146; see also LDB-III 2006, 165). One of the wrongfully exiled sons of the Roman emperor, Florent, is helped by Mausabille, daughter of the sultan of Babylon (Egypt) who "knew several languages" (scavoit pluiseurs langaiges), including French, and later by friar Clemens: "when I was in Jerusalem, I remained for three years over there and I learned to speak Arabic very well" (quant je fuch en Jherusalem, je demouray trois ans par dela et appris tres bien a parler le langage sarasinoys).[64]

The main character of the *History of the Lords of Gavre*, Louis of Gavre, ascends to the Duchy of Athens, through his marriage to the duke's daughter Ydorie, and in the process he becomes trilingual, speaking French and Flemish and learning Greek. The romance is very aware of cultural difference: "Sire, customs are according to lands! Now you are in Greece, and it behooves you to feast according to the manner and custom of Greece" (Sire, selonc les paÿs les coustumes! Maintenant estes en Grece, et pour ce selon la maniere et coustume de Grece vous convient faire la feste). Louis will assimilate completely into the Greek court. Years later, when he makes his way back to France for a royal tournament, the splendor of Louis's ducal court is blinding for the French West: "they seemed to be celestial beings, on account of the great splendor of gold and precious stones on their clothes" (sambloyent estre choses celestyeles, pour la grant resplendisseur de l'or et des pierryes que sur leurs vestemens avoyent; Stuip 1993, 137, 197). Louis of Gavre does the reverse passing: he returns home hiding behind his linguistic and cultural disguise, and no one recognizes him. His identity is revealed only when his father's wrongs, which sent him into exile, have been corrected.

In the *Romance of the Count of Artois*, the conflict is between the king of Castille and the king of Granada. Multilingualism is implicit: "Without

spies or dragomans military men can never be harrowed" (Sans espiez
ne truchemenz ne sont a painez jamais gens de guerre"). The romance
explains the advantages of an ethno-linguistic community abroad: "ex-
patriates are friends like brothers; and certainly they should be, for as
friends they are more cherished and more feared by others" (gens hors
de leurs paiis sont amis comme frerez; et certez sy doivent il estre, car ilz
en sont amis et plus chiers tenus et plus doubtez dez aultrez). Most strik-
ingly, this romance stages another example of a female fixer, the wife of
the estranged Count of Artois, who plays an intermediary between him
and his love interest at the court of Castille, where he resides, ultimately
succeeding in substituting herself for the other woman. The fact that she
has learned "the local language" (le langage du paiis) enables her to play
this role at the court of Castille. It is particularly striking that this female
fixer, like the daughter of the Count of Ponthieu, remains anchored in a
domestic situation (Seigneuret 1966, 81, 108, 107).

Two of Wavrin's commissions, *Gillion de Trazegnies* and *Paris and Vienne*, complete this summary picture. They are both quite exceptional in
their treatment of languages. Instead of simply dealing with the circumstances of becoming a fixer, they provide a double vision of fixers and
interpreters. Wavrin's copy of *Gillion de Trazegnies* is the earliest extant of
the copies. The Hainaut knight, Gillion, on pilgrimage to Jerusalem, hires,
in the port of Jaffa, guides and "the dragoman of Ramallah" (le tourche-
man de Rennes). Later in the narrative, another Christian knight from
Hainaut, Amaury, will hire a local interpreter in Jerusalem to take him
across the desert to Cairo. When, on his return from Jerusalem, Gillion is
captured by the sultan of Egypt, the sultan speaks to the ship's passengers
"through a dragoman" (par ung syen drugheman). Gillion is brought to
Cairo, where he learns Arabic so well that, when he finds himself at the
head of the sultan's army disguised as the sultan of Egypt, he is able to
address the troops in a rousing speech as if he were the sultan: "When
the Saracens heard my lord Gillion speaking thus, they all believed it was
the sultan who spoke to them" (Quant les sarasins oyrent Gillion ainsy
parler tous cuiderent que ce fust le souldan qui a eulx parlast).[65] The long
version—copied in the manuscripts of Philip the Good's advisers, Louis
of Gruuthuse (Los Angeles, JPGM, MS 111) and of Anthony of Burgundy
(Dülmen, MS 50)—contains one significant mention of "trucheman" that
did not exist in Wavrin's short copy, since the narrative ended prior to the
episode. After twenty-six years in Egypt, Gillion is able to return home to
Hainaut. The sultan sends him "one of his dragomans who spoke Greek,
Latin, French, German, and several other different languages that he had
learned in lands where he had lived in his youth" (ung sien trucheman

lequel sçavoit parler grec, latin, franchois, allemant et autre plusieurs divers langaiges qu'il avoit aprins es paijs ou il avoit demouré ou temps de sa jennesse),[66] who, in an acknowledgment of Gillion's fluency in Arabic, "threw himself at Gillion's feet and kissed his hand and coat, then greeted him in the Saracen language" (Il se jetta a ses pies et luy baisa la main et la robe, puis en langue sarrazine le salua; JPGM, MS 111, fol. 202).

Paris and Vienne's double presentation of fixers and interpreters is by far the most complex. Wavrin's copy is also the only one to contain the Burgundian version with two unique interpolations, one of which extends Paris's adventures in the East.[67] Unable to marry Vienne, daughter of the Dalfin of Vienne, Paris goes east into self-imposed exile, first on an obligatory pilgrimage from Jerusalem to Sainte Catherine's and Cairo. From there, he leaves with merchants for Tabriz in Persia and completely assimilates in a short time: "After a year, he knew how to speak Arabic as if he had been raised and born in it. He then started wearing Islamic garb and frequenting Moors and Turks as if he himself had been a Saracen. He went from one city to another, and everyone believed that he was a Turk and a Muslim" (Au bout d'un an il sceust aussi bien parler langue mourisque comme s'il y eust esté nourris et nez. Lors il se vestit de robes mourisques et commença à hanter avecq les Mores et avecq les Turques ne plus ne mains comme se il fust sarrazin. Et aloit de une ville en autre et tout le monde pensoit que il fust Turques et sarrazin).[68] Later, as the sultan's master falconer, he disguises the vagueness of his origins and his excellent knowledge of Arabic behind a purported kidnapping when he was a child (a common Mamluk practice). Even after his return to the Christian West, Paris continues to pass as an Arab: "he always spoke Arabic and wore Muslim Arabic clothes with a long beard" (tousjours parloit en morisque et portoit robes morisques atout une grant barbe), and "his skin was very tanned and darkened by the sun" (il estoit moult taint et noircy du soleil; De Crécy and Brown-Grant 2015, 265, 286, 307). This linguistic and cultural assimilation enable him to act as a fixer and save the Dalfin, captured by the sultan. This act will also allow him to win Vienne's hand because he never reveals his true identity and speaks to the Dalfin only through an interpreter (truchement), a friar minor: "Paris did not give away by any sign that he understood what he had said. So the friar repeated in Arabic what the Dalfin had originally told him" (Paris ne faisoit nul semblant qu'il eust entendu rien de ce qu'il avoit dit. Mais le frere ly redit en mourisque ainsi comme le daulphin ly avoit premierement dit; De Crécy and Brown-Grant 2015, 287, 284; see also 288). Paris's decision to learn Arabic is produced in conditions of dispossession and at a point of no return—a desperate situation of survival. It resembles the situations of the daughter of the Count of Ponthieu and Jean of Ponthieu. Similarly, Paris's ability to pass—linguistically and culturally—is a trait shared with Gillion, Blancandin, and Louis of Gavre.

The deliberate fashioning of Burgundy as a fixer between the Kingdoms of England and France, and between the East and the West, is accompanied by narratives produced for and around the court of Burgundy that are falsely presented as translations; all the while, they make fixers instrumental to their plotlines, if not main protagonists. This fixer literature, the literature of pseudotranslation, was commissioned by the duke's counselors for the duke's use. Why did political counselors adapt the mode of pseudotranslation? Specifically, these books were copied to explore possible crusading scenarios for an imperial Burgundy. The ducal counselors were political fixers through literary means. The function of literary advisers was in no way separate from the role of political counselors (see also Devaux 2010; Coste 2021a). Quite the opposite, literature was a policy, library a policy institution; and fixers—characters, romances, counselors—were the vehicle of the Burgundian crusade and imperial expansion.

Fixers: Translation as Process in Manuscript Illumination

As we saw, not only did Burgundians place translation at the center of daily governance and dynasty building, but writers and artists positioned translation as primary and originary. Translation was the inaugural moment. If Valois Burgundy saw itself as a fixer and the literature commissioned by the ducal counselors was the literature of fixers, then what can be said about the visualization of translation in Burgundian luxury secular manuscripts? Their representation of translation differs from that in manuscripts made in the thirteenth and fourteenth centuries. We saw earlier that the discourse on translation as primary exists already in French translations for Charles V: the translator's prologue comes first. But Burgundian illumination points to a different conception of the link between commissions and translations, patrons, and translators. Burgundian artists departed from the standard portrayal of patronage, which pictured the translator in the frontispiece presenting the completed book to the patron. Instead, they showed the process: translators at work and translation in the making, exhibiting a move from a static to a more dynamic representation of translation. For a time, artists even seemed to have viewed translation as emancipated from patronage. Yet, other artists developed ways of visualizing translation as a pivot, that is, as the central activity of cultural production, portraying the "original" as an antecedent. This view seems to characterize the late Burgundian model, even in cases where the patron was well known, though it does not concern manuscripts produced for the duke (fig. 4.1).

We know little about the Master of Wavrin, who illuminated most of Jean de Wavrin's commissions in the 1450s and early 1460s.[69] Several of the frontispieces to Wavrin's books, including *Gérard de Nevers* (Brussels, KBR, MS 9631), *History of the Lords of Gavre* (Brussels, KBR, MS 10238), *Jean d'Avesnes* (Paris, BnF, MS fr. 12572), and *The Count of Artois* (Paris, BnF, MS fr. 11610), show a dynamic translator's workshop, with at least three characters in the image. They appear to be already at a remove from the singular image of the translator enclosed, alone, in his study, surrounded by his books, often with the closest book to him open, indicating the translation source.[70] The frontispiece to the *Romance of the Count of Artois* (fig. 4.2) is reminiscent of the one in *Gerard de Nevers*, showing the lord consulting or picking up his commission inside the book/translation workshop.[71] The dynamism of the picture comes from the fact that the translator is not in a singular relationship with the patron or the client; rather, he is helped by his assistant, unless there is an even larger crowd of lord's courtiers present, as is the case in *Gérard de Nevers*.

With the frontispiece to *Florimont*, the Wavrin Master goes the furthest. He paints a different and unique take on translation when he transports the translator out of the study into the world. The prose *Florimont* is one of the earliest to have been produced for Jean de Wavrin, perhaps as early as 1448 (Timelli et al. 2014, 259), about the time when Wauquelin finished his *Deeds and Conquests of Alexander*. Alternatively, it is thought to have been completed in the early 1450s (Brown-Grant 2015). The prologue explains how the story's translator, an anonymous Picard, set out at the age of eighteen on a pilgrimage to Jerusalem. With his traveling companions from Burgundy, he was waylaid by a sea storm at a Mediterranean port of Thessalonica in Greece. During a monthlong stay, he purportedly found the Latin translation of *Florimont* in a library. The choice of this "small manuscript" is attributed to the writer's desire "to examine and learn the customs and marvels of Greece" (de enquerir et savoir les coustumes et merveilles du pais de grece) and "the histories and marvelous adventures that happened and the great deeds accomplished by Greek knights who once were the most distinguished among all reigns" (les histoires et merveileuses adventures et haulz fais advenus et acheves par la chevalerye grigoise qui jadis fu moult hault eslevee par tous rengnes; Paris, BnF, MS fr. 12566, fol. 1v). His translation is inspired by a desire to offer both a

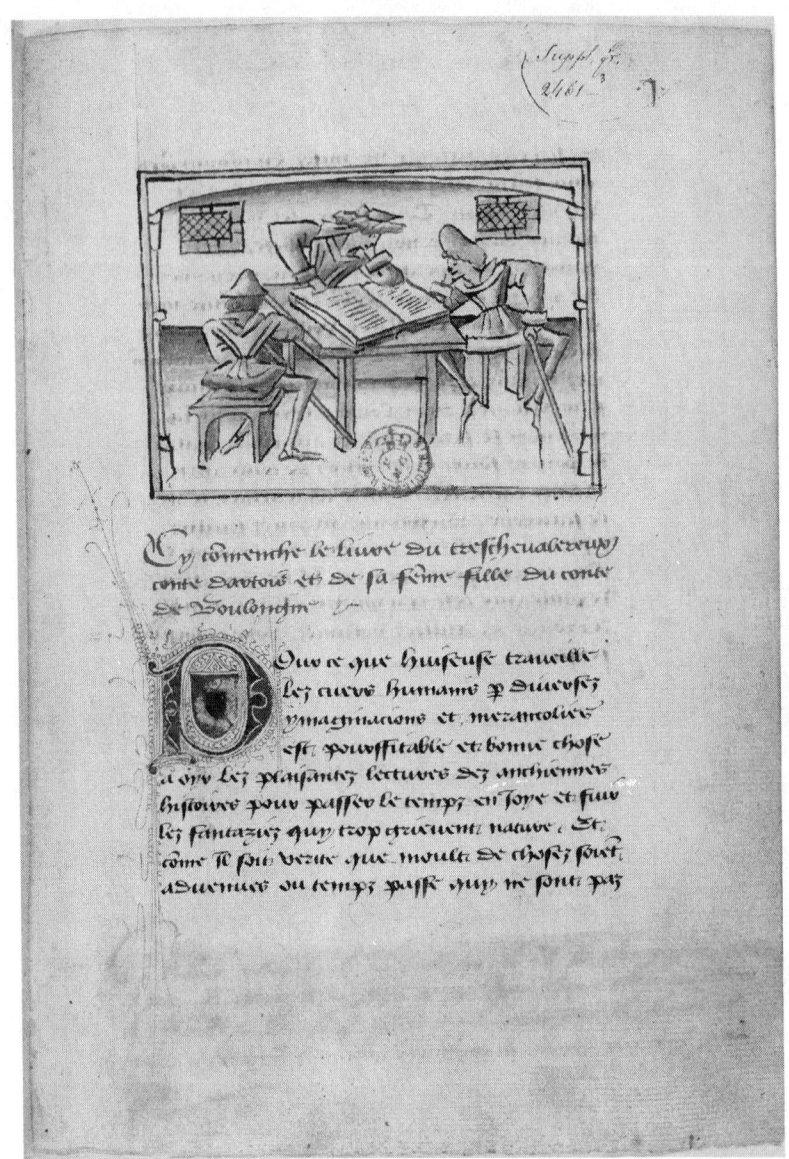

FIGURE 4.2: Master of Wavrin, *Patron Visiting the Translator in His Book Workshop.* From *Le roman du Comte d'Artois*, Lille, 1450–60. BnF, MS fr. 11610, fol. 1r. Photograph: Bibliothèque nationale de France.

cultural history and the genealogy of the greatest conqueror, "the most illustrious Emperor Alexander the Great" (le treshault empereur Alixandre le conquerant; fol. 2). Indeed, *Florimont* is a prequel to the history of Alexander: Florimont, Duke of Albania, was Alexander's grandfather. Side by side, the prologue thus tells a double story of travel and books, of a pilgrim's itinerary and the discovery of a library, of travel and knowledge collecting, and of pilgrimage and ethnographic curiosity. Accordingly, the Wavrin Master combines travel and translation in an exceptional way in the manuscript's frontispiece (fig. 4.3). In a continuous narrative, it shows, on the left, the pilgrim's vessel approaching the port and, on the right, the writer-translator being shown the "original" manuscript (the Latin translation of a Greek work) by the librarian at the window of the library. Despite the crowded space of the library's window, the book is painted open—and prominently—on the sill of the window. Like the prologue that tells a double story, the frontispiece shows how books travel and how, in turn, their translation inspires travel as a pilgrimage ("peregrinatio" was a common early medieval term for a crusade).

Although art history treats them as antipodes, the Wavrin Master, working for a minor noble on paper manuscripts, and Lieven van Lathem, painting for the greatest Burgundian nobles only on parchment, worked with a similar idea of dynamic translation as process. Van Lathem was active between 1454 and 1493, entering Duke Philip's service in 1456 and becoming one of the most favored illuminators of the Burgundian nobility. He also worked for Duke Charles, for regent and Archduke Maximilian, and, during the lifetime of Duke Philip the Good, for his courtiers Louis of Gruuthuse and Anthony of Burgundy. Among Louis of Gruuthuse's commissions figure three manuscripts illuminated by Lieven van Lathem in the mid-1460s and early 1470s: *Romance of Gillion de Trazegnies* (Los Angeles, JPGM, MS 111, 1464), Raoul Lefèvre's *History of Jason* (Paris, BnF, MS fr. 331, after 1472), and Pseudo-Aristotle's *Secret of Secrets* (*Secret des secrets*; Paris, BnF, MS fr. 562, ca. 1470–75), two of which are relevant to this discussion (see also Morrison and Stahuljak 2015).

The *Romance de Gillion de Trazegnies* is van Lathem's first known secular work and perhaps the first completed, in 1464, while he was in ducal service, for a member of the ducal entourage. Its frontispiece uses a continuous image of the writer-translator dressed in a blue robe (fig. 4.4). After he enters the monastery in the background, the "original" Italian book is offered to him as an open book in the central section, and in the final, upper-right section of the frontispiece, the translator is shown at work, the open book to his right. This technique is called continuous narrative, where more than one event happening to a single character is shown. In

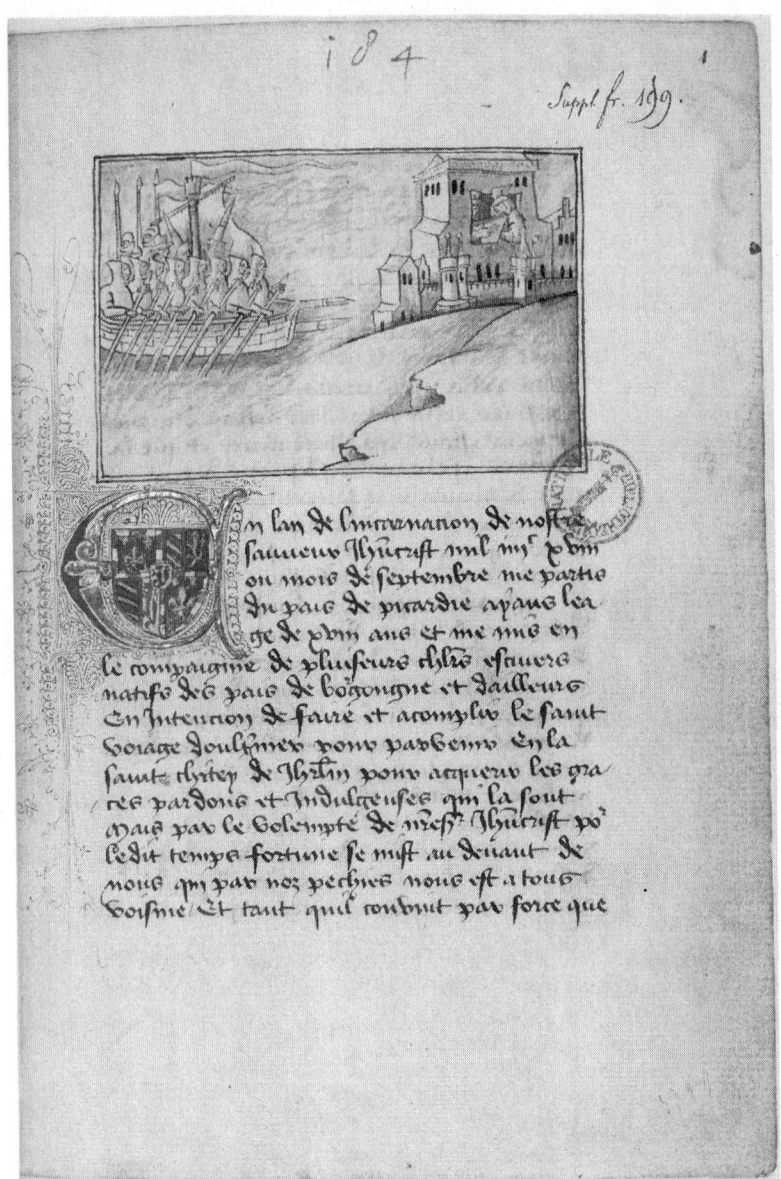

FIGURE 4.3: Master of Wavrin, *The Translator's Sea Voyage; The Translator Discovers a Book in a Thessalonica Library*. From *The Romance of Florimont*, Lille, 1450–60. Paris, BnF, MS fr. 12566, fol. 1r. Photograph: Bibliothèque nationale de France.

FIGURE 4.4: Lieven van Lathem, *The Translator Hearing the Story of Gillion de Trazegnies*. From *Roman de Gillion de Trazegnies*, Ghent or Antwerp, 1464. Los Angeles, J. Paul Getty Museum, MS 111, fol. 9r. Photograph: J. Paul Getty Museum.

other words, van Lathem showcases the idea of translation as a continuous process of transmission. He completely circumvents the standard scene of the presentation of the book, placing instead at the center the intermediary figure of the romance's "translator." His frontispiece is particularly interesting as the work's patron, Louis of Gruuthuse, is explicitly mentioned in the dedicatory prologue (fols. 8–8v), generally a rare feature of Louis's manuscripts (Stahuljak 2015). Despite the singling out of the patron, van Lathem does not opt for the presentation scene of the book to him.

Instead, van Lathem takes the translator outside his study; he places him in the world, making him into a fixer. The prologue makes it clear that the abbey is just one place on the map where the writer-translator stops in search of chivalric-crusading narratives. In the narrative, the fixer appears as a free agent—without a patron—and motivated by his curiosity. The agency rests with his desire rather than with a prince's or noble's order to translate. Accordingly, van Lathem paints translation as a process. Van Lathem's representation effaces the patron and points instead to the book as an object of exchange: having entered the monastery in the company of the abbot, the Italian book is offered to the fixer in the central section. And in the final, upper-right section of the frontispiece, he is watched by a monk in anticipation of the outcome. Van Lathem's pictorial choice arguably makes sense when considered in a larger context. His activity takes him outside the walls of the monastery (the gate and the road lead out in the lower-right corner). Out there in the secular world, the fixer will, upon completion of his translation, most likely engage in "trading" his book: as the dedication of *Gillion* signals, he will offer it as a gift to the duke, for which, in exchange, he can expect a countergift in the form of ducal payment, a fact perhaps underscored by the presence of the purse prominently hanging at his waist.[72] Van Lathem completely eliminated the patron and the typical presentation scene, placing at the center instead the intermediary figure of the fixer, who is the pivot of commercial circulation.

Translation as a commercial transaction is made explicit in the presentation scene of *Chronicles and Conquests of Charlemagne*, commissioned by Jean de Créquy for the Duke of Burgundy, where a market at the city gates occupies the foreground (Brussels, KBR, MS 9066; fig. 4.5). In the upper right-hand corner is located a more standard presentation scene, showing the manuscript being offered as a gift by the patron, Jean de Créquy, who is identified by the collar of the Order of the Golden Fleece and the short *cotte* worn by nobles (LDB-IV 2009, 128). Yet, this presentation scene is pushed into the background while trade is foregrounded in the urban marketplace at the city gates, where food, drink, clothes, and jewelry are all present. Other elements in the image marshal the idea of exchange: the

FIGURE 4.5: Jean le Tavernier, *Presentation Scene in a Town*. From *Croniques et conquestes de Charlemagne*, Audenarde, 1458–60. Brussels, Bibliothèque royale de Belgique, MS 9066, fol. 11r. Photograph: Bibliothèque royale de Belgique.

middle section shows courtiers engaged in a conversation, one of them holding a falcon and the duke's dwarf approaching the group, while the upper-left section presents two men exchanging something over the balcony. The inner courtyard sets the scene in a courtly tone. The artist, Jean le Tavernier, removed the inner wall of the duke's palace, thereby suggesting that the duke overlooks and enables the city and courtly exchanges, one adjacent to the other. All three communicate through the open gate and open facade of the palace. While the duke's "good government" encourages vigorous commercial activity and courtly exchange, the bustling urban marketplace offers a select arena for the courtiers to purchase gifts for the sovereign (Buettner 2001, 618). Le Tavernier thus saw translation as a circulation between the city market and the court, spurred by the middle section of courtiers.[73]

Van Lathem's *Gillion* frontispiece is not about patronage but about translation. Van Lathem undoes the fixed and static translator, making him into a mobile agent and creating a dynamic image. Translation seen as process turns the translator into a fixer. As he travels in the world, as he communicates in search of subjects and carries the book across space, rather than remaining in the isolation of his study and hence at the command and disposal of a prince, the translator is transformed into a fixer. From a passive translator of a bygone era, he becomes an active fixer of the Burgundian present: he chooses the artifact, which he proposes to a client, and he can reasonably expect a gain. He is a free agent in the world who sells his wares and collects the profits in his purse. He no longer needs the patron's authorization for his translation; rather it is the process of translation itself that authorizes his work. Furthermore, the Burgundian book market provides a form of self-authorization: the greater the demand for new narratives and translations, the greater the number of opportunities to create them. This is what le Tavernier comments on and what the case of the Master of the Vienna *Chroniques d'Angleterre* embodies.

The Master of the Vienna *Chroniques d'Angleterre* was active in Bruges around 1470–80 and seems to have illuminated primarily contemporary productions (appendix A, section 3). Although he worked for the biggest bibliophiles and courtiers (Louis of Gruuthuse, Anthony of Burgundy, Philippe de Clèves, Wolfert VI de Borssele), he also produced for the lesser nobility (Jan III de Baenst) and the bourgeois class (Pietro Villa). He made manuscripts in parchment and on paper for all tastes and purses. Most of his manuscripts contain spaces for coats of arms, some of which remain blank. This means that the artist's workshop created a stock of manuscripts for future clients, prefabricating and keeping manuscripts in high demand in stock for "off-the-shelf" sales.[74] Such is the case of two copies of Lucena's *Deeds of Alexander the Great* illuminated by this master: the first was purchased in 1475 by a knight of the Order of Saint John of Jerusalem and bailiff of Morea, Philippe de Cluys (London, BL, Burney MS 169); the second (Paris, BnF, MSS fr. 47–49) is currently known to have first been owned by Philippe de Béthune in the seventeenth century. Other examples of premade manuscripts by the same master include two copies of Wavrin's *Chroniques d'Angleterre* (Vienna, ÖNB, Cod. 2534; and Paris, BnF, Arsenal, MS 4750), and one copy of Raoul Lefèvre's *Collected Histories of Troy* (*Recueil des histoires de Troyes*; Wolfenbüttel, Herzog August Bibliothek, MS A.i. Aug. fol.).[75]

The translation market creates fixers out of translators and emancipates translation from patronage. Instead of within the scholastic ivory tower of his study inside the cloister or castle, the translator now participates as agent in the network of commerce and exchange in the secular world. The translator is thereby at least partially a reflection of the painter, who is himself a free agent in a painter's guild, offering his illuminations to patrons. It is perhaps not surprising that the Master of the Vienna *Chroniques d'Angleterre* painted Lefèvre with a purse for the frontispiece of a copy of the *Collected Histories of Troy* sold to the family de La Fontaine-Solare. This is a modern, urban take on the activity of translators and painters as fixers and on Burgundy's role and place in the world.

Van Lathem's frontispiece of Pseudo-Aristotle's *Secret of Secrets* shows a messenger presenting the Greek treatise to Alexander sent from Aristotle (Paris, BnF, MS fr. 562, ca. 1470; fig. 4.6). Alexander is bearded and is seated, in imperial crown, under a crescent, symbolizing Islam, painted in the middle of the archway. The messenger carries a sword typically seen in portrayals of Arab Muslims. The narrator states in the prologue that a certain "John, son of Patrick" (Jehan filz Patrice) translated "the book of Aristotle's secrets" (le livre des secretz Aristote; fol. 7) from Greek to Chaldean (Persian), and later into Arabic, at the request of the king of Arabia (possibly a reference to Abbasid Baghdad). Much later, "after a long time, a great cleric, Philip [of Tripoli], translated it into Latin from Arabic" (et apres long temps ung grant clerc appelle Phelippe le tranlatta de arabic en latin; fol. 7). "After that, another venerable cleric translated it from Latin in French, although not the whole book, but that which is most useful to the state and government of the princes" (Et depuis par ung venerable clerc il a este translate de latin en francois mais non pas tout le livre ainchois tout ce qui est plus prouffitable a l'estat et gouvernement des princes; fol. 7v).[76] While the prologue mentions a series of translations—from Greek, to Chaldean (Persian), to Arabic, all of which strangely evoke the variety of languages at work in Abbasid Baghdad (Classical and Byzantine

FIGURE 4.6: Lieven van Lathem, *Presentation Scene with the King of Arabia*. From Pseudo-Aristotle, *Secret of Secrets*, Ghent or Antwerp, ca. 1470. Paris, BnF, MS fr. 562, fol. 7r. Photograph: Bibliothèque nationale de France.

Greek, Middle Persian, Neopersian, Syriac), and then to Latin—van Lathem opts for the first presentation scene of the book to Alexander, the furthest removed in time: "And when Aristotle could not be with him, he would send him letters and epistles instructing him in governance and conduct. For this purpose, Aristotle composed and sent the book to Alexander" (Et quant il [Aristote] ne pouvoit estre avecques luy, il luy envoioit lettres et epistres comment il se devoit gouverner et maintenir. Et pour ce fist et composa Aristote ce livre et le envoia a Alixandre; fol. 7v). The distance from Greece is twice underlined: Aristotle, the writer and sender of the book, is absent from the presentation of the book, brought instead by a messenger. And Alexander is far away, possibly in Persia, in what will become Muslim lands under the king of Arabia. Van Lathem keeps the door to the outside open, just like in the *Gillion* frontispiece (fig. 4.4), and the path by which the messenger has just arrived—his white horse is without a rider in the right-center background of the image—meanders and fades in the distance across a bridge. The crescent does not merely signify Alexander's distant location to which the book has traveled; it is already a prefiguration of the Arabic translation of "the book of Aristotle's secrets." A book in Greek is already under the sign of Arabic. Van Lathem did not pinpoint one moment in this long process to the text's maturation into Middle French but created instead a layered image of Greek and superposed Arabic. It has been suggested that the kingly figure is not Alexander but the king of Arabia. Rather, it is possible that, just like there is superposition of languages because of the crescent, there may be a superposition of figures, of Alexander and the king of Arabia. Aristotle's absence and his messenger's presence furthermore accentuate the distance that the book has traveled. Although there is an overlayering of the Greek and the Arabic in the mixed signals that van Lathem plays with, the most striking is his removal of the starting point of the text, the text's writer, Aristotle. In his place, the messenger represents the portability of the book and of knowledge (no matter how secret), and the book's portability is already a sign of the portability of translation (from Greek into Arabic). In other words, van Lathem does not bring forward the book's origin but is interested in the messenger and the book as fixers who transport objects and knowledge (or secrets), across vast territories and languages. Lastly, van Lathem again skirts the representation of the patron of the vernacular translation.

Van Lathem's frontispieces for Louis of Gruuthuse display an architecture that seems to reflect the opening of Burgundy onto the world through translation: the walls have come down; the interior space is open onto the outside and not foreclosed to it; the interior communicates with the exterior. This architectural formula will dominate in the 1470s as van Lathem greatly influenced a number of Flemish painters working in Bruges, such as Loyset Liédet, the Master of Mary of Burgundy, the Master of Margaret of York, and the Rambures Master.[77]

Both the Master of Wavrin's and van Lathem's frontispieces display a high degree of textual consciousness and sensibility to translation and subvert the customary presentation scene of the completed manuscript to the patron. They show instead a translator transformed into a fixer. The fixer's mobility unifies the space. He carries the translated object across the space, and his movement shows that the portability of the object is the effect of translation. While translation is thought of as an activity that translates across time, their frontispieces focus on how translational objects that are the product of time move across space. Here, the translator is endowed with an agency and status that he had not been accorded previously. His authority no longer stems from a patron's commission but is instead created in the process of translation that responds to the needs of the book market and is authorized by it. The movement away from translators to fixers transforms the temporal moment into a spatial movement; it encapsulates the movement of writers, illuminators, and scribes in the new workshop template and the commercialization of the book market propelled by the demands for luxury vernacular translations. The translation movement, itself motivated by the expansionist politics of Burgundy, stimulates the book market and creates a new understanding of translation as both process and object of the work of fixers. Moreover, the object is commercial, monetized.

The frontispiece page becomes a translational space in which translation is shown as process and manuscript as a medium of communication. Incarnated in a portable object of the book that is seen moving continuously through architectural spaces of a single image, this visualization of the process that created the work now before the reader has the effect of transforming the very manuscript page from surface to space, from static (translator's desk in the *scriptorium*) to mobile (across several locales), from local (France or Burgundy) to global (Near East or Italy to France or Burgundy), from micro (image of the book) to macro (physical manuscript and library), from visual (image of the book) to tactile (manuscript held or leafed by the reader). This translational space is incarnated in the portable object that translation is. Ultimately, the image is not as much a visual translation of the text as it is an interstitial commentary (interlinear "gloss") on what the translators' prologues do not emphasize enough: the primacy of translation over an "original" (the vanishing of the original), the supersession of the maternal translational language over all others, and the mobility of material objects that create a globally interconnected space through a process of translation.

Translation and the Coming Burgundian Empire

Philip the Good's commission of *The Deeds and Conquests of Alexander* from Jean Wauquelin[78] in 1446 coincided with Burgundy's quest for the imperial title and growing involvement in the Mediterranean—in 1454, the duke made a crusade vow. When Vasco da Lucena presented a new translation of *Deeds of Alexander the Great* (*Les faits et gestes d'Alexandre le Grand*) to the new Duke Charles the Bold in 1468, the crusading dream of Burgundian dukes was still very much alive. Just as Wauquelin spoke of Alexander as "the most noble and valiant conqueror . . . in conquest of the world" ([le] hault noble et vaillant conquerant . . . conquerant le monde; Paris, BnF, MS fr. 9342, f. 1), so Lucena believed that the superiority of manpower, resources, and moral conduct in Charles made it easier for him than for Alexander to "conquer this whole Orient in order to subject it to the faith of Jesus Christ" (icelluy [tout orient] conquester pour le reduire a la foy de Jhesuscrist; BnF, MS fr. 22547, fol. 269v).

Most manuscript frontispieces of Lucena's translation follow the compositional formula of the standard presentation scene: Charles, seated on the left or the right, surrounded by his principal courtiers, receives the book from a kneeling Lucena.[79] But one (Paris, BnF, MS fr. 47) by the Master of the Vienna *Chroniques d'Angleterre* has an exceptional frontispiece, taking up translation as process (fig. 4.7). This is perhaps not surprising coming from a painter who embodies translators and bookmakers as fixers, as commercial agents of Burgundian towns. In the background in the upper left of the image, Charles enters a courtyard, surrounded by four courtiers, and appears to give an order to the kneeling Lucena. The courtyard serves as a connector between the building that Charles just exited and the building where Lucena will present his finished translation to Charles. Inside the hall, Charles takes the book from Lucena's hands, watched by four courtiers, while two other members of the entourage are distracted by the fool at the fountain. Even a monkey seated on the ground behind Lucena seems astonished gazing back to the scene at the fountain. Charles's and Lucena's concentration in the exchange of the book is contrasted with the foolishness of the two courtiers who look at the fool making a fool out of himself. Their distraction is the opposite of Charles's concentration and commitment to Alexander's imperial project of the conquest of the world. This frontispiece by the Master of the Vienna *Chroniques d'Angleterre* shows the process of the making of the book, from

FIGURE 4.7: Master of the Vienna *Chroniques d'Angleterre, Charles the Bold Ordering the Translation; Vasco da Lucena Presenting the Translation to Charles*. From Vasco da Lucena, *Deeds of Alexander the Great*, Bruges, ca. 1470–80. Paris, BnF, MS fr. 47, fol. 14r. Photograph: Bibliothèque nationale de France.

commission to the presentation of the finished object.[80] The continuity of space and time, between the commission and presentation, is ensured by Charles's and Lucena's figures, wearing the same clothes in the background as in the foreground. The courtyard appears as a transitional-translational space, joining the two bookend moments in the book-making process; the passage across the courtyard spatializes the temporality of translation.

With Charles's internal political problems intensifying by the mid-1470s, the imperial dream in the manner of Alexander receded. While Charles managed to finish the illumination programs for manuscripts described in the 1467–69 inventory of the ducal library as "Declaracion des parties a mectre encore en l'inventoire" (List of parts yet to be added to the inventory; Falmagne and van den Abeele 2016), the Burgundian crusade never materialized, nor did the new imperial Lotharingia. After Charles the Bold's unexpected death in January 1477 at the siege of Nancy, the window during which translation was painted as a process closed. In the aftermath of Charles's death, in the 1480s, it seems that Burgundian-Flemish artists returned to more traditional compositions that no longer highlighted translation in innovative ways; but they left us with a small and fascinating group of manuscript frontispieces that accompanied a mature and complex literature of the fixers, by the fixers, and for the fixers.

But the symbolic power of translation and the objects (manuscripts) that carry the (pseudo)translations in the Burgundian library—an empire of books—were the agent of the coming empire. The manuscripts of the Burgundian library opened up a horizon of expectation (also chapter 5). They posited translation as primary and a process, making translation into an agent of the new world order: the one that ultimately came into being for the last Valois descendant of Burgundy who was to rule over the world's largest Habsburg empire. Charles's daughter, Mary of Burgundy, did marry the Archduke Maximilian the year of Charles's death and gave birth to a son, Philip, in 1478. Duke Philip the Fair's ascension to the Spanish throne in 1506 culminated in the coronation of his own son, Charles V, first as king of Spain (1516), then as Holy Roman emperor (1519).[81] It is in that sense that translation as non-originary but as inaugural could carry the claims for an imperial Burgundy: the Spanish Empire was Burgundian not by (dynastic) origin, but by translation.

It is the fixer literature that imagined, enabled, and created this Valois-Habsburg Empire. Contrary to Huizinga's vision of the "waning of the Middle Ages," Burgundy is seen as the start of a new era, not the decline or end of Burgundian continuity. But it is only thanks to the lens of fixers that we can read this continuity of Burgundy in its final accomplishment as empire, rather than have focus fixed on the incompletion or illusion of

Burgundy as kingdom (Lecuppre-Desjardin 2016 / Lecuppre-Desjardin 2019). This goes, of course, against the grain of history and of literary history, which have been grounded in national conceptions of history and literature, dynastic conceptions of art and political history, and notions of modern nation-state borders. Burgundy is incomplete because it did not attain the status of an independent state in its ancestral site, uniting the historical time of its being to its land possessions. Fixers enable a different reading of imperial Spain: first, 1492—the year of the fall of the Muslim Kingdom of Granada and the year of Christopher Columbus's arrival in the Caribbean—can be seen not as a break, but as part of a continuity in the making of the Valois-Habsburg Empire; and second, we can see the agentive role of the literature of the fixers in it. Beyond imperial history, literary history is also at stake: where there is a decline for a national history, there is flourishing of a fixer literature that shapes the world, regardless of national boundaries or dynastic changes. This alternative literary history is the focus of the next chapter.

The Hermeneutics of Translation

AUTHORSHIP AND GENRE
(THE FIFTEENTH-CENTURY COURT OF BURGUNDY)

In the preceding chapter, we observed how the apparatus of the fixer reveals a late medieval understanding of translation as primary and originary, culminating in the vogue of pseudotranslation. In contrast, modern translation has been subsidiary to authorship and is considered a mere conduit of literary genres. The discipline of literary history has been shaped by this secondary and derivative placement of translation. That is, the construction of national literary histories of Europe imposed creative authorship and originality of form as categories of classification of medieval literature. When medieval literature was assimilated into national European literary histories, starting in the nineteenth century, it was defined and evaluated through the standards of modern aesthetic literary canons. National literatures thus acquired national author figures of international prestige (Dante, Petrarch, Boccaccio, Chaucer, Christine de Pizan) and exemplary forms of national expression (*Song of Roland*, Arthurian romance, *Song of the Nibelungs*). The advantage of having authors and genres in medieval literature was that the Middle Ages could be integrated into the history of the emerging European nation-states. In asking how originary translation impacts our understanding of basic literary categories of author and genre, this chapter pushes against the modern definitions of these two categories that have been applied to the medieval period. For, before there were authors, fixers were there first. And before there were aesthetically defined genre categories, there was situational genre within collections. In other words, there is an uncomfortable fit between literary and aesthetic categories of "author" and "genre" and medieval writing.

And that is what I mean by the "hermeneutics of translation": how the paradigm of the fixer, because it places translation and communication at the heart of medieval literacy and literary activity, radically changes the way we read European medieval literature.[1] In proposing translation as a hermeneutics, I write the history of medieval literature from the end, as it were. Usually, literary history is written from the beginning, that is from the origin. However, in his seminal 1969 essay "What Is an Author?," Michel Foucault explained that authority was made through the reception of "discursive initiation" (Foucault 1997, 220; see also Gavoille 2015). An "origin" is constructed in its reception. In other words, any designation of "initiation" as "origin" is a retrospective construction. The designation of "origin" is a retrospective gesture that bestows on the source the force of the act, the performative force of origination, what the nineteenth century called genius and we now call creativity. Initiation, origin(ation), inaugural gesture, emergence, invention, and foundation of a tradition are all histories that invert this retrospective gesture to posit it as original and proper to an author, who is a creator, a fount, a source. Modernity designates what was a discursive potential—that took a particular direction and shape in its reception—as discursive initiation, and moreover, as ownership, property rights, as if bestowed on the author at the moment of the discursive production. It transforms the potential, an uncertain future, into a certain history. And it is the certainty that history could only proceed the way in which it did that assigns an origin. To write from the end, that is to posit translation as the source of literature, means writing about the (long) death of the fixer rather than the emergence (or slow birth) of the author; it means thinking about genre as the existence of a situational cluster rather than as the invention of form. A hermeneutics of translation is a lens that offers a different view of the Middle Ages: one that was in its time but one that did not know its ultimate future outcome; and one that could only produce possible, speculative futures. The horizon of what it became—if at all there is a proper genealogy—is not the prism of what it was. To erect the ultimate outcome into a linear, genealogical (and teleological) history is to neglect what it was in its time when it had multiple possible, speculative futures. It is to unshed the light on the medieval world and thought. The crusades (chapter 1) provide a perfect example of what we lose with writing from the origin: after Acre fell in 1291 and Western Christians left the shores of Asia and withdrew to Rhodes, still in the 1330s no one thought that 1291 would remain the last moment in time that Christians had a hold in the Near East. Rather, European Christians thought that the recovery of the Holy Land would happen in the future, and that is exactly why and how they wrote, in relation to this potential and speculative future. They did not know that the "last" crusade had indeed been the last.

Thinking through this analogy with the history of the crusades, how can we write a new literary history from the medieval perspective of the fixer, and what kind of literary history can it be? This chapter takes steps toward a new literary history written through the lens of translation and with the fixer paradigm: it proposes a situational reading of authorship and genre rather than the explanation through individual genius or form. While several scholars have recently complicated the question of medieval authorship through translation, collective authorship (Coste 2021b; Cornish 2011), scribal authorship (Fisher 2012), and reader authorship,[2] my wager is that the literary history of the European Middle Ages must take up simultaneously the concordant questions of authorship and form at the site where they emerged, namely, in translation. There has been one constant in scholarly attempts at understanding the transition from medieval "auctor" to modern author, from authority to authorship: a disregard for the fact that vernacular authorship grew out of translation (Delsaux 2019). While I acknowledge that medieval writers have been first and foremost author names that conveniently gathered works of similar features into a corpus, ready-made to be studied by modern literary history, I wish to foreground the fact that they were first translators in the medieval sense of the activity (engaging in commentary, compilation, emendation, interpolation, abbreviation, amplification, etc.). We have been naming "authors" where there were first translators. Because medieval literary production was about memory, transmission, and reception, medieval literary history should be written from that point of view rather than from the vantage point of original creation and original creator. Adopting such a stance will allow us to analyze writers in two distinct positions: whereas translation is about the man and the world, authorship is about the man and the work. Failure to attempt a hermeneutics of translation—in other words, not to analyze writers as fixers and literature of the period as the literature of fixers—closes off a possible avenue of access to the medieval world.

Unmooring ourselves from the notion of "author" as the organizing principle of literary creation or library classification also gives visibility to a different notion of genre that concerns the form that clusters of works make within a collection, rather than the form in and of individual works. Anchoring ourselves instead in the notion of translator or fixer allows us to perceive translation as the giver and maker of forms rather than as a mere conduit of forms. This thereby alters the notion of genre as literary form. We no longer deal with the aesthetics of genre of individual works or exterior genre criteria applied to individual works but with clusters of works whose very fact of making a cluster gives shape to a situational genre within a collection. If we no longer see authors as creative origin or author names as organizing principles of works, this allows us to resituate a corpus of works within a collection. We will see that a "corpus," identified with certain genre characteristics or with a certain author name, does not always correspond to the situational genre—and also the practice, the use—of a library. Situational genre and fixer literature—literature of the fixers and by the fixers—emancipate medieval writing from the modern literary categories of genre and author, and they provide benchmarks for a new literary history written from the medieval point of view true to its time.

From Translators to Writers (Bonaventure, Albert the Great, John of Antioch, Nicole Oresme, the Apocalypse Tapestry)

In "What Is An Author?" Michel Foucault described the author function as an identifiable set of discourses that can be attached to a proper name, whether or not the person existed: "The author's name manifests the appearance of a certain discursive set and indicates the status of this discourse within a society and a culture" (Foucault 1997, 211). Foucault then drew a difference between authorship defined by law (acts) and that defined by market (goods). "Texts, books, and discourses really began to have authors . . . to the extent that authors became subject to punishment, that is, to the extent that discourses could be transgressive" (Foucault 1997, 212). Authors were responsible for their acts. But at the end of the eighteenth and beginning of the nineteenth century, a modern system of ownership of writing and texts—author's rights, intellectual property, copyright, and so on—came into being, whereby authors became owners of discourses as goods. Authors went from being juridical subjects to being economic subjects. From culpability to profit, from guilt to trademark, ownership changed literature from a relationship between a work and the world to a relationship between man, his intentionality, and his work (and, less commonly, a woman and her intentionality and work). The work was now attributed to a living individual, to *bios*, and was connected to his or her life (*vita*); the work was the issue of an autonomous creative self. Author was a creator and owner of an original work. In contrast, an author function was a field of discursivity but one that operated in a disconnect from the biological or psychological life of a historical person. The author function was first and foremost a signifier—author name—uniting a network of signifieds, a set of traits that characterized "a certain mode of being of discourse" (Foucault 1997, 211). Because it was not linked to the individual, to his or her life, the medieval author function, "auctor," was grounded in authority and could even accommodate anonymity since it did not depend on demonstrability in relation to *bios*. In juridical terms, before ownership, the medieval *auctor* was the responsible agent. Ancillary to his responsibility was that a medieval *auctor* acted as a guarantor of truth, at a remove from any kind of production of truth or new discourse. The medieval *auctor* was responsible but not necessarily the "origin."

I argue that in the Middle Ages "translator" is the other name for the Foucauldian author function. It would seem quite remarkable to propose such a shift away from authors to translators when neither "translateor" nor "interpreteor" actually appears in the list of agents engaged in intellectual activity and transmission in one of the authoritative medieval works that produced categories of writing agents for modern scholarship: Bonaventure's prologue to the *Commentary on the Sentences of Peter Lombard* (1250–52). Bonaventure lists writing agents as "scriptor," "compilator," "commentator," and "auctor."[3] On the one hand, it has been tempting to assimilate "auctor" with the modern notion of "author," and, on the other, it has been easy to miss the importance of "compilator," "commentator," or even "scriptor." Yet Bonaventure's list reveals a gradation of labor with increasing levels of autonomy and its hierarchy in medieval knowledge systems, from copyist (*scriptor*), who has no agency, to *auctor*, who has the most (but who is not yet an individuated "author"). This nuanced distribution of labor emerges from a very basic breakdown grounded in Scripture, in the Bible as Word (text) and God as Creator. In medieval theology, a writer is a transmitter, and transmission is an activity that is far from being an act of creation. God is the source of utterances, while human agents reproduce the Word (text) with varying degrees of agency.

Bonaventure's *scriptor* copies passively or blindly, so to speak, without change (apart from errors); he repeats and reproduces faithfully, without intervention. His agency is reduced to the activity of the writing hand, and he is "indeed someone [who] writes the matter of another without adding or changing anything" (aliquis enim scribit alienam materiam nihil addendo, vel mutando; Bonaventure 1864, 20). *Compilator's* agency consists only in the selection and gathering of texts or their parts written by others, which he otherwise copies blindly. His intervention is wholly contained in the selection he makes; he is "someone [who] writes the things of another, with additions but none of his own" (aliquis scribit aliena addendo, sed non de suo; Bonaventure 1864, 20). Both *scriptor* and *compilator* are reduced to the manual reproduction of the letter in manuscripts—literally, copying by hand (Lat. *manus*) the letters of the alphabet. We find a further degree of autonomy in the *commentator*, who deals with the spirit of the letter in that he interprets the text before him. The gloss—whether interlinear or marginal—that he produces consists of quotes from others and his words, although he does not have the initiative of his own doctrine or philosophy. He is "someone [who] writes the things of another, and his own; but such that those of the other are primary, and such that his own have been added for the purpose of clarity" (Aliquis scribit et aliena, et sua; sed aliena tanquam principalia, et sua tanquam annexa ad evidentiam; Bonaventure 1864, 20). The intellectual material of commentary is still the result of manual reproduction of prior content elevated to elucidation. Commentary (but not interpretation) is placed under the authority of another. A commentator is an appendix. The practice of writing, understood in its literal, instrumental sense of the manual reproduction of content by hand, made all three, *scriptor, compilator,* and *commentator,* into "actores" (Lat. actor), "doers" (from Lat. agere)—that is, hand writers. The same held for "auctor." But, contrary to the *commentator, auctor's* words form a doctrine and philosophy, while the words of others serve as verification and a guarantee. "Someone [who] writes his own things and those of another; but such that his own are primary, and those of the other have been added for the purpose of corroboration: such a man ought to be called an *auctor*" (Aliquis scribit et sua, et aliena; sed sua tanquam principalia, aliena tanquam annexa ad confirmationem: et talis debet dici auctor; Bonaventure 1864, 20). An *auctor* had agency; he was a writer, albeit some distance from being an author in the modern sense of the word.

Before the thirteenth century, no contemporary could lay claim to being an *auctor. Auctor* "denoted someone who was at once a writer and an authority, someone not merely to be read but also to be respected and believed" (Minnis 2010, 10). In the thirteenth century, Roger Bacon, Bonaventure's contemporary and fellow Franciscan, harshly criticized another contemporary, the Dominican theologian Albert the Great, for his claim to being an *auctor:* "And especially that man who is still alive, has the title of Doctor of Paris, and is designated with eagerness as *auctor,* which cannot happen without confusion and destruction of knowledge" (Et maxime ille qui vivit, habet nomen doctoris Parisiis, et allegatur in studio sicut *auctor,* quod non potest fieri sine confusione et destruction sapientiae; Bacon, *Opus minus,* qtd. in Chenu 1927, 85). For a contemporary to claim authority equaled, in Bacon's eyes, the destruction of knowledge. The claim of doctrine or philosophy came from historical stature: an *auctor* was an *actor,* a doer who had authority (*auctoritas;* Chenu 1927, 83; see also Gavoille 2015). He was a writer whose authority came from being ancient and from a long tradition of reception, hence Bacon's critique of Albert the Great. Moreover, something was "authentic" because it could be attributed to a recognized authority (Minnis 2010, 9). In essence, authority was circular: "the work of an *auctor* was a book worth reading; a book worth reading had to be the work of an *auctor*" (Minnis 2010, 12; see also Ziolkowski 2009, 427). *Auctoritas* had a double meaning "between a quality that empowers deed and deed itself" (Ziolkowski 2009, 424), just like *auctor* had a double function of doing (activity, role) and being (stature, authority); it was both performative and statutory.

While the autonomous—agentive—activity of writing, worthy of a claim to authority, allows us to speak of authorship, "auctors" are not yet authors but writers with agency (more than the doers, the "hand writers"). Namely, writer is not the center of enunciation, the origin of discourse; rather *writer* is still an interface of multiple functions, situated between multiple discourses (of works, writers, but also princes, nobles, knights, government officials) and the world. Specifically, writers become authors with the evolution of a self-conscious awareness that has juridical and commercial implications, aesthetic and stylistic markers. "Author" will be a creator and owner; "auctor" was a writer.

From *scriptor* to *auctor*, from doer to writer, medieval writers thus held the position of mediators, as actors between the divine word and the human object (text, book). We see this in a striking visual and textual example of the Apocalypse Tapestry, displayed at the Castle of Angers in France. It was commissioned in the early 1370s (ca. 1372) by Duke Louis I of Anjou, the brother of Charles V of France, Duke John of Berry, and Duke Philip the Bold. Unlike his brothers, who collected illuminated manuscripts, from an early age Louis promoted tapestries as a new model of graphic narrative art. The weaving of the Apocalypse Tapestry had begun by April 1377, and the accounts record payments through 1382. The tapestry is a monumental visual translation of the Apocalypse written by Saint John at the end of the first century CE; the images were painted by Hennequin of Bruges, the royal painter. Scholarly reconstitution efforts have established that it was composed of six series of tapestries, each of fourteen tableaux, adding up to eighty-eight tableaux: each series was approximately twenty-two meters long and six meters high, and each opened with a "reader" figure. Today sixty-seven out of eighty-eight tableaux survive, with four reader figures out of six series (readers 2 and 6 are missing). Also missing are the captions relating the scene for the viewers at the foot of each tableau. The textual aspect of the tapestry is preserved today in the figure of readers, seated in front of an open book or roll manuscript (in the form of scroll); their gaze is directed to the space where the inscriptions used to be.[4] The textual aspect of the tapestry remains in another way: the book as object appears in many individual scenes. Saint John is present in each tableau of the series, either as a (passive) witness or as an (active) scribe and/or participant in the scene. In most scenes, he carries either an open or a closed book of the Apocalypse. The interplay between seeing and reading is thus immediate in the tapestry.

Two tableaux stage specifically John's activity as a writer: tableau 27 and 28 of the second series. They are continuous: tableau 27 (fig. 5.1) shows the angel bringing the scroll with the revelation to John who is writing the book. The other angel holding the open book points to the heavens. Tableau 28 (fig. 5.2) shows the angel giving the book to John and pushing him to devour it: the ingested book is the revelation that he must transcribe and transmit. Although John eats the book, it consumes him; he becomes the book he transmits. He becomes the flesh of the book, the living (body of the) Word. The incorporation of the divine book indicates that John holds no agency beyond the action of his writing hand. Saint John is thus visually shown in the typical posture of evangelists, the scribes of the divine word, that was developed in iconography over centuries. The tapestry composition is closest to the iconography of Saint Matthew writing under the dictation of an angel (fig. 5.3), where the angel—as a kind of a fixer—enables the transmission from the divine to the human.[5] John's doing, his "authorship," is in the manual labor of reproduction and not in a creative act of production. John is a scribe; if he is a witness, his act of testimony consists in his faithful, blind reproduction. But Saint John was also an authority, a guarantor of the truth. Saint John's prophecy is recognized as one of the books of the Bible, the book of the canon, in other words, authentically inspired. On the scale of writing agents, John was neither a simple doer or writer since he was an authority, a reference; nor was he a creator, since he was a consumer of the divine book, which he "transcribed."

John of Antioch, in his translation of Cicero's *De inventione* (*On Invention*) and the anonymous *Rhetorica ad Herennium* (*Rhetoric for Herennius*; ca. 1282), sheds a light on Saint John's ingestion of the book: "all languages share this, because each language has its properties, and its manner of speaking. For this reason, no translator or interpreter could ever translate well from one language to another, were he not formed to the manner and properties of the language into which he translates" (ce est comunaument en toute lengue, quar chascune lengue si a ses proprietez et sa maniere de parler et por ce nul translateor o interpreteor ne porroit jamais bien translater d'une lengue a autre s'il ne s'enformast a la maniere et as proprietez de cele lengue en qui il translate).[6] A translator must take the shape of the target language into which he is translating, slip into the skin of the language into which he translates, embody the target language, as does Saint John when he swallows the book of the Apocalypse. In other words, the incorporation of the book signals John's position of translator, the book becoming the flesh of the target language, giving the book body in his writing. To ingest the divine book, John of Antioch suggested, means that the translator molds it to the target language of translation.

FIGURE 5.1: *Angel with a Book*. Apocalypse Tapestry, section 2, scene 27 (verso), ca. 1373–82. Angers Castle, France. Photograph: © Antoine Ruais / CMN Dist., Art Resource, New York.

FIGURE 5.2: *Saint John Eats the Book*. Apocalypse Tapestry, section 2, scene 28 (verso). 1373–82. Musée des Tapisseries, Angers, France. Photograph: © Antoine Ruais / CMN Dist., Art Resource, New York.

FIGURE 5.3: *Evangelist Saint Matthew Writing under the Dictation of the Angel.* Lime-
stone sculpture. Chartres, ca. 1230. Paris, Louvre RF 1388. Photograph: Louvre, Paris.

But the problem for the translator, according to John of Antioch, is that
each language has its "manner of speaking," and "the manner of speaking
in Latin is generally not similar to that in French, nor are the properties of
words or syntax similar to that of French" (la maniere dou parler au latin
n'est pas semblable generaument a cele dou françois, ne les proprietez
des paroles ne les raisons d'ordener les araisonemez et les diz dou latin ne

sont pas semblables a celes dou françois). There is furthermore "a discordance between letters and syllables found between the two languages" (la
discordance de letres et de sillabes qu'il trova entre les II lengues). In this
dissimilarity, room opens up for the translator's action that exceeds the
blind copy:

> For this reason, it behooves the translator of this body of knowledge
> sometimes to translate word for word, other times and more often
> sentence for sentence, and yet other times on account of the impen-
> etrability of the sentence, it is necessary to supplement and augment;
> otherwise, it is necessary in some places of elocution to change and
> modify the examples on account of the discordance between letters
> and syllables found between the two languages.

> (Por laquel chose il covint au translateor de ceste science de translater
> aucune fois parole por parole, et aucune fois et plus sovent sentence
> por sentence et aucune fois por la grant oscurté de la sentence li covint
> il sozjoindre et acreistre; autresi li covint en aucun leu en l'elocution
> de changer et muer exemples por la discordance de letres et de sillabes
> qu'il trova entre les II lengues.)

And it is indeed in that move between a straightforward "to translate"
(*translater*) and an entrepreneurial "to supplement-augment-change-
modify" (*sozjoindre-acreistre-changer-muer*) that an opening for the agency
of the translator appears, even as the injunction is always to translate "according to the discursive manner of the *auctor*" (sauvant la maniere dou
tratter de l'auctour; Monfrin 1963, 169).

This translational space finds its equivalent in the *causa efficiens* (efficient cause) of the scholastic method of exegesis in the early thirteenth
century, taken from Aristotle's *Physics*. Analyzed alongside *causa materialis*
(matter), *causa formalis* (form), and *causa finalis* (intention, end), *causa
efficiens* was defined as "the motivation, the driving force that turns a po-
tentiality into an act" (la motivation, la force motrice qui fait passer ce
qui est en puissance à ce qui est en acte; Compagnon, n.d.). In the same
period when John of Antioch is translating, Albert the Great—against
whom Roger Bacon railed—commented on Saint John in this way in his
Ennarationes in Ioannem:

> Indeed, the first efficient cause is divine knowledge manifesting itself to
> John within the uncreated Word, and in the incarnated Word instructing

and moving John to write. Matt. 10:20: *For it is not you who speak, but the Spirit of your Father who speaks in you.* The Spirit of the Father, however, is the Spirit of the speaking knowledge: on account of which the authority of his scripture is undoubted. . . . The nearest external efficient cause is John, who drank the secret Words from the spring of that sacred Lord's breast. John 21:20: *[the disciple] who also had leaned on His breast at the supper.* Ps. [45:1]: *My tongue is the pen of the swiftly writing scribe.* And again, Ps. [85:9]: *Would that I hear what the Lord God should speak unto me.* And thus it is loyal. John 19:35: *And he who has seen has testified, and his testimony is true; and he knows that he is telling the truth.* In this way therefore this scripture out of the internal *Auctor* is authentic, and out of the external loyal to it.

(Efficiens enim causa prima, sapientia divina est se in Verbo increato Joanni manifestans, et in Verbo incarnato Joannem erudiens et movens ad scribendum. Matth. x, 20: *Non vos estis qui loquimini, sed Spiritus Patris vestri qui loquitur in vobis. Spiritus* autem *Patris,* Spiritus est sapientiae loquentis: propter quod indubitata scripturae hujus est auctoritas. . . . Causa vero efficiens proxima exterius est Joannes, qui arcana Verbi ab ipso sacro Dominici pectoris fonte potavit. Joan. xxi, 20: *Qui et recubuit in coena super pectus Domini.* Psal. xliv, 2: *Lingua mea calamus scribae velociter scribentis.* Et iterum, Psal. lxxxiv, 9: *Audiam quid loquatur in me Dominus Deus.* Et ideo est fidelis. Joan. xix, 35: *Qui vidit, testimonium perhibuit, et verum est testimonium ejus. Et ille scit quia vera dicit.* Sic ergo haec scriptura ex interno Auctore est authentica, et ex exteriori est fidelis.)[7]

Causa efficiens was now seen as double in Bible commentaries: on the one hand, God the Father, or the Spirit, and on the other hand, man. Saint John was no longer an instrument, a writing hand; the agency of the external efficient cause belonged to him; the internal cause was authentic, but the external loyal and true. It is thus in the fault line of the internal and the external efficient cause, in the process of the ingestion of the divine book by its translator, John, that medieval authorship emerged.[8]

Through the conversion of the divine word, the passage from internal to external *causa efficiens*, one accedes to agency and greater autonomy. In his prologue to the *Commentary on the Sentences*, Bonaventure attributes authorship of the *Sentences* to Peter Lombard, the Magister, on the model of *causa efficiens* of Saint John: "Such was the Magister, since he puts down his own ideas and confirms the ideas of the Fathers. Hence, he truly ought to be called the *auctor* of his own book" (Talis fuit Magister, quoniam sententias suas ponit, et Patrum sententiis confirmat. Unde vere debet dici auctor hujus libri). This is because

> teaching is double, just as making someone see is double. That is, he who restored vision makes someone see; otherwise, he who points out with his finger that something is visible also makes someone see: God accomplishes the first; man the second. Similarly, he who teaches the body of knowledge, which he has, offers or extends it to another in speech or script; in other words, he who imprints the form of knowledge is all the same called a doctor and *auctor*; but God is primary, just as in the intention.

> (docere est dupliciter, sicut dicitur dupliciter aliquis facere videre. Aliter enim facit videre, qui visum restitui; aliter qui visibile digito ostendit: primum facit Deus; secundum, homo. Similiter, aliter docet qui scientiam, quam habet, in alium verbo vel scripto offert, vel ostendit; aliter, qui habitum scientiae imprimit: uterque tamen dicitur doctor, et auctor; sed Deus principalius, sicut in proposito.) (Bonaventure 1864, 20)

Although "God has not written this work with his own finger, but had another doctor" (Deus hoc opus non scripsit digito suo, ergo habuit alium doctorem), the doctor or *auctor* "has composed this work out of the knowledge that he had acquired over a long time, or through work, and he has confirmed his ideas through the doctrines of the Fathers. Even though there are many sayings of others, this does not take authority away from the Magister but rather commends his authority and humility" (a scientia, quam acquisierat longo tempore, vel labore, hoc opus composuit, et per doctrinas Patrum suas sententias confirmavit. Et quod sunt ibi multa dicta aliorum, hoc non tollit Magistro auctoritatem, sed potius ejus auctoritatem et humilitatem commendat; Bonaventure 1864, 20). As noted at the outset, Bonaventure's list of writing agents did not feature translators. On the surface, Bonaventure was not concerned with translating between languages, nor with commenting on vernacular writing, but with writing in one and the same language, Latin. But Bonaventure applied to Peter Lombard the thirteenth-century awareness of the breach that translation—"to supplement-augment-change-modify"—opened for agency of writers and, later, authorship.

A hundred years later, translators of Charles V of France (see chapter 4) will echo John of Antioch's idea that the singular ways of being of languages are compounded by the lack of equivalence between languages, namely between Latin and the vernaculars. Foremost among them was Nicole Oresme:

> At present, Latin is a more perfect and richer language than French, for the strong reason that one could not translate adequately all Latin into French. Among countless examples, this can be made clear with this common proposition: *homo est animal*, where *homo* signifies man and woman, and no word in French has the same equitable coverage. And *animal* signifies all beings that have a sensory soul and a sensory experience when touched. No word in French has this precise meaning. And that is why the [Latin] proposition *mulier est homo* is true, but [its French translation] "woman is man" is false. Likewise this [Latin] proposition is true: *homo est animal*, and this one [in French] is false: "man is a beast."

> (Latin est à present plus parfait et plus habondant langaige que françois, par plus forte raison l'en ne pourroit translater proprement tout latin en françois. Si comme entre innombrables exemples peult apparoir de ceste très commune proposition: *homo est animal*; car *homo* figure homme et femme, et nul mot de françois ne signifie equipollemment. Et *animal* signifie toute chose qui a ame sensitive et sent quant l'en la touche. Et il n'est nul mot en françois qui signifie precisement. Et pour ce ceste proposition est vraye: *mulier est homo*, et ceste est fausse: "femme est homme." Semblablement ceste proposition est vraye: *homo est animal*, et ceste est false: "homme est beste.") (Oresme 2013)

The translator's predicament only grows when it comes to science, an episteme. Although the text of Aristotle was "obscure in several places" (est en plusieurs lieux obscur), Oresme did not dare to "distance his language from Aristotle's text . . . so as not to distance myself from the intended meaning and fail" (eslongier mon parler du texte de Aristote . . . affin que je ne passe pas hors son intencion et que je ne faille). That is why "I must be forgiven in part if I do not speak of this matter as precisely, clearly, and stylishly as should be the case" (doy estre excusé en partie se je ne parle en ceste matiere si proprement, si clerement, si aornement comment il fust mestier; Oresme 2013). Confronted with Aristotle's obscurities, Oresme forgoes John of Antioch's entrepreneurial "sozjoindre-acreistre-changer-muer," just as he forgoes being precise, clear, and stylish in the language of the translation. Instead, Oresme resorts to the abundant creation of neologisms and of the new vocabulary in French: "it is necessary to use often the terms and proper words in science that are not commonly understood nor known to everyone" (il convient souvent user de termes ou de motz propres en la science qui ne sont pas communement entendus ne congneus de chascun; Oresme 2013). Indeed, Marie de France established already in the second half of the twelfth century that obscurity has been making translators into commentators, if not writers with agency: "As Priscian testifies, [the ancients], in the books they used to make, said rather obscurely, for those who were to come and who were to learn them, that there they could gloss the letter, and there they could place the surplus of their understanding" (Ceo testimoine Precïens / [Li ancient] es livres ke jadis feseient / Assez oscurement diseient / Pur ceus ki a venir esteient / E ki aprendre les deveient, / K'i peüssent gloser la lettre / E de lur sen le surplus mettre).[9]

Whether he is translating from Latin into a vernacular or from divine into human language, inventing new vocabulary or emending the text, the translator is creating equality rather than equivalence. Equality is Oresme's point on commensuration (see the introduction). In equality lies the room for agency and ultimately authorship. The modern focus on authors and their textual, original production has obscured the work of fixers and the role of translation in the emergence and articulation of vernacular authorship. But translation is the fault line of authorship. This imbrication of authorship in translation, the slow emergence of authorship from (vernacular) translation, must be understood as a very long process that is not interrupted by sudden appearances of author figures with a strong consciousness like Guillaume de Machaut or Jean Froissart (or Petrarch or Chaucer), but that continues past them into the modern era.

The Master Fixers (Machaut, Mézières, Froissart)

The hermeneutics of translation allows us to understand that "authorship" in this period is a literature of translation, or writing produced in translation. Translation commensurates and creates equality—in it lies the agency of writers. As we saw in chapter 3, Guillaume de Machaut, Philip of Mézières, and Jean Froissart are held as the fourteenth century's greatest writers in the French language. They were also emissaries, personal secretaries to great lords, and government officials—that is, intermediaries by virtue of their professional positions. In other words, they brought intermediation and commensuration to their writing as they positioned themselves as fixers in life and in their writings. Moving between Latin and different Romance languages and different parts of western Europe and the Mediterranean, they translated the world and brought narratives to their publics as fixers: what they did directed and shaped how they wrote about it. Thus, the writing they produced was for the most part engaged with its time and the world, clearly so in the case of Froissart and Mézières, while Machaut's late turn to historiography was more of an exception—albeit a striking one. Yet, these writers—and especially Froissart and Machaut—have been the focus of literary and historical study as "authors." Scholarship has until now, as a reflection of the overall devaluation of translation, privileged a mainly textual understanding of author or of authorial persona. In that, it was aided by the modern retrospectivity of author as (creative) origin. What has been neglected in this construction of authorship is the worldly aspect: the writer in the world, along the lines of visual narratives that develop in the fifteenth century around writers as fixers, as translators in and of the world (see chapter 4). By speaking of their being in the world, I do not wish to signal their biography, their professional career or statesmanship, or the list of patrons, but their position as an interface, the writer's positioning as a fixer. That these writers were among the first to have self-consciously developed the notion of something approaching "authorship" was a direct consequence of their individual positions as fixers at courts and in government and as fixers in search of eyewitness accounts across the world. They wrote with authority, that is, they were "auctors," since their authority came from being in the world, compared to church fathers, whose *auctoritas* came from a long tradition of citation practice. Fixers enabled the vernacularization of authority by their action in the world. ·

In that time period, there was no writer, "auctor," without the consciousness of being a fixer. Froissart presents, perhaps, the most transparent case in the way he positioned himself as a fixer rather than as an author. Froissart, as we saw in chapter 3, highlights his rewriting of the *Chronicle* by Jean le Bel (for the years 1325–50) in the first three versions of his *Chronicles*.[10] He supplemented le Bel's source by adding his collection of eyewitness testimonies, "And so I have always within my power investigated and inquired justly of the war's exploits and of the events that resulted from it" (si ay tousjours à mon pouvoir enquis et demandé du fait des guerres justement et des aventures qui en sont avenues; second and third redactions; Froissart 1867–77, 2:5). By the fourth (last) redaction, le Bel was no longer mentioned, and testimonies now constituted Froissart's sole acknowledged source of information, "the true information that I received from valiant men, knights, and squires, who contributed to increasing the deeds of arms and also by some kings of arms, known as heralds or marshals, who by right are and should be fair investigators and reporters of such undertakings" (la vraie information que ja ay eu des vaillans hommes, chevaliers et esquiers, qui les dittes armes ont aidiet a acroistre, et ausi par auquns rois d'armes nommés hiraux et lors marescaux qui par droit sont et doient estre juste inquisiteur et raporteur de tels besongnes).[11] Throughout the versions of the prologue, Froissart's stated goal of committing to "perpetual memory" (en memo[i]re perpetuel) the events of the Hundred Years' War between England and France "and of the neighboring kingdoms related to and allied with them" (et des roi-aulmes voisins conjoints et aliees avoecques euls; Froissart 1867–77, 2:11) remained stable. But just as the description of his source material evolved ultimately to give a unique emphasis to eyewitness testimony, so changed Froissart's relationship to the world. In the earliest Amiens redaction, Froissart inscribed himself as the translator in the world, that is as a fixer:

> I have expanded this book and this history with the just inquiry that I conducted in laboring across the world and inquiring about the truth of the events with brave men, knights, and squires who contributed to multiplying them, and also with some kings of arms and their marshals, in France as in England, where I worked with them to obtain the truth of the matter.

> (Or ay-je che livre et ceste histoire augmentée par juste enqueste que j'en ay fit en travillant par le monde et en demandant as vaillans hommes, chevaliers, escuyers, qui les ont aidiet à acroistre, la vérité des avenues, et ossi à aucuns rois d'armes et leurs mareschaus, tant en Franche comme en Engleterre où j'ay travillié apriès yaux pour avoir la vérité de la matère.) (Froissart 1867–77, 2:2)

For Albert the Great, the exterior efficient cause makes one loyal and true; for Froissart, he is a loyal (fidelis) transmitter because he is outside (exterius), collecting eyewitness reports from persons in the world. Translation is a relation between a man and the world, not a man and a text; in a relationship between persons, translation is loyal (rather than faithful to an "original"). But by the third and fourth redactions of the *Chronicles*, the very description of the world has changed:

> And the world is broken down and differentiated [differentiated and concealed] in several ways. First, valiant men exercise their bodies and arms to conquer glory and worldly renown [exercise their members in arms to advance themselves and increase their honor]. People talk, repeat, and describe their condition [and their fortunes]. Certain clerics write and record their deeds [events] and chivalries [third redaction stops here], whereby they are put and laid down in perpetual memory,

for by writing we can have the knowledge of all things, for good and evil are recorded, as are prosperities and fortunes of predecessors.

(Or se débrise et disfère [Ensi se diffère et dissimule] li mondes en pluisseurs manières. Premièrement li vaillans hommes travellent lors corps en armes pour conquérir la glore et renommée de che monde [traveillent leur membres en armes pour avancier leurs corps et acroistre leur honneur]. Li peuples parole, remember, et devise de lors estas [et de leurs fortunes]. Auquns clers escripsent et registrent lors œuvres [avenues] et baceleries, par quoi elles soient misses et couchies en mémores perpétuelles, car par les escriptures peut-on avoir la congnissance de toutes coses et sont registré li bien et li mal, les prospérités et les fortunes des ancyens.)[12]

Here, the chronicler is again portrayed as a fixer and not as an author. He is identified as a third element in the creation of "perpetual memory." The clerics, of which Froissart is one—"I, Jean Froissart, treasurer and canon of Chimay" (je, Jehan Froissarts, trésoriers et channones de Chimay; Froissart 1867–77, 2:11)—are the final link in a chain of transmission that would be incomplete without any of the preceding elements, actors and events, people and stories. The world is a fragmentation and a discernment (se debrise et disfere), a difference and a veiling (diffère et dissimule): the work of fixers is the work of translation. Froissart's authority, but not a claim to authorship, comes from his being in the world and being part of the chain, an element that participates in worldly circulation and transmission.

Mézières cuts another striking figure as a scholar and mystic, mercenary and soldier, as well as diplomat and chancellor of Cyprus. His worldly inscription as a statesman, politician, counselor, and envoy could not be greater. His literature of exhortation toward peace and reform of Christianity, with the purpose of a new crusade, is a quintessential literature of a fixer. Mézières's entire life as a fixer informed his own work. In the *Chivalry of the Order of the Passion* (*La chevalerie de l'Ordre de la Passion*, 1368–96), his experience foregrounds his proposals (see chapter 3). Life experience and firsthand information justify his *Letter of Lament and Consolation* (*Une epistre lamentable et consolatoire*, 1397): "by overall accounts public and private . . . the root and the cause of the defeat can be identified" (par les relacions doncques generales, publiques et privees, il se peut dire . . . la racine et l'occasion de la desconfiture; Mézières 2008, 121). Even in his advanced age, he receives information "by hearsay and by accounts of several men who do not all tell the same tale" (par oyr dire et par relacions de pluseurs qui ne tiennent pas tous une voie; Mézières

2008, 120–21). In the *Letter of Lament and Consolation*, "l'aucteur," the term used to identify Mézières in the rubrics to the chapters, is the one who "writes only by hearsay and by the accounts of others" (ne escript que par oyr dire et par relacions de pluseurs; Mézières 2008, 120), "by the accounts of those who were there on the woeful day" (par la relacion de ceuls qui se trouverent a la journee lacrimable; Mézières 2008, 119). Mézières paints himself as a weary, experience-worn, lifelong intermediary who "translates" the sources to his public, "the old solitary who has had no cease to write, shout, and scream that the stable be closed before the horse got away" (cestui viel solitaire qui grant temps a ne fina d'escrire, de crier et de braire que l'estable feüst close avant que le cheval ne s'eschappast; Mézières 2008, 120).

The firsthand information is translated into an elaborate allegory in each of Mézières's works. In *The Old Pilgrim's Dream* (*Le songe du Vieil Pelerin*, 1389), an index of allegories identifies "Burning Desire and his sister Good Hope [who] figuratively stand in for the Old Pilgrim, writer of this book called Dream or Vision, representing the persons of all those who desire the reform of the whole world and Christianity, and especially the reform of the Kingdom of France" (Ardant Desir et sa suer Bonne Esperance sont prins en figure pour le Vieux Pelerin, aucteur de cestui livre, appelle songe ou vision, representans les personnes de tous ceulx qui desirent la reformacion de tout le monde et de toute la crestiente et par especial du royaume de France).[13] On the one hand, Mézières the "aucteur" receives firsthand and relayed information; on the other, he is an emissary. "By the grace and command of Divine Providence, we have undertaken such a great voyage and a solemn embassy, a challenging delegation; that is, to find in this world Truth accompanied, as stated, by Peace, Mercy, and Justice" (Par la grace et commandement de Providence Divine nous avons emprins si grant voyage et une solennelle messagerie, ou une legacion de grant difficulte; c'est assavoir de trouver en ce monde cy Verite acompaignee comme dist est de Paix, de Misericorde et de Justice; Mézières 1969, 1:190–91). Mézières's language could not be clearer: an "aucteur" is the interface between "accounts of those who were there" and his own action in the world, his movement of voyage, embassy, and delegation.

The Old Pilgrim is named Burning Desire and Good Hope. He deploys all his writerly skills to advance a moral reform and crusading agenda. Allegory may be an expression not of his creativity, but precisely of his fixer's experience. It is a way to agentivize the future (as did Stanegrave; see chapter 3), a way to effect action, by appealing not to his past personal experience, but to the future of an universal order, freeing the future from the past, if not from the present:

Because this Old Solitary, for his sins, has sometimes been stricken and infected by the poison of the aforesaid wound, he feels pity now for those who have died by reason of it and still more concern and compassion for his Christian brethren who are now alive, lest they should, in time to come, be infected by the poison of this wound which has not yet been healed at all. (Mézières 1976, 8)

(Et pour ce que cestui vieil solitaire pour ses pechiez a este aucunesfoys ferus et envenimes du venim souvestesfoiz repete de la dicte plaie, et a present, par la bonte de Dieu, il a aucune compassion des trespassez pour la dicte plaie, et encores plus grand doubte et compassion de ses freres crestiens qui sont en vie et que en temps advenir ilz ne soient entechez du dit venim mortel de la plaie, qui n'est pas encore du tout estanchiee.) (Mézières 1969, 80)

The Hundred Years' War is the past and present wound, but the future, "temps advenir," is what matters. Putting to work the apparatus rather than the biography of the fixer, Mézières's experience and interpretation of the complexities of the world are a machine of translation into allegory, rather than the subject of the narrative. Allegory frees the future from the past in Mézières's universalizing and forward-looking projection. Mézières and Froissart both commensurate, but for Mézières allegory is the best measure.

It is interesting to speculate whether Machaut deployed allegory to similar ends in *The Taking of Alexandria*, a verse chronicle that stands apart from Machaut's poetic and musical production. Such a claim would run, at first sight, counter to the billing that Machaut has received as a preeminent (medieval) French author. Several generations of scholars shaped Machaut into the French national equivalent of England's Chaucer or Italy's Petrarch.[14] To achieve this goal, scholars advanced arguments on Machaut's status of "author" that would have been contemporary with his oversight of the making of codices of his collected works (five in number), and they likewise attributed to the French nobility the visionary power of financial support of creativity.

One manuscript of Machaut's works (Paris, BnF, MS fr. 1584 [MS A]) that has held the attention of scholars for a long time was collected toward the end of his life in the 1370s (ca. 1372–77). It is considered authoritative because it is late and is accompanied by two framing devices, two directional scripts, an index and a prologue: "A scribal-authorial hybrid, Machaut's prologue introduces a book made of many items but emphasizes their authorial and thematic unity and the relation of the parts to

the whole project of the manuscript book" (Leach 2011, 87). The index
has a virtue to draw attention to Machaut's name: "the order that G. de
Machau[t] wants his book to have" (Vesci lordenance que G. de machau
wet quil ait en son livre; BnF, MS 1584, fol. Av). The naming is thought
to reveal the self-consciousness of his corpus as *œuvre*. The prologue is
furthermore accompanied by two miniatures in which Machaut receives
the gifts of the God of Love (Sense/Meaning, Rhetoric, and Music; fol. D)
and of Lady Nature (Sweet Thought, Pleasure, and Hope; fol. E). Even
recent scholarship sees "the use of these allegorical offspring in the practice of authorship" (Leach 2011, 88), as Machaut rewrites "the exchange
narrative that typically focuses on the transfer of the œuvre to the patron
so as to focus on the gifts received by the poet that allow him to create
his œuvre": "This frontispiece replaces the intellectual's call to translate
ancient works with a poet called upon to translate and shape emotions
through verse. Affect replaces intellect; verse and music override prose
translation. The double frontispiece further identifies poetry and music
as divine callings that cause the patron-figures to express physically their
reverent support for the author's efforts" (McGrady 2019, 95, 127).

While we may recognize in Machaut a French version of a modern author, neither his immediate reception by contemporaries nor the staging
of his persona justifies this completely. In *The Writer's Gift or the Patron's
Pleasure?*, Deborah McGrady has presented a novel argument that the
production of manuscripts not of Machaut's making gives a more accurate
picture of "authorship" in the fourteenth and fifteenth centuries: "This
strong visual endorsement of a competing concept of literary creation
found in the first two illuminations in MS 1584 would not become the
standard and, instead, miniatures decorating later copies of Machaut's prologue would reserve a far more humble position for the poet" (McGrady
2019, 127). If we were tempted to proclaim the emergence of the full-
fledged author figure, as some of the earlier scholars have, we would be
amiss, she cautions. Machaut may have been a financially independent
poet without need for a patron for his works because of church benefices
his first "employer" obtained for him—this explains the particularity of his
independent positioning as a poet who finds that patronage is a menace
to his poetic freedom. He protects his self-conscious creativity (much
as Petrarch did). But in his immediate legacy, before being proclaimed
a canonical author in modern times, his single-author manuscripts were
subsumed into courtly dynamics of clientelism. Likewise, alongside
single-author codices, multiauthor codices—sometimes coherent compilations sometime miscellanies—either integrated Machaut into company
of other poets or made him into something else than the love poet that he

projected himself to be: "Artists responsible for later copies of Machaut's prologue proposed complex visual narratives that reinserted the poet into a conventional patronage dynamic that would become the standard in books produced for Valois princes and their entourage" (McGrady 2019, 128; see also McGrady 2012). It is indeed this tension between Machaut's intention and his reception that is of interest here, for it draws the horizon of expectations within which an "author" could be received. There was basically no room for Machaut as author, not because he may not have seen himself as one, but because authorship was still perceived as (a breach in) translation and a position of relationality to the world. Consequently, what is in scholarship referred to as his *œuvre* may be more accurately called a *corpus* or collected works.

It is in this context that we can return to Machaut's *The Taking of Alexandria* (*La Prise d'Alexandre*), which has never fitted neatly into a cohesive presentation of the poetic authorial persona or Machaut's purported *œuvre* (although it may fit into a corpus). As we saw in chapter 3, Machaut uses allegory in *The Taking of Alexandria* to inscribe new experiences into history and to make himself a translator of historical events. He presents himself, much like Froissart in the *Chronicles*, as the final link in a long chain of transmission, as a fixer for his audience. His use of allegory signals a historical consciousness and an acute awareness of the contemporary political events that have an effect on the world order. And yet allegory is a veil over Machaut's inscription in current events, as it distances contemporaneity and enables a metahistorical reflection on the *longue durée*. It has been impossible to conclude definitively whether *The Taking of Alexandria* is an anomaly or a seismic shift for Machaut; it comes too late in his career. Its exceptionalism conveys the shock of an extraordinary event of royal assassination by a Christian king's own liegemen: "I think that from London to Frisia, for the last thousand years nothing this evil has been plotted or carried out" (je croy que de londres en frige / passe a mil ans ne fu fais / ne penses si tres mauvais fait" (Machaut 2002, lines 8830–32). Machaut is writing after the murder of a king, an inconceivable act and fact, but from the perspective of the "after" the event.[15] The divergence of this verse chronicle and the lack of cohesion it introduces into the poetic-musical whole is remarkable for us only if we insist on Machaut the author and his *œuvre*. If, instead, we consider him to be a fixer, how much contradiction is there to Machaut's corpus? If we see him as a fixer, not as an author, Machaut's work was infinitely modulable, by Machaut himself and by his readers. An event of the proportion of royal murder reveals the "author" as a fixer in the world. As we will see in the next section, this has consequences for how we see Machaut in the larger context of European medieval writing. Terminology—moving away from the author and toward the fixer—changes effectively our analytical viewpoint and our comprehension of European medieval literatures.

Fixer Literature: Literature of the Fixers, by the Fixers, for the Fixers

Machaut's MS A (Paris, BnF, MS fr. 1584; Durand and Giovannoni 2012, 209) was purchased by Louis of Gruuthuse (ca. 1427–92), Philip the Good's counselor and governor general (*stadhouder*) of Holland, Zeeland, and West Frisia from 1463 to 1477.[16] Gruuthuse likewise had a copy of Froissart's *Chronicles* (Paris, BnF, MSS fr. 2643–46), also owned by most Burgundian nobles. Anthony of Burgundy (ca. 1421–1504), one of sixteen bastard sons sired by Philip the Good, who held the title of the Great Bastard (*le Grand Bâtard*) starting in 1452 and was governor of the Duchy of Luxembourg, commissioned an even more lavish copy of Froissart (Berlin, Staatsbibliothek, MS Dep. Breslau 1, vols. 1–4, ca. 1468–69). Both Louis of Gruuthuse and Anthony of Burgundy were pillars of the Burgundian state, one a governor and the other a top military commander. Machaut and Froissart found places in the book collections of these men, not as trophy "authors," but because of what their works told their owners about the world in which they lived. In fact, the hermeneutics of translation dictates a different reading of the medieval library, not as a collection of authors but as a collection of translators, not as a collection of works but as a collection of translations. Thanks to this lens, we will also see that the content of the works (fixer literature), the method (translation), and the agency of patrons who acted as fixers connect Louis of Gruuthuse and Anthony of Burgundy at least as effectively as their social status of being the duke's closest counselors and allies. Seen through the apparatus of the fixer, translation emerges as the central nerve of the library; it also makes the library a primary tool of state building and governmentality. Social status alone, symbolized in the ownership of the library, does not crystallize this instrumental and constitutive role of the library, since social status has most often been read as representation, whereby impressive library acquisitions and displays of lavish manuscripts in public readings are said to embody the patron's status. In contrast, the lens of translation reveals the library as the site and mechanism of counselors' political and social agency, laboratory and articulation of their political projects and policies: library is the policy-making body, as it were.

As we saw in chapter 4, Philip the Good and his entourage elevated translation into a massive cultural and political undertaking of rewriting, recomposing, as well as governing and state building. This project was sustained by whole range of intermediaries engaged in the work of translation, as David Aubert's prologue to the 1462 *Abbreviated History of Emperors*, or the *Chronicle of Baudouin d'Avesnes* (*Histoire abrégée des empereurs*, or *Chronique dite de Baudouin d'Avesnes*) indicated: "several translators, principal secretaries, skilled readers, illuminators, and writers, working diligently in great numbers in different provinces" (plusieurs translatteurs, grans clers, expers orateurs, ystoriens et escripvains et en diverses contrees en groz nombre dilligamment labourans; Paris, Bibliothèque de l'Arsenal, MS 5089, fols. Qr). Similarly, Aubert writes in the prologue to the 1463 *History of the Three Sons of Kings* (*Histoire des trois fils de roy*) that the duke "keeps in his daily employ and in different provinces principal secretaries, readers, translators, and writers charged with enlarging [the library]" (il a journellement et en diverses contrees grans clercs, orateurs, translatteurs et escripvains a ses propres gages occupez a ce; Palumbo 2001). The duke's counselors, governors, and commanders like Louis and Anthony, but also Jean de Créquy and Jean de Wavrin (see chapter 4), who were also patrons, consumers, and promoters of narratives, complete this network that manufactures and integrates culture at the level of policy and politics. Translation was not only a dominant form of cultural production but also the political road map of the Duchy of Burgundy toward an imperial title. This instituted the vogue of pseudotranslations, whereby all works and their writers had an interest in presenting and "selling" their works as translations and themselves as translators; instead of being new "authors," they could benefit as translators from the claim to *auctoritas* of the past. The market for narratives and manuscripts was fueled by the whole middle section of courtiers and counselors who were the pivot of city economies, where nonroyal nobles and bourgeois crossed paths, as we saw in Jean le Tavernier's frontispiece to *Chronicles and Conquests of Charlemagne* (see chapter 4, fig. 4.5). This new literature—of pseudotranslation—produced narratives whose main characters were fixers. The Burgundian fixer state produced a fixer literature: literature of the fixers by the fixers for the fixers. Given the negligence that the Burgundian fixer state had for "authors," what then was the place of Machaut and Froissart, to whom modern scholarship has granted the status of "author," in the Burgundian library? First, we will examine a Machaut manuscript (BnF, MS fr. 1584) acquired, not commissioned, by Louis of Gruuthuse. Then we will look at Anthony of Burgundy's new commission of the Froissart manuscript, written and illuminated by two of the duke's employees, scribe David Aubert and illuminator Lieven van Lathem.

Louis of Gruuthuse began collecting around 1460 to create the largest surviving collection owned by a nonroyal noble in the European West, representative of overall Burgundian bibliophilic interests: it contained 150 manuscripts in two hundred volumes (Morrison and Stahuljak 2015; Hans-Collas and Schandel 2009). About 150 were his own commissions; the rest were acquisitions of older manuscripts. His book collection was largely narrative prose and only exceptionally narrative verse (most notably of Christine de Pizan).[17] Other than Machaut's manuscript of lyric poetry, music, and narrative verse, Gruuthuse owned works by only one other writer whom we identify as a poet: Petrarch. But in line with Gruuthuse's interests, it was a prose work, *De remediis utriusque fortunae*, in its French translation by Jean Daudin (*Remèdes de l'une et l'autre fortune*; Paris, BnF, MS fr. 593). Louis's prose library was very much a copy of Philip's library, essentially of the section identified as "Library. Chronicles of France" in the 1467–69 ducal inventory compiled by the duke's secretary David Aubert.[18] Thus, many of Louis's manuscripts are connected to the Hundred Years' War, and its causes and effects (appendix B, section 1). Another group of works, dedicated to ancient and medieval Near East, stands out. *Gillion de Trazegnies* (Los Angeles, J. Paul Getty Museum, MS 111) is a crusade-themed work that follows the adventures of a Christian knight in the lands of the Muslims, and it has the distinction of being the sole original story in Louis's library of a Burgundian chivalric hero fighting in the East (cf. Jean de Wavrin; see chapter 4).[19] *Gillion*, despite being a historically inspired fictional narrative, falls in with at least two other Eastern-themed works, Vasco da Lucena's *The Deeds of Alexander the Great* (*Les fais du grand Alexandre*; Paris, BnF, MS fr. 257) and Raoul Lefèvre's *History of Jason* (*Histoire de Jason*; Paris, BnF, MS fr. 331). The stories of Jason and the Golden Fleece link the Crusader East and antiquity into one. If Jason is the founding figure associated with the chivalric Order of the Golden Fleece, whose task is also the defense of the Christian faith, then stories of antiquity set the stage for the contemporary Muslim East where Christian holy sites are occupied. The *Book of Heraclius* (*Livre d'Eracles*) and the *Chronicle of Baudouin d'Avesnes* (*Chronique dite de Baudouin d'Avesnes*; Paris, BnF, MS fr. 279, ca. 1470) were two other crusade-themed works in Louis's collection, and the addition of a history, *The Siege of Rhodes by the Turks* (*Le siège de Rhodes par les Turcs*; Paris, BnF, MS fr. 5646, after 1482), was in response to the unsuccessful Turkish siege of Rhodes in 1480.[20] Given this brief survey of his collecting proclivities, I venture that Guillaume de Machaut's *The Taking of Alexandria*, rather than his corpus of lyric poetry, was the reason for Louis's acquisition of MS A, aligning with his other crusade-themed works set in the East. Moreover, its crusade content was not the sole reason; Machaut's work, because of Pierre of Lusignan's dynastic and historical connections to France, also fit the category of "Chronicles of France." In other words, the acquisition of Machaut's manuscript, whatever the intention of the manuscript's prologue and miniatures, was not to grace Gruuthuse's library with a coveted author (and poet to wit), but rather to complement the contents of his manuscript collection dedicated to French and crusading history in overlapping ways. In that, it corresponded with Machaut's final inscription of his role as fixer to his audiences.

Much like Machaut's, the Burgundian reception of Froissart was dominated by issues relating to the position and function of fixers. Anthony of Burgundy commissioned his manuscript of Froissart's *Chronicles* (Berlin, Staatsbibliothek, MS Dep. Breslau 1, vols. 1–4, ca. 1468–69) from scribe David Aubert and illuminator Lieven van Lathem. The same scribe-illuminator team copied Louis of Gruuthuse's *Gillion de Trazegnies* (JPGM, MS 111, 1464), *Secret of Secrets* (*Secret des secrets*; BnF, MS fr. 562, ca. 1470), and *History of Jason* (BnF, MS fr. 331, after 1472). In chapter 4, we saw how van Lathem made translators into fixers and showed translation as a process, as an action of fixers in the world, in the frontispieces to Louis of Gruuthuse's *Gillion de Trazegnies* and Pseudo-Aristotle's *Secret of Secrets*. Similarly, in Anthony's *Chronicles*, the collaboration between the scribe and the illuminator produced a visual commentary on Jean Froissart's function as a fixer.

Anthony of Burgundy's book collection has forty surviving manuscripts. The greater part of the collection was produced between 1460 and 1477.[21] Most titles in Anthony's library were historical, and thirty were contemporary illuminated copies. Froissart's *Chronicles* were the only manuscripts in Anthony's collection illuminated by Lieven van Lathem. The Froissart manuscript that Aubert and van Lathem produced is a stunning visual feast, painted in a style referred to as *semigrisaille*, wherein part of the miniature is rendered in shades of gray and white with other elements portrayed in full color.[22] For our purposes, volumes 3 and 4 of the Breslau manuscript are the most interesting because the frontispiece of each volume features Froissart.[23] In the opening of book 3, alongside a frontispiece of Froissart's presentation of his book of poetry to Gaston de Foix (fig. 5.4), van Lathem painted a series of four illuminations of Froissart's arrival to Foix, accompanied and guided by one of the nobles of the court, Espaing de Lyon (fols. 11, 18, 19v). Van Lathem thus enhanced Froissart's role as fixer in the world, in search of information from eyewitnesses. In the frontispiece to book 3, van Lathem created a composition, used in the later frontispiece of Louis's *Secret of Secrets* (fig. 4.6). He placed Froissart in the same position that the messenger from Aristotle to Alexander will occupy, and put Gaston de Foix in Alexander's (or the king

FIGURE 5.4: Lieven van Lathem, *Jean Froissart Presenting His Book of Poems to Count Gaston de Foix*. From Jean Froissart, *Chronicles*, Ghent or Antwerp, 1468–69. Berlin, Staatsbibliothek zu Berlin—Preussischer Kulturbesitz, Handschriften und Historische Drucke, Dep. Breslau 1, vol. 3, fol. 1r. Photograph: Staatsbibliothek zu Berlin.

of Arabia's) position. On the right side of the Breslau frontispiece, two horses with only one rider signal the recent arrival of the person kneeling in front of Gaston de Foix. We find the same composition—two horses, one rider—in the background of the *Secret of Secrets* frontispiece. The open space on the right in the Breslau frontispiece, which does not exist in the other frontispiece (BnF MS 562), takes up another of van Lathem's compositions that we saw in the earlier frontispiece of the Getty *Gillion de Trazegnies* (fig. 4.4): a lone figure looking out to the horizon, outside the city gates.[24] In short, van Lathem's frontispieces convey the mobility and the communicative role of the fixer. The anonymous "translator" of *Gillion de Trazegnies*, Aristotle's messenger, and Froissart are all of this type.

The frontispiece to volume 4 of the Breslau manuscript is also of interest as it seems to translate visually the final version of Froissart's prologue (fig. 5.5). The left side of the miniature, which occupies only about a third of it, shows Froissart inside his *scriptorium*, at his desk. Froissart looks up into the space, as if collecting his thoughts or remembering. But to his right, we also see an open book, possibly a reference to le Bel's *Chronicle*. Froissart is seated in a typical position of translators surrounded by their books, often with an open book next to them, from which they are translating. We saw this standard portrayal of the translator also reproduced in the final third of the image sequence of the *Gillion* frontispiece (fig. 4.4), featuring a translator in his study, translating from an open book on his right. A great, earlier, example of this standard portrayal of translators is Jean le Tavernier's 1456 illumination of Jean Miélot's translation of *Miracles of Notre Dame* (*Miracles de Notre Dame*; Paris, BnF, MS fr. 9198). Two miniatures portray Saint Jerome and Jean Miélot in their study, surrounded by books. But while the miniature on folio 2 shows Saint Jerome in a similar posture to that in Froissart, looking up, the miniature on folio 19 depicts Miélot in a humbler posture with his eyes fixated on the manuscript before him.[25] In the frontispiece to book 4 of the *Chronicles*, van Lathem only moderately modulates the standard and static posture of the translator, possibly indicating in Froissart's free gaze an emancipation from the immediate source before him, similarly to Saint Jerome. Van Lathem's originality lies in what he does with the other two-thirds of the miniature, which shows the royal entry of Isabeau of Bavaria into Paris for her coronation (1389). Thus, the same frame holds Froissart on the interior next to the events happening in the exterior. The historical event flows from his writing, as it were. In juxtaposing the two bookends of a process, the event and its commission to memory via writing, the frontispiece translates the sequence described in the last version of the prologue in the Rome manuscript that we saw in chapter 4: it shows the breakdown of world making into its constituent parts, from the makers of actions to the transmitters of narratives to their recorders in manuscripts. As with many of van Lathem's compositions, this one will be influential on other Burgundian artists, notably the Master of Margaret of York.[26] In other words, the frontispiece shows Froissart as a link in the chain of transmission—his audience's fixer—recording for

FIGURE 5.5: Lieven van Lathem, *Jean Froissart Writing; Royal Entry of Isabeau of Bavaria into Paris for Her Coronation in 1389*. From Jean Froissart, *Chronicles*, Ghent or Antwerp, 1468–69. Berlin, Staatsbibliothek zu Berlin—Preussischer Kulturbesitz, Handschriften und Historische Drucke, Dep. Breslau 1, vol. 4, fol. 1r. Photograph: Staatsbibliothek zu Berlin.

posterity just as Machaut positioned himself in *The Taking of Alexandria*. Nevertheless, van Lathem positions Froissart not as the last link in the chain of transmission, but, as the narrative flows to his right from the pages of the manuscript, as a link in the continued transmission of the event that the audience will read or hear in the following pages. A writer is a fixer.[27]

Genre: From Literary to Situational

Literature of the fixers by the fixers is a literature of translation. I have been suggesting that a literature of translation cannot be aligned with the same categories of analysis as author-defined literature. This is especially true in the enlarged context that the understanding of fixer literature introduces, in which author literature, a literature of ownership and creative genius, does not have the same purchase on literary history. The analysis of Machaut's (Paris, BnF, MS 5184) and Froissart's (Berlin, Staatsbibliothek, MS Dep. Breslau 1) manuscripts opens the possibility that "Machaut" and "Froissart" belong in the later Middle Ages to a genre apart from their (not only authorial) persona, but even author function. In the case of Froissart, the hermeneutics of translation resolves a complex issue of representation. While it appears unclear why the same image composition would apply to a writer like Froissart and to an anonymous pseudotranslator of *Gillion*, there is no contradiction in using the same composition if Froissart, *Gillion*'s pseudotranslator, and Aristotle's messenger are all three perceived as fixers. In the case of Machaut, the genre of lyric poetry loses its acuity in the cluster of Louis of Gruuthuse's book collection, similarly to how Froissart finds his right place in the "world," just as he described in the prologue, in the constellation of David Aubert and Lieven van Lathem's collaboration. It is just such clusters in which we find "Machaut" and "Froissart" that I call "the situational genre." The situational genre becomes visible in the hermeneutics of translation. To accept these writers as fixers reveals, then, a horizon of expectations, not of one work or of an *œuvre* organized around the name of the author, but of a horizon of expectations for a cluster of works in which we find them. I claim that it is this horizon of expectations—this situational genre—that describes European medieval literature: what it does and says, the action and the discourse of medieval writing. Unmooring ourselves from the notion of author as the organizing principle of medieval literary creation or library classification, relinquishing the notion of literary genre based on individual formal and stylistic characteristics of a work, allows us to read medieval literature not according to an *œuvre* identified with certain genre characteristics or with a certain author name, but according to its uses and the practice of books, and according to its collective—albeit always situational—horizon of expectations. A library of translations is thus a library organized by situational clusters, not literary genres.

Genre has been a feature of analysis of European medieval literature, commonly split between romance, epic, lyric, chronicle, and so on. But genre theory is flawed because it is an expression of nineteenth- and twentieth-century canons of aesthetic and literary-historical thought, grounded in contemporaneous European national thinking. In a much-needed corrective to the construction of medieval genres, Simon Gaunt suggested taking up Keith Busby's *Codex and Context* and returning to the manuscripts, or more precisely codices, "in order to rethink the history of medieval literary genres" (Gaunt 2013a, 37; Busby 2002). To rephrase Gaunt and Busby, in their codicological contexts, medieval "texts" can be understood only as utterances, instances of discourse. Hence each manuscript is a variant (whence Paul Zumthor's *mouvance*) without the possibility of one's ever finding the initial text or establishing the first source or master text. A manuscript of a text or a work is the inscription of an utterance; a codex—codices often combine several manuscripts (texts)—is an instance of discourse. What we have commonly called a "compilation" is a configuration of a larger thought—and yet each codex is only one of the thought's possible articulations, that is, is an instance of discourse. Sometimes the compilation takes the form of a less cohesive *florilegium*, and sometimes it is intended as a coherent whole (e.g., Paris, BnF, MS fr. 2810, which contains Marco Polo's description of his travels).[28]

Much of the 150 years since the inception of medieval studies has been spent on tracing the "utterances" of a single work (or a cycle), that is, on establishing the textual tradition of a work in one language and its ramifications for other languages via translation. More recently, instead of genealogies, we have followed the itineraries, that is, the mobilities of these works (agents, sites, exchanges).[29] Busby advocated a codicological definition of genre—reading the text within the codex. Gaunt, moreover, read codices in the context of the time and place of their production—which he called "provenance" (Gaunt 2013a, 40)—and, when applicable, of their subsequent history. Between Busby and Gaunt, a double redefinition of genre, in the "historical and material manifestations" (Gaunt 2013a, 39), is at work in the notion of utterance: first, reading the work in a codex, then reading the codex in context (hence *Codex and Context*). *Provenance* is an important term in manuscript studies, indicating not only the manuscript's place of origin (in Gaunt's usage), but also its subsequent history of ownership. It adds to the codicological definition of genre—based on a single work in a codex or on a single codex in a context—a dimension of ownership, that is, a dimension of reception. Focus on ownership, and by extension on book collecting, furthermore opens up a single work to the notion of a cluster in which the work finds itself. To study the provenance of a codex means to grasp a manuscript not only within the cluster in which the codex was created (context), but also within the cluster of other works acquired or commissioned by the owner (library / book collection).

I thus propose a library approach to genre that reinforces the (historical and material) notion of the work as an utterance in the medieval context: a literary work connected to its place and connected to the other works in the cluster of the collection in which we find the manuscript. The "place" to which it is connected at any particular moment, its discursive instance, is a book collection, a library. The "cluster" is a collectivity of manuscripts, whose analysis stands in contrast to the study of individual works or cycles, or their genealogies. We find such clusters in the categories of the library inventory. What is the network each work constitutes along with the other works in that category? And how are we to read the instance of discourse of the cluster, a situational genre as it were, that the inventory proposes? I focus on the inventory of the library of Duke Philip the Good, written between 1467 and 1469, after the duke's death, by his secretary David Aubert. I trace how what we have defined as a genre of the *chanson de geste* is distributed across the inventory of the late medieval Burgundian library. *Chanson de geste* never constitutes a genre in the way we have been defining it; rather, it blends into several categories of the inventory.[30] At the same time, I observe how the inventory distributes the genre we call "romance" and redefines the coverage of "chronicle."

When Philip succeeded to the head of the duchy after the assassination of his father, John the Fearless, the ducal library had 248 volumes according to the 1420 inventory. At the time of his own death, the library had grown to 875 volumes, according to the 1467–69 inventory.[31] Because scholars have found a varying number of manuscripts that bear the marks of Philip but do not appear in the inventory, it is safe to say that the library may have contained around nine hundred manuscripts at the time of Philip's death.[32] Aubert's inventory records the following categories: no title (175 items); "Bonnes meurs, ethiques et politique" (Good morals, ethics, and politics; 193 items); "Chapelle" (Chapel; 56 items); "Meslée" (Miscellany; 33 items); "Livres de gestes" (Books of deeds; 72 items); "Livres de ballades et d'amours" (Books of ballades and love; 103 items); "Chapelle" (Chapel; 7 items); "Librairie. Croniques de France" (Library. Chronicles of France; 110 items); "Oultremer, medecines et astrologie" (*Outremer*, medicine, and astrology; 75 items); "Chapelle" (Chapel; 33

items); additional entries in "Declaracion des parties a mectre encore en l'inventoire" (List of parts yet to be added to the inventory; 18 items; Falmagne and van den Abeele 2016).

The categories of the inventory are instructive on late medieval thinking and are not based on our modern notions of genre. But these categories have been set aside by the modern understanding of literary genres—romance, chronicle, lyric (poetry), epic—that define literary history and literary studies. To emancipate ourselves from the modern genres allows us to assume the medieval genre. The argument that there is a "medieval genre" different from the modern one is reinforced by the fact that the categories of the inventory were not necessarily built in situ, in one centralized ducal library, but that the inventory was "the result of a stocktaking of books from at least four depositories" (Falmagne and van den Abeele 2016, 41). Its organization was thus deliberate and based on a set of criteria. That is, this organization that the inventory presents does not emerge out of Aubert's notational process but out of the practice of the library—its use—such as Aubert could have observed during his time as Philip's "escripvain" from 1459 to 1467. For instance, the first category, without a title, is a collection of books that seems to have been Philip's portable library that traveled with him (Wijsman 2020). Based on the number of works, "meslee," a "mixed" category, was also perhaps a portable collection. One category stands out, repeatedly, as a clear-cut practice: "chapelle." Each of its three iterations in the inventory testifies to a mix of what we consider different genres: books of hours, psalters, breviaries, saints' lives, missals, antiphonals, and so on. These three instances of "chapel" are not respectively subcategories of "Good morals, ethics, and politics," "Books of ballads and love," "Library. Chronicles of France," the categories that they follow, but individual categories on the same footing with other categories of the inventory (Wijsman 2022). The fact that the three were kept separate possibly related to their different in situ practice. It is therefore all the more striking that, if the hypothesis of four library sites is correct, Aubert would not have cataloged all the other manuscripts according to their in situ arrangement, but, as I propose, according to the practice that bound them together—much in the same way that the portability of the untitled collection or the three in situ iterations of the "chapelle" were a practice of (a medieval) genre. In other words, since we do not find poetry entirely separate from romance, and *chansons de geste* apart from chronicles, instead of a set of stylistic and formal characteristics I propose the practice of books as a genre.[33]

A whole section of the ducal library was dedicated to the lands overseas, "*Outremer*, medicine, and astrology." It contained a variety of what we call histories, travel reports, crusade treatises, and didactic works, several mappemondes (appendix B, section 2). I wish to point out that "Oultremer," "beyond the sea," which is a geographic category, was in this case reserved specifically for the crusades in the Holy Land, in the Near East. The East was otherwise well integrated into the library and the collectors' minds.[34] If it is not surprising that the category "Books of deeds" also contains narratives concerning the East, such as Machaut's *The Taking of Alexandria* (no. 489), a sizable presence of the narratives taking place in the east in the category "Library. Chronicles of France" is unexpected.

The contents of the category "Library. Chronicles of France" ostensibly traverse the Francophone space of northwestern Europe—the Kingdoms of England and France and the Burgundian Netherlands—as they include the compilation of the *Chronicles and Conquests of Charlemagne*, histories of the British Isles, chronicles of the Burgundian Low Countries (Brabant, Flanders, Hainaut, Holland), and numerous chronicles of the Kingdom of France. In no way does this "France" correspond to its modern namesake, the Hexagon. But there is more, for this category also contains works dealing with the East. We thus find histories *Godefroy of Bouillon* and *Baudouin of Jerusalem*, several histories of Alexander, Jean Mansel's *The Flower of Histories*, the *Moralized Bible*, Voragine's *The Golden Legend*, and Augustine's *The City of God* (appendix B, section 2). "Library. Chronicles of France" is thus composed of many types of narratives. If we conceptualize this category less in terms of a polity then as a language sphere, then the Near East—that is the Holy Land conquered by the armies that were by and large French speaking—fits perfectly in this category. It signals a continuity between "France" and the East, and between periods in the library— antiquity, Judeo-Christianity, and the contemporary period of crusades, and during the wars between England and France. There is, then, an even larger concept of the history of France at work here, one that stretches from Great Britain to the Near and Middle East. Narratives relating the conquest of medieval Syria, or the Holy Land, primarily by crusaders who spoke French (Morreale and Paul 2018), a conquest whose theologico-juridical justification lay in the life of Christ and the lives of saints, unite biblical and crusading history into a contiguous Francophone area and a continuous temporality.

The inventory thus allows us to read the library not as a form giving to a text—the form of romance, lyric, epic, and so on—but as an instance of the organization of the world, of the political, historical vision of the world: the East is in the chronicles of France just as "France" is a matter of the East. Here an additional example of the richest nonroyal library in the European West, that of Louis of Gruuthuse, Philip's chamberlain, is particularly instructive: as we saw, Louis copied much of Philip's library in his two hundred volumes, of which about 150 were his own commissions. According to our modern criteria of analysis, Louis's book collection seems to divide this category between the "Chronicles of France" and the "Outremer,"[35] but in fact it mostly equals one single category, "Library. Chronicles of France," in the ducal inventory, where the East is germane to the chronicles of France. I consider the medieval inventory classification to be, despite its variety and lack of uniformity, or perhaps thanks to it, a medieval genre. It is a situational genre not merely in relation to where the books were assigned, but in the sense of the situation that they describe for us, the instance of discourse and its intrinsic vision of the world. A cluster is a vision of the world and a statement of state policy.

Taking up the example of the *chansons de geste*, the first observation is that they do not constitute a well-defined or separate category in the library inventory of 1467–69. Rather, the works that we have defined for almost 150 years as *chansons de geste* are strewn across several large categories. Titles we associate with the *chansons de geste* are included in "Chronicles of France" (traditionally considered to be histories), "Books of deeds" (works we traditionally call romances), and "Books of ballades and love" (again, traditionally considered to be romances) (appendix B, section 3). The greatest number of titles associated with high medieval works that we understand to be the *chansons de geste* is found among "Books of deeds": prose versions of *Renault de Montauban, Huon de Bordeaux, Beuve de Hantone*, and *Garin le Loherain*,[36] and verse versions of the *Geste des Lorrains* ("old song," "vielle chansson"), *Guillaume d'Orange, Ayméri de Narbonne*, and *Garin de Monglane*.

In contrast, in "Chronicles of France," we find a single *chanson de geste*, albeit in multiple variants: "*The Book of Girard of Roussillon*, Duke of Burgundy, in Verse" (*Le livre de Gerard de Roucillon, duc de Bourgogne, en ryme*; no. 676), and again in Gascon verse (*rymé en gascon*; no. 680), then two volumes (presumably in prose) of "*L'istoire de Gerard de Roucillon*" (nos. 677–78), and "another small manuscript of *Girard of Roussillon*" (*un autre livre petit . . . le rommant de Gerard de Roucillon, duc* etc.; no. 679). Within the larger history of France that this category incorporating England, Scotland, France, and the Low Countries outlines, the presence of copies of a prosified *Girard of Roussillon* can be easily explained: Girard was the first historical Duke of (southern) Burgundy, who at once validated the claim of the Dukes of Burgundy to autonomy from the French crown and legitimized their ducal title; in literature, Girard valiantly fights to maintain his lands and title against Charles the Bald, until reconciliation and submission to the king, much like Philip's 1435

Treaty of Arras with Charles VII of France (which marked the beginning of the end of the Hundred Years' War between the Kingdoms of France and England; see chapter 4).[37] But, as we saw, this category also contains works dealing with the East. *Girard* is part of a larger French-language vision of the world, in which Carolingian Lotharingia might correspond to a part of the western Roman Empire.

The other category with few, but significant, *chansons de geste* titles is "Books of ballades and love," where we find *Ogier the Dane* (*Ogier le Danois*). It existed in several manuscripts, both in verse (no. 536, nos. 540–41) and in prose (no. 537). The description of another manuscript (no. 535) does not specify whether it is verse or prose. *Ogier the Dane* is accompanied by a version of the cycle of the *chanson de geste* hero William of Orange, "the book of Aimery of Narbonne, William of Orange, Vivian and Rainouart au tinel" (li livres de Eymery de Nerbonne, de Guillaume d'Orenges, de Vivien et de Renouart au tyner; no. 571). Both find themselves in the mix with, for instance, Ovid's *Metamorphoses* and *Ars amatoria*, the *Romance of the Rose*; the *Romance of Reynard the Fox*; Christine de Pizan's *One Hundred Ballads* and *Letter to the God of Love*; Guillaume de Machaut's and Charles d'Orléans's poetry; the series of works of chivalric vows continuing the alexander cycle, *The Vows of the Peacock* (*Vœux du paon*) and *The Restoration of the Peacock* (*Restor du paon*); and the *Knight of the Swan* (*Chevalier au cygne*). At entry 593 seems to begin a subcategory of "ballades" (the rubric title is above the margin),[38] where the majority of the works, though not all, are in verse, "en rime."

"Books of ballads and love" is the only category that seems to be defined by a combination of form and content: verse and love themes in narrative and lyric poetry. Yet, when *Ogier the Dane* appears in both verse and prose, it stands out. The verse versions may be Adenet le Roi's *Enfances Ogier* (*Childhood Exploits*; no. 536); and "the book of Ogier the Dane, in verse" (le livre d'Ogier le Danois, en rime; nos. 540–41) may represent the *chanson de geste* relating Ogier's rebellion, *La Chevalerie Ogier* (*Knightly Exploits*), since its inventory entry indicates that no matter the consequences, Ogier will do battle: "Charles, may all my land be devastated" (Charles que toute soit / ma terre gastee; no. 540). There is another "rommant Ogier" (no. 535), whose inventory entry points to a love story, "the maiden said" (dist la pucelle), perhaps a second volume of number 536, since they are both described as "a little book" (un petit livre[t]); we know that the *Enfances* had a love story. However, we do not know if number 535 is also in verse, or in prose. But the prose version of number 537 is likely the now-lost manuscript of the prosification of the *Chevalerie Ogier* containing the liberation of Rome and Jerusalem and adventures in the east, without Ogier's rebellion, known today thanks to the first printed editions of Antoine Vérard. Adenet le Roi's two other works, *Bertha Broadfoot* (*Berthe aux grands pieds*) and *Cléomadés*, were also placed in this category of "Books of Ballads and Love" (nos. 552–53). Of all the *Ogier the Dane* manuscripts, only number 535 also carries in margins "gestes," at odds with its category. For example, in this category both *Floire and Blanchefleur* (in a codex with *The Lady and the Unicorn*; no. 572) and *William of Palermo* (no. 585), neither now considered to be a *chanson de geste*, also carry the scribal notation of "gestes" in the margin. The category of ballads and love challenges our notion—very much influenced by the traditional scholarship of the *Song of Roland* (and its quasi-nonexistent love story between Aude and Roland)—that the *chansons de geste* are stories of military and historical import but also "loveless."[39] While it may be unclear why all of *Ogier* is in the category of "Books of Ballads and Love," the works centering on Guillaume d'Orange (listed both in "Books of love," no. 571; and in "Books of deeds," no. 526)—despite being full of battles against "Saracens"—also feature many Christian-Muslim love stories.[40] Thus we have works relating to William of Orange in two categories; and this could have been—though it is not—also the case of *Ogier the Dane*, the two different branches whose high medieval versions, one centered on courtly action, the other on rebellious battles, could have been split between two different categories, like the *chanson* of William of Orange.

What becomes apparent is that the *chanson de geste* is not a genre in the inventory of the fifteenth-century medieval library; in any case, it is not a genre according to our commonly accepted parameters. Instead, inventory categories emerge as an active and agentive genre. The function, if not form, of narratives that we would normally classify as *chansons de geste* seems to vary according to the cluster that they are in. The name of the category in which they appear—"chronicles"—and the works in whose company we find them emphasize, even produce the historical quality of the two versions of *Girard of Roussillon*, in verse and in prose. We can note in the historicity of this category a strong degree of presentism: many of the geopolitical areas in these chronicles are of importance to the Burgundian present, as part of the Burgundian sphere of influence or rule, and they are somehow connected to and even dependent on the speakers of the French language. In other words, the historical quality of the prose *chanson de geste* of *Girard of Roussillon*—the ancient claims to the autonomy of Burgundy—and its connection to Carolingian history, make it a part of the "history of France"—of France's larger, even global history— that is still active or being reactualized geopolitically in the Burgundian present.

A corollary is that "romance" as genre also suffers in this analysis. The coexistence of categories of "Books of deeds" and "Books of ballads and love" indicates that there was no such thing as a stable genre of "romance." It is thus that *Lancelot of the Lake*, known to us for the love of Lancelot and Guinevere, is not in the category of "ballads and love" but in that of "deeds." According to the inventory's marginal notations, different types of narratives qualify as "gestes," among them some we traditionally define as "romances" (e.g., *Floire and Blanchefleur* and *William of Palermo*, mentioned above), although they actually found their place in "Books of love" despite their marginal notation of "gestes."[41] Another example of negotiating the situational genres of the library inventory is the case of Guillaume de Machaut. The duke owned several manuscripts of Machaut: *The Taking of Alexandria* (no. 489) is in "Books of deeds." But of the three Machaut manuscripts (nos. 530–32) that are in "Books of ballads and love," numbers 530 and 531 bear in the margins a surprising notation: "gestes."[42]

Most narratives that we call *chansons de geste* have found their place in the "Books of deeds" category (with the exception of *Girard of Roussillon* in "Chronicles," and *Ogier le Danois* and a version of *William of Orange* under "Books of love"). It is as if the narratives associated with *chansons de geste* are more easily fitted within "Books of deeds" than in "Chronicles," the "history" genre (appendix B, section 2). But what does this appellation, *livres de gestes*, mean for the *chansons de geste*? The different narratives of the "Books of deeds" category, verse and prose, and whether they represent high or late medieval compositions, share the fact that they are an object, a book, regardless of narrative type or form. Put differently, what defines them is that they are a book, not what narrative the book contains. And they share a quality of "deed": *geste* derives from the Latin past participle *gesta*, things done. Not unlike the "Chronicles of France" category, works in "Books of deeds" could also be seen as histories. What distinguishes them then from those in the "Chronicles of France" category? First, they are not connected to "France": while written in French, they concern parts of the world that were not necessarily at the time under Burgundian influence, such as Greece. The most outstanding characteristic seems to be that the action of most narratives, if not all, takes place wholly or partially in the contact with "Saracens"—in Spain, Sicily, Greece, the Holy Land, Egypt—or in ancient Greece. One-third of narratives, mostly Arthurian, are books of chivalry. Crusades were also a matter of chivalry: Lefèvre's *History of Jason* is perhaps a quintessential work here. Since Jason was the founding figure of the ducal chivalric Order of the Golden Fleece, whose task was the defense of Christian faith, this category poses a foundational link between Jason and the Order of the Golden Fleece, between Troy and the crusades, between past *gesta* (things done) and future chivalric action in the "eastern" sphere (for example, in the form of a Burgundian crusade, launched in 1464 but failed in 1465). Thus, if we understand "gestes" not only in the Latin past value of the term but in terms closer to their contemporary meaning of "feat, action," it is possible to conceive the category "Books of deeds" as an action genre, intended for the future.

This then is a prospective action genre: what is told as "things done,"— events of ancient Greece, combat against Muslims, and, crucially, acts that may again be done, future action, "gestes," or indeed, what never did but may yet happen (Burgundian crusade or imperial title), under French-speaking rule. The East was conquered once, and it will be again; Lotharingia existed once, as it may again; Spain and Sicily were never Burgundian but may be; and so on. The "Books of deeds" category describes what will have been, a future anterior. The thrust of this category is in its agency and impact on the world, rather than in any stylistic or formal quality that would qualify its literariness. It takes the form of a future anterior because it contains works that are histories, but its force is projective, its potential in the chivalric deed. This category is beyond the "genre" of the *chansons de gestes*, for any narrative can be a book of deeds.[43]

The library is an archive of possibles—a past archive of the future possibles—where the rewriting of the *chansons de geste* projects a future anterior of the Burgundian state. Let us take the examples of *Girard of Roussillon* (in "Library. Chronicles of France") and *Garin le Loherain* (in "Books of deeds").[44] Together they reconstruct the ancient Carolingian Kingdom of Lotharingia, defended by Girard of Roussillon against the claims of Charles the Bald and incorporating Lorraine, the fief of the Loherain clan, allied to Germany but loyal to France. Between these two works, Burgundian Lotharingia stretches from the North to the Mediterranean Sea. This is consistent with Burgundian imperial policy, begun under Philip the Good and enacted under Charles the Bold, to unite the Burgundian Low Countries and the Duchy of Burgundy into a continuous territory inclusive of Lorraine and Liège (see chapter 4).[45] The future anterior of works in "Books of deeds" makes this category a medieval genre: a genre defined by a chronotopography—a site (Lotharingia and the East) and a time (simultaneously ancient, contemporary, and prospective)—rather than by literary style or form. Questions of (aesthetic) genre do not motivate the organization of the library, but rather its organization turns around the conception of the world and agency in the world. This category mixes antiquity (Rome, Greece, Judea), Arthurian matter, and the crusades, and it spans an area from the North Sea to the

Mediterranean Sea and across it to the Near East. Over and over again, the library demonstrates the connectivity of the world system from Persia and Syria to Greece and Rome to Burgundy as well as the continuity of the past to the present. And if this category mixes past and present, because the present reactualizes the past, so it mixes also fact and fiction as well as prose and verse. This is agency of a cluster, rather than of a single work or cycle. The category "Books of deeds" thus allows us to see the library as a living matter; the library is not yet an institution, but it is a policy-making body.

With this agency in mind, it is interesting to observe that the majority of commissions in the book collections of the duke's entourage were made of the works that belong in the "Books of deeds" category, which they offered to the duke. This is especially true of the collections of Jean de Créquy, Jean de Wavrin, and Jean de Croÿ, less of the rich collection of Louis of Gruuthuse, for, as mentioned, his library imitated the duke's category "Library. Chronicles of France." These men were all important political counselors to Philip; it is from that perspective that their role as literary counselors should not be set apart from their political counsel. The claim of chapter 4, that literature was a policy, is renewed from this angle as well.

A New Literary History: The Horizon of the Expectations of a Cluster

The idea of library as a set of clusters or networks, of the library as providing a genre based in practice and connected to the world, of the library as the driver of a future anterior, sets the stage for another corrective. In 1970, Hans Robert Jauss wanted to "bridge the gap between literature and history, between historical and aesthetic approaches" (Jauss 1982, 5.18). Namely, his influential *Toward an Aesthetic of Reception* was an attempt "to solve the problem of how the isolated literary fact or the seemingly autonomous literary work could be brought back into the historical coherence of literature and once again be productively conceived as evidence of social process or as a moment of literary evolution" (Jauss 1982, 9–10). This could be achieved thanks to "a dimension that inalienably belongs to its aesthetic character as well as to its social function: the dimension of its reception and influence" (Jauss 1982, 18). To reconstitute reception and influence of a work within "the horizon of expectations" meant for Jauss to reconstruct the preunderstanding of the genre, the form and themes of already familiar works, and the opposition between poetic and practical language. It is when a new work departs from the horizon of expectations that a modification of the horizon can occur and over time construct a new horizon of expectations. Jauss offered a linear reading of the history of a single work that influences and acts on history, specifically the history of its publics and of aesthetics. He also thought of the (aesthetic) description of the horizon of expectations as something that did happen, "evidence of social process or . . . a moment of literary evolution," thus giving aesthetics a material, historical presence. But a single work of literature did not only represent: it was not merely "evidence." What Jauss posited implicitly is that a single work acted and influenced; it had effects, and it could change the horizon of expectations. In other words, it was not just evidence of social process: it *was* the social process. This hermeneutics of translation expands therefore Jauss's horizon of expectations from a linear and diachronic to a synchronic and rhizomic—from single work as object to a network of multiple and interconnected works and objects (books, manuscripts, artifacts). This is neither about intertextuality—placing texts into an interrelated network—nor is it about the horizon of expectations of a public. Rather, it concerns the potential effective power that objects constitute together in a cluster, and, therefore, it pertains to the horizon of expectations of a cluster as a network (and no longer the horizon of expectations of a single work or cycle).

The categories of the Burgundian library do not merely redraw our genre distinctions but show that the library as network is an actor in and of the world. This is because the clusters in the categories of the inventory are not just a historical record of a culture and its practices (whether conscious or unconscious, visible or repressed). They are not merely a representation but are also agentive; in the proper sense of "cultural production," the clusters "produce" events, generate actions into happening. Beyond representation, the Burgundian library and its literature of translation are active and effective of a future event, a new world order.[46] In that sense, works are not merely objects of knowledge or material objects of desire; but as a cluster, as a network, they have a life of effectivity. They are connected to the world as actors of it; they effect action in the world.

The hermeneutics of translation interrogates a blind spot of nineteenth-century foundation of European medieval studies, the foundation of all literary history as teleological progression: from *chanson de geste* to *roman*, from verse to prose, from orality to writing. This forces us to undertake a new literary history. Literature of the fixers by the fixers for the fixers is a literature of the world, in which we learn to read not the genealogy of the man and the work, but the action of the works in the world. Indeed, we should once and for all abandon the genealogical thinking of literature and of medieval origins. Many recent efforts at inscribing the Middle Ages as a field of relevance in the humanities today have implicitly valorized the Middle Ages as the site of origin: the formative moment of modern discourses on nation, race, sexuality, and so on. To this list, I would un-hesitatingly add genre. I do not see what is to be gained today with a demonstration that the romance genre is the precursor of the novel or that the notion of "author" was fully fledged already in the Middle Ages (or for that matter, in the Renaissance). To show that modernity has its origins in the medieval period has not sufficed to make the medieval modern. In the age of global studies, perhaps we can be focused less on the stylistic and aesthetic formalism of the literary genre, and its place in the development of national literature, and more on the proximity and synchronicity of works in clusters that are a kind of a provisional genre, acting or interim, as it were: a situational genre enacting a discursive instance of a vision of the world. In our global moment, the question may very well be reformulated: in what ways can the medieval make the modern—and the moderns— grasp what we have until now failed to understand about modernity. How can the medieval be read as modernity's future anterior, rather than as precursor to or as origin of, as "premodern?" (Agamben 2009c; Stahuljak 2020a). Modernity would then be the speculative future of the medieval instead of the medieval being modernity's past.

Fixers

EARLY WORLD LITERATURE
IN THE AGE OF THE GLOBAL

The concept of fixer literature—literature of the fixers by the fixers for the fixers—provides us with a new vantage point on the writing of literary history. A different history of translation, to which interpreting in its dimensions of communication and commensuration is intrinsic, creates the conditions for an alternative history of literature. Our objects of study are transformed and our narratives renewed with different categorizations; in this case, the fixer paradigm unbinds us from reading medieval literature through the lens of aesthetic qualifications of author and genre defined by the modern nation-state. Not only are these categories ill adapted to the medieval literature of Europe, but across the globe, they are the legacy of nation-states' colonial enterprises that have left behind a problematic inheritance of Eurocentric categories of "literary translation," "literature," and "literary space," something that postcolonial critique and comparative theories of world literature have attempted to redress for several decades by focusing on the literature of a language—Anglophone, Francophone, Hispanophone, Sinophone, Lusophone, and so on—rather than on the literature of a nation-state or, more precisely, on the literature of modern imperial nation-states. Similarly, Indigenous scholars and activist interpreters have been advocating for the inclusion of other forms and narratives of translation, from storytelling (oral history) to decentering translations (adopting local, rather than the accepted, "universal," viewpoints). In the previous chapter, we read European medieval literature, the precolonial literature of Europe, without modern literary categories of national and colonial provenance. When reading through the lens of translation and the fixer paradigm, the tie between "author" and writing loosens, as does the bind between authors and the nation-states that claim them. This is the first step in the task of formulating a world literature of the early and precolonial worlds: the first, and necessary, one because, on the one hand, modern aesthetic categories do not apply to precolonial

European literature and, on the other, they also often do not apply to the literary traditions of the non-Western, precolonial parts of the world. Moreover, a departure from the modern national and colonial models of literary analysis, this conclusion shows, will also entail a realignment in the global approaches to early world literatures.

When the integration of the Middle Ages into national history occurred in nineteenth-century Europe, it was rooted in the same set of criteria applied to all periods. In the post-Romantic, post-Bonapartist European world, the spirit of national literature transcended the specificities of time periods and historical circumstances:

> I desired to show the already thriving tendencies that will form, through their combinations and struggles, in very large part, the complex life of modern centuries. In returning to these more known, or at least more studied centuries . . . we will perhaps better understand the development of the modern spirit, after having come across its seed in the vigorous womb of the Middle Ages.

> (J'ai voulu montrer déjà vivantes les tendances dont les combinaisons et les luttes formeront, en très grande partie, la vie complexe des siècles modernes. En arrivant à ces siècles plus connus, ou du moins plus étudiés . . . peut-être comprendra-t-on mieux le développement de l'esprit moderne, après en avoir surpris l'embryon dans les flancs vigoureux du Moyen Âge.) (Ampère 1839, 193)

According to this view, national unity of literature had always been there, albeit in embryonic form in the Middle Ages. The task of literary critics was to create a nation's literary genealogy and to support a national chronology in literature. On the European scale, the (long) thirteenth century became the locus of the eclipse of *auctoritas* and of the emergence of the modern author, in the modern sense of a creator and owner of original work. The literary thirteenth century coincided with the genealogies of the modernity of the nation, that is, the beginning of state centralization and royal territorial expansion and consolidation in northwestern Europe, namely France and England, the two medieval monarchies that will also be powerful imperial nation-states of the nineteenth century (Strayer 1970). In turn, the making of the nation was slowly aligned with the emergence of the strong vernacular and its cultural, written production, the first groundwork of ethno-linguistic identity on which nation-states rest: "When we return to listen to this naive language . . . we believe to be hearing the stutter of childhood. . . . This child who is already the great French people also speaks the great French language" (quand nous revenons écouter ce langage naïf... il nous semble entendre le bégaiement de l'enfance.... Cet enfant qui est déjà le grand peuple français parle aussi la grande langue française; Paris 1885, 117). This tendency was particularly striking in the case of the French language, the influence of whose medieval chivalric literature was claimed across the Continent's noble cultures, although each nation experienced a similar "originary" point of its ethno-linguistic identity that was quickly assimilated to an author name (Chaucer; Dante) or, second best, to the name of a work and genre (*chanson de geste*, *The Song of Roland*, Arthurian literature, *Song of the Nibelungs*).

Thus, medieval writing was ordered through the lens of author names and genres that made the Middle Ages and its cultural production legible to modern national audiences.[1] Disciplinary legacies of literary study in the time of nation-states have made it preferable to construct modern literary history with names of authors. Author and nation are caught up in an inextricable interdependency with each other. While national authors enhance a nation's status on the world literary scene, nations promote their authors and thus lay claim to different forms of intellectual property. For the medieval period, France had fewer author names to offer than its Italian (Dante, Petrarch, Boccaccio) or English (Chaucer, Malory) competitor nations. This dearth of author names still haunts early French literature (with the exception of Christine de Pizan today). But French medieval literature could set itself as the inventor of genres. In 1839, Jean-Jacques Ampère, a professor at the Sorbonne and later at the Collège de France, divided French medieval literature into categories of "chivalric inspiration" (inspiration chevaleresque), "religious inspiration" (inspiration religieuse), "independence of thought" (l'indépendance de la pensée), and "satirical power" (puissance satirique; Ampère 1839, 193). By the time of Gaston Paris, the founder of academic medieval studies in France, in the 1870s and 1880s, French literature was defined by two genres, romance and epic, that is, Arthurian chivalric romance and the Carolingian epic. After 1870 and the trauma of the Franco-Prussian War, the most famous epic, *The Song of Roland* (*La chanson de Roland*) assumed the role of "the most ancient of our French romances" (le plus ancien de nos romans français; Lacroix 1877, 412): "For, afterward, French literature was the queen and the initiator of neighboring literatures; no work of our classical era was translated into more languages, or exerted around us a larger and more durable influence, than our old *Song of Roland*" (Car dès lors ... la littérature de la France était la reine et l'initiatrice des littératures voisines; aucune œuvre de notre époque classique n'a été traduite en plus de langues, n'a exercé autour de nous une influence plus étendue et plus durable que notre vieille *Chanson de Roland*; Paris 1885, 117–18). In 1883, Gaston Paris redubbed "chivalric love," naming it "courtly love," and defined it as a French civilizational phenomenon, an art form developed in the northwestern Arthurian romances of chivalry (Paris 1883; see also Paris 1881, 468–69). By the turn of the twentieth century, "courtly love" (*amour courtois*) had become a part of the school curriculum in Gustave Lanson's *Histoire de la littérature française* (1895) and Ernest Lavisse's *Histoire de France* (1901). Over a period of time, courtly love became established as the French civilizational phenomenon and the *chanson de geste* as its national epic.

What kind of a place does translation have in this literary history of authors and genres? How is medieval translation "translated" into a national narrative and literary histories of emerging national literatures? The parallel and connected stories of William Caxton and Colard Mansion, who worked at the same time—and possibly together—in Bruges, in present-day Belgium, are a case in point. William Caxton, at once a translator, a printer, and a merchant, first in Bruges and later in Westminster, England, is considered an author, but Colard Mansion, who translated, compiled, and orchestrated manuscript and incunabula production in the fifteenth century Burgundian Netherlands, is not. Caxton is a household name of late fifteenth-century English literature; Mansion is known only to specialists of the history of the book as an early book printer in Flanders. What combination of circumstances of nation, language, name, and career have led to such divergent literary histories of two men who had likely worked, if not together, then at the same time and place and in the same profession?

The Master Narrative of Literary History: Author and Nation versus Translator and Agency

Colard Mansion is known to us as a "libraire."[2] *Libraires* were book producers and booksellers. Mansion is indeed first mentioned in 1457 in the accounts of the book producers' and merchants' guild in Bruges. From 1472 to 1474, he even presided over this book producers' guild. He is considered the most important early printer of Bruges, who tried to capitalize on Bruges as the prime location for the production of French-language luxury manuscripts in the Burgundian Netherlands. He invested in the mechanical production of manuscripts, known as incunabula, early printed books that combined aspects of manuscripts (printed medieval handwriting/script) and medieval illumination (printed woodcuts but colored by hand). Mansion was thus in the business of "printed manuscripts"; he used mechanical writing to accelerate production and make books more available, while still retaining the hand-painted properties of a luxury manuscript. The idea that the mechanical production of manuscripts could benefit from the spectacular increase in the demand and production of luxury manuscripts in the second half of the fifteenth century in the Burgundian Netherlands was informed by Mansion's long career as a scribe and translator in the manuscript workshops of Bruges.

In the course of his career, Mansion translated four works from Latin into French: a life of Adam and Eve, *La pénitence d'Adam* (*Adam's Penitence*); *Dialogue des créatures* (*The Dialogue of Creatures*), a translation of *Dialogus creaturarum* attributed to Mayno de Mayneri; *Le Donat espirituel*, a translation of Jean Gerson's *Donatus moralisatus* (*Moralized Donatus* [Aelius]); and Ovid's *Metamorphoses*, which Mansion adapted. He printed two of them, the *Metamorphoses* and *Le Donat esperituel* (Hauwaerts et al. 2018, 93–98; Timelli 1997). He produced five manuscripts of four works: two manuscripts were of his two translations *La pénitence d'Adam* and *Dialogue des créatures*, both for Louis of Gruuthuse; Jean Miélot's translation of Benevuto da Imola's *Romuléon* for Duke Philip the Good; and two manuscripts that were copies of Valerius Maximus in Simon de Hesdin and Nicolas de Gonesse's translation, one each for Philippe de Hornes and Abbot Jan Crabbe. Between 1475 and 1484, he printed twenty-four works: four large and twenty small folios.[3] In 1484, after the publication of the luxury edition of Ovid's *Metamorphoses* (Paris, BnF, Rés. G-YC-1002), Mansion departed Bruges and left no further records. It is commonly held that the luxury edition of Ovid was a failed experiment that led to his financial ruin, because it mistakenly targeted the buyers of luxury manuscripts. In the early days of printing, at the end of the fifteenth century, nobles acquired printed manuscripts, no matter how luxurious, only exceptionally rarely.

Like Mansion, William Caxton was both a translator and a printer. He is famous for his translation of Raoul Lefèvre's *Recuyell of the historyes of Troye*, which he began in Bruges in March 1468, continued in Ghent, and finished during his exile in Cologne in 1471, where printing had flourished since 1465.[4] The *Recuyell* would have been printed when he returned to Bruges in 1473, possibly in collaboration with David Aubert. It was the first book printed in English (San Marino, Huntington Library, MS Inv. RB 6222). By 1474, Caxton began preparing his move to England, and a press was set up in Westminster in 1475 or 1476, with the earliest confirmed date of a Westminster printing on December 13, 1476. Between 1473 and 1492, Caxton published about one hundred editions of which about twenty were his translations into English. He also wrote English prose, "the extensions of the *Chronicles of England* and the *Polychronicon*, . . . and most famously, the prologues and epilogues that accompanied many of his publications" (Hellinga 2010, 60). He added a prologue or an epilogue or both to all his translations of twenty works, ranging in size from the colossal *Golden Legend* to Alain Chartier's *Curial*, a pamphlet of six leaves, to his edition of Malory's *Morte d'Arthur*, and to some reeditions like the second edition of Chaucer's *Canterbury Tales* (Blake 1991, 1–18).

Before his career as a printer, Caxton was a merchant in Flanders, who by 1462 "had become Governor of the settlement of the English merchants in Bruges, known as the English Nation" (Hellinga 1982, 14). Perhaps unsurprisingly, then, the stroke of his genius was commercial printing, rather than the printing of luxury books, Mansion's fatal mistake. Caxton was deeply influenced by his merchant activities in Bruges: "Early printers depended for the distribution of their books on well-established networks, systems of agents and middle men; printing history is therefore inseparable from mercantile history" (Hellinga 2010, 10). But before returning to England, Caxton had also learned in Flanders another important lesson: his first two printed books, *Recuyell* and *Game of Chess*, the first dedicated to Margaret of York, the second to her brother the Duke of Clarence, failed to gain traction with his noble dedicatees (Hellinga 2010, 52). This commercial approach distinguished him from Mansion. Multiple printed copies did not (and would not) benefit from noble patronage, and Caxton understood that he had to rely on distribution far beyond individual networks of patronage or networks of affiliation; commercial networks could ferry goods far beyond a known audience of patrons to an unknown public. The other move that seems to have contributed to Caxton's commercial success was his choice of works to put in print and the style of language he used in his prologues and epilogues. He cultivated a plain style that seemed to work well for the unknown public, rather than the courtly ornate style for a select public of noble patrons (Hellinga 2010, 110). Likewise, his choice of works to print was made on the same basis of clear and simple language (Hellinga 2010, 108. See Caxton 1928). In the context of this book's argument, it could be said that it was not about publishing well-known "authors," but rather about translating and printing in a style that was appealing to the unknown public.[5]

Caxton's plainly styled prose and modest positioning corresponded to the broad notion of authorship that existed in medieval manuscript workshops: "In the first place, notions of authorship might include translation, editing, and compilation as well as writing original works. The scribe of a manuscript, often a courtier in the service of a patron, might also be its 'author' in this wider sense. Only the limners and painters of miniatures had a distinct function, and occasionally appear individually in accounts, apparently working under a separate arrangement" (Hellinga 2010, 35). In other words, Caxton's conception of his own writing was very much in line with the kinds of self-erasure (erasure perceived from our modern perspective) that we saw among Burgundian pseudotranslators and translators (see chapter 4). Similarly, Mansion presents himself as a "compiler" (*compileur*), a label that does not convey to our modern authorial sensibility the extent of Mansion's agency, but which Mansion emphasized visually and textually when he assigned himself a prominent place in image and word. This is true as much of his strong presence in the translation-compilation of Ovid as in his translation of the *Dialogue*.[6]

Colard Mansion and William Caxton were connected during the years 1475–76; Mansion's printing practice is identified with type 2 fount, typical of Caxton's printing. Mansion would have printed two books for Caxton, the *Cordiale* in French and a book of hours for Salisbury's use in Latin. In 1476, when Caxton left Bruges for Westminster, Mansion continued printing and using type 2 until his disappearance in 1484.[7] While Mansion had a limited production of his own prose in his translations and compilations, David Aubert, who also possibly worked with Caxton in 1473–74, had a large manuscript output (see chapters 4 and 5). Caxton's first two books, *Recuyell* and *Game of Chess*, were printed in Ghent in 1473–74 in type 1, imitating Aubert's hand. Aubert would have continued to print in French in type 1, printing the *History of Jason* (1477) and *Méditation* by Pierre d'Ailly (1474) (Hellinga 2010, 50–51). Yet, whether as translator or printer, and despite a considerable output that matches Caxton's, Aubert is no more than Mansion recognized in literary history as an "author."

So what is the difference between Caxton and Mansion or Caxton and Aubert? All three were literary fixers, writers, and businessmen. The difference between them lies in the construction of medieval authorship from the national perspective. Linguistic nationalism and national literature as cultural capital—the combination of nation and culture—drive the recognition of national figures. The recognition of Caxton is at least partially linked to his printing of Chaucer, the first major English "author." The prominence of both Chaucer and Caxton is the result of national narratives instituting them as figures of national importance, among the first "authors" of the English nation and language. But this description of "English" and "nation" is retrospective (Butterfield 2005, 63); Chaucer "never called himself an author, and he seems never even to have called himself a poet either" (Strohm 2014, 252). Rather, their "authorship" is a modern national narrative about two writers who, in their time, saw themselves as translators and compilers, and who were both heavily involved in the English trade: Chaucer as the comptroller of the Wool Custom and the Wool Subsidy, Caxton as mercer (trading in everything other than wool). In contrast, Mansion and Aubert are hardly the first writers in the French language; French vernacular writing has been flourishing since the second half of the twelfth century. Neither are they writers of the French nation, for they lived and worked in a Flemish-speaking part of present-day Belgium that was dominated by a Francophone noble elite in the fifteenth century. Mansion's status is so problematic in today's Belgium—divided politically, culturally, and linguistically between Flemish- and French-speaking populations—that a recent exhibition in Bruges of his works was accompanied by a catalog printed in English (Hauwaerts et al. 2018), an exhibition ceremony held entirely in Flemish (with only a few words in French thanking colleagues from the Bibliothèque nationale de France for an exceptional number of loans), and exhibition labels written in four languages (Flemish, French, German, and English, in that order, the first three being the official languages of the Belgian state). How could Aubert and Mansion be national figures if their language does not coincide with the ethno-linguistic dictate of the contemporary Belgian nation-state and is contrary to the local Flemish identity in Bruges? At the same time, France does not claim them as its national authors because of present-day territorial boundaries, nor does it need to claim them thanks to a rich and distinctive field of French-identified author names and genres that precede Aubert and Mansion by more than a century.

National literature is possible because there is an author name that coincides with language, and language with territory. In the extreme, we could say that there is no author without nation and no nation without author. In that process, translators and translations are not left much room for agency: (national) literary history supersedes the history of translation, while it also obscures the important fact that early writing issues from translational processes; conversely, literary history should be written from an alternative, decolonized history of translation. That is, the history of translation would provide categories of analysis, followed by the writing of an alternative literary history. It would be the inverse of the literary history as we know it, constructed in modern national and colonial times, which has instrumentalized translation and translators and relegated them to skill and occupation, rather than art and profession, elevating only literary translation and degrading interpreting. Since the very notion of literary history is national, thought and written with national-colonial literary categories, this new literary history, which would be written from the position of fixers, has the potential to be decolonized.

Nation-States and World Literature

The close traditional alignment of nation and author such as we saw in the cases of Chaucer-Caxton and Aubert-Mansion has recently been seriously tested. Not only are national narratives of medieval, precolonial literature not true to the time—witness the recent acknowledgment of multilingualism in European medieval literatures, especially of England[8]—but the national lens has for too long foreclosed the world vision that medieval literature created and contained. Precolonial literatures, while not unburdened from prejudice, observed and were penetrated by the (known) world, far more in resonance with the social and racial calls for inclusivity that mark the twenty-first century than the national lens, developed in the nineteenth century and brought to its summit in the twentieth century, would allow us to perceive. It is not surprising that the shift to medieval (and/or precolonial) world literature realigns the research toward translation, away from authorship as intellectual and national property, away from linguistic nationalism—in short, from nation to the world (Boucheron et al. 2017; Stahuljak 2020b).

For example, the Global Chaucers approach has been an important part of the scholarly endeavor of "rescuing" Chaucer from the grip of English nationalism. Global Chaucers is "a multilingual, multinational effort to locate, catalog, and study non-Anglophone translations and appropriations of Chaucer's corpus. Methodologically, Global Chaucers relies on . . . comparative translation, the philological study of a single author's work across various translations" (Barrington 2014, 464. See also Barrington and Hsy 2018). Through comparative translation, Global Chaucers reads Chaucer as a world author; in the process, it also returns to the notion of translation and borrowing prevalent in Chaucer's time and likewise typical of Chaucer. Although Chaucer's canonization by his admirers soon after his death as the "Father" of the English tradition was taken "to mean that he was the first poet in English (he wasn't), we can better understand Chaucer's immediate and long-term impact if we take that epithet to mean that he was the first English poet borrowing Continental topics and metrical practices to have lasting impact, locally and internationally" (Barrington 2019, 1). Indeed, "Chaucer's Englishness does not have as settled a character as was previously claimed" (Butterfield 2005, 64), and Chaucer was an "inveterate borrower and pillager of poetic material" (Wallace 2017, 49), which is exactly what made him the writer of the world:

The Canterbury Tales, Chaucer's best-known work, may take place along the 60-mile roadway between London's suburbs and Canterbury; however, its assemblage of tales recognizes a much broader world, reaching across Europe, around the Mediterranean Sea, into Africa, the Levant, and Asia. Some locales are associated with biblical stories, and some with Greek and Roman epics: Jerusalem and Troy are prominent settings that Chaucer shares with other European and English authors. He was also aware of Asia, Africa, and eastern Europe, and he placed some of his characters and stories there, too. Moreover, those stories set in England incorporate material from Scandinavian, Egyptian, Hebrew, Greek, and Arabic sources. His stories and sources reflect not only his own travels but also the confluence of peoples encountered in his everyday affairs. Chaucer drew from throughout the world as it was known to him for his characters and his stories; he thus introduced his readers to global literary influences. (Barrington 2019, 1–2)

Put together, Chaucer emerges as a world writer as much as a writer of a rich and diverse medieval world that was also sometimes "English." The lens of translation reveals medieval literature to be a world literature, rather than national literature.

Chaucer was a civil servant, a comptroller of customs, and at least twice the king's emissary; Caxton was a merchant, a head of the English nation in Flanders, and its emissary; Mansion was a businessman-*libraire* (though not an emissary). But Marco Polo too was a merchant and emissary (from the Great Khan to the pope, the kings of France and Spain, and other Christian kings; Polo 1982, 321 / Polo 2016, 8–9, 12). The "worlding" of Marco Polo provides another example of the denationalization of medieval authors.[9] Marco Polo has never fully attained the same stature of national "author" as "le tre corone" of Italy, like Dante, Petrarch, and Boccaccio, although, as a citizen of Venice, he is considered a national Italian treasure. This has not stopped Italy's neighbor across the Adriatic Sea, Croatia, from claiming to be the origin of the Polo family; according to those claims, Niccolò, Marco's father, would have come from the island of Korčula (Curzola) in present-day Croatia, at the time under Venetian control. In scholarship, Marco Polo has been a name fixture for a number of specialists of French medieval literature: the oldest manuscript is written in Franco-Italian, but there is a rich tradition of luxury illuminated manuscripts of *The Description of the World* (*Le devisement du monde*) that are all in French, thus influencing the trends in research of medieval literature written in the French language outside the bounds of medieval or even present-day France (Cruse 2015). In other words, based on geography and language, different national traditions have claimed Marco Polo. Whether Italian, Croatian, or Francophone, and possibly because all of those at once, Marco Polo may not be the national "author" that the postmedieval period made him.

In yet another way, his status of writer adjusts with difficulty to a more proprietary and singular modern notion of author. In the prologue to the *Devisement*, we learn about Marco Polo in the third person: "Then, being in prison in Genoa, he had all these things written down by Messer Rustichiaus of Pisa (who was in this same prison) in the year 1298 after the birth of Jesus Christ" (Le quel puis, demourant en le chartre de Jene, fist retraire toutes cestes chouses a messire Rusticiaus de Pise, que en celle meisme chartre estout, au tens qu'il avoit MCCXCVIII anç que Jesucrit nesqui; Polo 2016, 2 / Polo 1982, 306). Scholars have for a long time considered the double "authorship" of Rustichello of Pisa, writer of romances, and Marco Polo (Gaunt 2013b; Kinoshita 2016a). Marco Polo dictates, and Rustichello transcribes; Marco is a merchant and Rustichello a professional writer. A notion of collective authorship is here at work. Their "authorship" is complicated by the use of the word "retraire" by Rustichello to describe his contribution: "retraire" means "to translate."

Other new evidence that Marco Polo's "authorship" may have to be considered through forms of even wider participative authorship has emerged only recently, with the 2019 discovery of a 1323 document linking Marco to the Dominican convent of Saints John and Paul in Venice. The version Z of the Latin translation, produced in the first thirty years of the fourteenth century, may be attributed to a workshop of Dominican friars:

> The reception of the *Devisement du monde* on the part of the Dominicans would seem in fact to be a part of a complex and thought-out project: our working hypothesis is that the order intended to promote the figure of Marco Polo as an authority in the field of "anthropological" knowledge of eastern customs, essential to the implementation of evangelization and various campaigns of predication in the Holy Land at the turn of the thirteenth and fourteenth centuries. To tie the figure of the author of the *Devisement du monde* to the reading and the circulation of the text by the brothers is that much more significant in terms of the awareness of choices made in translations and in the optics of the history of the text's reception.

> (La ricezione del *DM* da parte dei Domenicani sembrerebbe in effetti far parte di un complessivo e meditato progetto: la nostra ipotesi di lavoro è che l'Ordine intenda promuovere la figura di Marco Polo quale

auctoritas nel campo della conoscenza "antropologica" dei costumi orientali, fondamentale per la messa in atto dell'evangelizzazione e delle
varie campagne di predicazione in Terrasanta negli anni a cavallo tra
XIII e XIV secolo. Affiancare la figura dell'autore del *DM* alla lettura del
testo e diffusione da parte dei frati è quanto mai significativo in termini
di consapevolezza delle scelte attuate nelle traduzioni, e in ottica di
storia della ricezione del testo.)[10]

The close connection between Marco Polo and the Dominicans builds
on and activates Polo's claim to be an unparalleled intermediary between
Christian Europe and the Mongol Khanate, a privileged translator of two
worlds unknown to each other. Among all the khan's envoys and civil servants, Marco Polo cut an exceptional figure that satisfied the khan's craving
for a narrative of the news of the world:

> And having often seen and heard the Great Khan say that the envoys
> he had sent to different parts of the world were fools and ignoramuses
> (when they returned and reported on the missions they had been sent
> on but were unable to say anything else about the countries they had
> visited) and that he would rather hear about the news and the customs
> and practices of the foreign country than about the affairs for which he
> had sent them, Marco, well aware of all of this, when he went on this
> mission, put a good deal of effort into being able to tell the Great Khan
> about all the novelties and strange things he had [seen]. (Polo 2016, 10)

> (por ce qu'el avoit veu et oi plusors fois que le grant kan, quant les mesajes
> k'il mandoit por les diverses partes dou monde, quant il retornoient a
> lui et li disoient l'anbasee por coi il estoit alés et no li savoient dir autres
> noveles de les contrees ou il estoient alés, il disoit elz qu'il estoient foux
> et non saiçhan[ç] et disoi[t] que miaus amoeroit oir les noveles et les
> costumes et les usajes de celle estranjes contree qu'il ne fasoit oir celç
> por coi il li avoit mandé, et Marc, ke bien saoie tout ce, quant il ala en
> cele mesajarie, toutes les nuvités et tutes les stranges chauses qu'il avoit,
> mettoit son entent por coi il le seust redire au grant kaan.) (Polo 1982, 318)

Polo's ability to accomplish his job as auditor of the imperial court, a
common position for foreign merchants at the Mongol court in which "he
fulfilled his tasks very well" (il achevoit moult bien la beisogne), combined
with his skill in the art of observation and gift for storytelling, by which he
"was able to relate many novelties and strange things" (li savoit dir mai[n]
tes novités et maintes estranges chouses), made Marco Polo equally excep-

tional back in Europe: "This was how Messer Marco came to know more about things in that country than any other man: he explored those foreign parts more than any man ever born, besides putting all his effort into this knowledge" (Or ço fui la raison por coi meser Marc seç plus de celes couses de celle contree que nulz autres home, qu'il cher[c]e plus de celes estranges parties ke nulz omes ke unques nasquist, et encore qu'il hi mettoit plus son entent a ce savoir; Polo 2016, 11 / Polo 1982, 319).[11] Polo was the sole interpreter of the world's diversity equally to the Great Khan as to the European publics, the sole fixer of the diversity of knowledge between the two worlds, "diverse races of men and the diversities of the diverse regions of the world" (les deverses jenerasions des homes et les deversités des deverses region dou monde; Polo 2016, 1 / Polo 1982, 305). This was possible only because Marco was his own fixer: "Now it so happened that Marco, Messer Niccolò's son, learned the Tartars' customs, languages, and writing so well that it was a marvel: for I tell you in all truth that not long after coming to the great lord's court, he learned to read and write [four] languages" (Or avint que Marc, le filz messer Nicolao, enprant si bien le costume de Tartars et lor langajes et lor leteres [que c'estoit mervoille]; car je voç di tout voiremant que, avant grament de tens puis qu'il vint en la cort dou grant segnor, il soit de [quatre] langaies et de quatre letres et scriture; Polo 2016, 10 / Polo 1982, 317–18; see the introduction). In other words, Polo was a fixer who brought a description of the world to the European courts, but his description was then used by the Dominicans, the Order of the Preachers, in a return into the world. Moreover, translation is key in this engagement with the world: first, from the languages of the Silk Road into Franco-Italian, from this hybrid Romance language into the Latin of the Dominicans, and from Latin back into the world via Dominican proselytization and dissemination.[12] Moreover, the very title of the *Description of the World* signals Marco Polo's work as world literature: his description divides the world (*deviser le monde*) with the same (merchant) categories evenly applied to different parts of the world. The world as commodity brings a previously unknown description of variety and diversity; the lens is not cultural or religious, but mercantile, providing a new objectivity to the description of the world. If Marco Polo is a world writer (Kinoshita 2013; see also Kinoshita 2016a), can we speak of an early precolonial world literature?

Translation and Early World Literature

Similar to the above translational argument of considering authors as fixers in the world, an argument for the existence of a precolonial world literature can also be made on the basis of clusters of medieval works that, in the analysis of Burgundian libraries of the fifteenth century (see chapter 5), I called the situational genre. These Burgundian clusters were principally made of translations and pseudotranslations. By the time of the death of Philip the Good, in one hundred years, the Dukes of Burgundy had collected almost nine hundred manuscripts. David Aubert, Philip's scribe and secretary, described this ducal library in 1463, in the prologue to the *History of the Three Sons of Kings* (*Histoire des trois fils de rois*): "Although he is the prince the best appointed with the most rich and noble library in the world, he is most inclined and desirous to enlarge it daily, as is the case" (Et nonobstant que ce soit le prince sur tous autres garny de la plus riche et noble *librairie du monde*, si est il moult enclin et desirant de chascun jour l'accroistre, comme il fait).[13] Aubert is saying two things: that the ducal library is the richest and noblest library *in the world* and also *of the world* (*librairie du monde*; cf. Chartier 1994). If the ducal library is a library of the world, it is a world library. The culture of the court of Burgundy was to collect an entire world of knowledge, the literature of the world—in translation. This world literature was organized in clusters, the situational genres, of the world library.

But contrary to accepted ideas about translation, Burgundian translation was not about domination. Modern translation, especially into the dominant English language, has been characterized as a colonial mode, a process of assumption and appropriation into the language of the rulers. For theorists of modern and contemporary world literature, English as the main language of world literature, whereby world literature ends up being literature in (English) translation, has been one of the thorniest problems to address (Mufti 2016). But this book's argument has been that in the precolonial period, translation did not operate in the colonial mode, and it was not a gesture of occupation and domination. As we saw in previous chapters, medieval Europe first displays a systematic sensitivity to the diversity of languages in the thirteenth century (see chapter 1). Foreign language acquisition was the desirable norm then. Those who wanted to engage with the other, the foreign, were supposed to learn the language of the other, because interpreters were inadequate for proselytism or conquest. Occupiers and preachers needed to learn the language of the conquered or of those intended for conversion if they were to succeed in their mission. In the Burgundian Valois-Habsburg imperial model, translation was a way of knowing the world, of world collecting (Stahuljak 2019b). Translation was imperial, not because the "colonizers" imposed their language on the conquered, but because they translated the conquered into their language. In contrast, modern-day colonization is usually associated with the imposition of the colonizer's language, through linguistic policies and strategies of domination-by-language on the part of modern imperial nation-states, such as England and France. Centralization and assimilation were accompanied by the expectation that the colonized would learn the dominant language. When medieval *translatio*(n), whose broad cultural range of signification motivated language acquisition among foreign arrivals on the new shores, receded in importance, translation—with principles of accuracy and fidelity—became a tool of enforcement of a single language's domination.

Translation—whether by Chaucer into English, or of Chaucer out of English and across the world; or by Marco Polo into Franco-Italian, or of Marco Polo out of Romance languages into non-European worlds—can be the principal mode of analysis of these world writers and their writing as world literature. When we add to the analysis their positionality as fixers—in their administrative, diplomatic, and trade roles—the fixer paradigm opens up early precolonial literature to world literature, since it emancipates it from the mold of national-colonial analyses and categories. Similarly to genres, medieval—precolonial—literature rapidly and easily accedes to the notion of world literature when we use the lens of translation to drop nationalist and colonial categories of literary analysis. Moreover, precolonial world literature reverses the teleology of national literary histories; rather than serving as the (genealogical) origin to national literatures, it can be read as world making, speculative futures; precolonial literature would not only represent and describe the world but would have imagined and shaped it. The clusters, those situational genres, made the world, either as categories through which the world was seen and understood, hence organizing and shaping the world, or as performatives that propelled men to action (see chapter 5). The fixer paradigm produces a nonproprietary, decolonized literature of the precolonial period, recentered outside of the modern. Hopefully the recentering also opens a door to categories that are non-Western, by displacing nineteenth-century European legacies that still dominate the world, so that we can study more easily alternative literacies and agencies.

Seeing precolonial writing as "world literature with agency" is important because two of the foundational works of world literature criticism, Pascale Casanova's *World Republic of Letters* and David Damrosch's *What Is World Literature?*, situate themselves within a traditional European national space and chronology: Casanova's study of autonomous literary spaces starts with Joachim du Bellay only to blossom with the analysis of the European nation-state (France), and Damrosch begins with Johann Wolfgang von Goethe and his elevation of German literature to the status of universal—world—literature.[14] In their wake, the bulk of the critical studies of world literature has been conducted by scholars of modern and contemporary literatures. Fixers and clusters of precolonial world literature expand and refresh the perspective on world literature beyond the modern period, and the study of clusters and situational genres may even provide a way out of the impasses in which world literature finds itself, unable to accomplish inclusive representation, and struggling to countenance the dominance of world literature in English or the dominance of translation into English.[15]

Early World Literature in the Age of the Global

To be clear, the fixer paradigm motivates the separation from Eurocentrically defined notions of literary genre, author, literary translation, national literary histories.[16] It enables the analysis of precolonial writing as world literature. It moreover rewrites disciplinary notions, for example in translation and medieval studies, as shown throughout this book. Finally, it also intervenes disciplinarily and methodologically in scholarly efforts toward a global Middle Ages and specifically in the epistemology of the "global" that is grounded in connectivity.

For many decades, humanistic and social science research has focused on temporal connectivity, that is continuity through time (linearity, genealogy, teleology). Recently, an epistemic corrective of European teleology has enabled spatial connectivity that in the last two decades has given rise to transnational, global, and connected-history approaches. Spatial connectivity has decentered Europe and brought the teleologies of its progress to a scale truer to historical phenomena. Yet, this idea of connectivity has been premised on the fact of the European circumnavigation of the globe that was first completed in 1522. Connectivity in this global sense is itself a colonial and national notion, based in the very definition of connectivity from the European perspective of circumnavigation, trade, and discovery of the world. Does that mean, on the one hand, that regional world systems were not global to the extent of the known worlds they connected; and on the other hand, that regional world systems cannot be studied globally just because they were not a part of a unified, total world system?[17] The other critique of spatial connectivity is that, just like connectivity through time, it is still based in linearity, that is, in contiguity. Both the temporal and the spatial models are premised on linearity, whether that linearity is continuous (time) or contiguous (space).

Many scholars of the early and medieval worlds acknowledge that, while "global" is a way to signal inclusivity, it means hemispheric, regional world systems: "A global Middle Ages cannot imply a total world system, which is often a tenet of globalization, because the period under consideration primarily witnessed intra-hemispheric contact."[18] In other words, we must recognize the profound globality of the early worlds and their simultaneous lack of total, universal connectivity: the precolonial is the time of global unconnected worlds. This raises the question for early world literature of how to do global studies in the age of unconnected worlds.

A move away from the Eurocentric definition of the global means that we need to reconsider the premise of connectivity, even in translation, that lies at the core of our scholarly literary histories. Translation, in its modern sense of accurate translation, is a model of connectivity. World literature has been premised on circulation or a literary arc of a single work (Damrosch 2003 and Shih 2015 respectively). In other words, the minimal unit of connectivity is the agency of a single work across national or linguistic lines, or both, and across time and space. For medievalists, who have been acutely aware of the globality of unconnected early worlds, the study of itineraries or of axes of transmission,[19] while pushing out the limits of national concepts, nevertheless maintains a spatial and temporal connectivity of works as foundation for literary study and literary history.

What this book proposes, in contrast to the linear model, is a paradigm of the fixer. An apparatus captures a mechanism, an operating system that is functional at a place in a time; it is a synchronic screen capture of a state of operations (Agamben 2009b; Agamben 2009a). In "profiling" the fixer apparatus, I proposed the possibility of the fixer paradigm in order to make intelligible a large historico-cultural domain. Through the fixer paradigm, we saw the notions of literary genre, author, literary translation, and literary history for the precolonial period be redefined. New categories replacing the old colonial and national categories enable us to see translation as a mode of world making. The fixer paradigm acknowledges a deep globality for each of the unconnected worlds, their capacity for speculative futures. It inflects the very notion of translation: the fixer apparatus is about commensuration, not accurate translation. Rather than follow linearity through time or space or both, the paradigm thus enables comparison on a larger scale. And since time and space are no longer the premise of comparison or of globality, we can compare both noncontinuously and noncontiguously. We can thus connect different apparatuses transperiodically (noncontinuously) and transspatially (noncontiguously). Global work is neither dependent on a connectivity of systems, nor is it as random as mere juxtaposition. This is commensuration, rather than translation: translation depends on forms of linearity, spatial, temporal, or both, but commensuration is a cosizing or comeasuring of clusters, apparatuses. Commensuration is a comparative method: fixers stand for connected methodologies in unconnected, but global early worlds. Commensuration thus connects regional world systems through comparison. But because commensuration rests neither on the logic of linearity nor on the teleology of globalization, it does not produce a total world literary history (cf. Beecroft 2015). It breaks with the civilizational and cultural approaches to literatures based on transfers and influences. Finally, discontinuous comparison of apparatuses in different places and different times on the globe gets around the problem of periodization in different parts of the globe.[20]

Fixers as a paradigm intervene in the notion of the global as an apparatus of translation in such a way that we can avoid national, colonial categories of author and genre. Fixers are a positionality, not a category that is European, a positionality that is often performed in the encounter of the European and the non-European. Fixers are global, not because they connect the world continuously and contiguously, but because they are the very measure of the commensuration that is our daily condition and lot.

Acknowledgments

Initial research time for work on what was at the time just a five-page project was provided in 2013 by the US Fulbright Research Grant and Fulbright Commission in Paris. My special thanks goes to Patricia Janin, former head of the American Section in Paris. A 2016 fellowship from the Guggenheim Foundation gave me a chance during the academic year 2017–18 to finalize the shape of the book and to explore new avenues emerging from it. Finally, research for and the writing of this book were supported in part by the "Research Cooperability" program of the Croatian Science Foundation, funded by the European Union from the European Social Fund under Operational Programme Efficient Human Resources 2014–20, within project PZS-2019-02-1624—GLOHUM—Global Humanisms: New Perspectives on the Middle Ages (300–1600).

Throughout these many years, I have been supported generously by travel grants and research funding from the University of California, Los Angeles, including the Academic Senate and the Office of the Dean of Humanities. My special thanks goes to Carole Goldberg, former vice chancellor of Academic Personnel, who made it possible to allow precious extra time for the completion of this book.

I am very grateful to colleagues at many national libraries who generously gave both access to manuscripts and their advice: Elizabeth Morrison (Los Angeles, J. Paul Getty Museum), Ann Kelders (Brussels, Bibliothèque royale de Belgique), Charlotte Denoël (Bibliothèque nationale de France–Richelieu), Nathalie Coilly (Bibliothèque de l'Arsenal and Bibliothèque nationale de France–Tolbiac); and staff at Berlin, Staatsbibliothek zu Berlin; Brussels, Bibliothèque royale de Belgique; Paris, Bibliothèque nationale de France; Vienna, Österreichische Nationalbibliothek; and London, British Library.

I also owe a deep debt of gratitude—that cannot be repaid but might be reciprocated—to all the colleagues who for the last ten years have offered invitations, listened to and shared with me, and provided precious islands of vigorous intellectual testing and exchange. I would not have written the same book without them: Emma Campbell and Bob Mills, without whose initial invitation in 2010 the question that this book attempts to answer may never have been asked, and Emma Campbell again, who gave me an opportunity to test the ideas in February 2019 at Warwick University in multiple venues with eager colleagues and students; Beth Morrison, whose 2013 invitation to write on *The Romance of Gillion de Trazegnies* (JPGM MS 111), along with our subsequent collaborative adventure of a lifetime, led me to the research on late medieval Burgundy and a realization of the stakes of a fixer project when it came to literary history; Patrick Boucheron, whose invitation to a visiting professorship at the Collège de France in June 2018 sealed the main themes of politics, economics, and ethics, and provided room for expansion of the project in ways that I had never imagined before; Torfi Tullinius and Sif Rikhardsdottir, whose invitation to teach a guest seminar at the University of Iceland in May 2022 pushed this book to completion in its final writing stages; Margaret Kim, whose invitation for a whirlwind tour of three top national universities in Taiwan in November 2022 provided the final test run for this book; and Gisèle Sapiro, whose invitation to the École des hautes études en sciences sociales in December 2022 gave me the confidence to send the book manuscript into production.

I owe a debt to many other colleagues who, over many years, offered venues to present my research and dispensed references, advice, and interpretations that enriched this book: Bill Burgwinkle and Miranda Griffin; Brian Catlos and Sharon Kinoshita; Christine Chism; Jocelyne Dakhlia; Marisa Galvez; Claire Gilbert; Jane Gilbert; Fiona Griffiths and Ivan Lupić; Noah Guynn; Anne D. Hedeman; Jennifer Jahner; Sarah Kay; Natalie Koble, Amandine Mussou, and Florent Coste; Sophie Marnette; Peggy McCracken; Deborah McGrady; Laura Morreale and Nick Paul; Thomas O'Donnell; Bruno Perreau; Natividad Planas; Yann Potin; Catherine Secretan; Mireille Séguy; Helen Solterer; Karen Sullivan; Luke Sunderland; Michelle Szkilnik; and Luke Yarbrough.

A very special thanks goes to my professor of Romance philology and Old French, August Kovačec, without whose patient passion I may never have discovered the beauty of a language that knows no rules.

I also wish to thank my research assistants and graduate students, who have made sure that my own language, that sometimes knows no rules, is kept in check when it comes to writing in English and translating from Latin: Shane Black, Christopher Gobeille, and Anne Le.

Through all that it takes to bring a book into this world, I remain deeply grateful to Laure Murat and Kathleen McHugh, and to my dear friends

Lynn Hunt and Peg Jacob, who have helped me and the book along in a myriad ways, professional and personal. I also want to acknowledge my lifelong friends Višnja Barbir, Andreja Orsag, and Janja Ružić, who all know what it is to live in exile from one's own language, in a third space, while providing a service for another. This book is dedicated to them, and to my mother, Ivanka (Althaller) Stahuljak, from whom I learned why and how I became who I am.

* * *

Some ideas in the introduction were originally explored in "Translation," in *Transnational Modern Languages: A Handbook*, edited by Jennifer Burns and Derek Duncan (Liverpool University Press, 2022), 313–21; and in "Afterword. Fixing Translation: Fixers as Paradigm for a Commensurate Social History of Translation," *Journal for Early Modern Cultural Studies* 21, no. 4 (December 2022): 164–77, Copyright © 2022 by University of Pennsylvania Press.

An earlier, shorter version of the section on Pierre Dubois in chapter 1 appeared in a section of "Medieval Fixers: Politics of Interpreting in Western Historiography," in *Rethinking Medieval Translation: Ethics, Politics, Theory*, edited by Robert Mills and Emma Campbell (D. S. Brewer, 2012), 147–63.

An earlier, shorter version of the discussion on "courtoisie" in chapter 2 appeared in "The Pilgrim Translation Market and the Meaning of *Courtoisie*," in *The French of Outremer: Communities and Communications in the Crusading Mediterranean*, edited by Laura Morreale and Nicholas Paul (Fordham University Press, 2018), 201–20.

An earlier, shorter version of the discussion on Machaut's *Taking of Alexandria* in chapter 3 appeared in "History's Fixers: Informants, Mediators, and Writers in the *Prise d'Alixandre*," in *A Companion to Guillaume de Machaut: An Interdisciplinary Approach to the Master*, edited by Deborah McGrady and Jennifer Bain (Brill, 2012), 277–92; and part of the section on Roger de Stanegrave appeared in "Merlin à Jérusalem: Un traité de croisade pour les rois d'Angleterre," in *Arthur après Arthur: La matière arthurienne tardive en dehors du roman arthurien, de l'intertextualité au phénomène de mode*, edited by Christine Ferlampin-Acher (Presses universitaires de Rennes, 2017), 491–500.

A shorter discussion on Lieven van Lathem and Jean le Tavernier originally appeared in Elizabeth Morrison and Zrinka Stahuljak, *The Adventures of Gillion de Trazegnies: Chivalry and Romance in the Medieval East* (Los Angeles: J. Paul Getty Museum, 2015).

A discussion similar to that in chapter 4 on fixers in Burgundian romances appeared in "Les langues du voyage: Le roman bourguignon et ses fixeurs méditerranéens," in *Écrire le voyage au temps des ducs de Bourgogne: Actes du colloque international organisé les 19 et 20 octobre 2017 à l'Université du Littoral—Côte d'Opale (Dunkerque)*, edited by Jean Devaux, Matthieu Marchal, and Alexandra Velissariou. Burgundica (Turnhout: Brepols, 2021), 233–41.

A discussion similar to that on genre and the *chansons de geste* in chapter 5 appeared in "Connected Literature: *Chansons de geste*, Burgundian *livres de gestes*, and the Writing of Literary Theory," in *The Futures of Medieval French*, edited by Jane Gilbert and Miranda Griffin (D. S. Brewer, 2021), 99–111. Reproduced with permission of the Licensor through PLSclear.

Appendix A (Chapter 4)

1. Crusade Treatises in the Ducal Library

- Two copies of Jean Miélot's French translation of Pseudo-Brocardus's / William of Adam's Latin *Directory for the Making of the Passage across the Sea* (*Advis directif pour faire le passage d'Outremer*; KBR, MS 9095).
- A Latin Pseudo-Brocardus's / William of Adam's *Directorium ad faciendum passagium transmarinum* with Burchard of Mount Sion's *Description of the Holy Land* (*Descriptio Terre Sancte*; KBR, MSS 9176–77).
- Hayton's *Flower of Histories of the East* (*La fleur des histoires d'Orient*).
- Two fourteenth-century Latin copies (one partially in old French) of Marino Sanudo's *The Book of the Secrets of the Faithful of the Cross* (*Liber secretorum fidelium crucis*; KBR, MSS 9347–48, and KBR, MSS 9404–5).
- Travel reports of Philip's spies (e.g., Ghillbert de Lannoy, *The Jerusalem Voyage* [*Le voyaige de Jhérusalem*]; Bertrandon de la Broquière, *Voyage in the Land of Outremer* [*Voyage en la terre d'Outremer*]). (LDB-V 2015)

2. Works Commissioned by Créquy and Wavrin and Found in Duke Philip's Library

- In addition to the historical works commissioned by Créquy, *Chronicles and Conquests of Charlemagne* (*Croniques et conquestes de Charlemaine*) before 1458, but volumes 2 and 3 were commissioned directly by Philip and completed in 1458 by Aubert (KBR, MSS 9066–68). Raoul Lefèvre, most likely Créquy's chaplain, wrote the *History of Jason* about 1460, consecrating Jason as the founding figure of the ducal Order of the Golden Fleece. Another of Créquy's scribes, Isidore du Ny, is thought to have copied for Philip the *Flower of Histories* (*Fleur des histoires*), Jean Mansel's universal history. Philip's library contained these commissions: *Blancandin and the Lady-Proud-in-Love* (Brussels, KBR, MSS

3576–77) was in the 1467–69 inventory (Greco 2002, 62), and a copy of the *History of the Sons of Three Kings* was made for Philip (Paris, BnF, MS fr. 92; Palumbo 2001, 11–13, 43). *Florent and Octavian* (Brussels, KBR, MS 10387) was commissioned by Créquy and offered as gift to the duke; it bears the duke's armorial.[1]

- Wavrin likely offered to Philip *Gérard de Nevers* (Brussels, KBR, MS 9631), the cycle of *Jean d'Avesnes* (*Jean d'Avesnes; La fille du comte de Ponthieu* [*The Daughter of the Count of Ponthieu*]; and *Saladin*; Paris, BNF, MS fr. 12572), and the *Romance of Florimont* (*Le roman de Florimont*; Paris, BnF, MS fr. 12566),[2] since they appear in the 1467–69 ducal inventory (Wijsman 2010c, 478, 479nn1129, 1131). The inventory also records, in a single volume, *Chastelain de Couci* and *Gilles de Chin* (Lille, BM, God. 50),[3] the *Romance of the Count of Artois* (*Roman du comte d'Artois*; Paris, BnF, MS fr. 11610), the *History of the Lords of Gavre* (*Histoire de seigneurs de Gavre*; Brussels, KBR, MS 10238), and *Oliver of Castille and Artus of Algarve* (*Olivier de Castille et Arthus d'Algarbe*; Ghent, UB 470), all of which came from Wavrin's library. Finally, *Gillion de Trazegnies* (Brussels, KBR, MS 9629) and, in a single volume, *Paris and Vienne / Apollonius of Tyre* (*Paris et Vienne / Apollonius de Tyr*; Brussels, KBR, MS 9632–33) also come from Wavrin's library, although they entered the ducal library later.[4]

3. *Manuscripts Illuminated by the Master of the Vienna* Chroniques D'Angleterre

- Five copies of books 1–2 of Wavrin's *Chroniques d'Angleterre* (one copy of books 1–2, BnF, MSS Fr. 74–77; one copy of book 1, ÖNB, Cod. 2534; three more copies of book 2).
- Two copies of Monstrelet's *Chronicles* (*Chroniques*).
- Three copies of Wauquelin's *Chronicles of Hainaut.*
- Five copies of Lucena's *Deeds of Alexander the Great.*
- Four copies of Lefèvre's *Collected Histories of Troy* (*Recueil des histoires de Troie*).
- Two copies of the anonymous *Chronicles of Pisa* (*Chroniques de Pise*).

Appendix B (Chapter 5)

1. Louis of Gruuthuse Manuscripts

- Related to the Hundred Years' War: Jean Froissart's *Chroniques*; *Chroniques de Hainaut*; Jean de Wavrin's *Chroniques d'Angleterre*; Jean de Bueil's *Le Jouvencel*; Enguerrand de Monstrelet's *Chroniques*; Jean Chartier's *Chroniques du règne de Charles VII*; Jean de Beka's *Chroniques de Hollande*; and the anonymous *Chronique des guerres advenues en France, en Angleterre et en Bourgogne depuis l'année 1444 jusqu'en 1471*; *Chroniques de Pise*; *Chroniques de Flandre*; *Justification de France contre Angleterre*; and a Latin *Processus factus ad coronationem regis Richard II post conquestum*.
- Works dealing with governance: *Statuts, ordonnances et armorial de l'Ordre de la Toison d'or* (Besançon, Bibliothèque municipale, Chifflet 91); *Ordonnance militaire de Charles le Téméraire* (Paris, BnF, N.a.f. 6219); Jean Boutillier, *La somme rural* (Paris, BnF, MSS fr. 201–2); [Ghillbert or Hugues] de Lannoy, *L'instruction d'un jeune prince* (London, BL, Cotton Vesp. B i, and Paris, BnF, MS fr. 1216); *Le gouvernement des princes* (Rennes, Bibliothèque municipale, MS 153).
- European chivalry or noble lifestyle: e.g., Gaston Phébus, *Livre de la chasse* (Cambridge, MA, Harvard University, Typ 130, and Geneva, BPU, fr. 169); Jacques Valère, *Traité de la noblesse* (London, BL Add. 18798, and Paris, BnF, MS fr. 1280); Jacques de Longuyon, *Vœux du paon* (Paris, BnF, MS fr. 2136, and BnF, MS fr. 20045); Christine de Pizan, *Livre des faits d'armes et de chevalerie* (Paris, BnF, MS fr. 585); *Tournoi de Bruges de 1393* (Paris, BnF, MS fr. 2692, and BnF, MS fr. 2693).
- Crusade-themed manuscripts: *Gillion de Trazegnies* (Los Angeles, J. Paul Getty Museum, MS 111); Vasco da Lucena, *The Deeds of Alexander the Great* (*Les fais du grand Alexandre*; Paris, BnF, MS fr. 257); Raoul Lefèvre, *History of Jason* (*Histoire de Jason*; Paris, BnF, MS fr. 331);

Book of Heraclius (*Livre d'Eracles*); the *Chronicle of Baudouin d'Avesnes* (*Chronique dite de Baudouin d'Avesnes*; Paris, BnF, MS fr. 279, ca. 1470); *The Siege of Rhodes by the Turks* (*Le siège de Rhodes par les Turcs*; Paris, BnF, MS fr. 5646, after 1482); the travels of Mandeville and Marco Polo (two copies); and literature produced for the members of the chivalric Order of the Golden Fleece, into which Louis was inducted in 1461: *Statutes of the Order*; Lefèvre's *History of Jason* and *Collected Histories of Troy*; Guillaume Fillastre's *History of the Golden Fleece* (*Histoire de la Toison d'or*); two copies of Jacques de Longuyon's *Vows of the Peacock* (*Vœux du paon*); Christine de Pizan's *Letter of Othea*.

2. Manuscripts in the Categories of the Inventory of the Dukes of Burgundy (1467–69)

- "*Outremer*, medicine, and astrology": "several mappemondes" (nos. 750–53); Hayton's *Flower of Histories of the East* (*La fleur des histoires d'Orient*; no. 777); *Chronicle of Morea* (*Chronique de Morée*; no. 782); *Mandeville's Travels* (no. 795); Marco Polo's *Description of the World* (*Devisement du monde*; no. 820); several "voiages d'oult-mer" (nos. 776, 779), including Ghillbert de Lannoy's (no. 819) and Bertrandon de la Broquière's (no. 756) travel reports; several chronicles and histories "de la terre d'oult-mer" (nos. 763, 776, 780); *History of Saladin* (*Histoire de Saladin*, no. 762); *Book of Heraclius* (*Livre d'Eracles*, no. 773); and finally different crusade treatises (nos. 755, 775, 778, 781, 816).
- "Library. Chronicles of France": the compilation of the *Chronicles and Conquests of Charlemagne* (nos. 748–49); histories of the British Isles (*Croniques de la Grant Bretaigne*, no. 666, or of the reign of Richard II, nos. 659, 686; *Croniques d'Escoce*, no. 668); chronicles of the Burgundian Low Countries (Brabant, no. 661; Flanders, nos. 671–72, 674; Hainaut, nos. 662–63; Holland, no. 673); numerous chronicles of the Kingdom of France (Monstrelet, no. 643; Froissart, nos. 655–58; *Les grans croniques*, nos. 649–50, etc.); histories of *Godefroy of Bouillon* (nos. 681–85); *Baudouin of Jerusalem* (nos. 704); several histories of Alexander (nos. 708, 709, 714), Jean Mansel's *The Flower of Histories* (*La fleur des histoires*; nos. 731–34), the *Moralized Bible* (*Bible moralisée*; nos. 736–37), Voragine's *The Golden Legend* (*La légende dorée*; nos. 739–40); Augustine's *The City of God* (*La cité de Dieu*; nos. 743–46).
- "Books of deeds": Guillaume de Machaut's verse history *The Taking of Alexandria* (no. 489); the romanced history of *Baudouin de Flandres* (no. 514); and Raoul Lefèvre's history of the founding figure of the ducal Order of the Golden Fleece, *History of Jason* (no. 494, this time with

a happy ending); the romanced *Belle Hélène de Constantinople* (nos. 495, 497, characterized in the margins as a "saint's life," "vie de sains"); Arthurian prose romances (*Lancelot of the Lake*, nos. 458–59; *Death of King Arthur* [*La mort le roi Artu*], no. 461, nos. 487–88; prose Tristan [*Tristan en prose*], nos. 466–69; *Perceforest*, nos. 472–76, nos. 477–82; *Erec en prose*, no. 501; the *Histoire du Saint Graal*, nos. 517–18); romances of Greco-Roman antiquity (*Brutus* [*Brut*], no. 513; *Eneas*, no. 510; *The Seven Sages of Rome* [*Les sept sages de Rome*], no. 462; *Buscalus*, no. 464; *Florimont*, a genealogy of Alexander the Great, no. 511; *Apollonius of Tyre* [*Apollonius de Tyr*], no. 519); Boccaccio's *Decameron* (no. 483–84, no. 486); and the Burgundian-made *One Hundred New Tales* (*Les cent nouvelles nouvelles*; no. 485); some of the historical exploits of the most famous Burgundian knight, Jacques de Lalaing (no. 523); and all the Burgundian prose chivalric narratives that deal with the East and the Crusades, such as *Jehan de Saintré* (no. 492), *Gilles de Chin* (no. 516), the *History of the Three Sons of Kings* (no. 515), the cycle of *Jean d'Avesnes* (no. 503), the *History of the Lords of Gavre* (no. 504), including the older romance of *Mélusine* (no. 493) and still others.

3. Chansons de Geste in Different Inventory Categories

- "Books of deeds": prose versions of *Renault de Montauban* (nos. 470–71), *Huon de Bordeaux* (no. 502), *Beuve de Hantone* (no. 499), and *Garin le Loherain* (no. 521); and verse versions of the *Geste des Lorrains* (no. 505, "old song," "vielle chansson"), *Guillaume d'Orange* (no. 526), *Ayméri de Narbonne*, and *Garin de Monglane* (no. 521).
- "Chronicles of France": "*The Book of Girard of Roussillon*, Duke of Burgundy, in Verse" (*Le livre de Gerard de Roucillon*, duc de Bourgogne, en ryme; no. 676), and again in Gascon verse (rymé en gascon; no. 680); two volumes (presumably in prose) of "*L'istoire de Gerard de Roucillon*" (nos. 677–78); "another small manuscript of *Girard of Roussillon*" (un autre livre petit . . . *le rommant de Gerard de Roucillon*, duc etc.; no. 679).
- "Books of ballades and love": *Ogier the Dane* (*Ogier le Danois*) in verse, "en rime" (no. 536, nos. 540–41), and in prose (no. 537); another Ogier manuscript (no. 535); "the book of Aimery of Narbonne, William of Orange, Vivian and Rainouart au tinel" (li livres de Eymery de Nerbonne, de Guillaume d'Orenges, de Vivien et de Renouart au tyner; no. 571); Ovid's *Metamorphoses* (nos. 542–43) and *Ars amatoria* (no. 569); the *Romance of the Rose* (*Roman de la Rose*; nos. 544–48); the *Romance of Reynard the Fox* (*Roman de Renart*; nos. 549–51); Christine de Pizan's *One Hundred Ballads* (*Les cent ballades*; nos. 554–57) and *Letter to the*

God of Love (*Épistre au dieu d'amour*; no. 625); Guillaume de Machaut's and Charles d'Orléans's poetry (nos. 530–32; no. 623); *The Bestiary of Love* (*Le bestiaire d'amour*; nos. 563–64), a manuscript of *The Lady and the Unicorn* (*La dame de la licorne*) and *Floire et Blanchefleur* (no. 572); a series of texts of chivalric vows continuing the Alexander cycle, *The Vows of the Peacock* (*Vœux du paon*) and *The Restoration of the Peacock* (*Restor du paon*; nos. 574, 575; no. 598, only the *Vows*); the *Romance of William of Palermo* (*Roman de Guillaume de Palerne*; no. 585), *Chastelain de Couci* (no. 624); the *Knight of the Swan* (*Chevalier au cygne*; no. 570; no. 609); *Bertha Broadfoot* (*Berthe aux grands pieds*) and *Cléomadés* (nos. 552–53).

Notes

Introduction

1. At the start of the twenty-first century, the term migrated into translation and interpreting studies, whence I borrowed it. See J. Palmer 2007; J. Palmer and Fontan 2007; Inghilleri 2012; Rafael 2015.

2. Von Harff 1946, 69 / von Harff 1860, 57; see Boyle 2021.

3. For *tangomão*, see Cook, forthcoming. For Mongol, see Sinor 1982; and Pegolotti 1970.

4. "Dragoman" and "latinier" can also mean "messenger"; see Merceron 1998, 27.

5. Mandeville 2011, 36 / Mandeville 2000, 164. See Greenblatt 1991; Higgins 1997; Khan-mohamadi 2014.

6. Froissart 1867–77, 15:325; 16:47. Also: "et parloit tous les jours le roy au conte de Nevers bien et largement voire par le moyen d'un latinier, qui les paroles de l'un et de l'autre remonstroit" (Froissart 1867–77, 15:430).

7. On Ottoman dragomans, Rothman 2012; on the Office of General Interpreter, see, e.g., Brewer-García 2020; Yannakakis, forthcoming; on Malintzin, see Townsend 2006; Spoturno 2014; on the Americas, see Karttunen 1994; Brickhouse 2015; Carayon 2019; on Mughal multilingual secretaries, see Kinra 2015; on tricksters, see Zemon Davis 2006; for an excellent overview of literature on interpreters as intermediaries with mixed loyalties, see de Jong 2018. For a broad overview of intermediation, see note 10 below in this chapter.

8. On third space instead of a middle ground, see White 1991, a ternary, rather than binary, analysis.

9. I first analyzed the fixer apparatus in a comparison between medieval fixers and contemporary Afghan fixers in a recent book, Stahuljak 2021a.

10. The literature is vast, and it is impossible to cite all the references. For general literature on intermediation, see Heimburger 2012, 23: "go-betweens are individuals who create and/or maintain connections between culturally and, practically always, linguistically distant social entities." For reviews of brokerage literature in social sciences, including history, see Stovel and Shaw 2012; Miklavcic and LeBlanc 2014; Lindquist 2015; Raj 2016; Hönke and Müller 2018. On cultural translation, see Asad 1986. On go-betweens in the medieval and early modern period, see Schaffer et al. 2009a; Rothman 2012; Höh et al. 2013; Karttunen 1994; Miović 2014. For a reciprocal analysis of intermediaries past and present, see de Jong 2018; Stahuljak 2021a.

11. I concur with the criticism of Dakhlia 2008 of the (biographical) exceptionalism of intermediaries in early modern history; see also Dakhlia and Kaiser 2013.

12. For an early interrogation on this, see Kelly 1997.

13. For a full list, see Berman 2012, 46, 69; Oresme 1940, 79–82.

14. Balibar 1998, 17–18; Brucker 2001. On Oresme, see also Brucker 2020; Babbitt 1985.

15. Oresme wrote the first treatise on monetary economy in the West, *On Mint: Treatise on the Origin, Nature, Law, and Alterations of Money* (*De moneta: De origine, natura, jure et mutationibus monetarum*) in 1356–57. By clearly delineating the destructive effects on a state's economy of a debasement of the currency, Oresme influenced Charles V's monetary and tax policies.

16. Money is intended to be a measure and a medium of commensuration. Jean Froissart says there is nothing that cannot be mediated by money: "Il n'est chose qui ne s'appaise et moyenne par or et par argent; Froissart 1867–77, 15:356); see chapter 3.

17. "Par le commun il faut entendre à la fois le banal, c'est-à-dire l'élément d'une égalité primordiale et irréductible à tout effet de dinstinction, et—indiscernablement—le partagé, c'est-à-dire ce qui n'a lieu que dans le rapport, par lui et comme lui: par conséquent, ce qui ne se résout ni en 'être' ni en 'unité'" (Nancy 2014, 12).

18. E.g., Sola 1988; Bennassar and Bennassar 1989; Abulafia 1994; Matar 1999; Kaiser 2008; Trivellato 2009; Greene 2010; Weiss 2011; Goldberg 2012; Mediano and García-Arenal 2013; Hershenzon 2018; Barker 2019; García-Arenal and Glazer-Eytan 2019.

19. Rothman 2012 focused on the office of dragoman in Ottoman Istanbul, an emerging institution for interpreting and diplomacy; Dakhlia 2008 studied the *lingua franca*, a shared language in the Mediterranean that never became anyone's native tongue; C. Gilbert 2020 studied on Arabic translators of early modern Spain; Subrahmanyam 2011 combines three case studies of the Mediterranean and Mughal India. This overview of the Mediterranean excludes the rich scholarship on the Americas; see notes 7 and 10 above in this chapter.

20. With some notable exceptions, see Wallace 2016; Morato and Schoenaers 2018; Mallette 2021; J. Gilbert, Gaunt, and Burgwinkle 2020.

21. Polo 2016, 10n32. On the multiplicity of languages, see Sinor 1995.

22. Carpini 1980, 4 / Carpini 1929, 1:28. For more on Benedict, see also Duque 2009.

23. For a longer reading of Marco Polo as fixer, see Stahuljak 2021a. For excellent studies of Polo, see Kinoshita 2013; Gaunt 2013b; Cruse 2015; Gadrat-Ouerfelli 2015; Kinoshita 2016b; Cruse 2017.

24. For multiple repercussions of this, see Stahuljak 2020a. On Columbus's readings, see Baschet 2004; Delaney 2006; Hamdani 1979; Nunn 1935; Watts 1985.

25. Chrétien de Troyes 2004, 123 / Chrétien de Troyes 1994, lines 30–39; see Stahuljak et al. 2011; Kinoshita 2008a.

26. Curtius 1953; Jongkees 1967; Kelly 1978; Freeman 1979; Gentry 1983; Beaune 1985.

27. For a reading of Walter Benjamin's "The Task of the Translator" and a comparative reading of multilingualism in the Middle Ages and contemporary discourses on multiculturalism, see Stahuljak 2004. On *translatio*, see Stahuljak 2005.

28. Wace 1877, vol. 1, part 1 and 2, lines 77–80. See the almost identical wording in vol. 2, part 3, lines 11–14.

29. Froissart 1867–77, 2:14. The quotation is from the fourth and last redaction of the *Chronicles* known as the Rome manuscript (ca. 1396–1400?). On Froissart and *translatio*, see Stahuljak 2001.

30. Several other scholars have offered correctives to this widely accepted general definition of *translatio*. *Translatio* is more complex geographically and its intellectual itinerary more diverse than what we have taught it to be: while its general trajectory goes from east to north/ northwest, it actually detours via the south, in North Africa (Akbari 2000). A similar southern inflection can be observed in the descriptions of merchant routes in the

very works that articulated the east-west linear trajectory; a passage via Spain, rather than Rome, offers a significant alternative geography (Kinoshita 2008a). Bynum 1991 emphasized fragmentation in the *translatio reliquiarum*. See Khanmohamadi 2017 on transfer of swords from the Muslim Empire to Charlemagne's empire in the epic genre. This in no way makes Charlemagne a descendant of Muslims, only their heir, unlike the romance *Saladin* or *Berte aux grands pieds*, which create fictional Muslim ancestry for Charlemagne. For a different way of reading *translatio*, not as global, but as maritime, see Batchelor 2018.

31. E.g., Manning and Owen 2018; Batchelor 2018; Burnett 1997; Lindberg 1978.

32. Bruni 1992, 82 / Bruni 2008, 30. Bruni introduces a new term, "traductio," "tradurre" (guiding, leading) vs. "volgarizzare" (Cornish 2011), but the term is a misreading of a Latin loan word from Greek (Berman 2012, 82).

33. Du Bellay 1939, 37 / du Bellay 1993, 214. Du Bellay borrows from Bruni, who introduced the idea of imitation, of transfer of forms and not of content (Berman 2012, 84).

34. Apter 2010, 59; see also Apter 2013; and Cassin 2006.

35. See the Stanford University web page on Plato, https://plato.stanford.edu/entries/african-ethics/.

36. "Translation is not secondary or incidental to these works. It is a condition of their production"; Walkowitz 2015, 5.

37. See the NPR item from June 29, 2020, https://www.npr.org/2020/06/29/884957240/afghan-interpreter-who-saved-u-s-troops-gets-american-citizenship.

38. See Baker 2006; Inghilleri 2012; Munday 2007; Tymoczko 2000.

39. The work of decolonizing the Middle Ages began two decades ago, when it became clear that the "medieval" had been a function of modernity. Having served as modernity's other, the Middle Ages became the "premodern" and were rapidly made irrelevant to modernity, whose explorations of the past now barely spill over into the "early modern." In this logic, the "premodern" is cut off from modernity; see Dagenais 2004; Stahuljak 2020a.

40. I began this work in Stahuljak 2020a. See also Werner and Zimmermann 2003. Cf. Subrahmanyam 1997; Heng 2021.

Chapter One

1. Some examples of dictionaries are Romanic-Germanic, Italian-Vulgar Greek, Latin-Basque, Latin-Hebrew, French-Arabic, German-Arabic. The information listed here is based on Bischoff 1961. Bullock-Davies 1966 wrote a fascinating study of French-Welsh, French-English, and French-Irish communication and the fixers employed at the courts of William I the Conqueror and Henry II and many baronial households in the eleventh and twelfth centuries.

2. Altaner 1924 described Dominican missions aimed at the Greeks, Jacobites, Nestorians, Maronites, Ethiopians, Armenians, Georgians, Tartars, Hungarians, Bulgarians, Albanians, Serbians, Prussians, Lithuanians, Latvians, Estonians, Finns, Russians and Poles. See also Delacroix-Besnier 1997; Rouxpetel 2015a and 2016b.

3. The following summary draws from Cortabarría 1969; Cortabarría 1970, Cortabarría-Beitia 1970. See also Zuili and Baddeley 2012; Balivet 1997; Richard 1976; Roncaglia 1953.

4. Qtd. in Cortabarría-Beitia 1970, 196, 216; see also Mérigoux 1986, 34; Lusignan 1987, 53–59.

5. Von Harff 1946, 69 / von Harff 1860, 57; see Boyle 2021.

6. Bratianu 1942, 353; Schein 1991; Leopold 2000; Meschini 2014.

7. Brandt 1956, 11; Schein 1991; Leopold 2000.

8. Humbert of Romans 1690; and Humbert of Romans 1968. For an essential study of Humbert and the Dominicans and on the integration of Eastern Christians, see Rouxpetel 2015a.

9. Brandt 1956, 7; Diotti 1977, 19; translation occasionally modified. I have not been able to consult a reedition with a new translation, P. Dubois 2019. On Dubois, see also Forcadet 2014; Mastnak 2002; Brandt 1930; Langlois 1891.

10. P. Dubois 2007. Dubois wrote two pamphlets against the Templars, "Remonstrance du peuple de France" (Remonstrance of the people of France) and "Populi Franciae ad regem supplicatio" (Plea of the people of France to the king; 1308), soon after completing *De recuperatione Terre Sancte*; Brandt 1956, 33 and P. Dubois 1956, 82n34.

11. Beattie 2019. See also Hames 2012; Johnston 2004; Hames 2003; Mastnak 2002; Beattie 1995.

12. This route was judged by Llull's contemporaries as impracticable and exhausting to the point of self-defeat, with the example of Louis IX's fatal crusade in Tunis; see Brocardus 1869, 420; Sanudo 1611, 39; Sanudo 2011, 75. A few years later, in the "Liber de acquisitione Terrae Sanctae," Llull proposed two land routes that converged in Egypt: a North African route and a route southward from a reconquered Constantinople.

13. This is consistent with Llull's position on forced conversion of nonbelievers in Christian lands; see Johnston 1995; Hames 2010.

14. This was not a novel idea; see Molay 2007.

15. This is a tried method from at least the time of the Fourth Crusade and the conquest of Constantinople in 1204; see Moore 2014.

16. Riccoldo of Monte Croce 1967, 168–69. For a more recent online edition, see Jensen 2014.

17. Riccoldo of Monte Croce 1997, 118/119. For an overview of the Dominicans' methods and Riccoldo's contributions, see Rouxpetel 2016a; see also Rouxpetel 2015b; and Booth 2021.

18. Not only interpreters don't know (Llull 1981, 254), but neither do the merchants: "Et quaerunt a mercatoribus christianis, qui sunt inter ipsos, de fide nostra catholica, et quia mercatores sunt laici, nesciunt satisfacere eis. . . . Unde si catholici bene litterati disputarent cum ipsis, tenendo modum praelibatum, tales converterentur ad fidem nostram" (Llull 1927, 272).

19. Bacon 1906–27, 1:267. See also Bourgain 1989; Bregola 1937.

20. Molay 2008, 184–85; Henri II 2008, 287–88; Brocardus 1869, 487–90. For a contrary opinion, see "Via ad terram sanctam" 2008, 176–77. Its Latin version proposes the same: "Memoria" 2008, 255, 267–70. See also Hayton 1906, 248–49. Hayton also recommends using Georgians; Hayton 1906, 246–47. On the Greeks, William of Adam 2012, 84/85–96/97, and Brocardus 1869, 372–73, are the most intransigent. For the view of the Armenians prior to the fourteenth century, see Rouxpetel 2018.

21. Mézières 2008, 141. See also Henri II 2008, 291; and "Memoria" 2008, 238.

22. A short memoir in Dubois's style was added shortly after the original treatise. A rubric, added still later, in a fifteenth-century hand, summarizes it as "The Opinion of One Urging the King of France to Acquire the Kingdom of Jerusalem and Cyprus for the Second of His Sons, and on the Invasion of the Kingdom of Egypt" ("Oppinio cujusdam suadentis regi Francie ut regnum Jerosolimitanum et Cipri acquireret pro altero filiorum suorum, ac de invasione regni Egipti"); see "Opinion" 1956, 205; and "Oppinio" 1891, 139.

23. On colonization, see Prawer 1986; Prawer 1992; Fernández-Armesto 1987.

24. Cf. Anderson 1991; see also J. Schwaller 2012; R. Schwaller 2012.

Chapter Two

1. E.g., Bacon 1906–27, 1:267; Llull 1975, 69–71; "Memoria" 2008, 249; Nogaret 1862.

2. The most common Latin terms were "peregrinatio" (pilgrimage) and "passagium."

3. William of Adam 2012, 26–27. See also Sanudo: While Christians want cotton and sugar, dates, wild cinammon and flax (bombis et zucharum; dactilis, cassia fistula, linõ; Sanudo 2011, 51–52 / Sanudo 1611, 24–25), Muslims want gold, silver, iron and other metals, oil, honey, oats, and wood (aurum, argentum, ferrum et catera metalla; oleum, mel, avellana; lignamen; Sanudo 2011, 51–53 / Sanudo 1611, 24–25). Especially condemnable is the slave trade, as William of Adam highlights; for more, see Barker 2019; Tolan 2019.

4. Richard 1984, 144. For the early opposition to pilgrimage, see Constable 1976.

5. John of Plano Carpini 1980 / John of Plano Carpini 1929; Benedict the Pole 1980 / Benedict the Pole 1929; Rubruck 2009 / Rubruck 1929.

6. Gucci 1948 / Gucci 1862; Lengherand 1861; Fabri 1896 / Fabri 1843–49.

7. For a substantial development on Marcel Mauss's gift exchange, Jacques Derrida's late twentieth-century critique of it, and representative late twentieth-century French anthropological thought on the gift, see Stahuljak 2021a.

8. Jackson 2009, 30. It is of some interest that Benedict, who was the official interpreter for German and Slavic languages, makes not a single mention of translation in his account; see the introduction. For more on Benedict, see Duque 2009.

9. Carpini had a good point of comparison as there were, according to him, four thousand emissaries present with innumerable gifts for the enthronement (Carpini 1980, 1:62 / Carpini 1929, 118; Carpini 1980, 1:64 / Carpini 1929, 120). For an excellent overview of the exchange between Carpini and the Mongols, and the signification of gifts in Mongol society, see Duque 2018.

10. Saint-Quentin 1965, 97. *Historia Tartarorum* is lost, known only from Vincent de Beauvais from his *Speculum historiale* because for Mongols he uses two sources: Simon of Saint-Quentin and John of Plano Carpini; see Richard 1965, 7.

11. Jackson 2009, 35–36; see also Duque 2018. Bertrandon de la Broquière observes the same custom in Turkish-controlled Syria, "car la coustume est par delà que nul ne parle aux princes, s'il ne porte quelque present"; de la Broquière 1892, 111. "Such is the custom of all who come to the lord, to give something, and thus respect the custom of giving and taking presents. Their greatness is considered according to the number of presents they give, in honour of the lord"; González de Clavijo 2001, 121. The Dominican Riccoldo of Monte Croce in his *Liber peregrinationis* (1300–1302) records the link between gifts to Mongol rulers and the right to live; Riccoldo of Monte Croce 1997, 80; for a reading of Riccoldo and the relationship between death and the gift of translation, see Stahuljak 2021a.

12. There is evidence for Latin interpreters at the Mongol court, in 1243 and 1268: "Verum mogalice signavimus, quia illo tempore scriba noster latinus presens non affuerat"; Meyvaert 1980, 251.

13. See Rubruck 2009, 144 / Rubruck 1929, 224; Rubruck 2009, 226 / Rubruck 1929, 289; see also Jackson 2009, 43–45; Pelliot 1931–32.

14. Riccoldo of Monte Croce 1967, 168–69. For a more recent online edition, see Jensen 2014.

15. For broader interpretations of missionary travel, see de Certeau 2005; Khanmohamadi 2014; and on travel experience in general, see Euben 2006.

16. The later missions to Asia, during the last quarter of the thirteenth century and the first half of the fourteenth century, make either superfunctory or no mention of a company

of an interpreter. It is a potentially rich area for the study of fixers, in light of the insights provided by Marco Polo and Benedict the Pole, who were their own fixers and did not make much mention of it. This applies, for example, to the Dominican Riccoldo of Monte Croce in *The Book of Peregrinations* (*Liber peregrinationis*, 1288–1300?) and the Franciscan John of Montecorvino, archbishop of Khanbaliq (Beijing) (1307–1328/1330?), in his *Letters* (*Epistolae,*), who respectively learned Arabic and Tartar. For more missionary accounts, see Gadrat-Ouerfelli 2021; Coulon and Gadrat-Ouerfelli 2017; Phillips 2014; Chareyron 2013; Gadrat-Ouerfelli 2013.

17. Burchard of Mount Sion 1864 / Burchard of Mount Sion 1896. But see the colorful account of Mandeville 2011 / Mandeville 2000.

18. For a list, see Graboïs 1998, 16, 213–14; and Chareyron 2005. This is a provisional list that continues to grow.

19. On the travelogues as a narrative genre, see Chareyron 2013; on the travelogues and pilgrimage guides, see Rajohnson 2014.

20. The case of narratives from East Asia is inversely proportional: references to communication and translation cease to appear in any significant number after the 1300s. Likewise, the number of pilgrimage narratives to Rome and Saint James of Compostella is fairly low; Richard 1984, 144.

21. Adorno 1978, 54, 460. This is my own translation.

22. Richard 1984, 144. On the rediscovery of the Holy Land after 1330, see Rouxpetel 2016b.

23. Ludolph von Sudheim, priest and parish rector who traveled in Syria from 1336 to 1341, was the first to attest the establishment of the Franciscans on Mount Sion; Sudheim 1884, 352.

24. Newett 1907, 26–28; Sumption 1975, 185–92. On "tolomaci," later Ger. Dolmetscher, borrowed from Slavic via Turkish, see Leptschy 1970.

25. Fabri, 1896, 1.1:84. (This is exceptionally my translation here because the English edition [1896] for some reason does not have a translation of this section.) On Fabri, see Beebe 2014. On German travelers in Venice, see Braunstein 2016.

26. Brasca 1481, fols. 48v–49. For the detail of twenty articles of this kind of contract signed with the ship's captain in Venice before the notaries, see Fabri 1896, 7:87–90 / Fabri 1843–49, 1:89–92.

27. *Le voyage* 1882, 25; see also Fabri 1986, 7:97, 7:152–58 / Fabri 1843–49, 1:97, 1:136–38. For cost of travel at the end of the fourteenth century, see for the year 1384, Gucci 1948, 149–56 / Gucci 1862, 419–38; and for the year 1392–93, Brygg 1884, 387–88.

28. For lodging, see, for example, "Itinerarium cuiusdem Anglici" 1906–27, 449; Brygg 1884, 388; Lengherand 1861, 115. For examples of Franciscans as guides, see for the year 1345–46 "Itinerarium cuiusdem Anglici" 1906–27, 4:454; for 1380, Bellorini and Hoade 1948, 16; for 1394–95, Martoni 1895, 613; for 1480, *Le voyage* 1882, 99.

29. Caumont 1858, 46. See also Coppart de Velaines 2007, 292 (for the year 1423); and de la Broquière 1892, 301–3 (for the year 1433); Tafur 1995, 39 / Tafur 1926, 54.

30. Rochechouart 1893, 239. Similarly in Lengherand 1861, 115: "comment ilz se y avoyent à conduire, et la passience qu'il failloit que chascun d'eulx supportast des Mores et aultres infidèles." Felix Fabri provides an exhaustive five-page description of twenty-seven articles of advice (Fabri 1896, 7:248–55 / Fabri 1843–49, 1:213–17).

31. De la Broquière 1892, 16. In 1384, the Florentines had "papers of presentation, for by skin and features we were noted" (la nostra carta della rappresentazione, perchè per pelo e per segno fummo rassegnati; Gucci 1948, 95 / Gucci 1862, 277).

32. Adorno 1978, 208, 209; Tafur 1995 / Tafur 1926.

33. Breydenbach 2010, 60 / Breydenbach 1486, 9. One can also consult the Italian translation, Breydenbach 1999. For other studies on Breydenbach, see E. Ross 2014; Boyle 2021.

34. Breydenbach 2010, 60 / Breydenbach 1486, 9. Cf. Fabri 1896, 7:87–90 / Fabri 1843–49, 1:89–91.

35. Von Harff 1946, 69 / von Harff 1860, 57; see Boyle 2021.

36. "Saetta," Poggibonsi 1945a, 120; "Saeto," Sigoli 1944, 185; see also Boldensele 1852, 274; Casola 1855, 65.

37. "Cocheca" in Anglure 2008; Poggibonsi 1945b, xvi; Jacobi de Verona, the Great Dragoman of Cairo, "el Trujaman mayor del Soldan" (in Tafur 1995, 52 / Tafur 1926, 72) was born in Seville, was taken by his Jewish father to Jerusalem, and, after his death, converted to Islam.

38. "Turchiusmagnus noster nomine Santaacha," Martoni 1895, 592; "Helya," Adorno 1978, 302, 316; "Bazella" or "Gatzelo," *Le voyage* 1882, xxxv.

39. "Myschier Vyncent," von Harff 1860, 57.

40. "Simone di Candia," Sigoli 1944, 202, 173; "Laurentio de Candia," Adorno 1978, 210.

41. Bellorini and Hoade 1948, 23. (This is cited from the editors' introduction, written in English; this is not a translation of the original Italian text.)

42. Poggibonsi 1945b, 6 / Poggibonsi 1945a, 8; "Itinerarium cuiusdem Anglici" 1906–27.

43. The Venetian archives attest to the amount of care that went into standardizing and enforcing the contracts, resolving any disputes, and sanctioning ship captains, in the attempt to preserve the monopoly on the pilgrim traffic; Newett 1907.

44. Poggibonsi 1945b, 98–99 / Poggibonsi 1945a, 115–16; Brygg 1884, 387–88; "Un pèlerinage en Terre Sainte 1905, 84–86; Adorno 1978, 210–16; Fabri 1896, 9:93–96 / Fabri, 1843–49, 2:100–101.

45. For the full contract, see Fabri 1896, 9:93–96 / Fabri 1843–49, 2:100–101.

46. For English, see Frescobaldi 1948; Gucci 1948; Sigoli 1948. For Italian, see Frescobaldi 1944; Gucci 1862; Sigoli 1944. There is a more recent edition of Gucci available; however, its editor mistakenly identifies it as Simone Sigoli's account; see Gucci 1999. Therefore, my references are to the 1862 edition of Gucci. I have not been able to consult a more recent edition, Lanza and Troncarelli 1990.

47. Gucci 1948, 150–56 / Gucci 1862, 421–36. Compare to a simpler budget, "la despence ordinaire et neccessaire," in "Un pèlerinage en Terre Sainte" 1905, 84–86; and in Brygg 1884, 387–88.

48. Dakhlia 2008, 343. Diplomatic registers from the sixteenth and the seventeenth centuries suggest that "mangerie" is an unofficial bargain intended to avoid creating a precedent and institutionalizing a new custom in contracts (Dakhlia 2008, 361).

49. Gucci 1948, 121 / Gucci 1862, 348; Frescobaldi 1948, 65–66 / Frescobaldi 1944, 117–20; Sigoli 1948, 178 / Sigoli 1944, 217–18; Fabri 1896, 9:64 / Fabri 1843–49, 2:77–78.

50. Also "Item et trucemannum, sive interpretem, nomine Helyam, christianum de centuria qui nos in itinere multiformiter tribulavit atque de manibus nostris pecunias cautelis dolosis extorsit, nobiscum habuimus" (Adorno 1978, 302; see also 316). Adorno's, Fabri's, and Pietro Casola's accounts are filled with similar scenes, too numerous to cite here in full, but see esp. Casola 1907, 270–74 / Casola 1855, 77–78, where pilgrims are taken hostage and ransomed by the governor of Jerusalem for a sum of a thousand ducats, ultimately reduced to twenty-five ducats.

51. For another version of the same event, see Frescobaldi 1948, 65–66 / Frescobaldi 1944, 117–20; and Sigoli 1948, 178 / Sigoli 1944, 217–18.

52. Lengherand 1861, 148; see also Lengherand 1861, 145–47, 150, 166. That said, Fabri also reports on constant thefts of relics by pilgrims; Fabri 1896, 10:625.

53. "The lord knights [Hospitaller] invited me and two of the Minorite fathers, two Jews, one Saracen and one Mamluke, to sup with them, and we supped merrily together—albeit we were of different faiths and customs. It is because of this converse with the infidels that a man is obliged to take leave from our lord the Pope when he wishes to make a pilgrimage to Jerusalem" (Fabri 1896, 9:132 / Fabri 1843–49, 2:129). See in contrast Barbatre 1972–73, 157, who recovers the feeling of "home" only on his return journey, in Rhodes.

54. Rochechouart 1893, 238; Fabri 1843–49, 1:193, 2:14; Gucci 1862, 423; Wey 1857, 7. Thomas Brygg seems to misunderstand the term as "curiositas," "pro" or "ex curiositate"; Brygg 1884, 387–88.

55. "Un pèlerinage en Terre Sainte" 1905, 86; "les aultres a pié qui chassoient les asnes, lesquieulx demandoient argent pour leurs courtoisies" (Barbatre 1972–73, 129).

56. Gucci 1948, 150 / Gucci 1862, 422; see also "Un pèlerinage en Terre Sainte" 1905, 86.

57. Haugeard 2006, 295; Boutet 1983; Duby 1973; Frappier 1973.

58. Zumthor 2000, 560; Payen 1966–67; Dupin 1931.

59. Brasca 1481, fol. 48v; Casola 1907, 225 / Casola 1855, 53.

60. The digital copy of the edition was not sufficiently legible to provide the full quote in Middle German.

Chapter Three

1. The number of interpreters is uncertain. See Lublinski-Bodenham 1978. References are to Froissart 1867–77, 14:151–59, 211–53, 269–80.

2. Once, the language of engagement is not specified; see Froissart 1867–77, 14:242–44.

3. For some of the most important scholarship on Machaut's life and work, see McGrady and Bain 2012; Butterfield 2002; Calin 2015; Cerquiligni-Toulet 1985; Earp 1995; Kelly 2014; Leach 2011; McGrady 2006; Plumley 2013. On Machaut and authorship, see chapter 5.

4. For some of the most important scholarship on Froissart's life and work, see Ainsworth 1990; Dembowski 1983; Figg 1995; Maddox and Maddox 1998; Soukupová 2021; Zink 1998. On Froissart and authorship, see chapter 5. The medieval French *dit* (thirteenth to fifteenth centuries) is a narrative or expository poem, most often written in octosyllabic verse couplets, although it was not a strict genre.

5. On Mézières's life and work, see Blumenfeld-Kosinski 2011b; Blanchard and Blumenfeld-Kosinski 2017; Blanchard et al. 2019; see also chapter 5.

6. Cyprus had been the dominion of the French Lusignan family since 1197, following the loss of Jerusalem in 1187.

7. Edward III may have refused the crusade by reminding Peter that his ancestor Richard I the Lionheart conquered Cyprus in 1191 before giving it in trust to Guy of Lusignan, the disgraced king of Jerusalem; Luce 1862, 128. On the details of Peter's trip in the West, see Iorga 1973.

8. Machaut 2002, lines 805–15. This citation includes a single reference to a bilingual edition that contains the original and a published translation. Machaut received a canonry at Reims in 1337; Edbury 2001, 8.

9. Edbury 1991, 166; Machaut 2002, lines 1894–914, 2428; Mézières 1954, 120–21, 127–28.

10. Mézières 1954; Makhairas 1932; al-Nuwayri al-İskandarāni 1968–76. See the later versions of events in Strambaldi 1893. On al-Nuwayri al-İskandarāni, see Wrisley 2011; on Makhairas, see Nicolaou-Konnari 2011.

11. Hardy 2011, cxxvi. Many writers cited Pierre, including Petrarch, who praises the "great and memorable achievement" of the conquest of Alexandria in a letter he wrote to Boccacio in 1367; Hazard 1975, 352, 357; see also de la Broquière 1892, 148; Adorno 1978, 353.

12. Froissart 1867–77, 11:231; also 16:32; See also Froissart 1869–75, 6:79, 82–86, 90, 277–80; 12:46, 208–10; Froissart 2007, 330.

13. See Chaucer in "The Monk's Tale," lines 401–6, qtd. in Hazard 1975, 360.

14. In the absence of any reference to the 1373–74 war between Cyprus and Genoa, some scholars prefer to date the work to ca. 1369–74 instead of to 1377, the year of Machaut's death.

15. This concords with the ambiguity as to the objective of the crusade: "Urban's bulls show a degree of ambiguity as to whether the immediate goal was the Mamluk sultanate or the areas in the Aegean and the Balkans under pressure from the Turks"; Edbury 1991, 165. It is possible that the raid on Alexandria had a strategic goal of reestablishing the Cypriot city of Famagusta as the port of call in the eastern Mediterranean trade; Edbury 2001, 2–3, 5.

16. Mézières 1969, 2:406, 405. This citation includes a single reference to a bilingual edition that contains the original and a published translation.

17. B. Palmer 2002, 23. See Ribémont 2002 for a similar argument that the poem is a literary space with an epic touch.

18. B. Palmer 2002, 20. See also Tarnowski 2006; Blumenfeld-Kosinski 2009a and 2009b.

19. Reminiscent of Machaut's most important work of narrative poetry, *Le Livre du voir dit* (*The Book of the True Dit*), which has over nine thousand lines of poetry (narrative and lyric) and combines narrative poetry with forty-six prose letters and sixty-three lyrics, seven of which have known musical settings. Of most interest to the *Taking of Alexandria* is the claim to truthfulness built on written and musical forms, including the epistolary.

20. For the outer limits of the geography of events covered in Froissart's *Chronicles*, see Medeiros 2003.

21. There are several episodes of interest: Froissart 1867–77, 15:216–31, 242–69, 309–52, 355–60; Froissart 1867–77, 16:29–67.

22. Froissart 1867–77, 15:316–17. Boucicaut's biographer preferred to blame it on "Fortune"; Lalande 1985, 99–100.

23. Contamine and Paviot 2008, 61; Delaville Le Roulx 1886, 1:297–98; Mézières 2008, 119–21; Lalande 1985, 104.

24. On the Créquy family, see Stahuljak 2015.

25. *Chevalerie de l'Ordre de la Passion*, Paris, Bibliothèque de l'Arsenal, MS 2251, fol. 12v. Andrew of Calabria, first husband of queen Joanna of Naples, whom Mézières served, was actually never crowned king.

26. Lalande 1985, 62; see also Lalande 1988, 26–28; Delaville Le Roulx 1886, 1:159–65.

27. Boucicaut's biography also confirms that the news of defeat and capture of Christian knights was brought by "les propres messages que le conte de Nevers envoya au duc de Bourgongne son pere" (Lalande 1985, 118).

28. On a similar use of this proverb, see Timelli 2019.

29. Cf. the word-for-word opposite version by a knight and marshal, Boucicaut; Lalande 1985, 125.

30. In the Froissart 1867–77 edition by Lettenhove, the first redaction corresponds to the Amiens manuscript in Froissart 1991–98. The second and the third redaction correspond to manuscripts A and B, in Froissart 1869–75. The fourth redaction corresponds to the Rome manuscript in Froissart 1972.

31. For a conclusive debate on the existence of a manuscript in verse and the referent of "cest livre," see Ainsworth 1990, 32–50.

32. See Ainsworth 1990, 123, 303; Ainsworth 2003a; Brownlee 2000, 82; Dembowski 1983, 16, 44; Stahuljak 2001; Stahuljak 2006; Zink 1998, 96, 100.

33. On allegory, see Tarnowski 2011; Strubel 1980.

34. Contamine 2009; see also Contamine 2015; Tarnowski 2006. On Mézières's political career, see Iorga 1973; Blumenfeld-Kosinski and Petkov 2011b.

35. Spiegel 1993. For a contrary view, see Damian-Grint 1999; and Ainsworth 2003b. For basic information on prosifications, see Doutrepont 1939.

36. See the list of Froissart's travels in Ainsworth 2003a. It certainly helped that he wrote his Arthurian romance in verse and poetry separately (although Ainsworth 2003a makes the argument that he stopped writing poetry after 1389 and imbued the *Chronicles* with lyricism in other ways).

37. This modern evaluation of Machaut's *Prise* stands in contrast to Louis de Mas Latrie, its first editor in 1877, who saw it as historically valuable, even if poetically unworthy. Mas Latrie saw the Machaut as a truthful historian: "L'auteur de tant de fictions et d'allégories ingénieuses est ici un historien, un écrivain véridique, impartial, au moins par l'intention, et presque scrupuleux"; Mas Latrie 1877, viii, xix.

38. However, a poem written in November 1349, the *Judgment of the King of Navarre* (*Jugement du roi de Navarre*), opens with 540 historical verses on the plague; Machaut 1988. Similarly, *Le Livre du voir dit* is interspersed with letters that mention historical figures, events, places, the Hundred Years' War, and the plague.

39. Gaullier-Bougassas 2011a; Schroeder 1971; Höltgen 1959; Meyer 1883.

40. Machaut 2002, lines 63–66, 7179–82, 8848–51. Machaut started the fashion of adding the tenth preux to the list (Hardy 2011, cxxiv, cxxvii; B. Palmer 2002, 12, 31).

41. Delogu 2008. Hardy 2011 considers it incongruous (ciii), but in terms of genre Machaut's choice this was perfectly resonant with the twelfth-century romances of antiquity, the earliest vernacular histories in verse.

42. Van Praet 1831; de Smedt 2000, 132–33; Vale 1995. For a full political and historical context as related to the Burgundian cultural and artistic output, see Morrison and Stahuljak 2015; see also chapters 4 and 5 below.

43. I take my cue from Chism 2009.

44. This goes far beyond the influence of Vegetius's *De re militari* for military strategy; Hardy 2011, cxxv (also p. cxxii for brief mention of "projets de croisade"). Bratianu 1942; Hayton 1906; de Villaret 2008; de Villaret et al. 2008; Sanudo 2011; William of Adam 2012; Stanegrave 2008.

45. Dopp 1958, vii. Even though after 1454 the crusading focus undeniably shifted to Constantinople at the Court of Burgundy, there was one major travel/spy report that treated Alexandria at length; de Lannoy 1878. Although Burgundian Bertrandon de la Broquière never went as far as Alexandria (1432–33), he makes a reference to Peter I; de la Broquière 1892, 148.

46. Stanegrave is a precursor to Mézières; Paviot 2008, 43n84.

47. Guard 2013; Krummel 2011, 13–14; Guard 2005.

Chapter Four

1. Huizinga 1954. For the new authoritative translation, see Huizinga 2020. For recent reconsiderations of Huizinga and the historiographic tradition, see Arnade et al. 2019; and Lecuppre-Desjardin 2019.

2. An *apanage* is a fief usually given to royal male children under the condition that it revert to the crown if the male line is extinguished; Blockmans and Prevenier 1999, 15.

3. Summary based on Vaughan 2002; Blockmans and Prevenier 1999.

4. Summary based on Blockmans and Prevenier 1999, 72–102; Vaughan 1970.

5. Summary for the years 1438–49 is based on Paviot 2003, 81–115; Paviot 1995, 105–26; Vaughan 1970, 270–73.

6. Chastellain 1865, 217. For a translation into modern French, see Thiry 1995, 751.

7. Summary for the years 1451–64 is based on Paviot 2003, 117–76; and Paviot 1995, 126–34.

8. Paviot 2003, 127–35; Caron 2003; Caron and Clauzel 1997; Moodey 2012, 125–48.

9. Summary based on Denoël 2004, 79–105, at 95; see also Beaune 1995, 1131–33. For an example that brings together Andrew's cross, Alexander the Great, and the knights of the Order of the Golden Fleece, see fig. 4.1. For information on the illuminator(s), see van Buren 1972 and 2000.

10. Blondeau 2009b, 19–20. She argues that the work is thus situated "d'emblée . . . dans l'optique d'un christianisme militant" (Blondeau 2009b, 249).

11. Falmagne and van den Abeele 2016, 257–65. On the ducal library and crusading, see Wrisley 2007–8.

12. Paviot 2003; Paviot 1995; Grunzweig 1956; Cartellieri 1929, 10, 247n10.

13. Vaughan 1970, 288–89; Bousmanne and Delcourt 2011, 75; Blockmans and Prevenier 1999, 104–7.

14. Vaughan 1973, 125–26. For an overview of Burgundian history, geography, and spheres of influence, consult Vaughan 1970; Vaughan 1973; Blockmans and Prevenier 1999; Schnerb 2005; Haemers 2009; Stein and Pollmann 2010; Lecuppre-Desjardin 2016 / Lecuppre-Desjardin 2022); Stein 2017.

15. Doutrepont 1909; Doutrepont 1939; Timelli et al. 2014.

16. It seems that *Girart of Roussillon* was the only one directly commissioned by the duke; Hériché-Pradeau 2006; Blondeau 2006; Timelli et al. 2014, 331–45. Translation of *Chronicles of Hainaut* was initiated by Simon Nockart, clerk of the bailiwick of Hainaut. The translation of this work participates in a larger movement of translation of regional histories, commissioned by local men who did not necessarily serve the duke, such as Nockart or Edmond de Dynter, who wrote the Latin *Chronica nobilissimorum ducum Lotharingiae et Brabantiae ac regum Francorum* that Wauquelin translated; Small 2000, 17–19. Although *Alexander* was originally commissioned, "a la requeste et principalement au commandement" of Jean de Bourgogne, Count of Étampes and Lord of Dourdan (1415–91), nephew of John the Fearless and cousin of Philip the Good, governor of Picardy, Philip treated Wauquelin's work as his own commission. Proof of their common commission lies in the records of a reimbursement made to Jean de Croÿ for payments made to Wauquelin and Jacotin du Bois for the first volume of *Chronicles*, *Girart*, and *Alexander*; Lemaire 2000, 29.

17. For a bilingual Latin-French edition of *Annales*, see de Guyse 1826–38.

18. Williams 1989; Hériché-Pradeau 2006. There is no edition of the Vienna manuscript that Wauquelin made for the duke. The 1880 Montille edition of Wauquelin's Beaune manuscript is the only available printed edition. The Beaune manuscript is the same, with few variants, as the Paris, BnF, MS fr. 852. The fourteenth-century alexandrine poem is a rewriting of the twelfth-century *chanson de geste*. Jean Wauquelin would have also written an abbreviated version, inserted by David Aubert in the *Histoire de Charles Martel* and by Jean Mansel in *La fleur des histoires*; Timelli et al. 2014, 475–93; Hériché-Pradeau 2006, 100; Naudet 2005; de Terre-Basse 1856.

19. The Duchy of Burgundy proper and the County of Burgundy (Franche-Comté, under the rule of German emperors) were definitely divided in 1032. The old Frankish kingdom of

Burgundy was founded in 843; Blockmans and Prevenier 1999, 18. The duke visited Pothières in 1433 and, in 1446, sent for the works in Latin and French on the life of Girart; Small 2006, 158.

20. Hériché-Pradeau 2008, 31; for a streamlined explanation of this complex tradition, see McKendrick 1996, 8; for a full history, see Gaullier-Bougassas and Bellon-Méguelle 2015, 1:7–56.

21. Paris, BnF, MS fr. 9342, fol. 127; fig. 4.1; for English translation, see Wauquelin 2012, 179.

22. BnF, MS fr. 9342, fol. 127v; Wauquelin 2012, 179.

23. BnF, MS fr. 9342, fols. 127–27v; see also Wauquelin 2012, 179–80.

24. This genealogy is exploited in the Burgundian romance *Perceforest*, transcribed by David Aubert in 1459–60 at the request of the duke. Jean Mansel in *La fleur des histoires*, in a luxury ducal copy, will also cite this story; Hériché-Pradeau 2006; Blondeau 2009b, 246; Ferlampin-Acher 2010. On the relationship of the library and crusade, see Wrisley 2007–8.

25. McGrady 2019; Veysseyre 2008; Babbitt 1985; Monfrin 1964; Monfrin 1963.

26. Potin 2020 has shown that the number of manuscripts is down from the 895 inventoried in 1380. For more information, see Delisle 1907; Doutrepont 1909, xv–xvi; Avril and Lafaurie 1968; Sherman 1995; Hedeman 2008.

27. Over six hundred manuscripts were acquired through commissions and gifts; Falmagne and van den Abeele 2016, 11; LDB-I 2000, 13–17. Doutrepont 1909, xliv, cites 876 volumes; see also Barrois 1830.

28. Originally written for the Avesnes family, at the end of the thirteenth century; Flutre 1974b, 25–42.

29. Chastellain 1865, 216, gives a more complete picture of political schemes; Thiry 1995, 750–51. In reality, Philip sought the title three times but either was unsuccessful or refused the conditions.

30. Paris, BnF, MS fr. 92, fol. 1v; edition Palumbo 2001, 82.

31. Literary works were offered to the duke by his entourage; see Paviot 2003; LDB-II 2003, 18–37.

32. LDB-IV 2009, 127–58. Jean may have had his own copy, which would be lost today, and intended *Croniques et conquestes* as gift for Philip (Charron and Gil 1999).

33. Lefèvre's claim that he was Philip's chaplain is not confirmed by otherwise substantial ducal accounts and registers; Gil 1998.

34. Wijsman 2010c, 477; see Visser-Fuchs 2018; Waurin [Wavrin] 1864, 1–4.

35. Waleran later served as counselor for the duke's 1464 crusade.

36. Wijsman 2010c, 472–76; Naber 1990a. Although they do not bear the usual marks of ownership, such as armorial marks or ex libris, we can add to Wijsman's list of thirty manuscripts two more stories of local chivalric heroes, *Gérard de Nevers* (Brussels, KBR, MS 9631) and *Jehan d'Avesnes* (Paris, BnF, MS fr. 12572), because they were illustrated by the Master of Wavrin, Wavrin's go-to illuminator. It is thought that *Gérard de Nevers* was made for Jean de Wavrin and passed to the duke's library; see Schandel in LDB-III 2006, 133–38. Wijsman also explains that *Jehan d'Avesnes* was in the 1469 inventory of the Duke of Burgundy, with other manuscripts offered by Wavrin; Wijsman 2010c, 478; see also Naber 1990b, 27. See also Naber 1990a; and Schandel 2002–3.

37. Devaux and Marchal 2018; Wijsman 2010c, 472–76; Naber 1990b.

38. Cf. the list presented in de Crécy and Brown-Grant 2015, 64, which does not include *Roman de Thebes* and *Histoire de Troie*, but includes *Buscalus* (*Compilation d'histoire romaine, suivie de l'histoire de Turnus et de la fondation de Tournay*; Paris, BnF, MS fr. 9343–44).

39. There are no editions available for the following from the Wavrin library: *Romuléon, Roman de Thèbes, Histoire de Troie*, and from the Créquy library, *Romance of Florent and Octavian*. I have not been able to consult the two doctoral thesis editions of the unedited *Le roman de Florimont* and *Histoire d'Olivier de Castille*: Bidaux 2007, and Régnier-Bohler 1994.

40. LDB-III 2006, 133–38; Devaux and Marchal 2018; Brown-Grant 2020.

41. For a full list, see appendix A, section 2. For an overview analysis of most Burgundian romances, see Brown-Grant 2008.

42. Monfrin 1963; Rychner 1963; Brucker 1987; Lusignan 1987, 129–71; Willard, 1989; Sherman 1995; Tesnière 2000; Hedeman 2008; Brucker 2020. See also Galderisi 2011.

43. Lechat 2012; Duval and Vielliard, n.d. While most manuscripts of Valerius Maximus do not prioritize the position of either *translateur* or *aucteur*, an incunabula, Paris, BnF, Rés Z-200, ca. 1475, does subordinate visually the entries by acteur to those of translateur. This seems particularly interesting at the threshold of the age of print.

44. A. Dubois 1994. See Paris, Bibliothèque nationale de France, Gallica Digital Library, https://gallica.bnf.fr/ark:/12148/btv1b9009640p/f31.item (MS 45), and https://gallica .bnf.fr/ark:/12148/btv1b8451116z/f5.item (MS 282), accessed May 3, 2023. For a parallel study of prologues for Charles V, with a similar conclusion of efforts to keep translator's and "author's" identities separate, see Hedeman 2019.

45. Paris, Bibliothèque nationale de France, MS 282, Gallica Digital Library, https:// gallica.bnf.fr/ark:/12148/btv1b90095492/f16.planchecontact, accessed May 3, 2023.

46. Paris, Bibliothèque nationale de France, MS 331, Gallica Digital Library, https:// gallica.bnf.fr/ark:/12148/btv1b9060022j/f6.item, accessed May 3, 2023.

47. Paris, Bibliothèque nationale de France, MS 5196, Gallica Digital Library, https:// gallica.bnf.fr/ark:/12148/btv1b55007803g/f17.item, accessed May 3, 2023.

48. Brussels, KBR MS 9242–44, Bibliothèque royale de Belgique, Belgica Digital Library, "La prologue de l'acteur" [*sic*] (MS 9242, fol. 2), http://uurl.kbr.be/1310113, accessed May 3, 2023.

49. Two more frontispieces take up this composition as a model, *Le Gouvernement des princes*, KBR, MS 9043, f. 2, by the Master of the Privileges of Ghent and Flanders, ca. 1450–52; and *L'instruction d'un jeune prince*, KBR, MS 10976, f. 2, by Dreux Jean, ca. 1452–60; Bousmanne and Delcourt 2011, 74.

50. LDB-IV 2009, 159–70, Brussels, KBR, MS 9242, Bibliothèque royale de Belgique, Belgica Digital Library, https://belgica.kbr.be, accessed May 3, 2023.

51. The attribution of the *Directorium ad faciendum passagium transmarinum / Advis directif* to William of Adam, traditional and widely accepted in French art historical scholarship and manuscript descriptions, has not been met with general scholarly approval; see Constable 2012, 5–8; Beazley 1907. *Directorium* is considered to be the work of Pseudo-Brocardus, but I have retained here the standard art historical manuscript attribution to William of Adam. The prologue of KBR, MS 9095, fol. 1, identifies Brocard as the author ("frere Brochart"); LDB-V 2015, 115.

52. Paris, Bibliothèque nationale de France, MS fr. 9087, Gallica Digital Library, https:// gallica.bnf.fr/ark:/12148/btv1b100215049/f13.planchecontact, accessed May 3, 2023.

53. *Débat d'honneur / Débat de vraie noblesse / Faits et miracles de saint Thomas*, Brussels, KBR, MS 9278–80, after 1450; *Traité des quatre dernières choses*, Brussels, KBR, MS 1129, after 1455; *Miracles de Notre Dame*, Paris, BnF, MSS fr. 9198, after April 1456; *Traité de l'oraison dominicale*, Brussels, KBR, ms. 9092, after 1457; *Miroir de la salvation humaine*,

Paris, BnF, MS fr. 6275, ca. 1450–60; Bousmanne and Delcourt 2011, 212–37; LDB-V 2015, 28–30.

54. Seigneuret 1966, 1. Its source may have been Boccaccio's novella III.9, which would have been available in French, since Laurent de Premierfait translated *Decameron* in 1414; see Hedeman 2008; cf. Brown-Grant 2012, 362, on the thirteenth-century *Histoire de Flore et Jehanne* as a source.

55. Ghent, UB 470, fol. 1v, is Wavrin's copy; Universiteits Bibliothek Gent, Creative Commons, https://lib.ugent.be/en/catalog/rug01:000990842, accessed May 3, 2023

56. Greco 2002, 150. *Blancandin* is a prosification of an anonymous verse romance from the first third of the thirteenth century; see chapter 1.

57. KBR, MS 10387, fol. 1v. Cf. "Icy fine la vraie hystoire de l'empereur Othovien le premier, et de ceulx qui de lui dessendirent, lequel livre fu mys en prose a la pryere et requeste de noble et puissant seigneur Jehan, seigneur de Crequi et de Canappes, lequel fu parfait et escript de ryme en prose le premier iour de may lan mil IIII^c LIIII"; Colophon, KBR, MS 10387, fol. 612; Timelli et al. 2014, 250; see also LDB-III 2006, 161. The prose version of *Othovien* combines the alexandrine verse version (ca. 1356) and the mid-fourteenth-century alexandrine version of the chanson de geste *Florence de Rome*.

58. Liétard-Rouzé 2010, 75. *Gilles de Chin* is a prose version of a thirteenth-century poem (1230–40) by Gautier de Tournai.

59. Of the romances in Wavrin's library not considered here, *Chastelain de Couci* is a prosification, but the writer makes no statement about prosification or translation. It does have an interest in the way characters act as fixers, in an extended development of epistolary exchange and messengers. *Jean de Saintré* is a new work without any pretense of translation or prosification. Just like for the *History of Jason* (BnF, MS fr. 12570), there is no mention of translation for *Apollonius of Tyre*, though the "translateur" is clearly indicated for its sister story in the manuscript, *Paris and Vienne* (KBR, MSS 9632–33, fol. 1). The other manuscripts from Wavrin's library to enter the ducal library are *Roman de Thèbes* and *Histoire de Troie* (KBR, MSS 9650–52). The prologue to the *Histoire de Troie* alludes to being a translation via compilation: "j'ay proposé . . . recueillier en brief histoire ainsy comme maistre Guy de Calompne l'a traictie" (KBR, MSS 9650–51, fol. 61).

60. For a longer development, see Stahuljak 2021b.

61. The fifteenth-century version adds an interesting twist on the role of intermediary: "Amours fu mediateur"; "je sercheray mediateur"; Fortune, "muable messagiere de perdicion"; Brunel 1923, 52, 75, 93.

62. This prosified epic continues to exploit the question of loyalty: the queen of France, who seduces Saladin, later convinces the king to go on a pilgrimage in order to see Saladin again and then tries to run away with him on the pretext of attempting to convert him. The queen sells her conversion project by positioning herself as a fixer.

63. Greco 2002, 200. Paris BnF, MS fr. 24371 was copied from ÖNB 3438; see Greco 2002, 13–14, 17–18; Timelli et al. 2014, 123–30.

64. Brussels, KBR, MS 10387, fols. 70, 108v.

65. Brussels, KBR, MS 9629, fols. 8, 8bisv, 22v.

66. There is a missing folio in JPGM, MS 111. Citation is from Dülmen, ms. 50, in Vincent 2010, 338.

67. Brown-Grant 2008; Brown-Grant 2010; Gaullier-Bougassas 2003, 158–64.

68. "Mourisque" and "sarrazinois" are here interchangeable to denote Arabic language.

69. Brown-Grant 2020; Devaux and Marchal 2018; Wijsman 2010c, 478; LDB-III 2006, 133–38; Schandel 2002–3; Schandel 1997; Naber 1990a; and Naber 1990b.

70. The oldest model was that of Saint Jerome translating in the intimate setting of his room. Saint Jerome in the intimate setting of his study first appears in the art of Trecento Italy, but the monumental setting that one finds throughout the fifteenth century was initiated by the Limbourg brothers in the early fifteenth century and imported back to Italy in the second half of the century; see Meiss 1963; and Metropolitan Museum of Art, New York, *The Art of Illumination* blog, https://blog.metmuseum.org/artofillumination/manuscript-pages/folio-187v/, accessed May 3, 2023. See also, e.g., Antonello da Messina (ca. 1475) at the National Gallery of Art, https://www.nationalgallery.org.uk/paintings/antonello-da-messina-saint-jerome-in-his-study, accessed May 3, 2023.

71. Gerard de Nevers, KBR, MS 9631, fol. 1, Bibliothèque royale de Belgique, Belgica Digital Library, https://uurl.kbr.be/1065669, accessed May 3, 2023.

72. See Martin le Franc, *Le Champion des dames* (Paris, BnF, MS fr. 12476, fol. 1v, 1451), in which Martin, wearing a purse, presents an unsolicited gift to the duke.

73. Many, although by no means all, presentation scenes to Duke Philip include a figure carrying a purse and dressed in a long robe: Chancellor Nicolas Rolin, a member of the bourgeois class who rose to become one of Philip's closest confidantes and the equivalent of Burgundy's prime minister (e.g., Paris, BnF, MS fr. 9342, f. 5; Brussels, KBR, MS 9043, fol. 2; Brussels, KBR, MS 9092, fol. 1; Brussels, KBR, MS 9242, fol. 1; Brussels, KBR, MS 10778, fol. 1; Vienna, ÖNB, Cod. 2549, fol. 6). The purse is worn by someone of the non-noble bourgeois class of citizens associated with the duke's court, a possible gesture to the middle section of courtiers.

74. On the creation of secular manuscripts in this time period, see Kren and McKendrick 2003, 59–78; Johan 2009.

75. Bousmanne and Delcourt 2011, 323, 326; McKendrick in Kren and McKendrick 2003, 77nn75–76. See McKendrick 1996, 19, for three manuscripts from this master's workshop (Paris, BnF, MSS fr. 47–49; Oxford, Laud. misc. 751; Stockholm, Skokloster 131) that were likely prefabricated for purchase.

76. Pseudo-Aristotle, n.d.; Lorée 2012; cf. van Buren 2008.

77. Bousmanne and Delcourt 2011, 289; Kren and McKendrick 2003, 217, 219, 239. On Bruges, see Wijsman 2010c, 62–71. For fr. 331 and fr. 562, van Lathem used his own formula and elements from the frontispiece (fol. 1) of vol. 3 of the Breslau Froissart (Berlin, Staatsbibliothek, SPK, MS Dep. Breslau 1, vols. 1–4) made for Anthony of Burgundy about 1468–69; see chapter 5.

78. On Wauquelin, see Hériché-Pradeau, 2008; de Crécy 2006.

79. E.g., Charles's copy, BnF, MS fr. 22547, Loyset Liédet and Master of Mary of Burgundy, 1468–70; copy for a member of the Croÿ family, JPGM, MS Ludwig XV 8, Master of the Jardin de vertueuse consolation and assistant, Lille and Bruges, ca. 1470–75. See also Paris, BnF, MS fr. 6440; London, BL, Royal 20 C iii; BL, Royal 17. F I; Geneva, BPU MS fr. 76. Also, four other frontispieces by the Master of the Vienna *Chroniques d'Angleterre*: London, BL, Burney MS 169, purchased in 1475 by Philippe de Cluys, Knight of the Order of Saint John of Jerusalem and Bailiff of the Morea; Copenhagen, Kongelige Bibliotek, Thott 540, for Anthony of Burgundy; Oxford, Bodleian, Laud. Misc. 751, made in the early 1470s for Engelbert II of Nassau; and Stockholm, Skokloster, MS 131, for Philippe de Clèves.

80. Although art historians suggest that the frontispiece of MS 47 is like the frontispiece of Paris, BnF, MS fr. 134, I would like to point out that MS 134 is a *mise en abyme* of the contents of the book, while fr. 47 shows the continuity of translation.

81. I developed these ideas in Stahuljak 2021a; Stahuljak 2020a; Stahuljak 2019a; and Stahuljak 2019b.

Chapter Five

1. Not the hermeneutics of translation—that is, translation as interpretive act—that has been proposed since Schleiermacher, Gadamer, and Steiner (see Stolze 2012), and most recently Venuti 2019, but instead that aligned with Ricœur 2006.

2. "Celui de cui le livre est et [sic] celui qui l'escrit" (Cornish 2011, 205n115).

3. Bonaventure 1864, 20. However, they do appear in one of the most commonly owned works in the fifteenth century, Valerius Maximus's *Faits et dits mémorables*, see chap. 4, note 43, and p. 164.

4. Summary based on Cailleteau and Muel 2015.

5. Schapiro 1973. On the image of the book appearing in manuscript painting as early as the Carolingian era, see Denoël et al. 2018.

6. Monfrin 1963, 169; see also Lusignan 1987, 143–45. There is only one surviving manuscript in Chantilly. John of Antioch's idea of transforming yourself, being a transmitter and an imitator, rather than the fount of the book, sheds an interesting light on Joachim du Bellay's *Défense et illustration de la langue française*, usually understood as promoting creative authorship through imitation (see the introduction).

7. Albertus Magnus 1899, 7–8. I have translated "fidelis" with "loyal" because it is about the relationship between beings—human to divine—rather than between a text and its translation.

8. Cementing the case for authorship, *causa finalis* gave another aspect to author's individuality, his individual moral activity in addition to his individual literary activity. Significantly, this extended to pagan authors; Minnis 2010, 75.

9. Marie de France 1966, lines 10–16. For commentary, see Stahuljak 2005.

10. All citations are from Froissart 1867–77, edition by Lettenhove. In Lettenhove, the first redaction corresponds to the Amiens manuscript in Froissart 1991–98. The second and the third redaction correspond to manuscripts A and B, in Froissart 1869–75. The fourth redaction corresponds to the Rome manuscript in Froissart 1972.

11. Froissart 1867–77, 2:11; Stahuljak 2001; Soukupová 2021.

12. Froissart 1867–77, 2:13, from fourth redaction with variants from third redaction, Froissart 1867–77, 2:9.

13. Mézières 1969, 1:106. Compare to "Cy commaince l'aucteur son livre intitule le Songe du Vieil Pelerin, adroissant au Blanc Faucon au bec et piez dorez, en recitant comment Ardant Desir, acompaigne de sa suer Bonne Esperance, prins en figure pour le Vieil Pelerin en la personne de tous ceulx qui desirent que le monde, et par especial la crestiene, soit reformee a bien fere, par le commandement de Providence Divine emprent son voyage pour trouver souverains arquemistes et multiplier le besant de l'evvangile" (1.190). This citation includes a single reference to a bilingual edition that contains the original and a published translation.

14. Poirion 1965 and many scholars since, e.g., Brownlee 1984; Cerquiligni-Toulet 1985; Huot 1987; Kelly 1987.

15. *The Taking of Alexandria* is not a first for Machaut; written in November 1349, in the *Jugement du roi de Navarre*, the poem opens with five hundred verses on the plague. *The Taking of Alexandria* presents the same dilemma as the *Jugement*: the stake is to write, or rather rewrite, "le monde d'avant d'après la peste"; Boucheron 2020–21, April 6, 2021. "D'après" plays on the double meaning of "after" and according to the murder.

16. De Smedt 2000; Van Praet 1831; Vale 1995.

17. Gruuthuse's manuscripts of Pizan are today in Brussels, KBR MS IV 1093; London, BL, Harley 4431; Paris, BnF, MS fr. 585; Paris, BnF, MS fr. 1177; Paris, BnF, MS fr. 1185.

18. Since all the contents of Louis's library are too numerous to be included, only representative works are cited here. For a fuller list, see appendix B, section 2.

19. Morrison and Stahuljak 2015. Louis preferred chivalric romances of the Arthurian world such as *Tristan and Isolde*; *Lancelot of the Lake* (*Lancelot du Lac*); *Perceforest* (Ferlampin-Acher 2010 and 2012b); *History of the Holy Grail* (*Histoire du saint Graal*); *Merlin*; *Artus de Bretagne* (Ferlampin-Acher 2021).

20. Hans-Collas and Schandel 2009, 11–18; Wijsman 2010c, 366; Wijsman 2007; Lafitte 1997, 249–50; Martens 1992; Baurmeister and Laffitte 1992. For a fuller list of Eastern-themed manuscripts in Louis's library, see appendix B, section 1.

21. Morrison 2023; Wijsman 2010c, 271–77; de Smedt 2000, 129–31; van den Bergen-Pantens 1993, 331.

22. Zenker 2018; Morrison 2015. Volume 1 was only partially illuminated by van Lathem.

23. Louis of Gruuthuse also owned a copy of Froissart's *Chronicles* (Paris, BnF, MSS Fr. 2643–46); the first two volumes were illuminated by Loyset Liédet, the last two by the Master of Anthony of Burgundy, the Master of the Dresden Hours, and the Master of Margaret of York; but Froissart is strangely absent, from the text and from the illuminations, except for one miniature of the presentation of his book to Richard II of England, MS 2646, f. 194v, Paris, Bibliothèque nationale de France, Gallica Digital Library, https://gallica.bnf.fr/ark:/12148/btv1b8438607b/f372.item, accessed May 4, 2023. One reason for this is that Louis's copy does not include the opening of book 3, Froissart's voyage and sojourn at the court of Gaston of Foix in Béarn, which were a major source of illumination in Anthony's copy. See Hans-Collas and Schandel 2009, 272–83.

24. Without the horses, the composition of the entire frontispiece resembles closely the frontispiece of Louis's *History of Jason*, fr. 331, fol. 1, the latest of the four manuscripts produced by Aubert and van Lathem.

25. Paris, Bibliothèque nationale de France, MS fr. 9198, Gallica Digital Library, https://gallica.bnf.fr/ark:/12148/btv1b8451109t/f15.item; https://gallica.bnf.fr/ark:/12148/btv1b8451109t/f49.item; accessed May 4, 2023. A copy of the second volume, BnF, MS fr. 9199, is in Oxford, Bodleian, MS Douce 374.

26. Master of Margaret of York, *Simon de Hesdin Presenting the Translation to Charles V* and *Simon de Hesdin Translating*, Valerius Maximus, *Faits et dits mémorables*, ca. 1470–80. Paris, BnF, MS fr. 288, fol. 1, Gallica Digital Library, https://gallica.bnf.fr/ark:/12148\/btv1b90095492/f16.item, and fol. 4, https://gallica.bnf.fr/ark:/12148/btv1b90095492/f22.item, accessed May 4, 2023.

27. Mézières's fate in the Burgundian libraries is interesting. Mézières was in the ducal library (no. 711; Brussels, KBR, MS 10486) because he wrote *The Letter of Lament* for Duke Philip the Bold. The copy was not illuminated. In Louis of Gruuthuse's library, Mézières appears only with *Livre de la vertu du sacrement de mariage*, a work that incorporates Petrarch's Griselda story that Mézières translated into French (Paris, BNF, MS fr. 1175). Anthony of Burgundy most likely did not own any of Mézières's writings.

28. Paris, BnF, MS fr. 2810 was a gift of Duke of Burgundy, John the Fearless, Philip's father, to the Duke of Berry.

29. Wallace 2016; Gaunt 2011–15; Gaunt 2015–20.

30. For an overview of the verse *chansons de geste*, their prosifications or compilations, or continuations at the court of Burgundy, see Doutrepont 1909. For an overview of late medieval French epic tradition, see Suard 1988, 1994, and 2005.

31. Over six hundred manuscripts were acquired through commissions and gifts; see Falmagne and van den Abeele 2016; Lemaire 2000; Doutrepont 1909; Doutrepont 1906.

32. Falmagne and van den Abeele 2016, 35. In comparison, by 1477, the year of the death of Philip's son, Duke Charles the Bold, the library had grown very moderately to around a thousand volumes; Bousmanne and Delcourt 2011, 104.

33. For an insight into the medieval mindset of classification, see Foucault 1970. For a distinction between category/categorization and class/classification, see Jacob 2004. Potin 2020 has shown brilliantly that the medieval inventory undermined the patrimonial idea of the library and highlights instead its functionality. Network analysis, based on library inventories, makes visible a nodal principle of library organization, counter to two modern tendencies, disciplinary or thematic organization and the search for a patrimonial function of the library. His conclusions on the library, the archive, and the inventory should lead to a reconsideration of institutional history and history of the French state.

34. Wijsman 2022; Wijsman 2013. For more on the presence of the East, as a "matter of the East," see Stahuljak 2019a.

35. This had been my earlier assumption in Stahuljak 2015, here corrected.

36. Garin le Loherain also figures in Aubert's *Histoire de Charles Martel* (no. add. 3–6 in Falmagne and van den Abeele 2016), in manuscript nos. 4 and no. 6. The general description of *Charles Martel* carries "gestes" in the margins.

37. The prose *Girard of Roussillon* exists in several versions. Jean Wauquelin, another of Philip's writers, completed one in 1448, as one of the first three major works of Philip's reign: the *Chronicles of Hainaut, Girard of Roussillon,* and *Deeds and Conquests of Alexander the Great.* On the vision of the world and policy that these simultaneous commissions (1446) give for Philip's reign, see chapter 4; and Stahuljak 2019a. Jean Wauquelin would have also written an abbreviated version, inserted by David Aubert in a vast romance-history-epic compilation known as the *Histoire de Charles Martel* (1463–65), and by Jean Mansel in *La fleur des histoires;* Timelli et al. 2014, 475–93; Hériché-Pradeau 2006, 100; Naudet 2005; de Terre-Basse 1856. In the abbreviated version, Aubert replaced Charles the Bald with Charles Martel. Aubert's *Charles Martel* also includes a different full-fledged prose version of *Girard of Roussillon* in book 3; Naudet 2005.

38. Falmagne and van den Abeele 2016, 238nA. The *Knight of the Swan* belongs to both subcategories, with one entry on each side, no. 570 and no. 609.

39. For a refutation, see Kay 1995.

40. This inventory classification proves the point made by Kay 1995 that such alliances characterize later *chansons de geste.*

41. Recent editors of the inventories of the ducal library, Falmagne and van den Abeele 2016, have been tempted to qualify the marginal notations as indications of "genre," but if it is possible to imagine "geste" as a genre, that is harder for a marginal notation of "Girart." Regardless of the inventory categories, other common marginal notations are "vie de sains" (saint's life) and "oultremer" (overseas/crusade).

42. No. 531 is Paris, Bnf, MS fr. 9221, that belonged to John of Berry. It has Machaut's prologue and ends with *The Taking of Alexandria,* but no music notation. Froissart (nos. 655–58) finds his place, predictably, in "Librarie: Chroniques de France."

43. That puts *Girard of Roussillon* in a new perspective: even though it is a *cronique* rather than a *geste,* it aims to bring about a new, greater Burgundy. The agentive aspects of the *livres de gestes* category bring to light this prospective aspect in other categories of the library inventory and enable a way of reading literature as history: *chapelle* incites, in addition to being a category of practice (see above), to piety and salvation, just as *Outremer* invites to crusade and conquest (see Stahuljak 2019a).

44. The *Histoire de Charles Martel* by David Aubert combines precisely those two great *gestes* into a single continuous narrative.

45. I have developed this argument for the advent of imperial Burgundy in the form of Valois-Habsburg Spain, first through the last Valois Duke of Burgundy, Philip the Fair, and then his son, Charles V, king of Spain and Holy Roman emperor, in Stahuljak 2019a and Stahuljak 2021a.

46. Coste 2017 finds that the question of action is the most neglected of literary studies.

Conclusion

1. For a full history of what follows, see Stahuljak 2013, chapters 5 and 6.

2. Hauwaerts et al. 2018, 11; Ruelle 1985, 39–45; Saenger 1975, 410; Van Praet 1829.

3. Coilly in Hauwaerts et al. 2018 claims twenty-four works in the list of incunabula; the appendix in Hauwaerts et al. 2018 indicates twenty-six works.

4. Summary based on Hellinga 2011; Hellinga 2010, 7–75, 99–113; Hellinga 1982; see also Van Praet 1829.

5. Style as brand is in many ways comparable to the acquisition preferences of Charles V, king of Spain and Holy Roman emperor, who sought Hieronymous Bosch not as an author, but for his style.

6. See frontispiece to *Dialogue des créatures*, Vienna, Österreichische Nationalbibliothek, Cod. 2572, fol. 1; and Hauwaerts 2018, 96; see also Bateman 2015, 145.

7. Summary based on Hellinga 2018; Hellinga 2011; Hellinga 2010.

8. Wogan-Brown 2009; Busby 2010; Cornish 2011; Morreale and Paul 2018.

9. Kinoshita 2013; Gaunt 2013b; Kinoshita 2016b.

10. Conte et al. 2020, 11–12; see also Gadrat-Ouerfelli 2015; Gadrat-Ouerfelli 2022. For participative authorship in Italy of the thirteenth and fourteenth centuries, see Cornish 2011.

11. Throughout the introductory, (auto)biographical portion of the book that frames the description of the world, Marco describes himself as an extraordinary intermediary; Polo 2016 10–14 / Polo 1982, 318–21. On auditors at the Mongol court, see Wolfe 2014, 411.

12. For medieval translations and languages, see Gaunt 2013b; Cruse 2022. For an inscription of Italian "authors," *le tre corone* of Dante, Petrarch, and Boccaccio, into the wider world, see, for example, Morosini 2020. Grévin 2020 describes Dante within the scribal tradition.

13. Paris, BnF, MS fr. 92, fol. 1v; Palumbo 2001, 82; my emphasis.

14. While Damrosch 2003 immediately circumvents the national boundaries with the idea of circulation of texts, analysis by Casanova 2008 (into the twentieth century) reads as a genealogy of autonomous literary spaces originating in the Renaissance. Damrosch has subsequently been sensitive to include medieval and ancient literatures into the idea of world literature.

15. Stahuljak 2020a provides avenues for asymmetrical, asynchronous, and heterotopic analyses of world literature.

16. And to this list, we can add the way that the focus on fixers rewrites notions such as orientalism, see Rothman 2021.

17. It is clear that the one unified world system is really a contemporary world phenomenon of the last fifty years, for the world was not connected in its totality until fairly recently.

18. Keene 2019, 7. See also Flood and Fricke 2023; Heng 2021; Holmes and Standen 2018; Heng 2014; Heng and Ramey 2014; Young and Mudan Finn 2022.

19. Wallace 2016; J. Gilbert, Gaunt, and Burgwinkle 2020; Morato and Schoenaers 2018.

20. Fixers put to work what I proposed and developed in Stahuljak 2020a. See also H-France Forum 2021.

Appendix A

1. Gil 1998; Timelli et al. 2014, 244–52; Marchal 2016. Chantilly, Mus. Condée, MS 652, has 125 miniatures by the Master of Wavrin. The Brussels manuscript would possibly be Créquy's manuscript, and the Chantilly manuscript would have been Wavrin's, made likely for one of the bibliophile members of the Croÿ-Chimay family (Jean, Philippe, or Charles). It may have been a gift of Wavrin to Jean de Croÿ; Timelli et al. 2014, 247; LDB-III 2006, 166; Gil 1998.

2. *Florimont* exists in a single manuscript. Scholars disagree as to whether it is a gift by Wavrin (Wijsman 2010c, 478) or if it is a manuscript commissioned by Philip (Dixon 2014); the manuscript bears the arms of Philip the Good.

3. The *Gilles de Chin* that Wavrin offered to Philip (Lille, BM, God. 50) was originally copied from Créquy's library (KBR, MS 10237); Gil 1998.

4. They were likely the purchase of Margaret of Austria from Charles de Croÿ, who inherited them from Philippe de Wavrin, Waleran's son, and were recorded in the 1523–24 inventory of Margaret of Austria; de Crécy and Brown-Grant 2015, 25–32; Wijsman 2010c, 328; Debae 1995; Debae 1987. They are interesting because Margaret of Austria was guided by the desire to complete the lacunae of the ducal library; Stahuljak 2019b.

Bibliography

Abulafia, David. 1994. *A Mediterranean Emporium: The Catalan Kingdom of Majorca*. Cambridge, UK: Cambridge University Press.

Adorno, Jean. 1978. *Itinéraire d'Anselme Adorno en Terre Sainte (1470–1471)*. Edited and translated by Jacques Heers and Georgette de Groer. Paris: Éditions du Centre national de la recherche scientifique.

Agamben, Giorgio. 2009a. *The Signature of All Things: On Method*. Translated by Luca D'Isanto with Kevin Attell. New York: Zone Books.

———. 2009b. "What Is an Apparatus?" In *What Is an Apparatus?, and Other Essays*. Translated by David Kishik and Stefan Pedatella, 1–24. Stanford, CA: Stanford University Press.

———. 2009c. "What Is the Contemporary?" In Agamben 2009b, 39–54.

Ainsworth, Peter F. 1990. *Jean Froissart and the Fabric of History: Truth, Myth, and Fiction in the "Chroniques."* Oxford, UK: Clarendon.

———. 2003a. "Contemporary and 'Eyewitness' History." In *Historiography in the Middle Ages*, edited by Deborah M. Deliyannis, 249–76. Leiden: Brill.

———. 2003b. "Legendary History: *Historia* and *Fabula*." In *Historiography in the Middle Ages*, edited by Deborah M. Deliyannis, 249–76. Leiden: Brill.

Akbari, Suzanne Conklin. 2000. "From Due East to True North: Orientalism and Orientation." In *The Postcolonial Middle Ages*, edited by Jeffrey Jerome Cohen, 19–34. New York: Palgrave.

———. 2009. *Idols in the East: European Representations of Islam and the Orient, 1100–1450*. Ithaca, NY: Cornell University Press.

Albertus Magnus. 1899. *Super Iohannem, Opera omnia*. Vol. 24. Edited by Émile Borgnet. Paris.

al-Nuwayri al-Iskandarāni, Muḥammad b. 1968–76. *Kitāb al-ilmām* [Book of knowledge relating what happened in the attack on Alexandria]. Edited by Aziz Atiya. Hyderabad: Da'irat al-Ma'arif al-'Utmaniyya.

al-Razi, the clinician. n.d. US National Library of Medicine, "Islamic Culture and Medical Arts." https://www.nlm.nih.gov/exhibition/islamic_medical/islamic_06.html. Accessed May 6, 2023.

Altaner, Berthold. 1924. *Die Dominikanermissionen des 13. Jahrhunderts: Forschungen zur Geschichte der kirchlichen Unionen und der Mohammedaner- und Heidenmission des Mittelalters*. Poland: Frankes Buchhandlung.

Ampère, Jean-Jacques. 1839. "Vue générale de la littérature française au Moyen-Age." *La Revue des deux mondes* 19:179–93.

Anderson, Benedict. 1991. *Imagined Communities*. Rev. ed. New York: Verso.

Angelo di Spoleto. 1906–27. "De fratribus minoribus visitantibus captivos in Babilonia." In Golubovich 1906–27, 3:60–72.

Anglure, Ogier d'. 2008. "Journal de voyage à Jérusalem et en Egypte (1395–1396)." In *Vers Jérusalem, Itinéraires croisés au XIVe siècle*, translated by Nicole Chareyron, 231–320. Paris: Les Belles Lettres.

Armstrong, C. A. J. 1983. *England, France and Burgundy in the Fifteenth Century*. London: Hambledon.

Arnade, Peter. 2010. "The City Defeated and Defended: Civism as Political Identity in the Habsburg-Burgundian Netherlands" In Stein and Pollmann 2010, 195–216.

Arnade, Peter, Martha Howell, and Anton van der Lem, eds. 2019. *Rereading Huizinga: Autumn of the Middle Ages, a Century Later*. Amsterdam: Amsterdam University Press.

Apter, Emily. 2010. "Philosophical Translation and Untranslatability: Translation as Critical Pedagogy." *Profession*, no. 1:50–63.

———. 2013. *Against World Literature: On the Politics of Untranslatability*. London: Verso.

Asad, Talal. 1986. "The Concept of Cultural Translation in British Social Anthropology." In *Writing Culture: The Poetics and Politics of Ethnography*, edited by James Clifford and George E. Marcus, 141–64. Berkeley: University of California Press.

Avril, François, and Jean Lafaurie. 1968. *La librairie de Charles V*. Exh. cat. Paris: Bibliothèque nationale de France.

Babbitt, Susan M. 1985. "Oresme's 'Livre de Politiques' and the France of Charles V." *Transactions of the American Philosophical Society*, n.s., 75, no. 1:1–158.

Bacon, Roger. 1906–27. "De situ Terrae Sanctae (1267)." In Golubovich 1906–27, 1:266–69.

Baker, Mona. 2006. "Translation and Activism: Emerging Patterns of Narrative Community." *Massachusetts Review* 47:462–84.

Baker, Mona, and Gabriela Saldanha, eds. 2020. *Routledge Encyclopedia of Translation Studies*. 3rd ed. New York: Routledge.

Balibar, Renée. 1998. "La communication en langue française." *Langage et société* 83–84:15–37.

Balivet, Michel. 1997. "Avant les jeunes de langues: Coup d'œil sur l'apprentissage des langues turques en monde chrétien, de Byzance à Guillaume Postel (VIe–XVIe siècles)." In *Istanbul et les langues orientales: Actes du colloque, Istanbul, 29–31 mai 1995, organisé par l'IFEA et l'INALCO à l'occasion du bicentenaire de l'École des langues orientales*, edited by Frédéric Hitzel, 67–77. Paris: L'Harmattan.

Barbatre, Pierre. 1972–73. "Le voyage de Pierre Barbatre à Jérusalem en 1480." Edited by Pierre Tucco-Chala. *Annuaire-Bulletin de la Société de l'histoire de France*, 75–172.

Barker, Hannah. 2019. *That Most Precious Merchandise: The Mediterranean Trade in Black Sea Slaves, 1260–1500*. Philadelphia: University of Pennsylvania Press.

Barrington, Candace. 2014. "Traveling Chaucer: Comparative Translation and Cosmopolitan Humanism." *Educational Theory* 64, no. 5:463–77.

———. 2019. "The Global Pilgrimage of Geoffrey Chaucer's Canterbury Tales." In *The Wiley-Blackwell Companion to World Literature*, vol. 2, *600 C.E. to 1450 C.E.*, edited by Christine Chism, general editor Kenneth Segneurie, 1–12. Oxford: Wiley-Blackwell.

Barrington, Candace, and Jonathan Hsy. 2018. "Editors' Introduction: Chaucer's Global Orbits and Global Communities." *Literature Compass* 15:e12457.

Barrois, Joseph. 1830. "Inventaire de la librairie qui est en la maison à Bruges, circa 1467." In *Bibliothèque protypographique, ou, Libraries des fils du roi Jean, Charles V, Jean de Berri, Philippe de Bourgogne et les siens*, 123–26. Paris: Treuffel et Würtz.

Baschet, Jérôme. 2004. *La Civilisation féodale: De l'an mil à la colonisation de l'Amérique.* Paris: Aubier.

Batchelor, Robert. 2018. "The Global and the Maritime: Divergent Paradigms for Understanding the Role of Translation in the Emergence of Early Modern Science." In Manning and Owen 2018, 75–90.

Bateman, J. Chimène. 2015. "The Hybrid Art of the Compiler: Text/Image Relations in the *Ovide moralisé* of Colard Mansion." In *Text/Image Relations in Late Medieval French and Burgundian Culture (14th–16th Centuries)*, edited by Rosalind Brown-Grant and Rebecca Dixon, 143–63. Turnhout: Brepols.

Baudot, Georges, ed. 1985. *Historia de los indios de la Nueva España (1541)*, by Fray Toribio de Motolinía. Madrid: Castalia.

Baurmeister, Ursula, and Marie-Pierre Laffitte. 1992. *Des livres et des rois: La bibliothèque royale de Blois*. Paris: Bibliothèque nationale de France.

Beattie, Pamela. 1995. "'Pro exaltation sanctae fidei catholicae': Mission and Crusade in the Writings of Ramon Llull." In *Iberia and the Mediterranean World of the Middle Ages: Studies in Honor of Robert I. Burns*, edited by Larry J. Simon, 113–29. Leiden: Brill.

———. 2019. "Ramon Llull's Crusade Treatises." In *A Companion to Ramon Llull and Lullism*, edited by Amy M. Austin, Mark D. Johnston, and Alexander Ibarz, 176–213. Leiden: Brill.

Beaune, Colette. 1985. *Naissance de la nation France*. Paris: Gallimard.

———, trans. 1995. *Les Vœux du Faisan*. In *Splendeurs de la cour de Bourgogne: récits et chroniques*, edited by Danielle Régnier-Bohler, 1131–63. Paris: Robert Laffont.

Beazley, C. R. 1907. "*Directorium ad faciendum passagium transmarinum.*" *American Historical Review* 12:810–57; 13:66–115.

Beebe, Kathryne. 2014. *Pilgrim and Preacher: The Audiences and Observant Spirituality of Friar Felix Fabri (1437/8–1502)*. Oxford: Oxford University Press.

Beecroft, Alexander. 2015. *An Ecology of World Literature: From Antiquity to the Present Day*. New York: Verso.

Beer, Jeanette M. A. 1976. *A Medieval Caesar*. Genève: Droz.

Bellorini, Theophilus, and Eugene Hoade. 1948. "Preface." In *Visit to the Holy Places of Egypt, Sinai, Palestine, and Syria in 1384, by Frescobaldi, Gucci and Sigoli*, translated by Theophilus Bellorini and Eugene Hoade, 1–28. Jerusalem: Franciscan.

Benedict the Pole. 1929. "Relatio Fr. Benedicti Poloni." In *Sinica franciscana: Itinera et relationes fratrum minorum saeculi XIII et XIV*, edited by Anastasius van den Wyngaert, 1:135–43. Firenze: Quaracchi.

———. 1980. "The Narrative of Brother Benedict the Pole." In *Mission to Asia*, translated by Christopher Dawson, 77–84. Toronto: University of Toronto Press / Medieval Academy of America.

Benjamin, Walter. 1969. "The Task of the Translator." 1923. In *Illuminations*, edited by Hannah Arendt, translated by Harry Zohn, 69–82. New York: Schocken Books.

Bennassar, Bartolomé, and Lucile Bennassar. 1989. *Les chrétiens d'Allah: L'histoire extraordinaire des renégats, XVIe et XVIIe siècles.* Paris: Perrin.

Berman, Antoine. 1984. *L'Épreuve de l'étranger: Culture et traduction dans l'Allemagne romantique; Herder, Goethe, Schlegel, Novalis, Humboldt, Schleiermacher, Hölderlin.* Paris: Gallimard.

———. 2012. *Jacques Amyot, traducteur français: Essai sur les origines de la traduction en France.* Edited by Isabelle Berman and Valentina Sommella. Paris: Belin.

Bidaux, Hélène. 2007. "Le Florimont en prose, édition critique du manuscrit BN 12566." PhD diss., Université de Lille III.

Bischoff, Bernhard. 1961. "The Study of Foreign Languages in the Middle Ages." *Speculum* 36, no. 2:209–24.

Blake N. F. 1991. *William Caxton and English Literary Culture.* London: Hambledon.

Blanchard, Joël, ed., with Renate Blumenfeld-Kosinski and Antoine Calvet. 2019. *Philippe de Mézières: Rhétorique et poétique.* Geneva: Droz.

Blanchard, Joël, and Renate Blumenfeld-Kosinski, eds. 2017. *Philippe de Mézières et l'Europe: Nouvelle histoire, nouveaux espaces, nouveaux langages.* Genève: Droz.

Blockmans, Wim, et al., eds. 2013. *Staging the Court of Burgundy: Proceedings of the Conference "The Splendor of Burgundy."* Turnhout: Brepols.

Blockmans, Wim, and Walter Prevenier. 1999. *The Promised Lands: The Low Countries under Burgundian Rule, 1369–1530.* Translated by Elisabeth Fackelman. Philadelphia: University of Pennsylvania Press.

Blondeau, Crystèle. 2006. "Jean Wauquelin et l'illustration de ses textes: Les exemples des *Faicts et conquestes d'Alexandre le Grand* (Paris, BnF, MS Fr. 9342) et du *Roman de Girart de Roussillon* (Vienne, ÖNB, MS 2549)." In de Crécy et al. 2006, 213–24.

———. 2009a. "L'Antiquité grecque, une passion bourguignonne." In *L'Antiquité entre Moyen Âge et Renaissance: L'Antiquité dans les livres produits au nord des Alpes entre 1350 et 1520, actes de colloque (INHA, Paris, 8–10 mars 2006)*, edited by Chrystèle Blondeau and Marie Jacob, 207–29. Nanterre: Presses de l'université de Nanterre.

———. 2009b. *Un conquérant pour quatre ducs: Alexandre le Grand à la cour de Bourgogne.* Paris: CTHS/INHA.

Blumenfeld-Kosinski, Renate. 2009a. "Philippe de Mézières's Ghostly Encounters: From the 'Vie de Saint Pierre de Thomas' (1366) to the 'L'epistre Lamentable' (1397)." *Romania* 127:168–89.

———. 2009b. "Philippe de Mézières's *Life of Saint Pierre de Thomas* at the Crossroads of Late Medieval Hagiography and Crusading Ideology." *Viator* 9:223–48.

Blumenfeld-Kosinski, Renate, and Kiril Petkov. 2011a. "Introduction." In Blumenfeld-Kosinski and Petkov 2011b, 1–16.

———, eds. 2011b. *Philippe de Mézières and His Age.* Leiden: Brill.

Boldensele, Guilielmus de. 1852. "Epistola Guillelmi de Boldensele ad Petrum abbatem Aulae Regiae." Edited by Dr. Grotefend. In *Zeitschrift des Historischen Vereins*, 226–86. Hannover, 1855.

Bonaventure. 1864. "Proœmium." In *Opera Omnia*, vol. 1, *Liber sententiarium*, edited by Adolphe C Peltier, 9–20. Paris: Vivès.

Booth, Philip. 2021. "The Dominican Educational and Social Contexts of Riccoldo of Monte Croce's Pilgrimage Writing." *Journal of Medieval and Early Modern Studies* 51, no. 1:49–78.

Bossuat, Robert. 1943. "Traductions françaises des *Commentaires* de César à la fin du XVᵉ siècle." *Bibliothèque d'Humanisme et Renaissance* 3:253–411.

———. 1946. "Vasque de Lucène, traducteur de Quinte-Curce (1468)." *Bibliothèque d'Humanisme et Renaissance* 8:197–245.

Boucheron, Patrick. 2016. *Ce que peut l'histoire, Leçons inaugurales du Collège de France.* Paris: Fayard.

———. 2020–21. Cours, La Peste Noire, "Après la peste, ou le temps défait." Collège de France. https://www.college-de-france.fr/agenda/cours/la-peste-noire /apres-la-peste-ou-le-temps-defait.

Boucheron, Patrick, Nicolas Delalande, Florian Mazel, Yann Potin, and Pierre Singaravélou, eds. 2017. *Histoire mondiale de la France.* Paris: Seuil.

Bourel, Guillaume. 1997. "La géographie des voyageurs à la fin du Moyen Âge." *Hypothèses* 1:149–55.

Bourgain, Pacale. 1989. "Le sens de la langue et des langues chez Roger Bacon." In *Traduction et traducteurs au Moyen âge: Actes du colloque international du CNRS organisé à Paris [par l'] Institut de recherche et d'histoire des textes les 26–28 mai 1986*, edited by Geneviève Contamine, 317–31. Paris: Éd. du Centre national de la recherche scientifique.

Bousmanne, Bernard, and Thierry Delcourt, eds. 2011. *Miniatures flamandes, 1404–1482.* Exh. cat. Brussels: Bibliothèque royale and Bibliothèque nationale de France.

Boutet, Dominique. 1983. "Sur 1'origine et le sens de la *largesse* arthurienne." *Le Moyen Âge* 89:397–411.

Boyle, Mary. 2021. *Writing the Jerusalem Pilgrimage in the Late Middle Ages.* Woodbridge, UK: Boydell and Brewer.

Brandt, Walther I. 1930. "Pierre Dubois: Modern or Medieval?" *American Historical Review* 35, no. 3:507–21.

———. 1956. "Introduction." In P. Dubois 1956, 3–65.

Brasca, Santo. 1481. *Viaggio in Terra Santa.* Milan.

Bratianu, G. I. 1942. "Le conseil du roi Charles." *Revue historique du sud-est européen* 19, no. 2:291–361.

Braudel, Fernand. 1972–73. *The Mediterranean and the Mediterranean World in the Age of Phillip II.* Translated by Siân Reynolds. New York: Harper and Row.

Braunstein, Philippe. 2016. *Les Allemands à Venise, 1380–1520.* Rome: École française de Rome.

Biegola, Giacomo. 1937. "Il valore delle lingue e delle scienze nell'apologetica di Ruggero Bacone." *La Scuola Cattolica* 65:372–91.

Brewer-García, Larissa. 2020. *Beyond Babel: Translations of Blackness in Colonial Peru and New Granada.* Cambridge: Cambridge University Press.

Breydenbach, Bernhard von. 1486. *Bernhardi de Breydenbach opusculum sanctarum peregrinationum ad sepulcrum Christi venerandum.* Mainz.

———. 1999. *Peregrinationes: Un viaggiatore del quattrocento a Gerusalemme e in Egipto.* Translated by Gabriella Bartolini and Giulio Caporali. Rome: Vecchiarelli Editore.

———. 2010. *Peregrinatio in terram sanctam: Eine Pilgerrreise ins Heilige Land; Frühneuhochdeutscher Text und Übersetzung.* Edited and translated by Isolde Mozer. Berlin: de Gruyter.

Brickhouse, Anna. 2015. *The Unsettlement of America: Translation, Interpretation, and the Story of Don Luis de Velasco, 1560–1945*. New York: Oxford University Press.

Brocardus. 1869. "Directorium ad passagium faciendum." In *Recueil des historiens des croisades: Documents arméniens*, edited by Académie royale des inscriptions et des belles-lettres, 2:367–517. Paris: Impr. impériale.

Brown-Grant, Rosalind. 2008. *French Romance of the Later Middle Ages: Gender, Morality, and Desire*. Oxford: Oxford University Press.

———. 2010. "Adolescence, Anxiety and Amusement in Versions of Paris et Vienne." *Cahiers de recherches médiévales et humanistes* 20:59–70.

———. 2012. "Narrative Style in Burgundian Prose Romances of the Later Middle Ages." *Romania* 130:355–406.

———. 2015. "How to Wield Power with Justice: The Fifteenth-Century *Roman de Florimont* as a Burgundian 'Mirror for Princes,'" 43–63. In *Textual and Visual Representations of Power and Justice in Medieval France: Manuscript and Early Printed Books*, edited by Rosalind Brown-Grant, Anne D. Hedeman, and Bernard Ribémont. Farnham, Surrey: Ashgate.

———. 2020. *Visualizing Justice in Burgundian Prose Romance: Text and Image in Manuscripts of the Wavrin Master (1450s–1460s)*. Turnout: Brepols.

Brownlee, Kevin. 1984. *Poetic Identity in Guillaume de Machaut*. Madison: University of Wisconsin Press.

———. 2000. "Mimesis, Authority, and Murder in Jean Froissart's *Voyage en Béarn*." In *Translatio Studii: Essays by His Students in Honor of Karl D. Uitti for His Sixty-Fifth Birthday*, edited by Renate Blumenfeld-Kosinski et al., 65–85. Amsterdam: Rodopi.

Brucker, Charles. 1987. *Denis Foulechat: Tyrans, princes et prêtres (Jean de Salisbury, policratique IV et VIII)*. Montreal: Editions Ceres.

———. 2001. "Aspects du vocabulaire politique et social chez Oresme et Christine de Pizan." *Cahiers de recherches médiévales* 8:227–49.

———. 2020. *Anthologie commentée des traductions françaises du XIVe siècle: Autour de Charles V. Culture, pouvoir et spiritualité*. 2 vols. Paris: Champion.

Brun, Laurent. 2010. "Le Miroir historial de Jean de Vignay: Édition critique du livre I (Prologue) et du livre V (Histoire d'Alexandre le Grand)." PhD thesis, University of Stockholm.

Brunel, Clovis. 1923. *La fille du comte de Pontieu: Conte en prose; Versions du XIIIe et du XVe siècle*. Paris: H. Champion.

Bruni, Leonardo. 1992. "On the Right Way to Translate." In *Translation/History/Culture: A Sourcebook*, edited and translated by André Lefevere, 82–86. New York: Routledge.

———. 2008. *De interpretatione recta*. Edited by Charles le Blanc. Ottawa: Les Presses de l'Université d'Ottawa.

Brygg, Thomas. 1884. *Itinerarium in Terram Sanctam domini Thomae de Swynburne (1392–93)*. Edited by Conte P. Riant. *Archives de l'Orient latin* 2:378–88.

Buettner, Brigitte. 2001. "Past Presents: New Year's Gifts at the Valois Courts, ca. 1400." *Art Bulletin* 83:598–625.

Bullock-Davies, Constance. 1966. *Professional Interpreters and the Matter of Britain*. Cardiff: Wales University Press.

Bumke 2000. Bumke, Joachim. *Courtly Culture: Literature and Society in the High Middle Ages*. 1986. Translated by Thomas Dunlap. New York: Overlook.

Burchard of Mount Sion. 1864. "Descriptio Terrae Sanctae." In *Peregrinatores medii aevi quatuor*, edited by J. C. M. Laurent, 1–100. Leipzig.

———. 1896. *A Description of the Holy Land*. Translated by Aubrey Stewart. Vol. 12. London: Palestine Pilgrims Text Society.

Buridant, Claude. 1980. "Jean de Meun et Jean de Vignay, traducteurs de *l'Epitoma Rei Militaris* de Végèce: Contribution à l'histoire de la traduction au Moyen âge." In *Etudes de langue et de littérature françaises offertes à André Lanly*, 51–69. Montreal: Editions Ceres.

Burnett, Charles. 1997. *Introduction of Arabic Learning into England*. London: British Library.

Busby, Keith. 2002. *Codex and Context: Reading Old French Verse Narrative in Manuscript*. 2 vols. Amsterdam: Rodopi.

———. 2010. "Vernacular Literature and the Writing of History in Medieval Francophonia." In Morrison and Hedeman 2010, 27–41.

Butterfield, Ardis. 2002. *Poetry and Music in Medieval France: From Jean Renart to Guillaume de Machaut*. Cambridge: Cambridge University Press.

———. 2005. "Nationhood." In *Chaucer: An Oxford Guide*, edited by Steve Ellis, 50–65. Oxford: Oxford University Press.

Bynum, Caroline Walker. 1991. *Fragmentation and Redemption: Essays on Gender and the Human Body in Medieval Religion*. New York: Zone Books.

Cailleteau, Jacques, and Francis Muel. 2015. *Apocalypse: La tenture de Louis d'Anjou*. Paris: Éditions du Patrimoine-Centre des monuments nationaux.

Calin, William. 2015. *A Poet at the Fountain: Essays on the Narrative Verse of Guillaume de Machaut*. Lexington: University Press of Kentucky.

Carayon, Céline. 2019. *Eloquence Embodied: Nonverbal Communication among French and Indigenous Peoples in the Americas*. Williamsburg, VA: Omohundro Institute of Early American History and Culture.

Caron, Marie-Thérèse. 2003. *Les vœux du faisan, noblesse en fête, esprit de croisade: Le manuscrit français 11594 de la Bibliothèque nationale de France*. Turnhout: Brepols.

Caron, Marie-Thérèse, and Denis Clauzel. 1997. *Le banquet du faisan*. Arras: Artois Presses Université.

Carpini, John of Plano. 1929. "Ystoria Mongalorum." In *Sinica franciscana: Itinera et relationes fratrum minorum saeculi XIII et XIV*, edited by Anastasius van den Wyngaert, 1:27–143. Firenze: Quaracchi.

———. 1980. *History of the Mongols*. In *Mission to Asia*, translated by Christopher Dawson, 1–76. Toronto: University of Toronto Press / Medieval Academy of America.

Cartellieri, Otto. 1929. *The Court of Burgundy*. New York: Routledge.

Casanova, Pascale. 2008. *La République mondiale des lettres*. 1999. Éd. revue et corrigée. Paris: Le Seuil.

Casola, Pietro. 1855. *Viaggio di Pietro Casola a Gerusalemme tratto dall'autografo esistente nella Biblioteca Trivulzio*. Edited by Giulio Porro. Milan: Tipografia di Paolo Ripamonti Carpano.

———. 1907. *Canon Pietro Casola's Pilgrimage to Jerusalem in the Year 1494*. Edited by Margaret Newett. Manchester: Manchester University Press.

Cassin, Barbara. 2006. *Vocabulaire européen des philosophies: Dictionnaire des intraduisibles*. Paris: Le Seuil.

Caumont, Nompar de. 1858. *Voyaige d'oultremer en Jhérusalem par le seigneur de Caumont l'an MCCCCXVIII*. Edited by Marquis de La Grange. Paris: Aubry.

Cavagna, Mattia. 2014. "Jean de Vignay: Actualités et perspectives." *Cahiers de recherches médiévales ethumanistes* 27:141–49.

Cavallo, Adolfo Salvatore. 1993. *Medieval Tapestries in the Metropolitan Museum of Art*. New York: Metropolitan Museum of Art.

Caxton, William. 1928. *Caxton's Prologues and Epilogues*. Edited by W. J. B. Crotch. London:. Pub. for the Early English Text Society by H. Milford, Oxford University Press.

Cerquiligni-Toulet, Jacqueline. 1985. *"Un Engin si soutil": Guillaume de Machaut et l'écriture au XIVe siècle*. Paris: Champion.

Chareyron, Nicole. 2005. *Pilgrims to Jerusalem in the Middle Ages*. Translated by W. Donald Wilson. New York: Columbia University Press.

———. 2013. *Ethique et esthétique du récit de voyage à la fin du Moyen Âge*. Paris: Champion.

Charron, Pascale, and Marc Gil. 1999. "Les enlumineurs des manuscrits de David Aubert." In Quéruel 1999, 81–100.

Chartier, Roger. 1994. *The Order of Books: Readers, Authors, and Libraries in Europe between the Fourteenth and Eighteenth Centuries*. 1992. Stanford, CA: Stanford University Press.

Chastellain, Georges. 1865. *Les hauts faits et glorieuses adventures du duc Philippe de Bourgongne, celuy qui se nomme le Grand duc et le Grand lyon*. In *Œuvres diverses*, vol. 7, edited by Kervyn de Lettenhove, 213–36. Brussels.

Chenu, M.-D. 1927. "*Auctor, actor, autor*." *Bulletin Du Cange: Archivum Latinitatis Medii Aevi* 3:81–86.

Chism, Christine. 2009. "Romance." In *The Cambridge Companion to Middle English Literature: 1100–1500*, edited by Larry Scanlon, 57–69. Cambridge: Cambridge University Press.

Chrétien de Troyes. 1994. *Cligès*. Edited and translated by Charles Méla et Olivier Collet. Paris: Le livre de poche.

———. 2004. *Cligés*. In *Arthurian Romances*, translated by William W. Kibler, 123–205. New York: Penguin Books.

Cifarelli, Paola, Maria Colombo Timelli, Matteo Milani, and Anne Schoysman, eds. 2017. *Raconter en prose: XIVe–XVIe siècle*. Paris: Classiques Garnier.

Clark, Gregory. 2000. *Made in Flanders: The Master of the Ghent Privileges and Manuscript Painting in the Southern Netherlands in the Time of Philip the Good*. Turnhout: Brepols.

Cockshaw, Pierre. 1974. "A propos des Pays de par deçà et des Pays de par delà." *Revue belge de philologie et d'histoire* 52:386–88.

———. 1977. "Les manuscrits de Charles de Bourgogne et de ses proches." In *Charles le Téméraire, 1433–1477, Catalogue*, edited by P. Cockshaw, C. Lemaire, and A. Rouzet, 3–19. Brussels: Bibliothèque royale Albert Ier.

———, ed. 1996. *L'Ordre de la Toison d'or, de Philippe le Bon à Philippe le Beau, 1430–1505*. Turnhout: Brepols.

———. 2000a. "A propos des 'éditeurs' à la cour de Bourgogne." In *Le statut du scripteur au Moyen âge: Actes du XIIe Colloque scientifique du Comité international de paléographie latine, Cluny, 17–20 juillet 1998*, edited by Marie-Clotilde Hubert, Emmanuel Poulle, and Marc H. Smith, 281–89. Paris: École des chartes.

————, ed. 2000b. *Les Chroniques de Hainaut, ou les ambitions d'un prince bourguignon.* Turnhout: Brepols.

Coleman, Joyce. 2013. "The First Presentation Miniature in an English-Language Manuscript." In *The Social Life of Illumination: Manuscripts, Images, and Communities in the Late Middle Ages,* edited by Joyce Coleman, Mark Cruse, and Kathryn A. Smith, 403–37. Turnhout: Brepols.

Compagnon, Antoine. n.d. "Cinquième leçon: L'auctor medieval." https://www.fabula.org/compagnon/auteur5.php. Accessed May 6, 2023.

Constable, Giles. 1976. "Opposition to Pilgrimage in the Middle Ages." *Studia Gratiana* 19:125–46.

————, ed. and trans. 2012. "Introduction." In William of Adam, *How to Defeat the Saracens,* 1–19. Washington, DC: Dumbarton Oaks Research Library and Collection.

Contamine, Philippe. 2004. "De Chypre à la Prusse et à la Flandre: Les aventures d'un chevalier poitevin; Perceval de Couloigne, segneur de Pugny, du Breuil-Bernard et de Pierrefitte (133–41)." In *Chemins d'outre-mer: Études d'histoire sur la Méditerranée médiévales offertes à Michel Balard,* edited by Damien Coulon, Catherine Otten-Froux, Paule Pagès, and Dominique Valérian, 149–57. Paris: Publications de la Sorbonne.

————. 2009. "'Les princes, barons et chevaliers qui a la chevalerie au service de Dieu se sont ja vouez': Recherches prosopographiques sur l'ordre de la Pasion de Jésus-Christ (1385–1395)." In *La noblesse et la croisade à la fin du Moyen âge: France, Bourgogne, Bohême,* edited by Martin Nejedlý and Jaroslav Svátek, 43–68. Toulouse: FRAMESPA-UMR 5136.

————. 2015. *L'ordre de la Passion de Jésus-Christ de Philippe de Mézières: Une utopie de chevalier.* In *Élites et ordres militaires au Moyen Âge: Rencontre autour d'Alain Demurger,* edited by Philippe Josserand, Luís Filipe Oliveira, and Damien Carraz, 125–34. Madrid: Casa de Velázquez.

Contamine, Philippe, and Jacques Paviot. 2008. "Introduction." In Mézières 2008, 11–94.

Conte, Maria, Antonio Montefusco, and Samuela Simion. 2020. *"Ad consolationem legentium": Il Marco Polo dei Dominicani.* Venice: Edizioni Ca'Foscari.

Cook, Lexie. Forthcoming. "The Silent *Tangomão*: Fictions of Intermediation along the Rivers of Guinea." *Journal of Early Modern Cultural Studies.*

Coppart de Velaines. 2007. "Le manuscrit 'Coppart de Velaines' (BNF, ms. nouv. acq. fr. 10058)." Edited by Jacques Paviot. In *Campin in context: Peinture et société dans la vallée de l'Escaut à l'époque de Robert Campin, 1375–1445; Actes du Colloque international; Tournai, Maison de la culture, 30 mars–1er avril 2006,* edited by Ludovic Nys and Dominique Wanwijnsberghe, 277–309. Valenciennes: Presses universitaires de Valenciennes; Bruxelles: Institut royal du patrimoine artistique / Koninklijk Instituut voor het Kunstpatrimonium; Tournai: Association des guides de Tournai.

Cornish, Alison. 2011. *Vernacular Translation in Dante's Italy: Illiterate Literature.* Cambridge: Cambridge University Press.

Cortabarría, Angel. 1969. "Originalidad y significacion des los "studia linguarum" de los dominicos españoles des los siglos XIII y XIV." *Pensamiento* 25:71–92.

————. 1970. "El *estudio de las lenguas* en la Orden dominicana." *Estudios Filosóficos* 19:79–127.

Cortabarría-Beitia, A. 1970. "L'études des langues au Moyen Âge chez les Dominicains." *L'Institut dominicain d'études orientales du Caire: Mélanges* 10:189–248.

Coste, Florent. 2017. *Explore: Investigations littéraires.* Paris: Questions théoriques.

———. 2021a. *Gouverner par les livres: Les légendes dorées et la formation de la société chrétienne (XIIIe–XVe siècles).* Turnhout: Brepols.

———. 2021b. "La littérature médiévale est-elle bien un atelier d'écriture?" *COnTEXTES* 2021. http://journals.openedition.org/contextes/10334. Accessed May 6, 2023.

Coulon, Damien, and Christine Gadrat-Ouerfelli. 2017. *Le voyage au Moyen Âge: Description du monde et quête individuelle.* Aix-en-Provence: Presses universitaires de Provence.

Crist, Larry S. 1972. *Saladin: Suite et fin du deuxième Cycle de la Croisade.* Genève: Droz.

Croizy-Naquet, Catherine. 1999. *Écrire l'histoire romaine au début du XIIIe siècle: L'"Histoire ancienne jusqu'à César" et les "Faits des Romains."* Paris: Honoré Champion.

Cruse, Mark. 2015. "Marco Polo in Manuscript: The Travels of the *Devisement du monde*." *Narrative Culture* 2:171–89.

———. 2017. "A Quantitative Analysis of Toponyms in a Manuscript of Marco Polo's *Devisement du monde* (London, British Library, MS Royal 19 D 1)." *Speculum* 92:247–64.

———, ed. 2022. "The Medieval and Early Modern Reception of Marco Polo's *Description of the World*." Special issue, *Digital Philology: A Journal of Medieval Cultures* 11, no. 2.

Curtius, Ernst Robert. 1953. *European Literature and the Latin Middle Ages.* Translated by Willard R. Trask. New York: Pantheon Books.

Dagenais, John. 2004. "The Postcolonial Laura." *Modern Language Quarterly* 65:365–90.

Dakhlia, Jocelyne. 2008. *Lingua franca: Histoire d'une langue métisse en Méditerranée.* Arles: Actes Sud.

Dakhlia, Jocelyne, and Wolfgang Kaiser. 2013. "Introduction: Une Méditerranée entre deux mondes, ou des mondes continus." In *Les Musulmans dans l'histoire de l'Europe*, vol. 2, *Passages et contacts en Méditerranée*, edited by Jocelyne Dakhlia and Wolfgang Kaiser, 7–31. Paris: Albin Michel.

Damian-Grint, Peter. 1999. *The New Historians of the Twelfth-Century Renaissance: Inventing Vernacular Authority.* Rochester, NY: Boydell.

Damrosch, David. 2003. *What Is World Literature?* Princeton, NJ: Princeton University Press.

Debae, Marguerite. 1987. *La Librairie de Marguerite d'Autriche: Catalogue d'exposition, du 18 septembre au 5 décembre 1987.* Bruxelles: Bibliothèque Royale Albert Ier.

———. 1995. *La bibliothèque de Marguerite d'Autriche: Essai de reconstitution d'après l'inventaire de 1523–1524.* Leuven: Editions Peeters.

de Certeau, Michel. 2005. *L'Étranger ou l'union dans la différence.* New ed. Edited by Luce Giard. Paris: Éditions du Seuil.

de Crécy, Marie-Claude, Gabriella Parussa, and Sandrine Hériché-Pradeau, eds. 2006. *Jean Wauquelin, de Mons à la cour de Bourgogne.* Turnhout: Brepols.

de Crécy, M.-Cl., and Rosalind Brown-Grant, eds. 2015. *Paris et Vienne*. Paris: Classiques Garnier.

de Gruben, Françoise. 1996. "Les chapitres de la Toison d'or à l'époque bourguignonne (1430–1477)." In Cockshaw 1996, 80–83.

de Guyse, Jacques. 1826–38. *Histoire de Hainaut*. 22 vols. Edited by Marquis de Fortia d'Urban. Paris: Sautelet; Bruxelles: Lacrosse.

de Jong, Sara. 2018. "Brokerage and Transnationalism: Present and Past Intermediaries, Social Mobility, and Mixed Loyalties." *Identities: Global Studies in Culture and Power* 25:610–28.

de la Broquière, Bertrandon. 1892. *Le Voyage d'Outremer de Bertrandon de la Broquière premier écuyer tranchant et conseiller de Philippe le Bon, duc de Bourgogne (1432–1433)*. Vol. 2 of *Recueil de voyages et de documents pour servier à l'histoire de la géographie depuis le XIIIe siècle jusqu'à la fin du XVIe siècle*, 2 vols., edited by Charles Schefer, Paris: Leroux.

Delacroix-Besnier, Claudine. 1997. *Les dominicains et la chrétienté grecque aux XIVe et XVe siècles*. Rome: École française de Rome, Palais Farnèse.

Délaissé, L. M. J. 1959. *Le siècle d'or de la miniature flamande: Le mécénat de Philippe le Bon; Exposition organisée à l'occasion du 400e anniversaire de la fondation de la Bibliothèque royale de Philippe II à Bruxelles, le 12 avril 1959*. Exh. cat. Brussels.

de Lannoy, Ghillbert. 1878. *Œuvres de Ghillbert de Lannoy, voyageur, diplomate et moraliste*. Edited by Charles Potvin and Jean-Charles Houzeau. Louvain, Lefever.

Delaney, Carol. 2006. "Columbus's Ultimate Goal: Jerusalem." *Comparative Studies in Society and History* 48, no. 2:260–92.

Delaville Le Roulx, J. 1886. *La France en Orient au xive siècle: Expéditions du maréchal Boucicaut; Par J. Delaville Le Roulx*. 2 vols. Paris: E. Thorin.

Delisle, Léopold. 1907. *Recherches sur la librairie de Charles V*. 3 vols. Paris: Honoré Champion.

Delogu, Daisy. 2008. *Theorizing the Ideal Sovereign: The Rise of the French Vernacular Royal Biography*. Toronto: University of Toronto Press.

Delsaux, Olivier. 2019. "Quand les auteurs étaient des nains: L'auctorialité des traducteurs à l'aube de la modernité." In *Quand les auteurs étaient des nains: Stratégies auctoriales des traducteurs français de la fin du Moyen Âge*, edited by Olivier Delsaux and Tania van Hemelryck, 9–31. Turnhout: Brepols.

Dembowski, Peter F. 1983. *Jean Froissart and His Meliador: Context, Craft, and Sense*. Lexington, KY: French Forum.

Denoël, Charlotte. 2004. *Saint André: Culte et iconographie en France, Ve–XVe siècles*. Paris: École des chartes.

Denoël, Charlotte, Anne-Orange Poilpré, and Sumi Shimahara, eds. 2018. *"Imago libri": Représentations carolingiennes du livre*. Turnhout: Brepols.

de Schryver, Antoine. 1957. "Lieven van Lathem, een onbekende grootmeester van de Vlaamse miniatuurschilderkunst." In *Handelingen van het XXIIe Vlams Filologencongres*, 338–42. Leuven: Uitgegeven door de Vlaamsche Philologencongressen.

de Smedt, Raphaël, ed. 2000. *Les Chevaliers de l'Ordre de la Toison d'or au XVe siècle: Notices bio-bibliographiques*. 2nd rev. ed. New York: P. Lang.

de Terre-Basse, Alfred, ed. 1856. *Gerard de Roussillon: S'ensuyt l'hystoire de monseigneur Gerard de Roussillon, jadis duc et conte de Bourgongne et d'Acquitaine*. Lyon.

Devaux, Jean. 2010. "Introduction: Littérature et politique sous les premiers Valois." In *Le Prince en son "miroir": Littérature et politique sous les premiers Valois*, edited by Jean Devaux and Alain Marchandisse. Special issue, *Le Moyen Âge* 116:33–543.

Devaux, Jean, and Mattieu Marchal, eds. 2018. *L'art du récit à la cour de Bourgogne: L'activité de Jean de Wavrin et de son atelier; Actes du colloque international organisé les 24 et 25 octobre 2013 à l'Université du Littoral-Côte d'Opale, Dunkerque*. Paris: Honoré Champion éditeur.

de Villaret, Foulques. 2008. "Informatio et instruction super faciendo generali passagio pro recuperatione Terre Sancte." In Paviot 2008, 189–98.

de Villaret, Foulques, et al. 2008. "Coment la Terre Sainte puet ester recouvree par les Crestiens." In Paviot 2008, 221–33.

Diotti, Angelo. 1977. "Premessa." In P. Dubois 1977, 7–114.

Dixon, Rebecca. 2014. "Consuming the Past and Dressing the Stage in the Burgundian *Roman de Florimant*: Codex, Costume, and Courtly Aspiration." In *Marqueurs d'identité dans la littérature médiévale: Mettre en signe l'individu et la famille (XIIe–XVe siècles); Actes du colloque tenu à Poitiers les 17 et 18 novembre 2011*, edited by Catalina Girbea, Laurent Hablot, and Raluca Radulescu, 39–52. Turnhout: Brepols.

Dogaer, Georges. 1987. *Flemish Miniature Painting in the 15th and 16th Centuries*. Amsterdam: B. M. Israël.

Donovan, Erin K. 2011. "A *Livre d'Eracles* within the Library of the Fifteenth-Century Flemish Bibliophile, Louis de Bruges: Paris, BnF MS fr. 68 in Context." In *Collections in Context: The Organization of Knowledge and Community in Europe*, edited by Karen L. Fresco and Anne D. Hedeman, 191–207. Columbus: Ohio State University Press.

———. 2013. "Imagined Crusaders: The *Livre d'Eracles* in Fifteenth-Century Burgundian Collections." PhD diss., University of Illinois, Urbana-Champaign.

Dopp, Pierre-Herman. 1958. "Introduction." In Piloti 1958, v–l.

Doutrepont, Georges. 1906. *Inventaire de la "librairie" de Philippe le Bon (1420)*. Brussels: Kiessling.

———. 1909. *La littérature française à la cour des ducs de Bourgogne: Philippe le Hardi, Jean sans Peur, Philippe le Bon, Charles le Téméraire*. Paris: Honoré Champion.

———. 1939. *Les Mises en prose des épopées et des romans chevaleresques du XIVe et XVe siècle*. Brussels: Palais des académies.

du Bellay, Joachim. 1939. *The Defence and Illustration of the French Language*. Translated by Gladys M. Turquet. London: J. M. Dent.

———. 1993. "La Défense et illustration de la langue française." 1967. In *Les Regrets: Les Antiquités de Rome*, edited by S. de Sacy, 197–267. NRF/Poésie. Paris: Gallimard.

Dubois, Anne. 1994. "Tradition et transmission: Un exemple de filiation dans les manuscrits enluminés de Valère Maxime." *Revue des archéologues et historiens d'art de Louvain* 27:51–60.

Dubois, Pierre. 1956. *The Recovery of the Holy Land*. Translated by Walther I. Brandt. New York: Columbia University Press.

———. 1977. Dubois, Pierre. *De recuperatione terre sancta*. Edited by Angelo Diotti. Florence: Leo Olschki.

———. 2007. Dubois, Pierre. "Populi proclamationes." 1923. In *Le Dossier de l'affaire des Templiers*, edited and translated by Georges Lizerand, 84–101. Paris: Les Belles Lettres.

————. 2019. Dubois, Pierre. *De la reconquête de la Terre Sainte*, edited by Charles-Victor Langlois, translated by Marianne Sághy and Alexis Léonas; and *De l'abrègement des guerres et procès du royaume des Francs, et la réforme de l'État universel de la République des chrétiens*, introduction by Marianne Sághy and Alexis Léonas, edited and translated by Pierre-Anne Forcadet. Paris: Les Belles Lettres.

Duby, Georges. 1973. *Guerriers et paysans, VIIIe–XIIe siècles: Premier essor de l'économie européenne*. Paris: Gallimard.

Dumolyn, Jan. 2001. "Les conseillers flamands au Xve siècle: Rentiers du pouvoir, courtiers de pouvoir." In *Powerbrokers in the Late Middle Ages: The Burgundian Low Countries in a European Context*, edited by Robert Stein, 67–85. Turnhout: Brepols.

————. 2006. "Justice, Equity and the Common Good: The State Ideology of the Councillors of the Burgundian Dukes." In *The Ideology of Burgundy: The Promotion of National Consciousness: 1364–1565*, edited by D'Arcy Jonathan Dacre Boulton and Jan R. Veenstra, 1–20. Leiden: Brill.

Dumolyn, Jan, and Élodie Lecuppre-Desjardin. 2010. "Le Bien commun en Flandre médiévale: Une lutte discursive entre princes et sujets." In Lecuppre-Desjardins and van Bruaene 2010, 253–66.

Dupin, Henri. 1931. *La courtoisie au Moyen Âge*. Paris: Picard.

Duque, Adriano. 2009. "The Carpino [*sic*] Mission to Mongolia in 1246." In *Travels and Travelogues in the Middle Ages: Essays on Symbolic Engagement in Early Drama*, edited by Jean Kosta Théphaine, 233–48. New York: AMS.

————. 2018. "Gift-Giving in the Carpini Expedition to Mongolia (1246–1248 C.E.)." In *Remapping Travel Narratives (1000–1700): To the East and Back Again*, edited by Montserrat Piera, 187–200. Leeds, UK: Arc Humanities.

Durand, Jannic, and Dorota Giovannoni, eds. 2012. *Chypre, entre Byzance et Occident, IVe–XVIe siècle: Catalogue de l'exposition au musée du Louvre*. Paris: Louvre éditions.

Duval, Frédéric, and Françoise Vielliard. n.d. *Miroir des classiques*. Éditions en ligne de l'École des chartes. Paris, École nationale des chartes. http://elec.enc .sorbonne.fr/miroir_des_classiques/xml/classiques_latins/factorum_dicto rum_memorabilium_libri_ix_valerius_maximus.xml#presentation. Accessed May 6, 2023.

Earp, Lawrence. 1995. *Guillaume de Machaut: A Guide to Research*. New York: Garland.

Edbury, Peter W. 1991. *The Kingdom of Cyprus and the Crusades, 1191–1374*. Cambridge: Cambridge University Press.

————. 2001. "Introduction." In *Guillaume de Machaut: The Capture of Alexandria*, translated by Janet Shirley, 1–16. Aldershot, UK: Ashgate.

Elst, Stefan Vander. 2009. "'Tu es pélérin en la sainte cité': Chaucer's Knight and Philippe de Mézières." *Studies in Philology* 106:379–401.

Emerson, Catherine. 2006. "La double vie d'Olivier de La Marche." In *L'écrit et le manuscrit à la fin du moyen âge*, edited by Tania van Hemelryck and Céline van Hoorebeeck, 111–20. Turnhout: Brepols.

Euben, Roxanne Leslie. 2006. *Journeys to the Other Shore: Muslim and Western Travelers in Search of Knowledge*. Princeton, NJ: Princeton University Press.

Ludmilla Evdokimova. 2014. "Le directoire de Jean de Vignay, une traduction littérale au début du XIVe siècle." *Cahiers de recherches médiévales et humanistes* 27:177–98.

Fabri, Fratris Felicis [Felix]. 1843–49. *Evagatorium in Terrae Sanctae, Arabiae et Egypti peregrinatione*. Edited by Konrad Dieterich Hassler. 3 vols. Stuttgart.

———. 1896. *The Book of the Wanderings (1480–1483)*. Translated by Aubrey Stewart. Vols. 7–10. London: Palestine Pilgrims Text Society.

———. 2000–2006. *Les errances de frère Félix, pèlerin en Terre Sainte, en Arabie et en Égypte*. Edited by Jean Meyers and Nicole Chareyron. Montpellier: Université Paul-Valéry, CERCAM.

———. 2013–20. *Les errances de frère Félix, pèlerin en Terre Sainte, en Arabie et en Égypte*. Edited by Jean Meyers and translated by Jean Meyers and Michel Tarayre. Paris: Classiques Garnier.

Falmagne, Thomas, and Beaudouin van den Abeele, eds. 2016. *Corpus catalogorum Belgii: The Medieval Booklists of the Southern Low Countries*. Vol. 5. Louvain: Peeters.

Ferlampin-Acher, Christine. 2010. *Perceforest et Zéphir: Propositions autour d'un récit arthurien bourguignon*. Geneva: Droz.

———. 2012a. "Introduction." In *Guillaume de Palerne*, translated by Christine Ferlampin-Acher, 7–112. Paris: Garnier Classiques.

———, ed. 2012b. *"Perceforest": Un roman arthurien et sa réception*. Rennes: Presses universitaires de Rennes.

———. 2021. *Artus de Bretagne* Paris: Honoré Champion.

Fernández-Armesto, Felipe. 1987. *Before Columbus: Exploration and Colonization from the Mediterranean to the Atlantic, 1229–1492*. Philadelphia: University of Pennsylvania Press.

Fidentius of Padua. 2008. *Liber recuperationis Terre Sancte*. In Paviot 2008, 53–169.

Figg, Kristen Mossler. 1995. *The Short Lyric Poems of Jean Froissart: Fixed Forms and the Expression of the Courtly Ideal*. New York: Garland.

Fisher, Matthew. 2012. *Scribal Authorship and the Writing of History in Medieval England*. Columbus: Ohio State University Press.

Fitzsimon, Simon. 1960. *Itinerarium Symonis Semeonis ab Hybernia ad Terram Sanctam*. Edited and translated by Mario Esposito. Dublin: Dublin Institute for Advanced Studies.

Flood, Finbarr Barry, and Beate Fricke. 2023. *Tales Things Tell: Material Histories of Early Globalisms*. Princeton, NJ: Princeton University Press.

Flutre, Louis Ferdinand. 1974a. *Les Manuscrits des "Faits des Romains."* 1932. Geneva: Slatkine.

———. 1974b. *"Li Fait des Romains" dans les littératures française et italienne du XIIIe au XVIe siècle*. 1932. Geneva: Slatkine.

Forcadet, Pierre-Anne. 2014. "Le *De recuperatione Terre Sancte* de Pierre Dubois: Prétexte de croisade et pouvoir royal." In *Les projets de croisade: Géostratégie et diplomatie européenne du XIVe au XVIIe siècle*, edited by Jacques Paviot, 69–86. Toulouse: Presses universitaires du Mirail.

Foucault, Michel. 1970. *The Order of Things: An Archaeology of the Human Sciences*. 1966. New York: Vintage Books.

———. 1997. "What Is an Author?" In *The Essential Works of Foucault, 1954–1984*, edited by Paul Rabinow, vol. 2, *Aesthetics, Method, and Epistemology*, edited by James D. Faubion, 205–22. New York: New Press.

Frappier, Jean. 1973. "Le motif du 'don contraignant' dans la littérature du Moyen Âge." 1969. In *Amour courtois et Table ronde*, 225–64. Genève, Droz.

Freeman, Michelle A. 1979. *The Poetics of Translatio Studii and Conjointure: Chrétien de Troyes's "Cligès."* Lexington, KY: French Forum.

Frescobaldi, Lionardo. 1944. "Viaggio in Terrasanta di Lionardo di N. Frescobaldi." In *Viaggi in Terrasanta di Leonardo Frescobaldi e Simone Sigoli,* edited by Cesare Angelini, 39–167. Florence: F. Le Monnier.

———. 1948. "Pilgrimage of Lionardo di Niccolò Frescobaldi to the Holy Land." In *Visit to the Holy Places of Egypt, Sinai, Palestine, and Syria in 1384, by Frescobaldi, Gucci and Sigoli,* translated by Theophilus Bellorini and Eugene Hoade, 31–90. Jerusalem: Franciscan.

Froissart, Jean. *Chroniques.* 1867–77. 25 vols. In *Œuvres de Froissart,* edited by Kervyn de Lettenhove. Brussels: Académie royale de Belgique.

———. 1869–75. *Chroniques de J. Froissart, publiées pour la Société de l'histoire de France.* Edited by Siméon Luce. 15 vols. Paris: J. Renouard.

———. 1972. *Chroniques: Début du premier livre; Édition du manuscript de Rome Reg. lat. 869.* Edited by George T. Diller. Geneva: Droz.

———. 1991–98. *Chroniques: Livre I; Le manuscrit d'Amiens.* Edited by George T. Diller. 5 vols. Geneva: Droz.

———. 2007. *Jean Froissart: Chroniques; Livre III; Le manuscrit de Besançon Bibliothèque municipale no. 865.* Edited by Peter F. Ainsworth. Geneva: Droz.

Fuchs, Barbara. 2001. *Mimesis and Empire: The New World, Islam, and European Identities.* Cambridge: Cambridge University Press.

Fulcher of Chartres. 1969. *A History of the Expedition to Jerusalem: 1095–1127.* Edited by Harold S. Fink, translated by Frances Rita Ryan. Knoxville: University of Tennessee Press.

Gadrat-Ouerfelli, Christine. 2013. "Le Voyage." In *La Terre: Connaissance, représentations, mesure au Moyen Âge,* edited by Patrick Gautier Dalché, 505–79. Turnhout: Brepols.

———. 2015. *Lire Marco Polo au Moyen Age: Traduction, diffusion et réception du Devisement du monde.* Turnhout: Brepols.

———. 2021. "Des carnets de voyage au Moyen Âge?" *Viatica* 5. https://revues-msh .uca.fr:443/viatica/index.php?id=837.

———. 2022. "Marco Polo, the Book, and the Dominicans." *Digital Philology: A Journal of Medieval Cultures* 11:286–301.

Galderisi, Claudio, ed. 2011. *Translations médiévales: Cinq siècles de traductions en français au Moyen Âge (XIe–XVe siècles); Étude et répertoire.* 3 vols. Turnhout: Brepols.

Gallet-Guerne, Danielle. 1974. *Vasque de Lucène et la Cyropédie à la cour de Bourgogne (1470).* Geneva: Droz.

García-Arenal, Mercedes, and Yonatan Glazer-Eytan. 2019. *Forced Conversion in Christianity, Judaism and Islam: Coercion and Faith in Premodern Iberia and Beyond.* Boston: Brill.

Gaullier-Bougassas, Catherine. 1998. *Les romans d'Alexandre: Aux frontières de l'épique et du romanesque.* Paris: Honoré Champion.

———. 2003. *La tentation de l'orient dans le roman médiéval: Sur l'imaginaire médiéval de l'autre.* Paris: Champion.

———. 2011a. *Les vœux du Paon de Jacques de Longuyon: Originalité et rayonnement.* Paris: Klincksieck.

———, ed. 2011b. *L'historiographie médiévale d'Alexandre le Grand.* Turnhout: Brepols.

Gaullier-Bougassas, Catherine, and Hélène Bellon-Méguelle. 2015. *La fascination pour Alexandre le Grand dans les littératures européennes (Xe–XVIe siècle)*. 4 vols. Turnhout: Brepols.

Gaunt, Simon. 2013a. "Genres in Motion: Reading the *Grundriss* 40 Years On." *Medioevo Romanzo* 27:24–43.

———. 2013b. *Marco Polo's Le Devisement du Monde: Narrative Voice, Language and Diversity*. Cambridge, UK: D. S. Brewer.

Gaunt, Simon, et al. 2011–15. *Medieval Francophone Literary Culture Outside France.* AHRC-funded research. http://www.medievalfrancophone.ac.uk/.

Gaunt, Simon, et al. 2015–20. The Values of French. Funded by the European Research Council (ERC), under the European Union's Horizon 2020 research and innovation programme (grant agreement no. 670726). http://www.medieval francophone.ac.uk/.

Germain, Jean. 1895. "*Le discours du voyage d'oultremer au très victorieux roi Charles VII*, prononcé, en 1452, par Jean Germain, évêque de Chalon." Edited by Ch. Schefer. *Revue de l'Orient latin* 3:303–42.

Gavoille, Élisabeth. 2015. "*Auctor* et *auctoritas*: Le paradigme latin de 'l'instauration discursive.'" In *L'autorité dans le monde des lettres*, edited by Élisabeth Gavoille, Marie-Paule de Weerdt-Pilorge, and Philippe Chardin, 21–38. Paris: Kimé.

Gentry, Francis G. 1983. "'Ex oriente lux': 'Translatio' Theory in Early Middle High German Literature." In *Spectrum Medii Aevi: Essais in Early German Literature in Honor of George Fenwick Jones*, edited by William C. McDonald, 119–37. Göppingen: Kümmerle.

Gil, Marc. 1998. "Le mécénat littéraire de Jean V de Créquy, conseiller et chambellan de Philippe le Bon." *Eulalie* 1:69–95.

Gilbert, Claire M. 2020. *In Good Faith: Arabic Translation and Translators in Early Modern Spain*. Philadelphia: University of Pennsylvania Press.

Gilbert, Jane, Simon Gaunt, and William Burgwinkle. 2020. *Medieval French Literary Culture Abroad*. Oxford: Oxford University Press.

Goldberg, Jessica. 2012. *Trade and Institutions in the Medieval Mediterranean: The Geniza Merchants and Their Business World*. Cambridge: Cambridge University Press.

Golubovich, Girolamo, ed. 1906–27. *Biblioteca bio-bibliographica della Terra Santa e dell'Oriente francescano*. 5 vols. Florence: Quaracchi, Collegio di S. Bonaventura.

González de Clavijo, Ruy. 2001. *Narrative of the Embassy of Ruy Gonzalez de Clavijo to the Court of Timour at Samarcand, A.D. 1403–6*. 1859. Translated by Clements R. Markham. New Delhi: Asian Educational Services.

Graboïs, Aryeh. 1998. *Le Pèlerin occidental en Terre Sainte au Moyen Âge*. Bruxelles: de Boeck.

Greco, Rosa Anna, ed. 2002. *Blancandin et l'Orgueilleuse d'amours: Versioni in prosa del XV secolo*. Alessandria: Ed. dell' Orso.

Greenblatt, Stephen. 1991. *Marvelous Possessions: The Wonder of the New World*. Chicago: University of Chicago Press.

Greene, Molly. 2010. *Catholic Pirates and Greek Merchants: A Maritime History of the Mediterranean*. Princeton, NJ: Princeton University Press.

Grévin, Benoît. 2020. *Al di là delle fonti "classiche": Le epistole dantesche e la prassi duecentesca dell'ars dictaminis*. Venice: Edizioni Ca'Foscari.

Grunzweig, A. 1956. "Le Grand duc du Ponant." *Le Moyen Age* 62, nos. 1–2:119–65.

Guard, Timothy. 2005. "Stanegrave, Sir Roger (*fl.* 1280s–1331)." In *Oxford Dictionary of National Biography*. Oxford: Oxford University Press. https://doi .org/10.1093/ref:odnb/92443.

———. 2013. *Chivalry, Kingship, and Crusade: The English Experience in the Fourteenth Century*. Cambridge, UK: D. S. Brewer.

Gucci, Giorgio. 1862. *Viaggio ai luoghi santi*. In *Viaggi in Terra Santa di Lionardo Frescobaldi et d'altri*, edited by Carlo Gargiolli, 269–438. Florence: G. Barbèra.

———. 1948. "Pilgrimage of Giorgio Gucci to the Holy Places." In *Visit to the Holy Places of Egypt, Sinai, Palestine, and Syria in 1384, by Frescobaldi, Gucci and Sigoli*, translated by Theophilus Bellorini and Eugene Hoade, 93–156. Jerusalem: Franciscan.

———. 1999. *Testimone a Gerusalemme: Il pellegrinaggio di un fiorentino del Trecento*. Edited by Alessandro Bedini. Rome: Città nuova.

Guenée, Bernard. 1976. "La culture historique des nobles: Le succès des *Faits des Romains*; XIIIᵉ–XIVᵉ siècles." In *La noblesse au Moyen Âge, XIe–XVe siècles: Essais à la mémoire de Robert Boutruche*, edited by Philippe Contamine, 261–88. Paris: Presses universitaires de France.

Robert Guiette, ed. 1940–51. *Croniques et conquestes de Charlemaine*. 3 vols. Bruxelles: Palais des Académies.

Haemers, Jelle. 2009. *For the Common Good: State Power and Urban Revolts in the Reign of Mary of Burgundy (1477–1482)*. Turnhout, Belgium: Brepols.

Haemers, Jelle, Céline van Hoorebeeck, and Hanno Wijsman, eds. 2007. *Entre la ville, la noblesse et l'état: Philippe de Clèves (1456–1528), homme politique et bibliophile*. Turnhout: Brepols.

Haggh, Barbara. 2013. "Between Council and Crusade: The Ceremonial of the Order of the Golden Fleece in the Fifteenth Century." In Blockmans et al. 2013, 51–58.

Hamdani, Abbas. 1979. "Columbus and the Recovery of Jerusalem." *Journal of the American Oriental Society* 99, no. 1:39–48.

Hames, Harvey J. 2003. "The Language of Conversion: Ramon Llull's Art as a Vernacular." In *The Vulgar Tongue: Medieval and Postmedieval Vernacularity*, edited by Fiona Somerset and Nicholas Watson, 43–56. University Park: Pennsylvania State University Press.

———. 2010. "Truly Seeking Conversion? The Mendicants, Ramon Llull and Alfonso de Valladolid." *Jahrbuch der Knorr-von-Rosenroth Gessellschaft* 20:41–62.

———. 2012. "Through Ramon Llull's Looking Glass: What Was the Thirteenth-Century Dominican Mission Really About?" In *Ramon Llull i el lul·lisme: Pensament i llenguatge; Actes de les Jornades en homenatge a J. N. Hillgarth i A. Bonner*, edited by Maria Isabel Ripoll and Margalida Tortella, 51–74. Palma de Mallorca: Universitat de les Illes Balears.

Hans-Collas, Ilona, and Pascal Schandel. 2009. *Manuscrits enluminés des anciens Pays-Bas méridionaux*. Vol. 1, *Manuscrits de Louis de Bruges*. Paris: Bibliothèque nationale de France.

Hardy, Sophie. 2011. "Édition critique de la Prise d'Alexandrie de Guillaume de Machaut." PhD thesis, Université d'Orléans.

Harper, James G. 2005. "Turks as Trojans; Trojans as Turks: Visual Imagery of the Trojan War and the Politics of Cultural Identity in Fifteenth-Century Europe." In *Postcolonial Approaches to the European Middle Ages*, edited by Ananya Jahanar Kabir and Deanne Williams, 151–79. Cambridge: Cambridge University Press.

Haugeard, Philippe. 2006. "L'enchantement du don: Une approche anthropologique de la largesse royale dans la littérature médiévale (XIIᵉ–XIIIᵉ siècles)." *Cahiers de civilisation médiévale* 195:295–312.

Hauwaerts, Evelien, Evelien de Wilde, and Ludo Vandamme, eds. 2018. *Colard Mansion: Incunabula, Prints and Manuscripts in Medieval Bruges.* Ghent: Uitgeverij Snoeck.

Hayton. 1906. "*La Flor des estoires de la terre d'Orient.*" In *Recueil des historiens des croisades: Documents latins et français relatifs à Arménie*, edited by Édouard Dulaurier and Charles Kohler, 113–253. Paris: L'Académie des inscriptions et de belles lettres.

Hazard, Harry W., ed. 1975. *The Fourteenth and Fifteenth Centuries.* Vol. 3 of *A History of the Crusades*, general editor Kenneth M. Setton. Milwaukee: University of Wisconsin Press.

Hedeman, Anne D. 2008. *Translating the Past: Laurent de Premierfait and Boccaccio's "De casibus."* Los Angeles: J. Paul Getty Museum.

———. 2019. "Translating Prologues and Prologue Illustration in French Historical Texts." In *Inscribing Knowledge in the Medieval Book: The Power of Paratexts*, edited by Rosalind Brown-Grant, Patrizia Carmassi, Gisela Drossbach, Anne D. Hedeman, Victoria Turner, and Iolanda Ventura, 197–223. Kalamazoo, MI: Medieval Institute.

———. 2022. *Visual Translation: Illuminated Manuscripts and the First French Humanists.* Notre Dame, IN: University of Notre Dame Press.

Heimburger, Franziska. 2012. "Of Go-Betweens and Gatekeepers: Considering Disciplinary Biases in Interpreting History through Exemplary Metaphors; Military Interpreters in the Allied Coalition during the First World War." In *Translation and the Reconfiguration of Power Relations: Revisiting Role and Context of Translation and Interpreting*, edited by Béatrice Fischer and Matilde Nisbeth Jensen, 21–34. Münster: LIT Verlag.

Hellinga, Lotte. 1982. *Caxton in Focus: The Beginning of Printing in England.* London: British Library.

———. 2010. *William Caxton and Early Printing in England.* London: British Library.

———. 2011. "William Caxton, Colard Mansion, and the Printer in Type 1." *Bulletin du Bibliophile* 1:86–114.

———. 2018. "William Caxton and Colard Mansion." In Hauwaerts et al. 2018, 63–69.

Heng, Geraldine. 2014. "Early Globalities, and Its Questions, Objectives, and Methods: An Inquiry into the State of Theory and Critique." *Exemplaria* 26:234–53.

———. 2015. "Reinventing Race, Colonization, and Globalisms across Deep Time: Lessons from the 'Longue Durée.'" *PMLA* 130:358–66.

———. 2021. *The Global Middle Ages: An Introduction.* Elements in the Global Middle Ages. Cambridge: Cambridge University Press.

Heng, Geraldine, and Lynn Ramey. 2014. "Early Globalities, Global Literatures: Introducing a Special Issue on the Global Middle Ages." *Literature Compass* 11, no. 7:389–94.

Henri II, roi de Chypre, et son conseil. 2008. "Informatio (1311)." In Paviot 2008, 281–92.

Hériché-Pradeau, Sandrine. 2006. "Girart de Roussillon: La stratégie hagiographique d'une compilation." In de Crécy et al. 2006, 89–109.

———. 2008. Hériché-Pradeau, Sandrine. *Alexandre le Bourguignon: Étude du roman "Les Faicts et les Conquestes d'Alexandre" le Grand de Jehan Wauquelin.* Genève: Droz.

Hershenzon, Daniel. 2018. *The Captive Sea: Slavery, Communication, and Commerce in Early Modern Spain and the Mediterranean.* Philadelphia: University of Pennsylvania Press.

Hesdin, Simon de. n.d. *Dits et faits memorables, traduzione di Simon de Hesdin.* Edited by Maria Cristina Enriello, vol. 1. http://www.pluteus.it/?page_id=12. Accessed May 6, 2023.

Heyder, Joris. 2014. "Corporate Design Made in Ghent/Bruges? On the Extensive Reuse of Patterns in Late Medieval Flemish Illuminated Manuscripts." In *Usage of Models in Medieval Book Painting,* edited by Monika Müller, 167–20. Newcastle upon Tyne: Cambridge Scholars.

H-France Forum on "Z. Stahuljak, *Médiéval contemporain: Pour une littérature connectée* (Macula 2020)." 2021. September. https://h-france.net/h-france -forum-volume-16-2021/.

Higgins, Iain Macleod. 1997. *Writing East: The "Travels" of Sir John Mandeville.* Philadelphia: University of Pennsylvania Press.

Hoernel, Alexandra. 2012. "Réécriture(s) et réception du *Perceforest* au XVIᵉ siècle." In Ferlampin-Acher 2012b, 317–33.

Höh, Marc von der, Nikolas Jaspert, and Jenny Rahel Oesterle, eds. 2013. *Cultural Brokers at Mediterranean Courts in the Middle Ages.* München: Wilhelm Fink.

Holmes, Catherine, and Naomi Standen. 2018. "Introduction: Towards a Global Middle Ages." *Past and Present* 238, no. 13:1–44.

Höltgen, Karl Josef. 1959. "Die 'nine worthies.' " *Anglia* 77:279–309.

Hönke, Jana, and Markus-Michael Müller. 2018. "Brokerage, Intermediation, Translation." In *The Oxford Handbook of Governance and Limited Statehood,* edited by Thomas Risse, Tanja A. Börzel, and Anke Draude, 333–52. Oxford: Oxford University Press.

Huizinga, Johan. 1954. *The Waning of the Middle Ages: A Study of the Forms of Life, Thought, and Art in France and the Netherlands in the XIVth and XVth Centuries.* Garden City, NY: Doubleday.

———. 2020. *Autumntide of the Middle Ages: A Study of Forms of Life and Thought of the Fourteenth and Fifteenth Centuries in France and the Low Countries.* Edited and translated by Graeme Small and Anton van der Lem. Leiden: Leiden University Press.

Humbert of Romans. 1690. *Opus tripartitum.* In *Appendix ad Fasciculum rerum expetendarum et fudiendarum,* edited by Edward Brown, 185–229. London.

———. 1968. Humbertus de Romanus. "Excerpta de tractandis in concilio Lugdun." 1724. In *Veterum scriptorum et monumentorum historicorum, dogmaticorum, moralium: Amplissima collectio,* edited by Domni Edmundi Martene and Domni Ursini Durand, 9 vols., 7:174–98. New York: B. Franklin.

Huot, Sylvia. 1987. *From Song to Book: The Poetics of Writing in Old French Lyric and Lyrical Narrative Poetry.* Ithaca, NY: Cornell University Press.

———. 2007. *Postcolonial Fictions in the "Roman de Perceforest": Cultural Identities and Hybridities.* Cambridge, UK: D. S. Brewer.

Informationes Massilie. 1872. "Informationes Massilie pro passagio transmarino." In "Projet de croisade du premier duc de Bourbon (1316–1333)," edited by A. de Boislisle. *Annuaire-Bulletin de la Société de l'histoire de France*, 246–55.

Inghilleri, Moira. 2008. "The Ethical Task of the Translator in the Geo-political Arena: From Iraq to Guantánamo Bay." *Translation Studies* 1:212–23.

————. 2012. *Interpreting Justice: Ethics, Politics and Language.* New York: Routledge.

Iorga, Nicolas. 1973. *Philippe de Mézières (1327–1405).* 1896. London: Variorum Reprints.

"Itinerarium cuiusdem Anglici." 1906–27. In Golubovich 1906–27, 4:435–60.

Jackson, Peter, with David Morgan. 2009. "Introduction." In Rubruck 2009, 1–55.

Jacob, Elin K. 2004. "Classification and Categorization: A Difference That Makes a Difference." *Library Trends* 52, no. 3:515–40.

Jacopo da Verona. 1950. *Liber peregrinationis.* Edited by Ugo Monneret de Villard. Rome: La Libreria dello stato.

Jauss, Hans Robert. 1982. "Literary History as a Challenge to Literary Theory." In *Toward an Aesthetic of Reception*, translated by Timothy Bahti, 3–45. Minneapolis: University of Minnesota Press.

Jensen, Kurt Villads. 2014. "Riccoldi Florentini, Libellus ad nationes orientales." Online edition. https://www2.historia.su.se/personal/villads-jensen/Riccoldo /paginaprincipalis.pdf. Accessed May 6, 2023.

Jerome n.d. *Epistola LVII: Ad Pammachium; De optimo genere interpretandi / Traité sur les devoirs d'un traducteur des livres sacrés: Au sénateur Pammaque*, sec. 5. http:// remacle.org/bloodwolf/eglise/jerome/pammaque4.htm. Accessed October 26, 2015.

Johan, Frédérique. 2009. "Les artisans du livre sous les gouvernements de Philippe le Bon et de Charles le Téméraire: En marge d'un projet d'édition de sources." In *Miscellanea in memoriam Pierre Cockshaw (1938–2008)*, edited by Frank Daelemans and Ann Kelders, 2:223–38. Brussels: Bibliothèque royale de Belgique.

Johnston, Mark D. 1995. "Ramon Llull and the Compulsory Evangelization of Jews and Muslims." In *Iberia and the Mediterranean World of the Middle Ages: Studies in Honor of Robert I. Burns*, edited by Larry J. Simon, 3–37. Leiden: Brill.

————. 2004. "Translation, Social Psychology, and Evangelism." In *The Medieval Translator / Traduire Au Moyen Age: V.8; The Theory and Practice of Translation in the Middle Ages; Proceedings*, edited by Rosalynn Voaden et al., 61–69. Turnhout: Brepols.

Jongkees, A. G. 1967. "Translatio Studii: Les avatars d'un thème médiéval." In *Miscellanea Mediaevalia in memoriam Jan Frederik Niermeyer*, 41–52. Groningen: J. B Walters.

"Journal d'un pèlerin français en Terre-Sainte (1383)." 1895. Edited by H. Omont. *Revue de l'Orient latin* 3:457–59.

Kaiser, Wolfgang, ed. 2008. *Le commerce des captifs: Les intermédiaires dans l'échange et le rachat des prisonniers en Méditerranée, XVe–XVIIIe.* Rome: École française de Rome.

Karttunen, Frances E. 1994. *Between Worlds: Interpreters, Guides, and Survivors.* New Brunswick, NJ: Rutgers University Press.

Kay, Sarah. 1995. *The "Chansons de Geste" in the Age of Romance: Political Fictions.* Oxford, UK: Clarendon.

Keene, Bryan C., ed. 2019. *Toward a Global Middle Ages: Encountering the World through Illuminated Manuscripts*. Los Angeles: J. Paul Getty Museum.

Kelly, Douglas. 1978. "*Translatio Studii: Translatio*, Adaptation, and Allegory in Medieval French Literature." *Philological Quarterly* 57:287–310.

———. 1987. "The Genius of the Patron: The Prince, the Poet, and Fourteenth-Century Inventions." *Studies in the Literary Imagination* 20, no. 1:77–97.

———. 1997. "The *Fidus interpres*: Aid or Impediment to Medieval Translation and *Translatio*." In *Translation Theory and Practice in the Middle Ages*, edited by Jeanette Beer, 47–58. Kalamazoo, MI: Medieval Institute, Western Michigan University.

———. 2014. *Machaut and the Medieval Apprenticeship Tradition: Truth, Fiction and Poetic Craft*. Woodbridge, UK: Boydell and Brewer.

Khanmohamadi, Shirin A. 2014. *In Light of Another's Word: European Ethnography in the Middle Ages*. Philadelphia: University of Pennsylvania Press.

———. 2017. "Durendal, Translated: Islamic Object Genealogies in the *chanson de geste*." *Postmedieval: A Journal of Medieval Cultural Studies* 8:321–33.

Kinoshita, Sharon. 2006. *Medieval Boundaries: Rethinking Difference in Old French Literature*. Philadelphia: University of Pennsylvania Press.

———. 2008a. "Chrétien de Troyes's *Cligés* in the Medieval Mediterranean." *Arthuriana* 18:48–61.

———. 2008b. "Translatio/n, Empire, and the Worlding of Medieval Literature: The Travels of *Kalila wa Dimna*." *Postcolonial Studies* 11, no. 4:371–85.

———. 2013. "The Worlding of Macro Polo." In *Cosmopolitanism and the Middle Ages*, edited by John M. Ganim and Shayne Legassie, 39–57. New York: Palgrave Macmillan.

———. 2016a. "Introduction." In Polo 2016, xiv–xxx.

———. 2016b. "The Painter, the Warrior, and the Sultan: The World of Marco Polo in Three Portraits." *Medieval Globe* 2, no. 1:101–28.

Kinra, Rajeev. 2015. *Writing Self, Writing Empire: Chandar Bhan Brahman and the Cultural World of the Indo-Persian State Secretary*. Oakland: University of California Press.

Kren, Thomas. 2005. "The Importance of Patterns in the Emergence of the New Style of Flemish Manuscript Illumination after 1470." In *Manuscripts in Transition: Recycling Manuscripts, Texts, and Images*, edited by Brigitte Dekeyzer and Jan van der Stock, 357–77. Leuven: Uitgeverij Peeters.

Kren, Thomas, and Scot McKendrick, eds. 2003. *Illuminating the Renaissance: The Triumph of Flemish Manuscript Painting in Europe*. Exh. cat. Los Angeles: J. Paul Getty Museum.

Krummel, Miriamne Ara. 2011. *Crafting Jewishness in Medieval English: Legally Absent, Virtually Present*. New York: Palgrave Macmillan.

Laborde, A. de. 1909. *Les Manuscrits à peintures de la cité de Dieu de Saint Augustin*. Vol. 1. Paris: Édouard Rahir.

Lacroix, Paul. 1877. *Sciences et lettres au Moyen Âge et à l'époque de la Renaissance*. Paris: Firmin-Didot.

"La Devise des chemins de Babylone." 2008. In Paviot 2008, 199–220.

Lafitte, Marie-Pierre. 1997. "Les manuscrits de Louis de Bruges, chevalier de la Toison d'or." In *Le Banquet du Faisan*, edited by Marie-Thérèse Caron and Denis Clauzel, 243–55. Arras: Artois Presses Université.

Laiou, A. 1970. "Marino Sanudo Torsello, Byzantium and the Turks: The Background to the Anti-Turkish League of 1332–1334." *Speculum* 45, no. 3:374–92.

Lalande, Denis, ed. 1985. *Le livre des fais du bon messire Jehan le Maingre, dit Bouciquaut, Mareschal de France et Gouverneur de Jennes*. Geneva: Droz.

———, ed. 1988. *Jean II le Meingre, dit Boucicaut (1366–1421): Étude d'une biographie héroïque*. Geneva: Droz.

Langlois, Charles-Victor, ed. 1891. Pierre Dubois, *De recuperatione terre sancta: Traité de politique générale*. Paris, Alphonse Picard.

Lanza, Antonio, and Marcellina Troncarelli, eds. 1990. *Pellegrini scrittori: Viaggiatori toscani del Trecento in Terrasanta*. Firenze: Ponte alle Grazie.

Leach, Elizabeth Eva. 2011. *Guillaume de Machaut: Secretary, Poet, Musician*. Ithaca, NY: Cornell University Press.

LDB-I. 2000. *La librairie des ducs de Bourgogne: Manuscrits conservés à la Bibliothèque royale de Belgique*. Vol. 1, *Textes liturgiques, ascétiques, théologiques, philosophiques et moraux*. Edited by Bernard Bousmanne and and Céline van Hoorebeeck. Turnhout: Brepols.

LDB-II. 2003. *La librairie des ducs de Bourgogne: Manuscrits conservés à la Bibliothèque royale de Belgique*. Vol. 2, *Textes didactiques*. Edited by Bernard Bousmanne, Frédérique Johan, and Céline van Hoorebeeck. Turnhout: Brepols.

LDB-III. 2006. *La librairie des ducs de Bourgogne: Manuscrits conservés à la Bibliothèque royale de Belgique*. Vol. 3, *Textes littéraires*. Edited by Bernard Bousmanne, Tania van Hemelryck, and Céline van Hoorebeeck. Turnhout: Brepols.

LDB-IV. 2009. *La librairie des ducs de Bourgogne: Manuscrits conservés à la Bibliothèque royale de Belgique*. Vol. 4, *Textes historiques*. Edited by Bernard Bousmanne, Tania van Hemelryck, and Céline van Hoorebeeck. Turnhout: Brepols.

LDB-V. 2015. *La librairie des ducs de Bourgogne: Manuscrits conservés à la Bibliothèque royale de Belgique*. Vol. 5, *Textes historiques*. Edited by Bernard Bousmanne, Tania van Hemelryck, and Céline van Hoorebeeck. Turnhout: Brepols.

le Bel, Jean. 1904. *Chronique*. Vol. 1. Edited by Jules Viard and Eugène Déprez. Paris: Renouard.

Lechat, Didier. 2012. "Sort et présentation des traductions de Valère Maxime." In *Accès aux textes médiévaux de la fin du Moyen Âge au XVIIIe siècle*, edited by Michèle Guéret-Laferté and Claudine Poulouin, 55–72. Paris: Honoré Champion.

Lecuppre-Desjardin, Élodie. 2016. *Le royaume inachevé des ducs de Bourgogne*. Paris: Belin.

———, ed. 2019. *L'odeur du sang et des roses: Relire Johan Huizinga aujourd'hui*. Villeneuve d'Ascq, France: Presses universitaires du Septentrion.

———. 2022. *The Illusion of the Burgundian State*. Translated by Christopher Fletcher. Manchester: Manchester University Press.

Lecuppre-Desjardin, Élodie, and Anne-Laure van Bruaene. 2010. *De bono communi: The Discourse and Practice of the Common Good in the European City (13th–16th C.)*. Turnhout: Brepols.

Legaré, Anne-Marie. 2007. "Les Bibliothèques de deux princesses: Marguerite d'York et Marguerite d'Autriche." In *Livres et lectures de femmes en Europe entre Moyen Âge et Renaissance*, edited by Anne-Marie Legaré, 253–64. Turnhout: Brepols.

Lemaire, Claudine. 1996. "La bibliothèque de Louis de Gruuthuse." In Cockshaw 1996, 206–8.

————. 2000. "Les pérégrinations des trois volumes des *Chroniques de Hainaut*." In Cockshaw 2000b, 29–32.

Lemaire, Claudine, and Antoine de Schryver. 1981. "De bibliotheek van Lodewijk van Gruuthuse." In *Vlaamse kunst op perkament* 1981, 207–77.

Lengherand, Georges. 1861. *Voyage de Georges Lengherand, Mayeur de Mons en Haynaut, à Venise, Rome, Jérusalem, Mont Sinaï & le Kayre, 1485–1486*. Edited by Godefroy Ménilglaise. Mons: Masquillier and Dequesne.

Leopold, Antony. 2000. *How to Recover the Holy Land: The Crusade Proposals of the Late Thirteenth and Early Fourteenth Centuries*. Aldershot, UK: Ashgate.

Leptschy, A. L. 1970. "Tholomacii not tholomarii." *Italian Studies* 25:79–80.

Le voyage de la saincte cyté de Hiérusalem: Avec la description des lieux, portz, villes, citez et aultres passaiges fait l'an mil quatre cens quatre vingtz, estant le siège du grant Turc à Rhodes et régnant en France Loys unziesme de ce nom. 1882. Edited by M. Ch. Schefer. Paris: E. Leroux.

Lewis, Bernard. 2004. *From Babel to Dragomans: Interpreting the Middle East*. Oxford: Oxford University Press.

Liétard-Rouzé, Anne Marie, ed. 2010. *Messire Gilles de Chin, natif de Tournesis*. Lille: Presses universitaires du Septentrion.

Lindberg, David C., ed. 1978. *Science in the Middle Ages*. Chicago: University of Chicago Press.

Lindner, Arthur. 1912. *Der Breslauer Froissart: Festschrift des Vereins für Geschichte der bildenden Künste zu Breslau, zum fünfzigjahrigen Jubilaeum verfasst im Auftrage des Vereins*. Berlin: Kommissions-Verlag von Meisenbach.

Lindquist, Johan. 2015. "Brokers and Brokerage, Anthropology Of." In *International Encyclopedia of the Social and Behavioral Sciences*, 2nd ed., edited by James D. Wright, 870–74. Amsterdam, Netherlands: Elsevier.

Lorée, Denis. 2012. "Édition commentée du *Secret des Secrets* du Pseudo-Aristote." PhD diss, Université Rennes 2.

Lublinski-Bodenham, Henry. 1978. "The Interpreter or Interpreters in Froissart's Account of the Siege of Mahdia (1390)." *Romanische Forschungen* 90:254–59.

Luce, Siméon, ed. 1862. *Chronique Des Quatre Premiers Valois (1327–1393)*. Paris: V. J. Renouard.

Llull, Ramon. 1927. "Liber de acquisitione Terrae Sanctae." Edited by P. E. Longpré. *Criterion* 3:265–78.

————. 1954. "Quomodo Terra Sancta recuperari potest / Tractatus de modo convertendi infideles." In *Beati Magistri R. Lulli opera latina*, vol. 3, edited by J. Rambaud-Buhot, 93–112. Palma de Mallorca: Gráficas Miramar.

————. 1975. *Liber natalis*. Vol. 7 of *Raimundi Lulli Opera Latina*, edited by Hermogenes Harada. Corpus Christianorum Continuatio Mediaeualis 32. Turnhout: Brepols.

————. 1981. "Liber de fine." In *Raimundi Lulli Opera Latina*, vol. 9, edited by Aloisius Madre, 250–91. Corpus Christianorum Continuatio Mediaeualis 35. Turnhout: Brepols.

————. 2010. *A Contemporary Life [Vita coaetanea]*. Edited and translated by Anthony Bonner. Woodbridge, UK: Tamesis.

Lusignan, Serge. 1987. *Parler vulgairement: Les intellectuels et la langue française aux XIIIe et XIVe siècles*. 2nd ed. Paris: Vrin.

Machaut, Guillaume de. 1877. *La Prise d'Alexandrie, ou Chronique du roi Pierre Ier de Lusignan*. Edited by Louis de Mas Latrie. Geneva: Droz.

———. 1988. *The Judgment of the King of Navarre*. Edited and translated by R. Barton Palmer. New York: Garland.

———. 2002. *La Prise d'Alixandre*. Edited and translated by R. Barton Palmer. New York: Routledge.

Maddox, Donald, and Sara Sturm-Maddox, eds. 1998. *Froissart across the Genres*. Gainesville: University Press of Florida.

———, eds. 2002. *The Medieval French Alexander*. Albany: State University of New York Press.

Makhairas, Leontios. 1932. *Recital concerning the Sweet Land of Cyprus*. Edited by R. M. Dawkins. Oxford, UK: Clarendon.

Mallette, Karla. 2021. *Lives of the Great Languages: Arabic and Latin in the Medieval Mediterranean*. Chicago: University of Chicago Press.

Mandeville, Jean de [John]. 2000. *Le Livre des merveilles du monde*. Edited by Christiane Deluz. Paris: CNRS Éditions.

———. 2011. *The Book of John Mandeville with Related Texts*. Translated by Iain Macleod Higgins. Indianapolis: Hackett.

Manning, Patrick, and Abigail Owen. 2018. *Knowledge in Translation: Global Patterns of Scientific Exchange, 1000–1800 CE*. Pittsburgh: University of Pittsburgh Press.

Marchal, Matthieu. 2013. *Histoire de Gérard de Nevers: Mise en prose du "Roman de la Violette" de Gerbert de Montreuil*. Villeneuve d'Ascq: Presses universitaires du Septentrion.

———. 2016. "Voyages et conflits militaires au Proche-Orient dans la mise en prose bourguignonne de *Florient et Octavien*." In *Pays bourguignons et Orient: Diplomatie, conflits, pélerinages, échanges (XIVe–XVIe siècles)*, 145–59. Publications du Centre Européen d'Etudes Bourguignonnes. Turnhout: Brepols.

———. 2017. "La réception de *l'Histoire de Gérard de Nevers* dans les imprimés du XVIᵉ siècle." In Cifarelli et al. 2017, 225–42.

Marchandisse, Alain. 2006. "Jean de Wavrin, un chroniqueur entre Bourgogne et Angleterre, et ses homologues bourguignons face à la Guerre des deux roses." *Le Moyen Age* 3:507–27.

Marie de France. 1966. "Prologue." In *Les lais de Marie de France*, edited by Jean Rychner, 1–3. Paris: Honoré Champion.

Martens, Maximiliaan P. J. 1992. *Lodewijk van Gruuthuse: Mecenas en Europees Diplomaat, ca. 1427–1492*. Bruges: Stichting Kunstboek.

Martoni, Nicolas de. 1895. "Relation du pèlerinage à Jerusalem de Nicolas de Martoni, notaire italien (1394–95)." Edited by Léon le Grand. *Revue de l'Orient latin* 3:566–669.

Mas Latrie, Louis de. 1877. "Préface." In Machaut 1877, vii–xxxvii.

Mastnak, Tomaž. 2002. *Crusading Peace: Christendom, the Muslim World, and Western Political Order*. Berkeley: University of California Press.

Matar, N. I. 1999. *Turks, Moors and Englishmen in the Age of Discovery*. New York: Columbia University Press.

Mediano, Fernando Rodriguez, and Mercedes García-Arenal. 2013. *The Orient in Spain: Converted Muslims, the Forged Lead Books of Granada, and the Rise of Orientalism*. Leiden: Brill.

Meyer, Paul. 1883. "Les neuf preux." *Bulletin de la Société des anciens textes français* 9:45–54.

McGrady, Deborah L. 2006. *Controlling Readers: Guillaume de Machaut and His Late Medieval Audience*. Toronto: University of Toronto Press.

———. 2012. "Machaut and His Material Legacy." In McGrady and Bain 2012, 361–85.

———. 2019. *The Writer's Gift or the Patron's Pleasure? The Literary Economy in Late Medieval France*. Toronto: University of Toronto Press.

McGrady, Deborah L., and Jennifer Bain, eds. 2012. *A Companion to Guillaume de Machaut: An Interdisciplinary Approach to the Master*. Boston: Brill.

McKendrick, Scot. 1990. "*La grande histoire Cesar* and the Manuscripts of Edward IV." In *English Manuscript Studies 1100–1700*, vol. 2, edited by Peter Beal and Jeremy Griffiths, 109–38. Oxford: Blackwell.

———. 1994. "*Romuléon* and Edward IV." In *England and the Fifteenth Century: Proceedings of the 1992 Harlaxton Symposium*, edited by Nicholas Rogers, 149–66. Stamford, UK: Paul Watkins.

———. 1996. *The History of Alexander the Great: An Illuminated Manuscript of Vasco da Lucena's French Translation of the Ancient Text by Quintus Curtius Rufus*. Los Angeles: J. Paul Getty Museum.

———. 2012. "Charles the Bold and Romuléon: Reception, Loss, and Infuence." In *Kunst und KulturTransfer zur Zeit Karls des Kühnen*, edited by Gramaccini Norberto and Marc Carel Schurr, 59–84. Bern: Peter Lang.

Medeiros, Marie Thérèse de. 2003. *Hommes, terres et histoire des confins: Les marges méridionales et orientales de la chrétienté dans les Chroniques de Froissart*. Paris: Honoré Champion.

Meiss, Millard. 1963. "French and Italian Variations on an Early Fifteenth-Century Theme: St. Jerome in His Study." In *Essais en l'honneur de Jean Porcher: Études sur les manuscrits à peintures*, edited by Otto Pächt, 147–70. Paris: Gazette des Beaux-Arts.

"Memoria." 2008. In Paviot 2008, 235–79.

Merceron, Jacques. 1998. *Le Message et sa fiction: La communication par messager dans la littérature française des XIIe et XIIIe siècles*. Berkeley: University of California Press.

Mérigoux, J.-M., ed. 1986. "L'ouvrage d'un frère prêcheur florentin en Orient à la fin du XIIIᵉ siècle." *Memorie domenicane* 17:3–144.

Meschini, Marco. 2014. "Penser la croisade après la chute de Jerusalem (1187): Le *De re militari et triplici via peregrinationis ierosolimitane* de Radulfus Niger." In *Les projets de croisade: Géostratégie et diplomatie européenne du XIVe au XVIIe siècle*, edited by Jacques Paviot, 31–59. Toulouse: Presses universitaires du Mirail.

Meyvaert, Paul. 1980. "An Unknown Letter of Hulagu, Il-Khan of Persia, to King Louis IX of France." *Viator* 11:246–61.

Mézières, Philippe de. 1954. *The Life of Saint Peter Thomas by Philippe de Mézières: Edited from Hitherto Unpublished Manuscripts*. Edited by Joachim Smet. Rome: Institutum Carmelitanum.

———. 1969. *Le songe du Vieil Pelerin*. Edited by George William Coopland. 2 vols. London: Cambridge University Press.

———. 2008. *Une epistre lamentable et consolatoire: Adressée en 1397 à Philippe le Hardi, duc de Bourgogne, sur la défaite de Nicopolis, 1396*. Edited by Philippe Contamine and Jacques Paviot. Paris: Société de l'Histoire de France.

Miklavcic, Alessandra, and LeBlanc, Marie Nathalie. 2014. "Culture Brokers, Clinically Applied Ethnography, and Cultural Mediation." In *Cultural Consultation Encountering the Other in Mental Health Care*, edited by Laurence J. Kirmayer, Jaswant Guzder, and Cécile Rousseau, 115–37. New York: Springer New York.

Miller, Marie-Hélène. 2019. "Nicole Oresme's Cultural *Translatio* in Question." *Digital Philology* 7:139–60.

Minnis, A. J. 2010. *Medieval Theory of Authorship: Scholastic Literary Attitudes in the Later Middle Ages.* 1984. 2nd ed. Philadelphia: University of Pennsylvania Press.

Minois, Georges. 2015. *Charles le Téméraire.* Paris: Perrin.

Miović, Vesna. 2014. "Dubrovački mladići jezika: Studenti osmansko-turskoga u vrijeme Dubrovačke Republike." *Književna smotra* 46:137–46.

Molay, Jacques de. 2007. "Enquête pontificale sur l'opportunité de la fusion des deux ordres des Templiers et des Hospitaliers: Réponse de Jacques de Molay (1306–1307)." 1923. In *Le Dossier de l'affaire des Templiers*, edited by Georges Lizerand, 2–15. Paris: Les Belles Lettres.

———. 2008. "Conseil sur le saint passage (1306)." In Paviot 2008, 183–88.

Monfrin, Jacques. 1963. "Humanisme et traductions au Moyen Âge." *Journal des savants*, 61–90.

———. 1964. "Les traducteurs et leur public au Moyen Âge." *Journal des savants*, 5–20.

Moodey, Elizabeth J. 2012. *Illuminated Crusader Histories for Philip the Good of Burgundy.* Turnhout: Brepols.

Moore, Megan. 2014. "Introduction." In *Exchanges in Exoticism: Cross-Cultural Marriage and the Making of the Mediterranean in Old French Romance*, 3–19. Toronto: University of Toronto Press.

Morato, Nicola, and Dirk Schoenaers. 2018. *Medieval Francophone Literary Culture Outside France: Studies in the Moving Word.* Turnhout, Belgium: Brepols.

Morgan, Nigel, Stella Panayotova, et al. 2009. *A Catalogue of Western Book Illumination in the Fitzwilliam Museum and the Cambridge Colleges.* Pt. 1, vol. 2, *The Meuse Region, Southern Netherlands.* Turnout: Harvey Miller.

Morosini, Roberta. 2020. *Il mare salato: Il Mediterraneo di Dante, Petrarca e Boccaccio.* Rome: Viella.

Morreale, Laura, and Nicholas Paul, eds. 2018. *The French of Outremer: Communities and Communications in the Crusading Mediterranean.* New York: Fordham University Press.

Morrison, Elizabeth. 2015. "The Genius of Visual Narrative." In Morrison and Stahuljak 2015, 103–39.

———. 2023. "None Touches It: The Library of Anthony of Burgundy." In *Collectors, Commissioners, Curators: Studies in Medieval Art for Stephen N. Fliegel*, edited by Elina Gertsman, 81–106. Boston: Medieval Institute Publications.

Morrison, Elizabeth, and Anne D. Hedeman. 2010. *Imagining the Past in France: History in Manuscript Painting, 1250–1500.* Exh. cat. Los Angeles: J. Paul Getty Museum.

Morrison, Elizabeth, and Zrinka Stahuljak. 2015. *The Adventures of Gillion de Trazegnies: Chivalry and Romance in the Medieval East.* Los Angeles: J. Paul Getty Museum.

Mufti, Amir. 2016. *Forget English! Orientalisms and World Literatures.* Cambridge, MA: Harvard University Press.

Munday, Jeremy, ed. 2007. *Translation as Intervention*. New York: Continuum.

Naber, Antoinette. 1987. "Jean de Wavrin, un bibliophile du quinzième siècle." *Revue du Nord* 59:281–93.

———. 1990a. "Les goûts littéraires d'un bibliophile de la cour de Bourgogne." In *Courtly Literature: Culture and Context*, edited by Keith Busby and Erik Kooper, 459–64. Amsterdam: John Benjamins.

———. 1990b. "Les manuscrits d'un bibliophile bourguignon du XV⁰ siècle, Jean de Wavrin." *Revue du Nord* 72:23–48.

Nancy, Jean-Luc. 2014. *La communauté désavouée*. Paris: Éditions Galilée.

———. 2016. *The Disavowed Community*. Translated by Philip Armstrong. New York: Fordham University Press.

Naudet, Valérie. 2005. "Introduction." In *Guérin le Loherain*, edited by V. Naudet, 5–46. Aix-en-Provence: Publications de l'Université de Provence.

Nesvig, Martin. 2012. "Spanish Men, Indigenous Language, and Informal Interpreters in Postcontact Mexico." *Ethnohistory* 59:739–64.

Newett, M. Margaret. 1907. "Introduction." In *Canon Pietro Casola's Pilgrimage to Jerusalem in the Year 1494*, edited by Margaret Newett, 1–113. Manchester: Manchester University Press.

Nicolaou-Konnari, Angel. 2011. "Apologists or Critics? The Reign of Peter I of Lusignan (1359–1369) Viewed by Philippe de Mézières (1327–1405) and Leontios Makhairas (ca. 1360/80–after 1432)." In Blumenfeld-Kosinski and Petkov 2011b, 451–73.

Nogaret, G. de. 1862. "Que sunt advertenda pro passagio ultramarino et que sunt petenda a papa pro prosecutione negocii." Edited by Gustave Dugat. *Notices et extraits des manuscrits de la Bibliothèque impériale et autres bibliothèques* 20:199–205.

Nunn, George E. 1935. "The Imago Mundi and Columbus." *American Historical Review* 40, no. 4:646–61.

Nuttall, Paula. 2004. *From Flanders to Florence: The Impact of Netherlandish Painting, 1400–1500*. New Haven, CT: Yale University Press.

———. 2013. *Face to Face: Flanders, Florence, and Renaissance Painting*. San Marino, CA: Huntington Library, Art Collections, and Botanical Gardens.

"The Opinion of One Urging the King of France to Acquire the Kingdom of Jerusalem and Cyprus for the Second of His Sons, and on the Invasion of the Kingdom of Egypt." 1956. In P. Dubois 1956, 199–207.

"Oppinio cujusdam suadentis regi Francie ut regnum Jerosolimitanum et Cipri acquireret pro altero filiorum suorum, ac de invasione regni Egipti." 1891. In Langlois 1891, 131–40.

Oresme, Nicole. 1940. *Le livre de Éthiques d'Aristote: Published from the Text of Ms. 2902, Bibliothèque royale de Belgique, with a Critical Introduction and Notes*. Edited by Albert Douglas Menut. New York: Stechert.

———. 2013. " 'Le Prologue du translateur' des *Éthiques* et des *Politiques* d'Aristote par Nicole Oresme (1370–1374)." Edited by Elisabetta Barale. In *Corpus Eve* (online resource), *Éditions de textes ou présentations de documents liés au vernaculaire*. https://journals.openedition.org/eve/643?lang=en.

Österreichische Nationalbibliothek (National Library of Austria). n.d. Vienna. http://data.onb.ac.at/rec/AL00166634.

Pächt, Otto, Ulrike Jenni, and Dagmar Thoss. 1983. *Die illuminierten Handschriften und Inkunabeln der Österreichischen Nationalbibliothek: Flämische Schüle I*. Vienna: Verlag der Österreichischen Akademie der Wissenschaften.

Palmer, Barton, R. 2002. "Introduction." In Machaut 2002, 1–37.

Palmer, Jerry. 2007. "Interpreting and Translation for Western Media in Iraq." In *Translating and Interpreting Conflict*, edited by Myriam Salama-Carr, 13–28. New York: Rodopi.

Palmer, Jerry, and Victoria Fontan. 2007. "'Our Ears and Our Eyes': Journalists and Fixers in Iraq." *Journalism* 8:5–24.

Les trois fils de rois. 2001. Edited by Giovanni Palumbo. Paris: H. Champion.

Paris, Gaston. 1881. "Études sur les romans de la table ronde." *Romania* 10:465–96.

———. 1883. "Études sur les romans de la table ronde: Lancelot du Lac." *Romania* 12:459–534.

———. 1885. "*La chanson de Roland* et la nationalité française: Leçon d'ouverture au Collège de France, le 8 décembre 1870." In *La poésie du Moyen Âge*, 1:87–118. Paris: Hachette.

Pastoureau, Michel. 1996. "Un nouvel ordre de chevalerie." In Cockshaw 1996, 65–66.

———. 2009. *L'art héraldique au Moyen Âge*. Paris: Seuil.

Paviot, Jacques. 1995. *Politique navale des ducs de Bourgogne, 1384–1482*. Villeneuve-d'Ascq: Presses Universitaires de Lille.

———. 1996. "L'Ordre de la Toison d'or et la Croisade." In Cockshaw 1996, 71–74.

———. 1999. "David Aubert à la cour de Bourgogne." In Quéruel 1999, 11–18.

———. 2003. *Les ducs de Bourgogne, la croisade et l'Orient: Fin XIVe siècle–XVe siècle*. Paris: Presses de l'Université de Paris–Sorbonne.

———, ed. 2008. *Projets de croisade (v. 1290–v. 1330)*. Paris: Académie des inscriptions et belles-lettres.

———. 2009. "Mentions de livres, d'auteurs, de copistes, d'enlumineurs, de miniaturistes ('historieurs') et de libraires dans les comptes généraux du duc de Bourgogne Philippe le Bon (1419–1467)." In *Miscellanea in memoriam Pierre Cockshaw, 1938–2008: Aspects de la vie culturelle dans les Pays-Bas méridionaux, XIVe–XVIIIe siècle,* edited by Frank Daelemans and Ann Kelders, 2:413–47. Brussels: Bibliothèque royale de Belgique.

Payen, M. 1966–67. *Les origines de la courtoisie dans la littérature française médiévale.* 2 vols. Paris: Centre de documentation universitaire.

Pegolotti, Francesco Balducci. 1970. *La pratica della mercatura*. 1936. Edited by Allan Evans. New York: Kraus Reprint.

Pelliot, P. 1931–32. "Les Mongols et la Papauté (chapitre 2)." *Revue de l'Orient chrétien* 28:3–84.

Perdrizet, Paul. 1907. "Jean Miélot, l'un des traducteurs de Philippe le Bon." In *Revue d'Histoire littéraire de la France* 14, no. 3:472–82.

Petit, Aimé, and François Suard, eds. 1994. *Le livre des amours du chastellain de Coucy et de la dame de Fayel, version en prose du XVe siècle*. Lille: Presses universitaires de Lille.

Phillips, Kim M. 2014. *Before Orientalism: Asian Peoples and Cultures in European Travel Writing, 1245–1510*. Philadelphia: University of Pennsylvania Press.

Piloti, Emmanuel. 1958. *Traité d'Emmanuel Piloti sur le passage en Terre Sainte (1420)*. Edited by Pierre-Herman Dopp. Louvain: Éditions E. Nauwelaerts; Paris: Béatrice-Nauwelaerts.

Pinkernell, Gert, ed. 1971. Raoul Lefèvre, *L'Histoire de Jason, ein Roman aus dem fünfzehnten Jahrhundert*. Frankfurt a/M: Athenäum.

———. 1973. "Die Handschrift B.N., MS Fr. 331 von Raoul Lefevres *Histoire de Jason und das Wirken des Miniaturisten Lieven van Lathem in Brügge*." *Scriptorium* 27, no. 2:295–301.

Pleij, Herman. 2010. "Printing as a Long-Term Revolution." In Wijsman 2010a, 287–307.

Plumley, Yolanda. 2013. *The Art of Grafted Song: Citation and Allusion in the Age of Machaut*. New York: Oxford University Press.

Poggibonsi, Niccolò da. 1945a. *Libro d'oltramare. 1346–50*. Edited by A. Bacchi della Lega and P. B. Bagatti. Jérusalem: Tipografia dei PP. Francescani.

———. 1945b. *A Voyage beyond the Seas (1346–1350)*. Translated by Theophilus Bellorini and Eugene Hoade, Jerusalem: Franciscan.

Poirion, Daniel. 1965. *Le Poète et le prince: L'évolution du lyrisme courtois de Guillaume de Machaut à Charles d'Orléans*. Paris: Presses universitaires de France.

Polo, Marco. 1982. *Milione: Il Milione nelle redazioni toscana e franco-italiana*. Edited by Gabriella Ronchi. Milan, Mondadori.

———. 2016. *The Description of the World*. Edited and translated by Sharon Kinoshita. Indianapolis: Hackett.

Potin, Yann. 2020. *Trésor, écrits, pouvoirs: Archives et bibliothèques d'État en France à la fin du Moyen Âge*. Paris: CNRS.

Prawer, Joshua. 1986. "The Roots of Medieval Colonialism." In *The Meeting of Two Worlds: Cultural Exchange between East and West during the Period of the Crusades*, edited by Vladimir P. Goss, 23–38. Kalamazoo, MI: Medieval Institute.

———. 1992. "The Crusading Kingdom of Jerusalem: The First European Colonial Society? A Symposium." In *The Horns of Hattin*, edited by B. Z. Kedar, 340–67. London: Variorum; Jerusalem: Israel Exploration Society.

Pseudo-Aristotle. n.d. *Le Secret des secrets*. http://www.sites.univ-rennes2.fr/celam /cetm/S2.htm#4. Accessed October 26, 2015.

Quéruel, Danielle. 1997. *L'istoire de tres vaillans princez monseigneur Jehan d'Avennes*. Villeneuve-d'Ascq: Presses universitaires du Septentrion.

———, ed. 1999. *Les manuscrits de David Aubert*. Paris: Presses de l'Université de Paris–Sorbonne.

———. 2000a. "Au carrefour de la chronique et du roman: Évocations et dénominations de la ville dans les récits bourguignons de la fin du Moyen Âge." *Revue belge de philologie et d'histoire* 78:393–407.

———. 2000b. "Pourquoi partir? Une typologie des voyages dans quelques romans de la fin du Moyen Âge." In *Guerres, voyages et quêtes au Moyen Âge: Mélanges offerts à Jean-Claude Faucon*, edited by Alain Labbé, Daniel W. Lacroix, and Danielle Quéruel. Paris: Honoré Champion.

———. 2006. "Du mécénat au plaisir de lire: L'exemple de quelques seigneurs bourguignons et en particulier de Louis de la Gruthuyse." *Cahiers du léopard d'or* 11:197–211.

Rafael, Vincente L. 2015. "Translation in Wartime." *Public Culture* 19:239–46.

Raj, Kapil. 2016. "Go-Betweens, Travelers, and Cultural Translators." In *A Companion to the History of Science*, edited by Bernard Lightman, 39–57. Chichester, UK: Wiley and Sons.

Rajohnson, Matthieu. 2014. "Les guides de Terre Sainte au Moyen Âge: Outils normatifs d'un voyage édifiant." *Hypothèses* 17:37–45.

Reboldi, Antonio de. 1906–27. "Itinerarium ad Sepulcrum Domini (1327) et ad Montem Sinai (1330)." In Golubovich 1906–27, 3:326–42.

Régnier-Bohler, Danielle. 1994. Édition et étude critique de 'L'histoire d'Olivier de Castille et Artus d'Algarbe.'" PhD diss., Université de Paris IV-Sorbonne.

Ribémont, Bernard. 1999. "Jean Corbechon, un traducteur encyclopédiste au XIVᵉ siècle." *Cahiers de recherches médiévales* 6:75–98.

———. 2002. "Une vision de l'Orient au XIVᵉ siècle: *La Prise d'Alexandrie* de Guillaume de Machaut." *Cahiers de recherches médiévales* 9:249–61.

Riccoldo of Monte Croce. 1967. "Libellus ad nationes orientales." In "Ricoldiana: Notes sur les oeuvres de Ricoldo da Montecroce," edited by A. Dondaine. *Archivum fratrum praedicatorum* 37:119–79.

———. 1997. *Pérégrination en Terre dite sainte et au Proche-Orient: Lettres sur la chute de Saint-Jean-d'Acre.* Edited and translated by René Kappler. Paris: H. Champion.

Ricœur, Paul. 2006. *On Translation,* translated by Eileen Brennan. London: Routledge, 2006.

Richard, Jean. 1965. "Introduction." In Simon de Saint-Quentin, *Histoire des Tartares* [*Historia Tartarorum*], edited by Jean Richard, 7–22. Documents relatifs à l'histoire des croisades publiés par l'Académie des inscriptions et belles-lettres 8. Paris: Paul Geuthner.

———. 1976. "*L'enseignement des langues orientales* en Occident au Moven Âge." *Revue des études islamiques* 46:149–64.

———. 1984. "Les relations de pèlerinages au Moyen Âge et les motivations de leurs auteurs." In *Wallfahrt kennt keine Grenzen,* edited by Lenz Kriss-Rettenbeck and Gerda Möhler, 143–53. Munich: Schnell und Steiner.

Rochechouart, Louis de. 1893. "Journal de voyage à Jérusalem de Louis de Rochechouart (1461)." Edited by C. Couderc. *Revue de l'Orient latin* 1:168–274.

Roncaglia, M. 1953. "I *Frati Minori e* lo *studio* delle lingue orientali nel secolo XIII." *Studi Francescani* 50:169–84.

Ross, David A. J. 1988. *Alexander historiatus: A Guide to Medieval Illustrated Alexander Literature.* 1963. Frankfurt am Main: Athenäum Verlag.

Ross, Elizabeth. 2014. *Picturing Experience in the Early Printed Book: Breydenbach's Peregrinatio from Venice to Jerusalem.* University Park: Pennsylvania State University Press.

Rothman, E. Natalie. 2012. *Brokering Empire: Trans-imperial Subjects between Venice and Istanbul.* Ithaca, NY: Cornell University Press.

———. 2021. *The Dragoman Renaissance: Diplomatic Interpreters and the Routes of Orientalism.* Ithaca, NY: Cornell University Press.

Rouse, Richard H., and Mary A. Rouse. 2000. *Manuscripts and Their Makers: Commercial Book Producers in Medieval Paris, 1200–1500.* 2 vols. Turnhout: Harvey Miller.

Roussineau, Gilles. 2012. "Réflexions sur la genèse de Perceforest." In Ferlampin-Acher 2012b, 255–67.

Rouxpetel, Camille. 2015a. *Occident au miroir de l'Orient chrétien: Cilicie, Syrie, Palestine et Égypte (XIIe–XIVe siècle).* Rome: École française de Rome.

———. 2015b. "Riccoldo da Monte Croce's Mission towards the Nestorians and the Jacobites (1288–ca. 1300)." *Medieval Encounters* 21, nos. 2–3:250–68.

———. 2016a. "Dominicans and East Christians: Missionary Method and Specific Skills (13th–14th Centuries)." In *Quis Est Qui Ligno Pugnat? Missionaries and Evangelization in Late Antique and Medieval Europe (4th–13th Centuries),* edited by Emanuele Piazza, 367–76. Verona: Alteritas.

———. 2016b. "Redécouvrir l'Orient après la conquête mamelouke: Chrétiens, Juifs et Musulmans dans deux récits des années 1330, *La Descriptio Terrae Sanctae* de Fra Giovanni di Fedanzola da Perugia et *Le Liber Peregrinationis* de Jacques de Vérone." *Revue des sciences religieuses* 90, no. 4:539–60.

———. 2018. "Les Arméniens, la 'nation' préférée des Latins partis pour la Terre Sainte entre XIIᵉ et XIIIᵉ siècles?" *Mélanges de l'École française de Rome—Moyen Âge* 130, no. 1:41–51.

Rowley, Anthony, and Fabrice d'Almeida. 2011. *Et si on refaisait l'histoire?* Rev. ed. Paris: Odile Jacob.

Royal Manuscripts: The Genius of Illumination. 2011. Edited by Scot McKendrick, John Lowden, and Kathleen Doyle. London: British Library.

Rubruck, William of. 2009. *The Mission of Friar William of Rubruck: His Journey to the Court of the Great Khan Möngke, 1253–1255.* 1990. Translated by Peter Jackson. Indianapolis: Hackett.

———. 1929. "Itinerarium Guillelmus de Rubruc." In *Sinica franciscana, Itinera et relationes fratrum minorum saeculi XIII et XIV*, edited by Anastasius van den Wyngaert, 1:164–332. Firenze: Quaracchi.

Ruelle, Pierre. 1985. *Le Dialogue des créatures: Traduction par Colart Mansion (1482) du Dialogus creaturarum (XIVe siècle).* Brussels: Académie royale de Belgique.

Rychner, Jean. 1963. "Observations sur la traduction de Tite-Live par Pierre Bersuire (1354–1356)." *Journal des Savants* 4, no. 1:242–67.

Saenger, Paul. 1975. "Colard Mansion and the Evolution of the Printed Book." *Library Quarterly: Information, Community, Policy* 45, no. 4:405–18.

Saint-Quentin, Simon de. 1965. *Histoire des Tartares* [*Historia Tartarorum*]. Edited by Jean Richard. Documents relatifs à l'histoire des croisades publiés par l'Académie des inscriptions et belles-lettres 8. Paris: Paul Geuthner.

Samoyault, Tiphane. 2020. *Traduction et violence.* Paris: Le Seuil.

Sanudo Torsello, Marino. 1611. *Liber secretorum fidelium crucis super Terrae Sanctae recuperatione et conservation.* In *Gesta Dei per Francos*, ed. J. Bongars, 2 vols.

———. 2011. *The Book of the Secrets of the Faithful of the Cross.* Translated by Peter Lock. Burlington, VT: Ashgate.

Schaffer, Simon, Lissa Roberts, Kapil Raj, and James Delbourgo, eds. 2009a. *The Brokered World: Go-Betweens and Global Intelligence, 1770–1820.* Sagamore Beach, MA: Science History.

———. 2009b. "Introduction." In Schaffer et al. 2009a, ix–xxxviii.

Schandel, Pascal. 1997. "Le Maitre de Wavrin et les miniaturistes Lillois a l'époque de Philippe le Bon et de Charles le Téméraire." PhD diss., Université des sciences humaines de Strasbourg.

———. 2002–3. "*Histoire des seigneurs de Gavre.*" *Art de l'Enluminure* 3 (December–February): 4–16.

Schapiro, Meyer. 1973. *Words and Pictures: On the Literal and the Symbolic in the Illustration of a Text.* The Hague: Mouton.

Schein, Sylvia. 1991. *Fideles Crucis: The Papacy, the West, and the Recovery of the Holy Land, 1274–1314.* Oxford, UK: Clarendon.

Schnerb, Bertrand. 2005. *L'État bourguignon, 1363–1477.* 1999. Paris: Perrin.

Schoysman, Anne. 2006. "Le statut des auteurs 'compilés' par Jean Miélot." In *L'écrit et le manuscrit à la fin du Moyen Âge*, edited by Tania van Hemelryck and Céline van Hoorebeeck, with Olivier Delsaux and Marie Jennequin, 303–14. Turnhout, Brepols.

Schroeder, Horst. 1971. *Der Topos der Nine Worthies in Literatur und bildender Kunst.* Göttingen: Vandenhoeck and Ruprecht.

Schwaller, John F. 2012. "The Expansion of Nahuatl as a Lingua Franca among Priests in Sixteenth-Century Mexico." *Ethnohistory* 59:675–90.

Schwaller, Robert C. 2012. "The Importance of Mestizos and Mulatos as Bilingual Intermediaries in Sixteenth-Century New Spain." *Ethnohistory* 59:713–38.

Scott, Margaret. 1980. *Late Gothic Europe, 1400–1500.* Atlantic Highlands, NJ: Humanities.

Seigneuret, Jean-Charles, ed. 1966. *Le roman du comte d'Artois.* Geneva: Droz.

Seth, Vanita. 2020. "The Origins of Racism: A Critique of the History of Ideas." *History and Theory* 59:343–36.

Sherman, Claire. 1995. *Imaging Aristotle: Verbal and Visual Representation in Fourteenth-Century France.* Berkeley: University of California Press.

Shih, Shu-Mei. 2015. "World Studies and Relational Comparison." *PMLA* 130:430–38.

Sigoli, Simone. 1944. "Viaggio al Monte Sinai di Simone Sigoli." In *Viaggi in Terrasanta di Leonardo Frescobaldi e Simone Sigoli,* edited by Cesare Angelini, 171–269. Florence: F. Le Monnier.

———. 1948. "Pilgrimage of Simone Sigoli to the Holy Land." In *Visit to the Holy Places of Egypt, Sinai, Palestine, and Syria in 1384, by Frescobaldi, Gucci and Sigoli,* translated by Theophilus Bellorini and Eugene Hoade, 163–201. Jerusalem: Franciscan.

Sinor, Denis. 1982. "Interpreters in Medieval Inner Asia." *Asian and African Studies* 16:293–320.

———. 1995. "Languages and Cultural Interchange along the Silk Roads." *Diogenes* 171, no. 43:1–13.

Small, Graeme. 2000. "Les Chroniques de Hainaut et les projets d'historiographie régionale en langue française à la cour de Bourgogne." In Cockshaw 2000b, 17–22.

———. 2006. "Of Burgundian Dukes, Counts, Saints and Kings (14 C.E.–c. 1500)." In *The Ideology of Burgundy: The Promotion of National Consciousness: 1364–1565,* edited by D'Arcy Jonathan Dacre Boulton and Jan R. Veenstra, 151–94. Leiden: Brill.

Sola, Emilio. 1988. *Un Mediterráneo de piratas: Corsarios, renegados y cautivos.* Madrid: Tecnos.

Soudavar, Abolala. 2008. *Decoding Old Masters: Patrons, Princes and Enigmatic Paintings of the 15th Century.* London: I. B. Tauris.

Soukupová, Věra. 2021. *La construction de la réalité historique chez Jean Froissart: L'historien et sa matière.* Paris: Honoré Champion.

Spiegel, Gabrielle M. 1993. *Romancing the Past: The Rise of Vernacular Prose Historiography in Thirteenth-Century France.* Berkeley: University of California Press.

Spoturno, María Laura. 2014. "Revisiting Malinche: A Study of Her Role as an Interpreter." In *Translators, Interpreters, and Cultural Negotiators: Mediating and Communicating Power from the Middle Ages to the Modern Era,* edited by Federico M. Federici and Dario Tessicini, 121–35. New York: Palgrave Macmillan.

Stahuljak, Zrinka. 1999. "The Violence of Neutrality: Translators in and of the War (Croatia, 1991–92)." *College Literature* 26:34–51.

———. 2001. "Jean Froissart's *Chroniques*: *Translatio* and the Impossible Apprenticeship of Neutrality." In *Politics of Translation in the Middle Ages and the Renaissance*, edited by Renate Blumenfeld-Kosinski, Luise von Flotow, and Daniel Russell, 121–42. Ottawa: University of Ottawa Press.

———. 2004. "An Epistemology of Tension: Translation and Multiculturalism." *Translator* 10:33–57.

———. 2005. *Bloodless Genealogies of the French Middle Ages: Translatio, Kinship, and Metaphor*. Gainesville: University Press of Florida.

———. 2006. "Neutrality Affects: Froissart and the Practice of Historiographic Authorship." In *The Medieval Author in Medieval French Literature*, edited by Virginie Greene, 137–56. New York: Palgrave Macmillan.

———. 2010. "War, Translation, Transnationalism: Interpreters in and of the War (Croatia, 1991–1992)." In *Critical Readings in Translation Studies*, edited by Mona Baker, 391–414. New York: Routledge.

———. 2013. *Pornographic Archaeology: Medicine, Medievalism, and the Invention of the French Nation*. Philadelphia: University of Pennsylvania Press.

———. 2015. "A Romance between the East and the West." In Morrison and Stahuljak 2015, 63–101.

———. 2017. "Merlin à Jérusalem: Un traité de croisade pour les rois d'Angleterre." In *Arthur après Arthur: La matière arthurienne tardive en dehors du roman arthurien, de l'intertextualité au phénomène de mode*, edited by Christine Ferlampin-Acher, 491–500. Rennes: Presses universitaires de Rennes.

———. 2019a. "L'empire des livres: Imagination, matière d'Orient, et archive du possible aux Pays-Bas bourguignons." *Tirant* 22:195–205.

———. 2019b. "World Collecting: Patronage, Spoliation, and Forms of Government." In *The Wiley-Blackwell Companion to World Literature*, vol. 2, *600 C.E. to 1450 C.E.*, edited by Christine Chism, general editor Kenneth Segneurie, 1181–89. Oxford: Wiley-Blackwell.

———. 2020a. *Médiéval contemporain: Pour une littérature connectée*. Paris: Éditions Macula.

———. 2020b. Review of Patrick Boucheron with Nicolas Delalande, Florian Mazel, Yann Potin, and Pierre Singaravélou, eds., *France in the World: A New Global History*, English-language editor Stéphane Gerson (Other Press, 2019). *H-Diplo* 22, no. 11 (November): 12–17.

———. 2021a. *Les Fixeurs au Moyen Âge: Histoire et littérature connectées*. Paris: Les Éditions du Seuil.

———. 2021a. "Les langues du voyage: Le roman bourguignon et ses fixeurs méditerranéens." In *Écrire le voyage au temps des ducs de Bourgogne: Actes du colloque international organisé les 19 et 20 octobre 2017 à l'Université du Littoral—Côte d'Opale (Dunkerque)*, edited by Jean Devaux, Matthieu Marchal, and Alexandra Velissariou, 233–41. Burgundica. Turnhout: Brepols.

Stahuljak et al. 2011. Stahuljak, Zrinka, Virginie Greene, Sarah Kay, Sharon Kinoshita, and Peggy McCracken. *Thinking through Chrétien de Troyes*. Cambridge, UK: D. S. Brewer.

Stanegrave, Roger de. 2008. *L'Escarboucle d'armes de la conquête précieuse de la Terre Sainte de promission*." In Paviot 2008, 293–387.

Stein, Robert. 2001. "Burgundian Bureaucracy as a Model for the Low Countries? The *Chambres des comptes* and the Creation of an Administrative Unity." In *Powerbrokers in the Late Middle Ages: The Burgundian Low Countries in a European Context,* edited by Robert Stein, 3–25. Turnhout: Brepols.

———. 2010a. "Introduction." In Stein and Pollmann 2010, 1–18.

———. 2010b. "An Urban Network in the Medieval Low Countries: A Cultural Approach." In Stein and Pollmann 2010, 43–71.

———. 2017. *Magnanimous Dukes and Rising States: The Unification of the Burgundian Netherlands, 1380–1480.* Oxford: Oxford University Press.

Stein, Robert, Anita Boele, and Wim Blockmans. 2010. "Whose Community? The Origin and Development of the Concept of *bonum commune* in Flanders, Brabant and Holland (Twelfth–Fifteenth Century)." In Lecuppre-Desjardins and van Bruaene 2010, 149–69.

Stein, Robert, and Judith Pollmann, eds. 2010. *Networks, Regions and Nations: Shaping Identities in the Low Countries, 1300–1650.* Leiden: Brill.

Stolze, Radegundis. 2012. "The Hermeneutical Approach to Translation." *Vertimo Studijos,* no. 5:30–41.

Stovel, Katherine, and Lynette Shaw. 2012. "Brokerage." *Annual Review of Sociology* 38:139–58.

Strambaldi, Diomedes. 1893. *Chroniques d'Amadi et de Strambaldi.* Edited by René de Mas Latrie. Vol. 2. Paris: Imprimerie nationale.

Straub, Richard E. F. 1986–87. "Contribution à l'étude de l'activité littéraire de David Aubert: Les manuscrits." *Romanica vulgaria: Quaderni* 10–11:233–68.

———. 1995. *David Aubert, escripvain et clerc.* Amsterdam: Rodopi.

———. 1997. "L'activité littéraire de David Aubert." In *Le moyen français: Philologie et linguistique; Approches du texte et du discours; Actes du VIIe colloque international sur le moyen français (Nancy, 5–6–7 septembre 1994),* edited by Bernard Combettes and Simone Monsonégo, 143–50. Paris: Didier Érudition.

Strayer, Joseph R. 1970. *On the Medieval Origins of the Modern State.* Princeton, NJ: Princeton University Press.

Strohm, Paul. 2014. *Chaucer's Tale: 1386 and the Road to Canterbury.* New York: Viking.

Strubel, Armand. 1908. "*Le songe du Vieil Pelerin* et les transformations de l'allégorie au quatorzième siècle." *Perspectives médiévales* 6:54–74.

Stuip, René, ed. 1993. *Histoire des seigneurs de Gavre.* Paris: H. Champion.

Suard, François. 1988. "L'Épopée," in *La Littérature française aux XIVe et XVe siècles,* edited by Daniel Poirion, 161–77, vol. 8:1 of *Grundriss der Romanischen Literaturen des Mittelalters,* ed. Jean Frappier, Martin de Riquer, Aurelio Roncaglia, Hans Robert Jauss und Erich Köhler. Heidelberg: C. Winter Universitätsverlag.

———. 1994. "L'Épopée française tardive (XIVe–XVe s.)." In *Chanson de geste et tradition épique en France au Moyen Âge,* 243–54. Caen: Paradigme.

———. 2005. "La tradition épique française du Moyen Âge au XIXe siècle." Special issue, *Cahiers de recherches médiévales* 12.

Subrahmanyam, Sanjay. 1997. "Connected Histories: Notes towards a Reconfiguration of Early Modern Eurasia." *Modern Asian Studies* 31:735–62.

———. 2011. *Three Ways to Be Alien: Travails and Encounters in the Early Modern World.* Waltham, MA: Brandeis University Press.

Sudheim, Ludolphus von. 1884. "De itinere terre sancta." Edited by G. A. Neumann. *Archives de l'Orient latin* 2:329–76.

Sumption, Jonathan. 1975. *Pilgrimage: An Image of Medieval Religion*. London: Faber and Faber.

Sunderland, Luke, and Thomas Hinton, eds. 2016. "The Medieval Library." Special issue, *French Studies* 70, no. 2.

Sweetser, Franklin P, ed. 1964. *Blancandin et l'Orgueilleuse d'Amour, roman d'aventure du XIIIe siècle*. Genève: Droz.

Tafur, Pero. 1926. *Travels and Adventures, 1435–1439*. Edited and translated by Malcolm Letts. London: G. Routledge.

———. 1995. *Andanças e viajes de un hidalgo español*. Edited by Marcos Jimenez de la Espada. Madrid: Miraguano Ediciones.

Tarnowski, Andrea. 2006. "Material Examples: Philippe de Mézières' Order of the Passion." *Yale French Studies* 110:163–75.

———. 2011. "The Consolations of Writing Allegory: Philippe de Mézières' *Le songe du Vieil Pelerin*." In Blumenfeld-Kosinski and Petkov 2011b, 237–54.

Taylor, Jane H. M. 2012. "Profiter du Perceforest au XVIe siècle: *La Plaisante et amoureuse histoire du Chevalier Doré et de la Pucelle surnommée Cœur d'Acier*." In Ferlampin-Acher 2012b, 355–69.

Tesnière, Marie-Hélène. 2000. "À propos de la traduction de Tite-Live par Pierre Bersuire: Le manuscrit Oxford, Bibliothèque Bodléienne, Rawlinson C 447." *Romania* 118:449–98.

Thiry, Claude, trans. 1995. *Déclaration de tous les hauts faits et glorieuses aventures du duc Philippe de Bourgogne, celui qui se nomme le Grand Duc et le Grand Lion*. In *Splendeurs de la cour de Bourgogne: Récits et chroniques*, edited by Danielle Régnier-Bohler, 749–63. Paris: Robert Laffont.

Timelli, Maria Colombo. 1997. *Le Donat espirituel de Colard Mansion: Etude et édition*. Milan: Istituto Lombardo si Scienze e Lettere.

———. 2004. "Pour une 'défénse et illustration' des titres de chapitres: Analyse d'un corpus de romans mis en prose au XVe siècle." In *Du roman courtois au roman baroque: Actes du colloque des 2–5 juillet 2002*, edited by Emmanuel Bury and Francine Mora, 209–32. Paris: Les Belles Lettres.

———. 2018. "Jean Miélot: Bilan et perspectives." *Carte Romanze* 6:105–20.

———. 2019. " 'Qui tient le moien, il va le seur chemin' (Songe du Viel Pelerin, 1133, 28–29): Les 'proverbes' dans le Songe de Philippe de Mézières." In Blanchard et al. 2019, 31–50.

Timelli et al. 2014. Timelli, Maria, Barbara Ferrari, Anne Schoysman, and François Suard. *Nouveau répertoire de mises en prose (XIVe–XVIe siècle)*. Paris: Classiques Garnier.

Tolan, John V. 2002. *Saracens: Islam in the Medieval European Imagination*. New York: Columbia University Press.

———. 2019. "Ramon de Penyafort's *Responses to Questions concerning Relations between Christians and Saracens*: Critical Edition and Translation." In *Convivencia and Medieval Spain Essays in Honor of Thomas F. Glick*, edited by Mark T. Abate, 159–92. Palgrave Macmillan.

Townsend, Camilla. 2006. *Malintzin's Choices: An Indian Woman in the Conquest of Mexico*. Albuquerque: University of New Mexico Press.

Trivellato, Francesca. 2009. *The Familiarity of Strangers: The Sephardic Diaspora, Livorno, and Cross-Cultural Trade in the Early Modern Period*. New Haven, CT: Yale University Press.

Trouilhet, Julien. 2014. "Les projets de croisade des dominicains d'Orient au XIVᵉ siècle: Autour de Guillaume Adam et Raymond Étienne." In *Les projets de croisade: Géostratégie et diplomatie européenne du XIVe au XVIIe siècle*, edited by Jacques Paviot, 151–81. Toulouse: Presses universitaires du Mirail.

Tyerman, Christopher J. 1982. "Marino Sanudo Torsello and the Lost Crusade: Lobbying in the Fourteenth Century." *Transactions of the Royal Historical Society* 32:57–73.

Tymoczko, Maria. 2000. "Translation and Political Engagement: Activism, Social Change and the Role of Translation in Geopolitical Shifts." *Translator* 6:23–47.

"Un pèlerinage en Terre Sainte et au Sinaï au XVᵉ siècle." 1905. Edited by H. Moranvillé. *Bibliothèque de l'École de chartes* 66:70–106.

Vagnon, Emmanuelle. 2014 "Géographie et stratégies dans les projets de croisade, XIII–XVᵉ siècle." In *Les projets de croisade: Géostratégie et diplomatie européenne du XIVe au XVIIe siècle*, edited by Jacques Paviot, 125–50. Toulouse: Presses universitaires du Mirail.

Vale, Malcolm. 1995. "An Anglo-Burgundian Nobleman and Art Patron: Louis de Bruges, Lord of la Gruthuyse and Earl of Winchester." In *England and the Low Countries in the Late Middle Ages*, edited by Caroline Barron and Nigel Saul, 115–31. New York: St. Martin's.

van Buren, Anne. 1972. "New Evidence for Jean Wauquelin's Activity in the *Chroniques de Hainaut* and for the Date of the Miniatures." *Scriptorium* 26:249–68.

———. 2000. "*Les Chroniques de Hainaut*: Texte, histoire et illustrations." In *Les "Chroniques de Hainaut" ou les ambitions d'un prince bourguignon*, edited by Pierre Cockshaw and Christiane van den Bergen-Pantens, 65–74. Turnhout: Brepols.

———. 2008. "Van Lathem's Costumes." In *Invention: Northern Renaissance Studies in Honor of Molly Faries*, edited by Julien Chapuis, 94–103. Turnhout: Brepols.

———. 2011. *Illuminating Fashion: Dress in the Art of Medieval France and the Netherlands, 1325–1515*. Exh. cat. New York: Morgan Library and Museum.

van den Bergen-Pantens, Christiane. 1993. "Héraldique et bibliophilie: Le cas d'Antoine, Grand Bâtard de Bourgogne (1421–1504)." In *Miscellanea Martin Wittek: Album de codicologie et de paléographie offert à Martin Wittek*, edited by Anny Raman and Eugène Manning, 323–54. Paris: Editions Peeters.

———. 1996. "Antoine, Grand Bâtard de Bourgogne, bibliophile." In Cockshaw 1996, 198–200.

Vanderjagt, A. J. 1981. "Qui sa vertu anoblist: The Concepts of 'Noblesse' and 'Chose Publicque' in Burgundian Political Thought." PhD diss., Groningen University.

Van der Linden, Herman. 1940. *Itinéraires de Philippe le Bon, duc de Bourgogne (1419–1467) et de Charles, comte de Charolais (1433–1467)*. Brussels: Palais des Académies.

Van Elslande, Rudy. 1992. "Lieven van Lathem, een onbekende belangrijke kunstenaar uit de 15de eeuw." *Jaarboek van de Heemkring Scheldeveld* 21:127–69.

Van Praet, Joseph. 1829. *Notice sur Colard Mansion, libraire et imprimeur de la ville de Bruges en Flandre, dans le quinzième siècle*. Paris: de Bure frères.

———. 1831. *Recherches sur Louis de Bruges, seigneur de la Gruthuyse*. Paris: de Bure frères.

Van Steenbergen, Jo. 2003. "The Alexandrian Crusade (1365) and the Mamluk Sources." In *East and West in the Crusader States III: Context, Contacts,*

Confrontations, edited by Krijna Nelly Ciggaar and Herman G. B. Teule, 123–37. Leuven: Uitgeverij Peeters.

Vaughan, Richard. 1969. *John the Fearless: The Growth of Burgundian Power*. London: Longman.

———. 1970. *Philip the Good: The Apogee of Burgundy*. Harlow: Longmans.

———. 1973. *Charles the Bold: The Last Valois Duke of Burgundy*. London: Longmans.

———. 2002. *Philip the Bold: The Formation of the Burgundian State*. 1969. Woodbridge, UK: Boydell.

Veenstra, Jan. 2006. "'Le prince qui se veult faire de nouvel roy': Literature and Ideology of Burgundian Self-Determination." In *The Ideology of Burgundy: The Promotion of National Consciousness; 1364–1565*, edited by D'Arcy Jonathan Dacre Boulton and Jan R. Veenstra, 195–221. Leiden: Brill.

Venuti, Lawrence. 1995. *The Translator's Invisibility: A History of Translation*. New York: Routledge.

———. 2019. *Contra Instrumentalism: A Translation Polemic*. Lincoln: University of Nebraska Press.

Veysseyre, Géraldine. 2008. "Le Livre des propriétés des choses de Jean Corbechon (Livre VI) ou la vulgarisation d'une encyclopédie latine." In *Science Translated: Latin and Vernacular Translations of Scientific Treatises in Medieval Europe*, edited by Michéle Goyens, Pieter de Leemans, and An Smets, 331–58. Leuven: Leuven University Press.

"Via ad terram sanctam" 2008. In Paviot 2008, 171–81.

Vincent, Stephanie, ed. 2010. *Le roman de Gillion de Trazegnies*. Turnhout: Brepols.

Visser-Fuchs, Livia. 2002. "Warwick and Wavrin: Two Case Studies on the Literary Background and Propaganda of Anglo-Burgundian Relations in the Yorkist Period." PhD diss., University College London.

———. 2006. "The Manuscript of the Enseignement de Vraie Noblesse Made for Richard Neville, Earl of Warwick, in 1464." In *Medieval Manuscripts in Transition: Tradition and Creative Recycling*, edited by Geert Claassens and Werner Verbeke, 337–62. Mediaevalia Lovaniensia, 1st ser., 36. Leuven: Leuven University Press.

———. 2018. *History as Pastime: Jean de Wavrin and His Collection of Chronicles of England*. Donnington: Shaun Tyas.

Viveiros de Castro, Eduardo Batalha. 2014. *Cannibal Metaphysics: For a Post-structural Anthropology*. Translated by Peter Skafish. Minneapolis: Univocal.

Vlaamse kunst op perkament: Handschriften en miniaturen te Brugge van de 12de tot de 16de eeuw. 1981. Exh. cat. Bruges: Gruuthusemuseum.

von Harff, Arnold. 1860. *Die pilgerfahrt des ritters Arnold von Harff von Cöln durch Italien, Syrien, Aegypten, Arabien, Aethiopien, Nubien, Palästina, die Türkei, Frankreich und Spanien, wie er sie in den jahren 1496 bis 1499 vollendet, beschrieben und durch zeichnungen erläutert hat*. Edited by E. von Groote. Cologne: J. M. Heberle H. Lempertz.

———. 1946. *The Pilgrimage of Arnold von Harff, Knight, from Cologne through Italy, Syria, Egypt, Arabia, Ethiopia, Nubia, Palestine, Turkey, France, and Spain*. Edited and translated by Malcolm Letts. London: Hakluyt Society.

Wace, 1877. *Roman de Rou*. Edited by Hugo Andresen. 2 vols. Heilbronn: Verlag von Gebr. Henninger.

———. 1999. *Roman de Brut*. Edited by Judith Weiss. Devon: University of Exeter Press.

Walkowitz, Rebecca L. 2015. *Born Translated: The Contemporary Novel in an Age of World Literature (Literature Now)*. New York: Columbia University Press.

Wallace, David. 2016. *Europe: A Literary History, 1348–1418*. Oxford: Oxford University Press.

———. 2017. *Geoffrey Chaucer: A New Introduction*. Oxford: Oxford University Press.

Watts, Pauline Moffitt. 1985. "Prophecy and Discovery: On the Spiritual Origins of Christopher Columbus's 'Enterprise of the Indies.'" *American Historical Review* 90, no. 1:73–102.

Wauquelin, Jean. 1880. *Chroniques des faiz de feurent monseigneur Girart de Rossillon, publiées pour la première fois, d'après le manuscrit de l'Hôtel-Dieu de Beaune*. Edited by L. de Montille. Paris: H. Champion.

———. 2000. *Les faicts et les conquestes d'Alexandre le Grand de Jehan Wauquelin*. Edited by Sandrine Hériché. Geneva: Droz.

———. 2012. *The Medieval Romance of Alexander: Jehan Wauquelin's "The Deeds and Conquests of Alexander the Great."* Translated by Nigel Bryant. Woodbridge: Boydell.

Waurin [Wavrin], Jehan de. 1864. *Recueil des croniques et anchiennes istories de la Grant Bretaigne, à présent nommé Engleterre*. Vol. 1. Edited by William Hardy. London.

Weiss, Gillian Lee. 2011. *Captives and Corsairs: France and Slavery in the Early Modern Mediterranean*. Stanford, CA: Stanford University Press.

Werner, Michael, and Bénédicte Zimmermann. 2003. "Penser l'histoire croisée: Entre empirie et réflexivité." *Annales: Histoire, Sciences Sociales* 58:7–36.

Wey, William. 1857. *The Itineraries of William Wey, Fellow of Eton College, to Jerusalem, A.D. 1458 and A.D. 1462, and to Saint James of Compostelle, A.D. 1456*. London.

White, Richard. 1991. *The Middle Ground: Indians, Empires, and Republics in the Great Lakes Region, 1650–1815*. Cambridge: Cambridge University Press.

Wijsman, Hanno. 2007. "Politique et bibliophilie pendant la révolte des villes flamandes des années 1482–1492: Relations entre les bibliothèques de Philippe de Clèves, Louis de Gruuthuse et la Librairie de Bourgogne." In Haemers, van Hoorebeeck, and Wijsman 2007, 245–78.

———. 2009. "Bibliothèques princières entre Moyen Âge et humanisme: A propos des livres de Philippe le Bon et de Matthias Corvin et de l'interprétation du XVᵉ siècle." In *Matthias Corvin: Les Bibliothèques princières et la genèse de l'état moderne*, edited by Jean-François Maillard, István Monok, and Donatella Nebbiai, 121–34. Budapest: Országos Széchényi Könyvtár.

———, ed. 2010a. *Books in Transition at the Time of Philip the Fair: Manuscripts and Printed Books in the Late Fifteenth and Early Sixteenth Century Low Countries*. Turnhout: Brepols.

———. 2010b. "Jean Miélot et son réseau: L'insertion à la cour de Bourgogne du traducteur-copiste." *Le Moyen français* 67:129–56.

———. 2010c. *Luxury Bound: Illustrated Manuscript Production and Noble and Princely Book Ownership in the Burgundian Netherland, 1400–1550*. Turnhout: Brepols. http://www.cn-telma.fr/luxury-bound/index/.

———. 2010d. "Northern Renaissance? Burgundy and Netherlandish Art in Fifteenth-Century Europe." In *Renaissance? Perceptions of Continuity and Discontinuity in Europe, c. 1300–c. 1550*, edited by Alexander Lee, Pit Péporté, and Harry Schnitker, 269–88. Leiden: Brill.

———. 2010e. "Philippe le Beau et les livres." In Wijsman 2010, 17–92.

———. 2010f. "Une bataille perdue d'avance? Les manuscrits après l'introduction de l'imprimerie dans les anciens Pays-Bas." In Wijsman 2010, 257–69.

———. 2013. "Book Collections and Their Use: The Example of the Library of the Dukes of Burgundy." *Queeste* 20, no. 2:83–98.

———. 2020. "Listes de livres à la cour de Bourgogne (XVᵉ–XVIᵉ)." In *Pouvoir des listes au Moyen Âge, III. Les listes d'objets et de personnes*, edited by Etienne Anheim, Laurent Feller, Madeleine Jeay, and Giuliano Milan, 83–104. Paris: Éditions de la Sorbonne.

———. 2022. "The Library as a Window: The Grand Duke of the West and the Fascination of the East." In *Horizons médiévaux d'Orient et d'Occident: Regards croisés entre France et Japon*, edited by Atsushi Egawa, Marc Smith, Megumi Tanabe, and Hanno Wijsman, 121–37. Paris: Éditions de la Sorbonne.

Willard, Charity Cannon. 1989. "Raoul de Presles's Translation of Saint Augustine's *De civitate Dei.*" In *Medieval Translators and Their Craft*, edited by Jeanette Beer, 329–46. Kalamazoo, MI: Medieval Institute.

———. 1996. "Patrons at the Burgundian Court: Jean V de Créquy and His Wife, Louise de la Tour." In *The Search for a Patron in the Middle Ages and the Renaissance*, edited by David G. Wilkins and Rebecca L. Wilkins, 55–62. Lewiston, NY: E. Mellen.

———. 1997. "Louis de Bruges, lecteur de Christine de Pizan." *Cahiers de recherches médiévales* 4:191–95.

William of Adam. 1869. "De modo Sarracenos extirpandi." In *Recueil des historiens des croisades: Documents arméniens*, edited by Académie royale des inscriptions et des belles-lettres, 2:521–55. Paris: Impr. impériale.

———. 2012. *How to Defeat the Saracens.* Edited and translated by Giles Constable. Washington, DC: Dumbarton Oaks Research Library and Collection.

William of Tripoli. 1883. *Tractatus de statu Saracenorum.* In *Kulturgeschichte der Kreuzzüge*, edited by Hans Prutz, 573–98. Berlin.

———. 2011. "Notice on Muḥammad: On The State of the Saracens." In *The Pseudo-historical Image of the Prophet Muhammad in Medieval Latin Literature: A Repertory*, edited by Michelina di Cesare, 349–64. Boston: de Gruyter.

Williams, G. S. 1989. "How to Make Friends: Burgundian Politics in Early Modern Prose Texts." *Sixteenth-Century Journal* 20, no. 2:277–95.

Wogan-Brown, Jocelyn, ed. 2009. *Language and Culture in Medieval Britain: The French of England, c. 1100–c. 1500.* Woodbridge, Suffolk, UK: York Medieval.

Wolf, Eva. 1996. *Das Bild in der spätmittelalterlichen Buchmalerei: Das Sachsenheim-Gebetbuch im Werk Lieven van Lathems.* Hildesheim: Georg Olms.

Wolfe, Alexander C. 2014. "Marco Polo: Factotum, Auditor; Language and Political Culture in the Mongol World." *Literature Compass* 11, no. 7:409–22.

Wrisley, David J. 2006. "L'Orient de Jehan Wauquelin." In de Crécy et al. 2006, 171–84.

———. 2007–8. "The Loss of Constantinople and Imagining Crusade at the Fifteenth-Century Court of Burgundy." *Al Abhath* 55:81–115.

———. 2011. "Historical Narration and Digression in al-Nuwairī al-Iskandarānī's Kitāb al-Ilmām." In Blumenfeld-Kosinski and Petkov 2011b, 451–73.

Yannakakis, Yanna. Forthcoming. "Interpreters and the Deep Layer of Spanish Colonial Justice." *Journal of Early Modern Cultural Studies.*

Young, Helen, and Kavita Mudan Finn. 2022. *Global Medievalism: An Introduction.* Cambridge: Cambridge University Press.

Zemon Davis, Natalie. 2006. *Trickster Travels: A Sixteenth-Century Muslim between Worlds*. New York: Hill and Wang.

Zenker, Nina. 2018. *Der Breslauer Froissart: Im Spiegel spätmittelalterlicher Geschichtsauffassung*. Petersberg: Michael Imhof Verlag.

Zink, Michel. 1998. *Froissart et le temps*. Paris: Presses universitaires de France.

Ziolkowski, Jan M. 2009. "Cultures of Authority in the Long Twelfth Century." *Journal of English and Germanic Philology* 108, no. 4:421–48.

Zuili, Marc, and Susan Baddeley, eds. 2012. *Les langues étrangères en Europe: Apprentissages et pratiques, 1450–1700*. Paris: Presses de l'Université Paris–Sorbonne.

Zumthor, Paul. 2000. *Essai de poétique médiévale*. 1972. Paris: Seuil.

Index

Page numbers in italics refer to figures.